LATIN AMERICA AND THE
UNITED STATES

LATIN AMERICA AND THE UNITED STATES

A Documentary History

❖

Robert H. Holden
OLD DOMINION UNIVERSITY

Eric Zolov
FRANKLIN & MARSHALL COLLEGE

New York   Oxford
OXFORD UNIVERSITY PRESS
2000

Oxford University Press

Oxford   New York
Athens   Auckland   Bangkok   Bogotá   Buenos Aires   Calcutta
Cape Town   Chennai   Dar es Salaam   Delhi   Florence   Hong Kong   Istanbul
Karachi   Kuala Lumpur   Madrid   Melbourne   Mexico City   Mumbai
Nairobi   Paris   São Paulo   Singapore   Taipei   Tokyo   Toronto   Warsaw

and associated companies in
Berlin   Ibadan

Copyright (c) 2000 by Oxford University Press, Inc.

Published by Oxford University Press, Inc.
198 Madison Avenue, New York, New York 10016
http://www.oup-usa.org

Oxford is a registered trademark of Oxford University Press

Library of Congress Cataloging-in-Publication Data
Latin America and the United States : a documentary history / edited
by Robert H. Holden, Eric Zolov.
p.   cm.
Includes index.
ISBN 0-19-512993-8 (cloth). — ISBN 0-19-512994-6 (pbk.)
1. Latin America—Foreign relations—United States Sources.
2. United States—Foreign relations—Latin America Sources.
I. Holden, Robert H.   II. Zolov, Eric.
F1418.L354   2000   327.7308'09—DC21   99-31523

5 7 9 8 6

Printed in the United States of America
on acid-free paper

Contents

Contents

II. THE COLOSSUS OF THE NORTH

Contents

III. BURYING THE BIG STICK

Contents

Contents

Contents

V. AFTER THE COLD WAR:
CONFLICT IN THE SEARCH FOR COMMON GROUND

Contents

Preface

Nearly two centuries have passed since the Latin American colonies of the European powers began to liberate themselves from colonial rule and to establish themselves as independent nations alongside the United States. Only in the last three to four decades, however, has the study of their interaction with the United States constituted a distinct academic subspecialty in this country. Until about the 1960s, the scholars who studied the history of that interaction were generally trained as experts in U.S. diplomatic history. As a result, their research was largely concerned with political and military matters, and their sources were chiefly, if not entirely, drawn from the archival records of the U.S. government.

In the last thirty years, however, the boundaries of inquiry into the history of relations between the United States and Latin America have expanded considerably. While diplomacy and politico-military matters have by no means been excluded, they are now more likely to be understood as components of a much broader field of interaction between the United States and Latin America, as well as components of a global context from which European, African and Asian influences and interests cannot be excluded.

A review of the literature over the last three decades discloses two prominent signs of that boundary expansion. First, scholars who specialize in the history of Latin America have joined historians of U.S. foreign policy as important contributors of knowledge about the history of hemispheric relations. Second, the field has come to depend increasingly on theories, methods and research derived from academic disciplines other than history itself, above all anthropology, literature, political science and sociology. This blending of area specialties and disciplinary approaches in the study of the relations between Latin America and the United States suggests that historians have become more sensitive to their thematic complexity. Historians now recognize that, in addition to the traditional subject of government-to-government interactions, a congeries of other kinds of linkages—demographic, legal, financial, commercial, environmental, literary, religious, ethnic, artistic and so on—join the inhabitants of the Americas. The most welcome result of these boundary changes is the increasing richness and originality of the interpretations that students of the subject now have to draw on. At the same time, historians have deepened our appreciation for the diversity of those linkages by producing many new studies focused on particular countries, groups of countries or regions within countries. The multidimensional and interactive character of the relations between the United States and Latin America is what now seems to stand out in the historical literature, whether those relations are constituted as ideologies, social movements, economic transformations, institutional violence or religious values, to name just a few examples.

As they have expanded their field of vision, historians of the relationship between Latin America and the United States have turned to an increasing variety of sources on which to base their interpretations. The purpose of this volume is to bring together a representative sample of those sources. The historiography has clearly sanctioned a particular canon, at the core of which is the Monroe Doctrine, followed by such others as the Olney Memorandum, the Roosevelt Corollary, the Clark Memorandum, the Rio Treaty, the Act of Bogotá and so on. Treaties, correspondence, memoirs, speeches, legislation, doctrinal pronouncements and the like—what might be called "official views"—are amply represented in this volume. In addition, we have included many other sources that may be taken to be broadly representative of certain sectoral or group values, opinions or interests. Some documents—such as excerpts from a particular article or book—were included for the widely acknowledged impact they had at the time they were published.

While quite a few of the documents we have selected stand outside the canon, the majority of them were chosen precisely because they make up that canon. Because they have been key sources for many historical interpretations and textbook accounts, our aim is to encourage both understanding and dissent, an appreciation of their significance that enables the reader to challenge the interpretations that draw on them.

Questioning the meaning of these documents and their relevance to the history of hemispheric relations is a vital part of their study. In assembling this collection, therefore, we also hoped to inspire discussions about how knowledge of relations between Latin America and the United States should be approached. In some ways, this basic question is the starting point that connects every course in the history of those relations. The question points to the conflicting interpretations at the heart of scholarship in this field. Which of many perspectives should be emphasized in the classroom? Should one stress the strategic aspect of the relationship, subsuming questions of intervention and military alliances within a broader global dynamic, of which Latin America is just one component? Or does one argue for the primacy of economic relationships? How important are cultural patterns like racism, paternalism, individualism or pragmatism? Others might stress the primacy of political and social forces within Latin America as well as in the United States; an example would be the power of nationalism, an "idea" strong enough that it has at times seemed to be the controlling, underlying force in the relationship. Our own view is that balance in teaching this field requires the consideration not only of the different dimensions of the relationship—strategic, economic, cultural, domestic and so on—but also of expressions of those dimensions in Latin America as well as in the United States. In this regard, we have sought to include in this collection documents that represent initiatives and responses originating in Latin America. Often acting against the grain of a U.S.–constructed Pan-Americanism, for example, Latin Americans have frequently expressed distinctive notions of national and American identity. Providing access to some of these claims should help correct a historical imbalance that still affects textbooks and monographs on the subject. In a sense, that imbalance reflects the obvious asymmetry in the relationship between the United States and Latin America. The very persistence of U.S. supremacy transformed it into a permanent premise of hemispheric relations, not only in the United States but in Latin America as well. One consequence was the silencing, within the historical record as it has been constructed in the United States, of Latin American initiatives aimed at addressing that asymmetry. We have sought to include some of the outstanding examples of such initiatives—among them, the Calvo and Drago doctrines, the Tlatelolco Treaty of 1967, the Esquipulas II agreement and of course the challenges to U.S. supremacy represented in certain social movements and revolutions, from Bolivia and Peru to Cuba and Nicaragua.

The kinds of documentation that historians call on to support their interpretations are, like the interpretations themselves, constantly evolving. We hope that this collection, therefore, will stimulate informed debate over the shifting character of relations between Latin America and the United States—shifts that, we believe, are disclosed in the documentary record that we have assembled here. Every student of the subject has to wrestle with the meaning of the changes that these documents point to, decade after decade. For example, one might interpret the Roosevelt Corollary to the Monroe Doctrine as evidence of the rising strategic stakes for control over the Panama Canal, or as a sign of imperialist economic designs in the Caribbean region, or as a reflection of a racist paternalism. While all are in some measure "correct," one of our goals in assembling this collection was precisely to stimulate discussion of the relative significance or insignificance of such politico-diplomatic events compared to other historical forces. How is it, for example, that the Monroe Doctrine had relatively scant impact at the time of its utterance, and yet much later, ripped from its original context, emerged as the core dictum of U.S. policy? Similarly, how did the Braden Report come to be associated with U.S. imperialism, turning Colonel Juan Domingo Perón's presidential campaign of 1946 into a test of Argentine national identity and pride? While this collection does point to some shifts in interpretations and meanings of hemispheric relations over time, it will also suggest some startling continuities in those relations.

When we have gone beyond the well-established boundaries of the documentary canon by introducing lesser-known and entirely novel sources from the historical record, we have tried to offer voices from the political and cultural margins of official decision making. An example was our decision to include not just the official platitudes of the Good Neighbor Policy, but the skepticism of a contemporary journalist, Carleton Beals. The purpose of adding such sources is to impress students with the variety of opinions and policy alternatives that are always at stake at any given moment in history. The proclamations and treaties hammered out by government leaders may only rarely represent a true consensus, either among elites themselves or among the populace as a whole. And even when they do, there have always been other voices. Who, indeed, gets to "speak" for the United States, or for any society, for that matter? How do answers to that question determine the shape of the "documentary record"? This collection should stimulate discussion of the shaping of both discursive "centers" and discursive "peripheries," and in doing so, raise the question of just what it is that constitutes a document suitable for historical analysis. The history of the human experience may largely be written by the powerful and their allies, but it would be a hopelessly distorted history were it to exclude the contributions of those at the margins of power. Yet perhaps the "marginal" voices represented in this volume were not so marginal after all, considering their capacity to have acted intentionally to influence policy choices, and to have done so in a way that was durable enough to produce a written record. It seemed appropriate to limit this book to the voices of those in or near the center of power. A very different collection of documents on hemispheric relations might be assembled that draws entirely on the words of those who have been powerless, as individuals, to influence the course of those relations, but who nevertheless lived them in ways that the voices in this volume have not. Copper miners, immigrants, soldiers, drug dealers, *maquiladora* employees, guerrilla fighters and African slaves are among those who could testify to results of decisions taken by many of the figures represented in this volume, and even at times to having influenced those decisions in a collective, if not individual, way.

Some of the lesser-known materials in this collection—from both government as well as nongovernmental sources, from both U.S. and Latin American perspectives—should broaden students' understanding of how historical investigation is itself pursued. Among the most exciting aspects of studying this subject is precisely the opportunity to discover for oneself new sources, whether they come from previously classified (or unexplored) governmental records, or from an unnoticed editorial in a small-town newspaper. In effect, anything—music, films, tourist advertisements, interviews, comic strips—might constitute a valid source. What ultimately matters is how those sources are interpreted within their historical context. Our selection of documents outside the canon represented, to us, evidence of important trends and key shifts in the relationship between the United States and Latin America. Our aim was not just to challenge the limits of the canon, but to illustrate the availability of multiple reference points in the construction of the relationship, while stimulating the creative instincts of our readers, both inside and outside the classroom.

Finally, this collection should make it easier for students to interpret for themselves—unencumbered by others' summary judgments—the meaning of the historical record. Analyzing documents is the fundamental way in which historians develop their interpretations. They approach the document not simply as a literal text, but more importantly, they seek to "read" the text in the fullest sense of the word: to go beyond the words on the page in order to understand the hidden (and sometimes not so hidden) context of rival interests and distinctive cultural orientations. Students of history, therefore, learn to interpret language, to go beyond its literal meaning and to understand it as a window onto both the overt and the hidden relationships of power, emotion and bias that frame all discourse. The documents assembled here are intended to support that process by providing a diversity of perspectives—U.S. and Latin American, strategic and cultural, the powerful and the less powerful. They should enhance the possibility for enriched interpretations not only of what governments do, but also of the behavior of groups of people and individuals as they themselves shape the relationship between the United States and Latin America. We think these documents demonstrate more than the obvious asymmetry of that relationship, of the hegemony of the United States "over" Latin America. They also reveal something of the character of the counterhegemonic movements that have shaped the relationship.

We have organized this collection into five chronological sections, spanning the period of early Latin American independence to the contemporary era. Needless to say, our periodization implies an argument as to when, why and how certain shifts occurred in the relationship. While the periodization we have chosen is broadly accepted by historians of the field, we hope that students will carefully consider the logic of the beginnings and endings selected for those periods. Certainly, other plausible chronologies can be found to challenge our own, and we hope that readers seize those differences as opportunities for discussion and debate. We have included a detailed index to enable readers to liberate themselves from what some may consider the rigid logic of the table of contents.

Each entry is preceded by a brief introduction aimed at explaining the larger context in which the document was produced. We have sought to refrain from offering in these introductions any interpretation of the document itself that might unfairly influence the reader's own analysis. For reasons of space, very few of the documents could be presented here in their entirety and therefore we were required to select what we considered to be their most relevant passages. This was a regrettable necessity that we hope our readers will accept. While it was relatively easy to edit out the repetitive, the trivial and the less germane parts of our documents, decisions about which sections to cut inevitably required us to make some difficult choices about what mattered most in a particular source. A citation to the full source of the document may be found at the foot of the first page of each entry. While we encourage readers to go back to the original source for the full text, we feel confident that the edited versions presented here provide ample basis for interpretation and discussion. We preserved the originals' grammar and spelling.

We could not have produced this book without the support of many other individuals. We are especially grateful for the advice and encouragement of John H. Coatsworth, Tom Klubock, Walter LaFeber, Nathaniel Smith and Peter H. Smith, and the numerous other colleagues who made suggestions for suitable documents; we would like to have been able to include them all! We thank Renée DiPilato, Maridith Hozier, Elizabeth Kerwin and Moira Oswalt for their expert research assistance and copy preparation. Oxford's anonymous reviewers helped us to improve the manuscript.

In addition, Robert H. Holden thanks Old Dominion University's Department of History and its College of Arts and Letters for essential material assistance for this project and for a supportive and collegial work environment. He is deeply grateful to Karen L. Gould and Chandra R. DeSilva. Old Dominion's Perry Library reference and interlibrary loan staffs responded to numerous requests for assistance in locating sources. Rina Villars contributed to this volume so abundantly and in so many different ways that it would be impossible to thank her adequately for her generosity. Finally, Robert Holden was fortunate to have been initiated into the history of Latin America and its relations with the United States by Charles D. Ameringer, whose high standards and expert knowledge have been a permanent inspiration to him.

Eric Zolov acknowledges the support of the History Department at Franklin & Marshall College and the reference and interlibrary loan staffs of the Shadek-Fackenthal Library. Special thanks also go to Carrie Sliver for helping to secure copyright permissions, Michael Socolow and Gillian McGillivray for helping to locate documents, and the staff of the National Security Archive. Emmy Avilés Bretón's unfailing moral and logistical support for this project, as always, deserve special mention; her honesty and passion have helped him understand still more clearly the meaning of *respect* in relations between the United States and Latin America.

Finally, as graduate students both of us shared a singular stroke of good luck. We were guided by two extraordinary scholar-teachers, John H. Coatsworth and Friedrich Katz, and we are happy to be able to acknowledge our gratitude to them.

LATIN AMERICA AND THE UNITED STATES

I.

TRANSITIONS OF EMPIRE

1811

No Transfer Doctrine

The Congress of the United States

The French invasion of the Iberian peninsula in 1808 increased the likelihood that Spanish colonial territories in the New World might become the property of another European power. Of immediate concern to the U.S. government was Florida, governed by Spain but occupied in its western areas by U.S. immigrants. On October 27, 1810, while Congress was in recess, President James Madison ordered the annexation of Florida territory between the Mississippi and Perdido Rivers, which Madison claimed were part of the Louisiana Purchase of 1803. Great Britain's vehement protests on behalf of Spain provided the impetus for Madison to send a message to a special, closed-door session of Congress in January 1811. Fearful of British designs on Spain's former colonies and recalling the secret transfer of Louisiana from Spain to France in 1800, Congress responded with the "No Transfer" bill, signed into law on January 15, 1811. A record of Congressional action, including a message from President Madison, is excerpted below. The No Transfer law was kept secret by Congress until 1818. The following year, under the terms of the Adams-Onís Treaty, Spain ceded all of Florida to the United States.

Thursday, January 3, 1811.

The following confidential Message was received from the President of the United States, by Mr. Coles, his Secretary:

To the Senate and House of Representatives of the United States:

. . . I recommend to the consideration of Congress, the seasonableness of a declaration that the United States could not see, without serious inquietude, any part of a neighboring territory, in which they have, in different respects,

Source: David Hunter Miller. "Proceedings in the Senate in Secret Session." In *Secret Statutes of the United States: A Memorandum*, pp. 11–17. Washington, D.C.: GPO, 1918.

so deep and so just a concern, pass from the hands of Spain into those of any other foreign Power.

I recommend to their consideration, also, the expediency of authorizing the Executive to take temporary possession of any part or parts of the said territory, in pursuance of arrangements which may be desired by the Spanish authorities; and for making provision for the government of the same, during such possession.

The wisdom of Congress will, at the same time, determine how far it may be expedient to provide for the event of a subversion of the Spanish authorities within the territory in question, and apprehended occupancy thereof by any other foreign Power.

James Madison.

Friday, January 11

[Taking into consideration the] peculiar situation of Spain and of her American provinces; and considering the influence which the destiny of the territory adjoining the southern border of the United States may have upon their security, tranquillity, and commerce: Therefore,

Resolved, by the Senate and House of Representatives of the United States of America in Congress assembled, That the United States, under the peculiar circumstances of the existing crisis, cannot, without serious inquietude, see any part of the said territory pass into the hands of any foreign Power; and that a due regard to their own safety compels them to provide, under certain contingencies, for the temporary occupation of the said territory; they at the same time, declare that the said territory shall, in their hands, remain subject to a future negotiation.

Sunday, March 3

Resolved, by the Senate and the House of Representatives of the United States of America in Congress assembled, That the act passed during the present session of Congress, entitled "An act to enable the President of the United States, under certain contingencies, to take possession of the country lying east of the river Perdido, and south of the State of Georgia and the Mississippi Territory, and for other purposes;" and the declaration accompanying the same, be not printed or published, unless directed by the President of the United States, any law or usage to the contrary notwithstanding.

NO. 2

1823

Cuba: "An Apple Severed by the Tempest From Its Native Tree."

John Quincy Adams

On April 28, 1823, Secretary of State John Quincy Adams wrote a 15,000-word letter of instruction to the new head of the U.S. mission to Spain, Hugh Nelson. In the brief excerpt that follows, Adams expresses some of the interests and concerns that will find their way, eight months later, into President Monroe's famous declaration (Document No. 3). As the Spanish empire collapsed, Washington feared British and French expansion, which it was ill-prepared to counter. As a result, while the United States publicly welcomed the new republican governments of Latin America, as a practical matter a more conservative policy toward the Spanish colonies of the Caribbean (especially Cuba) was indicated because political instability might have invited the transfer of Cuba to another, more powerful European nation. In effect, continued Spanish rule in the Caribbean favored U.S. interests, at least until the United States could augment its military and economic capacities. Adams's reference to Cuba as a ripening fruit that will fall inevitably into the lap of Uncle Sam was to become one of the premises of U.S. Latin American policy in the nineteenth century.

. . . It has been a maxim in the policy of these United States, from the time when their independence was achieved, to keep themselves aloof from the political systems and contentions of Europe. To this principle it is yet the purpose of the President to adhere: and in the war about to commence, the attitude to be assumed and maintained by the United States will be that of neutrality.

But the experience of our national history has already shown that, however sincerely this policy was adopted, and however earnestly and perseveringly it was maintained, it yielded ultimately to a course of events by which the violence and injustice of European powers involved the immediate interests and brought in conflict the essential rights of our own country.

Source: "To Hugh Nelson." Worthington Chauncey Ford, ed. *Writings of John Quincy Adams.* Vol. 7, 1820–1823, pp. 369–421. New York: The Macmillan Co., 1917.

Two of the principal causes of the wars between the nations of Europe since that of our own Revolution, have been, indeed, the same as those in which that originated—civil liberty and national independence. To these principles, and to the cause of those who contend for them, the people of the United States can never be indifferent. A feeling of sympathy and of partiality for every nation struggling to secure or to defend these great interests, has been and will be manifested by this Union; and it is among the most difficult and delicate duties of the general government, in all its branches, to indulge this feeling so far as it may be compatible with the duties of neutrality, and to withhold and restrain from encroaching upon them. So far as it is indulged, its tendency is to involve us in foreign wars, while the first and paramount duty of the government is to maintain *peace* amidst all the convulsions of foreign wars, and to enter the lists as parties to no cause, other than our own.

In the *maritime* wars of Europe, we have, indeed, a direct and important interest of our own; as they are waged upon an element which is the common property of all; and as our participation in the possession of that property is perhaps greater than that of any other nation. The existence of maritime war, itself, enlarges and deepens the importance of this interest; and it introduces a state of things in which the conflict of neutral and belligerent rights becomes itself a continual and formidable instigation to war. To all maritime wars Great Britain can scarcely fail of becoming a party; and from that moment arises a collision between her and these states, peculiar to the situation, interests and rights of the two countries, and which can scarcely form a subject of discussion between any other nation and either of them.

This cause then is peculiarly our own: and we have already been once compelled to vindicate our rights implicated in it by war. It has been too among the dispensations of Providence, that the issue of that war should have left that question unsettled for the future; and that the attempts which on the part of the United States have been repeatedly made since the peace for adjusting it by amicable negotiation, have in like manner proved ineffectual. There is therefore great reason to apprehend, that if Great Britain should engage in the war, now just kindled in Europe, the United States will again be called to support by all their energies, not excepting war, the rights of their national independence, enjoyed in the persons of their seamen.

But in the war between France and Spain now commencing, other interests, peculiarly ours, will in all probability be deeply involved. Whatever may be the issue of this war, as between those two European powers, it may be taken for granted that the dominion of Spain upon the American continents, North and South, is irrecoverably gone. But the islands of Cuba and of Porto Rico still remain nominally and so far really dependent upon her, that she yet possesses the power of transferring her own dominion over them, together with the possession of them, to others. These islands, from their local position, are natural appendages to the North American continent; and one of them, Cuba, almost in sight of our shores, from a multitude of considerations has become an object of transcendent importance to the political and commercial interests of our

Union. Its commanding position with reference to the Gulf of Mexico and the West India seas; the character of its population; its situation midway between our southern coast and the island of San Domingo; its safe and capacious harbor of the Havana, fronting a long line of our shores destitute of the same advantage; the nature of its productions and of its wants, furnishing the supplies and needing the returns of a commerce immensely profitable and mutually beneficial; give it an importance in the sum of our national interests, with which that of no other foreign territory can be compared and little inferior to that which binds the different members of this Union together.

Such indeed are, between the interests of that island and of this country, the geographical, commercial, moral, and political relations, formed by nature, gathering in the process of time, and even now verging to maturity, that in looking forward to the probable course of events for the short period of half a century, it is scarcely possible to resist the conviction that the annexation of Cuba to our federal republic will be indispensable to the continuance and integrity of the Union itself. It is obvious however that for this event we are not yet prepared. Numerous and formidable objections to the extension of our territorial dominions beyond the sea present themselves to the first contemplation of the subject. Obstacles to the system of policy by which it alone can be compassed and maintained are to be foreseen and surmounted, both from at home and abroad. But there are laws of political as well as of physical gravitation; and if an apple severed by the tempest from its native tree cannot choose but fall to the ground, Cuba, forcibly disjoined from its own unnatural connection with Spain, and incapable of self-support, can gravitate only towards the North American Union, which by the same law of nature cannot cast her off from its bosom.

In any other state of things than that which springs from this incipient war between France and Spain, these considerations would be premature. They are now merely touched upon, to illustrate the position that, in the war opening upon Europe, the United States have deep and important interests involved, peculiarly their own. The condition of Cuba cannot but depend upon the issue of this war. As an integral part of the Spanish territories, Cuba has been formally and solemnly invested with the liberties of the Spanish constitution. To destroy those liberties, and to restore in the stead of that Constitution the dominion of the Bourbon race, is the avowed object of this new invasion of the Peninsula. There is too much reason to apprehend that in Spain itself this unhallowed purpose will be attended with immediate, or at least with temporary success; the constitution of Spain will be demolished by the armies of the Holy Alliance; and the Spanish nation will again bow the neck to the yoke of bigotry and despotic sway.

Whether the purposes of France, or of her continental allies, extend to the subjugation of the remaining ultramarine possessions of Spain or not, has not yet been sufficiently disclosed. But to confine ourselves to that which immediately concerns us, the condition of the island of Cuba, we know that the republican spirit of freedom prevails among its inhabitants. The liberties of the constitution are to them rights in possession: nor is it to be presumed that they will be willing to surrender them, because they may be extinguished by foreign violence in the parent country. As Spanish territory the island will be liable to invasion from France during the war: and the only reasons for doubting whether the attempt will be made are the probable incompetence of the French maritime force to effect the conquest, and the probability that its accomplishment would be resisted by Great Britain. In the meantime and at all events, the condition of the island in regard to that of its inhabitants, is a condition of great, imminent, and complicated danger: and without resorting to speculation upon what such a state of things must produce upon a people so situated, we know that its approach has already had a powerful effect upon them, and that the question what they are to do upon contingencies daily pressing upon them and ripening into reality, has for the last twelve months constantly excited their attention and stimulated them to action.

Were the population of the island of one blood and color, there could be no doubt or hesitation with regard to the course which they would pursue, as dictated by their interests and their rights. The invasion of Spain by France would be the signal for *their* Declaration of Independence. That even in their present state it will be imposed upon them as a necessity is not unlikely; but among all their reflecting men it is admitted as a maxim fundamental to all deliberation upon their future condition, that they are not competent to a system of permanent self-dependence. They must rely for the support of protection upon some force from without; and as, in the event of the overthrow of the Spanish constitution, that support can no longer be expected from Spain, their only alternative of dependence must be upon Great Britain, or upon the United States.

Hitherto the wishes of this government have been that the connection between Cuba and Spain should continue, as it has existed for several years. . . .

The motives of Great Britain for desiring the possession of Cuba are so obvious, especially since the independence of Mexico, and the annexation of the Floridas to our Union; the internal condition of the island since the recent Spanish revolution, and the possibility of its continued dependence upon Spain, have been so precarious; the want of protection there; the power of affording it possessed by Great Britain, and the necessities of Spain to secure, by some equivalent, the support of Great Britain for herself; have formed a remarkable concurrence of predispositions to the transfer of Cuba; and during the last two years rumors have been multiplied, that it was already consummated. . . .

The transfer of Cuba to Great Britain would be an event unpropitious to the interests of this Union. This opinion is so generally entertained, that even the groundless rumors that it was about to be accomplished, which have spread abroad and are still teeming, may be traced to the deep and almost universal feeling of aversion to it, and to the alarm which the mere probability of its occurrence has stimulated. The question both of our right and our power to prevent it, if necessary, by force, already obtrudes itself upon our councils, and the administration is called upon, in the performance of its duties to the nation, at least to use all the means within its competency to guard against and forefend it.

It will be among the primary objects requiring your most earnest and unremitting attention, to ascertain and report to us any movement of negotiation between Spain and Great Britain upon this subject. We cannot indeed prescribe any special instructions in relation to it. We scarcely know where you will find the government of Spain upon your arrival in the country; nor can we foresee with certainty by whom it will be administered. . . .

An object of considerable importance will be to obtain the admission of *consuls* from the United States in the ports of the colonies, specially in the islands of Cuba and of Porto Rico. . . . The commerce between the United States and the Havana is of greater amount and value than with all the Spanish dominions in Europe. The number of American vessels which enter there is annually several hundreds. Their seamen from the unhealthiness of the climate are peculiarly exposed to need there the assistance which it is a primary purpose of the consular office to supply; nor is there any conceivable motive for continuing to maintain the pretension to exclude them, and to refuse the formal acknowledgment of consuls. Informal commercial agents have in many of the ports been allowed to reside, and partially to perform the consular duties; but as they are thus left much dependent on the will of the local government, and subject to control at its pleasure, they have neither the dignity nor authority which properly belongs to the office. . . .

❖

NO. 3

1823

The Monroe Doctrine

James Monroe

E ver since Brazil and most of the Spanish colonies of the Americas gained their independence in the 1820s, U.S. policy toward them has been influenced by a few core principles that were contained in President James Monroe's annual message to Congress on December 2, 1823. Two related series of events inspired

Source: James Monroe, "Seventh Annual Message." In *The State of the Union Messages of the Presidents, 1790–1966*. Vol. 1, 1790–1860, ed. Fred L. Israel, pp. 202–14. New York: Chelsea House Publishers in association with the R. R. Bowker Company, 1967.

Monroe's message: the successful wars for independence from Spain by her American colonies, and signs of a desire by some of the European powers—especially France and Russia—to colonize, or recolonize, the Americas. In the summer of 1823, Great Britain invited the United States to issue a joint declaration against further intervention in the New World by the other European powers. But Monroe's secretary of state, John Quincy Adams, argued forcefully in favor of a unilateral U.S. statement. Suspicious of Britain's motives, Adams convinced the president of the advantages of going it alone: "It would be more candid as well as more dignified to avow our principles explicitly to Russia and France, than to come in as a cock-boat in the wake of the British man-of-war." After reading Monroe's first draft of the declaration, Adams persuaded the president to make it less forceful and defiant; the resulting policy and wording were strongly influenced by Adams's views.

Fellow-Citizens of the Senate and House of Representatives:

Many important subjects will claim your attention during the present session, of which I shall endeavor to give, in aid of your deliberations, a just idea in this communication. I undertake this duty with diffidence, from the vast extent of the interests on which I have to treat and of their great importance to every portion of our Union. I enter on it with zeal from a thorough conviction that there never was a period since the establishment of our Revolution when, regarding the condition of the civilized world and its bearing on us, there was greater necessity for devotion in the public servants to their respective duties, or for virtue, patriotism, and union in our constituents. . . . A precise knowledge of our relations with foreign powers as respects our negotiations and transactions with each is thought to be particularly necessary. . . .

It was stated at the commencement of the last session that a great effort was then making in Spain and Portugal to improve the condition of the people of those countries, and that it appeared to be conducted with extraordinary moderation. It need scarcely be remarked that the result has been so far very different from what was then anticipated. Of events in that quarter of the globe, with which we have so much intercourse and from which we derive our origin, we have always been anxious and interested spectators. The citizens of the United States cherish sentiments the most friendly in favor of the liberty and happiness of their fellow-men on that side of the Atlantic. In the wars of the European powers in matters relating to themselves we have never taken any part, nor does it comport with our policy so to do. It is only when our rights are invaded or seriously menaced that we resent injuries or make preparations for our defense. With the movements in this hemisphere we are of necessity more immediately connected, and by causes which must be obvious to all enlightened and impartial observers. The political system of the allied powers is essentially different in this respect from that of America. This difference proceeds from that which exists in their respective Governments; and to the defense of our own, which has been achieved by the loss of so much blood and treasure, and matured by the wisdom of their most enlightened citizens, and under which we have enjoyed unexampled felicity, this whole nation is devoted. We owe it, therefore, to candor and to the amicable relations existing between the United States and those powers to declare that we should consider any attempt on their part to extend their system to any portion of this hemisphere as dangerous to our peace and safety. With the existing colonies or dependencies of any European power we have not interfered and shall not interfere. But with the Governments who have declared their independence and maintained it, and whose independence we have, on great consideration and on just principles, acknowledged, we could not view any interposition for the purpose of oppressing them, or controlling in any other manner their destiny, by any European power in any other light than as the manifestation of an unfriendly disposition toward the United States. In the war between those new Governments and Spain we declared our neutrality at the time of their recognition, and to this we have adhered, and shall continue to adhere, provided no change shall occur which, in the judgment of the competent authorities of this Government, shall make a corresponding change on the part of the United States indispensable to their security.

The late events in Spain and Portugal shew that Europe is still unsettled. Of this important fact no stronger proof can be adduced than that the allied powers should have thought it proper, on any principle satisfactory to themselves, to have interposed by force in the internal concerns of Spain. To what extent such interposition may be carried, on the same principle, is a question in which all independent powers whose governments differ from theirs are interested, even those most remote, and surely none more so than the United States. Our policy in regard to Europe, which was adopted at an early stage of the wars which have so long agitated that quarter of the globe, nevertheless remains the same, which is, not to interfere in the internal concerns of any of its powers; to consider the government *de facto* as the legitimate government for us; to cultivate friendly relations with it, and to preserve those relations by a frank, firm, and manly policy, meeting in all instances the just claims of every power, submitting to injuries from none. But in regard to those continents circumstances are eminently and conspicuously different. It is impossible that the allied powers should extend their political system to any portion of either continent without endangering our peace and happiness; nor can anyone believe that our southern brethren, if left to themselves, would adopt it of their own accord. It is equally impossible, therefore, that we should behold such interposition in any form with indifference. If we look to the comparative strength and resources of Spain and those new Governments, and their distance from each other, it must be obvious that she can never subdue them. It is still the true policy of the United States to leave the parties to themselves, in the hope that other powers will pursue the same course.

If we compare the present condition of our Union with its actual state at the close of our Revolution, the history of the world furnishes no example of a progress in improvement in all the important circumstances which constitute the happiness of a nation which bears any resemblance to it. At the first epoch our population did not exceed 3,000,000. By the last census it amounted to about 10,000,000 and, what is more extraordinary, it is almost altogether native, for the immigration from other countries has been inconsiderable. At the first epoch half the territory within our acknowledged limits was uninhabited and a wilderness. Since then new territory has been acquired of vast extent, comprising within it many rivers, particularly the Mississippi, the navigation of which to the ocean was of the highest importance to the original States. Over this territory our population has expanded in every direction, and new states have been established almost equal in number to those which formed the first bond of our Union. This expansion of our population and accession of new States to our Union have had the happiest effect on all its highest interests. That it has eminently augmented our resources and added to our strength and respectability as a power is admitted by all. But it is not in these important circumstances only that this happy effect is felt. It is manifest that by enlarging the basis of our system and increasing the number of States the system itself has been greatly strengthened in both its branches. Consolidation and disunion have thereby been rendered equally impracticable. Each Government, confiding in its own strength, has less to apprehend from the other, and in consequence each, enjoying a greater freedom of action, is rendered more efficient for all the purposes for which it was instituted. It is unnecessary to treat here of the vast improvement made in the system itself by the adoption of this Constitution and of its happy effect in elevating the character and in protecting the rights of the nation as well as of individuals. To what, then, do we owe these blessings? It is known to all that we derive them from the excellence of our institutions. Ought we not, then, to adopt every measure which may be necessary to perpetuate them? . . .

1824

The Congress of Panama

Simón Bolívar

S imón Bolívar was born in the Spanish colonial city of Caracas, Venezuela, in
1783, a descendant of one of the city's oldest and wealthiest families. By
1810, however, he had become a leader of the Venezuelan independence movement and within a decade had established himself as the single most prominent
advocate of independence for all of Spain's American possessions. The invitation to the first conference of American states, reproduced below, was issued
from Lima by Bolívar to the heads of state of the newly independent American
republics on December 7, 1824, on the eve of final victory over the Spanish.
Bolívar extended the invitation to Great Britain (which had lent material and
moral support to the independence cause), but not to Brazil, the United States
or Haiti. Bolívar hoped the conference would establish a pan-American confederation supported by a mutual security pact, a framework for resolving inter-
American disputes, and greater cooperation between the newly independent
states. Only Mexico, Central America, Gran Colombía and Peru sent delegates
to what became known as the Congress of Panama, which met from June 22 to
July 15, 1826. Invitations to Brazil and the United States were issued over Bolívar's opposition; two U.S. representatives eventually set course for Panama but
one died en route and the other arrived too late to participate.

Great and Good Friend: After fifteen years of sacrifices devoted to the liberty
of America to secure a system of guaranties that in peace and war shall be the
shield of our new destiny, it is time the interests and relations uniting the American Republics, formerly Spanish colonies, should have a fundamental basis
that shall perpetuate, if possible, those Governments.

To initiate that system, and concentrate the power of this great political body,
implies the exercise of a sublime authority, capable of directing the policy of

Source: "Circular Invitation Addressed by Simón Bolívar to the Governments of Colombia, Mexico, Central America, the United Provinces of Buenos Aires, Chile, and Brazil." Lima, December
7, 1824. In James Brown Scott, ed., *The International Conferences of American States, 1889–1928*,
pp. xix–xx. New York: Oxford University Press, 1931. Copyright by the Carnegie Endowment for
International Peace. Reprinted with permission.

our Governments, whose influence should maintain uniformity of principles, and whose name alone should put an end to our quarrels.

Such a respectable authority can exist only in an assembly of plenipotentiaries, appointed by each of our Republics, and called together under the auspices of the victory obtained by our arms over the Spanish power.

Profoundly imbued with these ideas, I invited, in 1822, as President of the Republic of Colombia, the Governments of Mexico, Peru, Chili, and Buenos Ayres to form a confederation, and hold on the Isthmus of Panama, or some other point agreeable to the majority, a congress of plenipotentiaries from each State "that should act as a council in great conflicts, to be appealed to in case of common danger, and be a faithful interpreter of public treaties, when difficulties should arise, and conciliate, in short, all our differences." . . .

Longer to defer the general Congress of the Plenipotentiaries of the Republics that in fact are already allied awaiting the accession of the others, would be to deprive ourselves of the advantages which that assembly will produce from its very incipiency.

These advantages are largely increased, if we but contemplate the spectacle that the political world, and particularly that of the European continent, presents to us. . . .

Considering the difficulties and delays presented by the distance separating us, together with other grave motives the general interest suggests, determines me to take this step with a view of bringing about an immediate meeting of our plenipotentiaries, while the rest of the Governments may conclude the preliminaries already gone through by us concerning the appointment and commissioning of their representatives.

With respect to the time of the opening of the Congress, I make bold to think that no obstacle can oppose its verification within six months from this date; and I shall also go so far as to flatter myself that the ardent desire animating all Americans to exalt the power of the world of Columbus will diminish the obstacles and delays that the ministerial preparations demand, and the distance separating the capitals of each state and the central point of the meeting. It seems that if the world should have to choose its capital, the Isthmus of Panama would be selected for this grand destiny, located as it is in the center of the globe, having on one side Asia, and on the other Africa and Europe. The Isthmus of Panama has been tendered for this purpose in existing treaties by the Colombian Government. The Isthmus is equally distant from the extremities of the continent, and on this account ought to be the provisional seat for the first meeting of the confederates. . . .

Nothing, certainly, can so realize the ardent desire of my heart as the agreement I hope for on the part of the confederated Governments to accomplish this august act of America.

Should your Excellency not adhere to this I foresee great delays and injuries, at a time, too, when the movement of the world hurries everything on, and may accelerate to our harm. . . .

The day our plenipotentiaries make the exchanges of their powers will stamp in the diplomatic history of the world an immortal epoch.

When, after a hundred centuries, posterity shall search for the origin of our public law, and shall remember the compacts that solidified its destiny, they will finger with respect the protocols of the Isthmus. In them they will find the plan of the first alliances that shall sketch the mark of our relations with the universe. What, then, shall be the Isthmus of Corinth compared with that of Panama?

❖

NO. 5

1829

The United States: "Destined to Plague America with Torments"

Simón Bolívar

In 1829, the year before his death, Simón Bolívar was facing the breakup of Gran Colombia, the new nation that he governed as president. He seemed now to be questioning his once militant faith in republican forms of government, and inclining toward a monarchical solution to the political chaos around him. The following letter to a British diplomat reveals not only Bolívar's doubts about how Gran Colombia should be governed, but how the great powers of Europe, and the new United States of America, might respond to the chaotic political situation. Colonel Campbell, the recipient of Bolívar's letter, represented the world's greatest naval and commercial power at the time, and the one with the most influence on the governments of the new Latin American republics.

Source: Simón Bolívar. "Letter to Colonel Patrick Campbell." In *Selected Writings of Bolívar,* comp. Vicente Lecuna, ed. Harold A. Bierek Jr., trans. Lewis Bertrand. Vol. 2, *1823–1830.* 2d ed., pp. 731–32. New York: The Colonial Press, 1951.

To: Colonel Patrick Campbell, British chargé d'affaires, Bogotá
Guayaquil, August [5], 1829.
My esteemed friend and Colonel:

. . . I can only begin by thanking you for the many fine things that you say in your letter respecting Colombia and myself. Yet do you not have every right to our gratitude? I am abashed when I recall how much thought you have given and how much you have done, since you came among us, to assist this nation and uphold her leader's glory. . . .

What you are good enough to tell me regarding the latest plan for appointing a European prince as successor to my authority does not take me by surprise. I had been informed of it in part, although with no little mystery and some trepidation, because my thoughts on the subject are well known.

I know not what to say to you about this plan, which is surrounded by a thousand drawbacks. You must know there is no objection on my part, as I am determined to resign at the next Congress. But, who will appease the ambitions of our leaders and the dread of inequality among the lower classes? Do you not think that England would be displeased if a Bourbon were selected? Will not all the new American nations, and the United States, who seem destined by Providence to plague America with torments in the name of freedom, be opposed to such a plan? I seem to foresee a universal conspiracy against our poor Colombia, which is already greatly envied by all the American republics. Every newspaper would issue a call for a new crusade against the ringleaders in the betrayal of freedom, those supporters of the Bourbons and wreckers of the American system. The Peruvians in the South, the Guatemalans and the Mexicans at the Isthmus, the peoples of the Antilles, Americans and liberals everywhere would kindle the flame of discord. Santo Domingo would not remain inactive; she would call upon her brothers to make common cause against a prince of France. Everyone would become our enemy, and Europe would do nothing to help us, for the New World is not worth the price of a Holy Alliance. We have good cause to think this way, judging from the indifference which greeted our launching and maintaining of the struggle for the liberation of half the world, which is soon to become the richest source of Europe's prosperity.

In short, I am far from being opposed to a reorganization of Colombia that conforms to the tested institutions of sagacious Europe. On the contrary, I would be delighted and inspired to redouble my efforts to aid an enterprise that might prove to be our salvation, one that could be accomplished without difficulty if aided by both England and France. With such powerful support we could do anything; without it we could not. I, therefore, reserve my final opinion until we hear the views of the English and French governments respecting the above-mentioned change in our system and the selection of a dynasty. . . .

❖

1845

U.S. Participation in the Brazilian Slave Trade

Henry A. Wise

In the nineteenth century, Brazil and the United States were the two largest slave-owning societies in the world. Until slavery was finally abolished (in the United States in 1865, in Brazil in 1888), the trade in African slaves was the most important issue in Brazilian-U.S. relations. Pressure on Brazil by Great Britain, which had taken the lead in ending the international slave trade, resulted in a Brazilian law outlawing the importation of African slaves in 1831. The law was unenforced, however, and the importation of slaves into Brazil continued unabated. By the 1840s, Brazilian slave importers were relying increasingly on U.S. ships to carry the slaves. Although the United States had outlawed the slave trade in 1808, and signed a treaty with Great Britain in 1842 agreeing to cooperate in the suppression of the trade, the United States failed to enforce both its own law and its treaty obligation. In 1845, Henry A. Wise of Virginia was the U.S. minister to Brazil; in the following dispatch to the secretary of state, John C. Calhoun, Wise described U.S. participation in the trade, and the response of the Brazilian imperial government to Wise's efforts to convince his own government to enforce the 1808 law.

Mr. Wise to Mr. Calhoun. Legation of the United States, Rio De Janeiro, February 18, 1845.

Sir: The African slave trade "thickens around us," and we are treading on its dragon's teeth. It is not to be denied, and I boldly assert it, that the administration of the imperial government of Brazil is forcibly constrained by its influences, and is deeply inculpated in its guilt. With that, it would seem, at first sight, the United States have nothing to do; but an intimate and full knowledge of the subject informs us that the only effectual mode of carrying on that

Source: U.S. Congress. House. 30th Cong., 2nd sess., 1849. Ex. Doc. No. 61. "Correspondence between the Consuls of the United States at Rio de Janeiro, &c., with the Secretary of State, on the subject of the African slave trade," pp. 70–86. Washington, D.C.: GPO, 1849.

trade between Africa and Brazil, at present, involves *our laws and our moral responsibilities* as directly and fully as it does those of this country itself. Our flag alone gives the requisite protection against the right of visit, search and seizure; and our citizens, in all the characters *of owners, of consignees, of agents and of masters and crews of our vessels* are concerned in the business and partake of the profits of the African slave trade, *to and from the ports of Brazil*, as fully as Brazilians themselves and others, in conjunction with whom they carry it on. In fact without the aid of our citizens and our flag, it could not be carried on with success at all. They furnish the protection; they are the common carriers; they sail over and deliver up to the trade *vessels* as well as *cargoes*; they transport the *supplies* of slave factories, the food and raiment of the slave trade's agents, and the goods which constitute the *purchase money* of the slave trade's victims; they carry the *arms* and the *ardent spirits* which are the hellish agents and instruments of the savage wars of African captivity; they afford safe passage to Brazilian masters and crews intended for the slave vessels when sold, and for the American masters and crews who have manned those vessels over to the coast; and they realize a profit in proportion to the risks of a contraband trade. In one word, the sacred principle of the inviolability of the protection of our flag is perverted in the ports of Brazil into a perfect monopoly of the unhallowed gains of the navigation of the African slave trade. And for the reason of this inviolability, our flag and vessels are sought and bought and our citizens, at home and here, *sail* them and *sell* them in the African slave trade to and from all the ports of Brazil. And in all those ports, and in this, the metropolitan port of Rio de Janeiro especially, our vessels are fitted out for the slave trade; and most of the crimes of that trade, in violation of the laws of the United States, openly have their inception under the very eye of the imperial government; and in them all, and in this port especially, *the consummation of those crimes is sheltered, as of right, by the sovereign jurisdiction of this empire.* This is fully shown by the facts of the case which it is now my duty to present, in addition to the other cases of which I have already given information; and it is left to the United States to determine *whether they permit any power upon earth to countenance, to connive at, and to encourage the inception of the crimes of their citizens against their laws in its jurisdiction, and then to shelter the consummation of those crimes and the violation of their laws, and of the sanctity of their flag, under the protection of that same jurisdiction?* . . .

[M. Cavalcanti, the Brazilian minister of marine, told me that] the only reason why England was so unpopular was that she opposed and interrupted the African slave trade; that if the United States prevented their flag and citizens from engaging in it, they too would become unpopular, and there could not be friendly relations with Brazil. I told him at once if it came to that, the United States would *elect any* honorable alternative rather than be compelled to allow the foreign slave trade to be carried on unmolested by their citizens, and that they would assume any justifiable responsibility to snatch their flag from its infamous uses. He said England would rejoice at this. I replied I knew Great Britain would rejoice, and, therefore, Brazil and the United States ought to aid each other to arrest the further prosecution of the African slave trade, and ought effectually to punish their own citizens engaged in it, in order to strip England of all pretext for visit and search on the high seas and on the coast; that the best defence of the lawful slavery already existing in Brazil and the United States, would be for both those powers to enforce, sternly and strictly, their own laws for the suppression of the contraband slave trade, and for them to aid each other in this high and humane duty. He said this was impossible. He was opposed to the slave trade himself; but it was impossible to do this and preserve kind feelings in Brazil towards the United States; . . .

I beseech, I implore, the President of the United States to take a decided stand on this subject. You have no conception of the bold effrontery and the flagrant outrages of the African slave trade, and of the shameless manner in which its worst crimes are licensed here. And every patriot in our land would blush for our country did he know and see, as I do, how *our own citizens sail and sell our flag* to the uses and abuses of that accursed traffic, in almost open violation of our laws. . . .

❖

NO. 7

1845

Texas, Mexico and Manifest Destiny

James K. Polk

Even before the colony of New Spain achieved its independence in 1821, Spanish colonial authorities were encouraging residents of the United States to establish settlements in the sparsely populated northern territories of the colony. The newly independent nation of Mexico at first continued the policy of attracting immigrants to settle its northern frontier, and as a result the state of Coahuila y Tejas quickly attracted the most U.S. immigrants. But as they poured into the state, they soon outnumbered the Mexican inhabitants. Political and cultural tensions between the U.S. settlers and the government of Mexico escalated, ex-

Source: "President's Message." *The Congressional Globe*, 29th Congress, 1st Sess. (Dec. 4, 1845), pp. 4–11.

ploding into a war that ended in a victory for the settlers, who declared the independence of the republic of Texas in 1836. Mexico was too weak to take its land back; U.S. citizens and U.S. capital continued to flow into Texas, which voted for annexation to the United States on July 4, 1845. The U.S. Congress welcomed Texas into the Union on December 29, shortly after President James K. Polk addressed the question of U.S. relations with Texas and Mexico in his annual message to Congress on December 2. With the spirit of "manifest destiny" running high in the United States, European efforts to keep the continent divided became the focus of Polk's address.

Fellow-Citizens of the Senate and House of Representatives:

. . . In performing, for the first time, the duty imposed on me by the constitution, of giving to you information of the state of the Union, and recommending to your consideration such measures as in my judgment are necessary and expedient, I am happy that I can congratulate you on the continued prosperity of our country. Under the blessings of Divine Providence and the benign influence of our free institutions, it stands before the world a spectacle of national happiness. . . .

A constitution for the government of the State of Texas, formed by a convention of deputies, is herewith laid before Congress. It is well known, also, that the people of Texas at the polls have accepted the terms of annexation, and ratified the constitution. . . .

This accession to our territory has been a bloodless achievement. No arm of force has been raised to produce the result. The sword has had no part in the victory. We have not sought to extend our territorial possessions by conquest, or our republican institutions over a reluctant people. It was the deliberate homage of each people to the great principle of our federative union.

If we consider the extent of territory involved in the annexation—its prospective influence on America—the means by which it has been accomplished, springing purely from the choice of the people themselves to share the blessings of our union, the history of the world may be challenged to furnish a parallel. . . . We may rejoice that the tranquil and pervading influence of the American principle of self-government was sufficient to defeat the purposes of British and French interference, and that the almost unanimous voice of the people of Texas has given to that interference a peaceful and effective rebuke. From this example European governments may learn how vain diplomatic arts and intrigues must ever prove upon this continent against that system of self-government which seems natural to our soil, and which will ever resist foreign interference. . . . I regret to inform you that our relations with Mexico, since your last session, have not been of the amiable character which it is our desire to cultivate with all foreign nations. On the sixth day of March last, the Mexican Envoy Extraordinary and Minister Plenipotentiary to the United States made a formal protest . . . against the joint resolution passed by Congress "for the annexation of Texas to the United States," which he chose to regard as a violation of the rights of Mexico, and, in consequence of it, he demanded his passports. . . . Thus, by the acts of Mexico, all diplomatic intercourse between the two countries was suspended.

Since that time Mexico has, until recently, occupied an attitude of hostility towards the United States—has been marshalling and organizing armies, issuing proclamations, and avowing the intention to make war on the United States, either by an open declaration, or by invading Texas. . . . The independence of Texas is a fact conceded by Mexico herself, and she had no right or authority to prescribe restrictions as to the form of government which Texas might afterwards choose to assume. But though Mexico cannot complain of the United States on account of the annexation of Texas, it is to be regretted that serious causes of misunderstanding between the two countries continue to exist, growing out of unredressed injuries inflicted by the Mexican authorities and people on the persons and property of citizens of the United States, through a long series of years. Mexico has admitted these injuries, but has neglected and refused to repair them. . . . Such a continued and unprovoked series of wrongs could never have been tolerated by the United States, had they been committed by one of the principal nations of Europe. Mexico was, however, a neighboring sister republic, which, following our example, had achieved her independence, and for whose success and prosperity all our sympathies were early enlisted. . . . We have, therefore, borne the repeated wrongs she has committed, with great patience, in the hope that a returning sense of justice would ultimately guide her councils, and that we might, if possible, honorably avoid any hostile collision with her. . . .

The rapid extension of our settlements over our territories heretofore unoccupied; the addition of new States to our confederacy; the expansion of free principles, and our rising greatness as a nation, are attracting the attention of the Powers of Europe; and lately the doctrine has been broached in some of them, of a "balance of power" on this continent, to check our advancement. The United States, sincerely desirous of preserving relations of good understanding with all nations, cannot in silence permit any European interference on the North American continent; and should any such interference be attempted, will be ready to resist it at any and all hazards. . . . The American system of government is entirely different from that of Europe. Jealousy among the different sovereigns of Europe, lest any one of them might become too powerful for the rest, has caused them anxiously to desire the establishment of what they term the "balance of power." It cannot be permitted to have any application on the North American continent, and especially to the United States. We must ever maintain the principle, that the people of this continent alone have the right to decide their own destiny. Should any portion of them, constituting an independent State, propose to unite themselves with our confederacy, this will be a question for them and us to determine, without any foreign interposition. . . .

❖

NO. 8

1846

President Polk's War Message to Congress

James K. Polk

A fter the U.S. Congress admitted Texas as a state in 1845 (see Document No. 7), President Polk claimed that Texas's southern boundary (and therefore the new southern boundary of the United States) should be the Rio Grande, or as Polk refers to it below, the Rio del Norte (called the Rio Bravo del Norte by the Mexicans). Mexico, however, insisted that the true boundary was the Rio Nueces, 150 miles to the north. The Mexican government turned away a U.S. offer in December 1845 to buy the territory between the Nueces River and the Rio Grande, as well as California and New Mexico. In response, President Polk ordered the U.S. Army to occupy the land between the Nueces and the Rio Grande, an act regarded by Mexico as an invasion of its national territory. Mexican and U.S. forces clashed on April 25, 1846. When news of the fighting reached Washington on May 9, Polk asked Congress for a declaration of war against Mexico two days later on the controversial grounds that Mexico had "shed American blood upon the American soil." Below is Polk's successful request to Congress.

To the Senate and House of Representatives:

The existing state of the relations between the United States and Mexico renders it proper that I should bring the subject to the consideration of Congress. In my message at the commencement of your present session, the state of these relations, the causes which led to the suspension of diplomatic intercourse between the two countries in March, 1845, and the long continued and unredressed wrongs and injuries committed by the Mexican government on citizens of the United States, in their persons and property, were briefly set forth. . . .

The strong desire to establish peace with Mexico on liberal and honorable terms, and the readiness of this government to regulate and adjust our boundary, and other causes of difference with that power, on such fair and equitable

Source: U.S. Congress. Senate. Senate Document No. 337. 29th Cong., 1st sess. *Public Documents Printed By Order of the Senate of the United States.* . . . Vol. 7. Washington, D.C.: Ritchie & Reiss, 1846.

principles as would lead to permanent relations of the most friendly nature, induced me in September last to seek the reopening of diplomatic relations between the two countries. Every measure adopted on our part had for its object the furtherance of these desired results. In communicating to Congress a succinct statement of the injuries which we had suffered from Mexico, and which have been accumulating during a period of more than twenty years, every expression that could tend to inflame the people of Mexico, or defeat or delay a pacific result, was carefully avoided. An envoy of the United States repaired to Mexico, with full powers to adjust every existing difference. But . . . the Mexican government not only refused to receive him, or listen to his propositions, but, after a long-continued series of menaces, have at last invaded our territory, and shed the blood of our fellow-citizens on our own soil. . . .

In my message at the commencement of the present session, I informed you that, upon the earnest appeal both of the congress and convention of Texas, I had ordered an efficient military force to take a position "between the Nueces and the Del Norte." This had become necessary, to meet a threatened invasion of Texas by the Mexican forces, for which extensive military preparations had been made. The invasion was threatened solely because Texas had determined, in accordance with a solemn resolution of the Congress of the United States, to annex herself to our Union; and under these circumstances, it was plainly our duty to extend our protection over her citizens and soil. . . .

Meantime Texas, by the final action of our Congress, had become an integral part of our Union. The Congress of Texas, by its act of December 19, 1836, had declared the Rio del Norte to be boundary of that republic. Its jurisdiction had been extended and exercised beyond the Nueces. The country between that river and the Del Norte had been represented in the congress and in the convention of Texas; had thus taken part in the act of annexation itself; and is now included within one of our congressional districts. Our own Congress had, moreover, with great unanimity, by the act approved December 31, 1845, recognized the country beyond the Nueces as part of our territory. . . . It became, therefore, of urgent necessity to provide for the defence of that portion of our country. Accordingly, on the 13th of January last, instructions were issued to the general in command of these troops to occupy the left bank of the Del Norte. . . .

The Mexican forces at Matamoras [sic] assumed a belligerent attitude. . . . A party of [U.S.] dragoons, of sixty-three men and officers, were . . . despatched from the American camp up the Rio del Norte, on its left bank, to ascertain whether the Mexican troops had crossed, or were preparing to cross, the river, "became engaged with a large body of these troops, and, after a short affair, in which some sixteen were killed and wounded, appear to have been surrounded and compelled to surrender."

The grievous wrongs perpetrated by Mexico upon our citizens throughout a long period of years remain unredressed; and solemn treaties, pledging her public faith for this redress, have been disregarded. A government either unable or unwilling to enforce the execution of such treaties, fails to perform one of its plainest duties. . . .

Upon the pretext that Texas, a nation as independent as [Mexico] herself, thought proper to unite its destinies with our own, she has affected to believe that we have severed her rightful territory, and in official proclamations and manifestos has repeatedly threatened to make war upon us, for the purpose of reconquering Texas. In the meantime, we have tried every effort at reconciliation. The cup of forbearance had been exhausted, even before the recent information from the frontier of the Del Norte. But now, after reiterated menaces, Mexico has passed the boundary of the United States, has invaded our territory, and shed American blood upon the American soil. She has proclaimed that hostilities have commenced, and that the two nations are now at war.

As war exists, and, notwithstanding all our efforts to avoid it, exists by the act of Mexico herself, we are called upon by every consideration of duty and patriotism to vindicate with decision the honor, the rights, and the interests of our country. . . .

In further vindication of our rights, and defence of our territory, I invoke the prompt action of Congress to recognise the existence of the war, and to place at the disposition of the Executive the means of prosecuting the war with vigor, and thus hastening the restoration of peace. . . .

❖

NO. 9

1846

Bidlack Treaty

The Governments of New Granada and the United States

Just as the United States was waging war against Mexico for possession of the territory that would shortly extend the boundaries of the United States to the Pacific Ocean, the U.S. chargé d'affaires in Bogotá, capital of Nueva Granada (later Colombia), began negotiating a treaty to ensure U.S. transit rights across the province of Panama. Benjamin A. Bidlack, the U.S. chargé, was convinced of the strategic necessity of such a treaty, but he had a difficult time convincing

Source: U.S. Department of State. "Treaty with New Granada," 12 December 1846. *U.S. Statutes at Large and Treaties of the United States of America From December 1, 1845, to March 3, 1851, . . .* Vol. 9, pp. 881–901. Boston: Little, Brown & Co., 1862.

President Polk. At the same time, Bogotá was eager for such an agreement because of its fears of British encroachment on Panama. Acting without instructions from Washington, Bidlack signed a treaty with Bogotá in December 1846 that gave the United States exclusive transit rights in exchange for a U.S. promise to defend the isthmus against any threat to New Granada's sovereignty over Panama. The treaty was ratified by the U.S. Senate on June 10, 1848, just in time to accommodate the demand for oceangoing passage to California that would be generated by the gold rush of 1849.

The United States of North America, and the republic of New Granada, in South America, desiring to make lasting and firm the friendship and good understanding which happily exist between both nations, have resolved to fix, in a manner clear, distinct, and positive, the rules which shall in future be religiously observed between each other, by means of a treaty, or general convention of peace and friendship, commerce and navigation. . . .

ARTICLE 3. [B]eing likewise desirous of placing the commerce and navigation of their respective countries on the liberal basis of perfect equality and reciprocity, mutually agree that the citizens of each may frequent all the coasts and countries of the other, and reside and trade there, in all kinds of produce, manufactures, and merchandise. . . .

ARTICLE 14. The citizens of the United States residing in the territories of the republic of New Granada shall enjoy the most perfect and entire security of conscience, without being annoyed, prevented, or disturbed on account of their religious belief. . . . provided that in so doing they observe the decorum due to divine worship and the respect due to the laws, usages, and customs of the country. . . .

ARTICLE 35. [T]he citizens, vessels, and merchandise of the United States shall enjoy in the ports of New Granada, including those of the part of the Granadian territory generally denominated Isthmus of Panama . . . all the exemptions, privileges, and immunities concerning commerce and navigation, which are now or may hereafter be enjoyed by Granadian citizens, their vessels, and merchandise; and that this equality of favors shall be made to extend to the passengers, correspondence, and merchandise of the United States, in their transit across the said territory. . . . And, in order to secure to themselves the tranquil and constant enjoyment of these advantages, and as an especial compensation for the said advantages, . . . the United States guaranty [sic], positively and efficaciously, to New Granada, by the present stipulation, the perfect neutrality of the beforementioned isthmus, with the view that the free transit from the one to the other sea may not be interrupted or embarrassed in any future time while this treaty exists; and in consequence, the United States also guaranty [sic], in the same manner, the rights of sovereignty and property which New Granada has and possesses over the said territory. . . .

❖

1847

The United States:
"An Inconceivable Extravaganza"

Domingo Faustino Sarmiento

B orn and raised in Argentina during its struggle for independence from Spain, Domingo Faustino Sarmiento (1811–88) was a prominent liberal and a strong advocate of compulsory public education to overcome what he regarded as Latin America's backwardness. During his political exile in Chile in 1840, Sarmiento wrote *Facundo: Civilization and Barbarism* (1845), in which he denounced the Argentine dictatorship of Juan Manuel Rosas, who had sent him into exile. In 1845 the Chilean government sent Sarmiento to Europe and the United States on a three-year mission to study educational institutions and methods. While in the United States, Sarmiento wrote the letter excerpted below to Valentín Alsina (1802–69), an Argentine politician and journalist who was also exiled by Rosas. Returning to Chile favorably impressed by the strength of representative government and the nonhierarchical nature of public education in the United States, Sarmiento wrote a two-volume memoir of his travels, *Viajes en Europa, Africa, i América, 1845–1847* (1849–51), which was widely read throughout Latin America and included the letter to Alsina. In 1852 Sarmiento briefly returned to Argentina to join a successful movement against Rosas, and served as president of Argentina from 1868 to 1874.

Don Valentín Alsina:

I am leaving the United States, my dear friend, in that state of excitement caused by viewing a new drama . . . I want to tell you that I am departing sad, thoughtful, pleased, and humbled, with half of my illusions damaged while others struggle against reason to reconstitute again that imagery with which we always clothe ideas not yet seen. . . . The United States is without precedent, a

Source: Domingo Faustino Sarmiento, "Travels in the United States in 1847," November 12, 1847. In Allison Williams Bunkley, *A Sarmiento Anthology*. Copyright © 1948, renewed 1976 by Princeton University Press. Reprinted by permission of Princeton University Press. Pp. 193–266.

sort of extravaganza that at first sight shocks and disappoints one's expectations because it runs counter to preconceived ideas. Yet this inconceivable extravaganza is grand and noble, occasionally sublime, and always follows its genius. It has, moreover, such an appearance of permanence and organic strength that ridicule would ricochet from its surface like a spent bullet off the scaly hide of an alligator. . . .

You and I, my friend, having been educated under the iron rod of the sublimest of tyrants . . . have prided ourselves and taken renewed courage from the aureola of light shining over the United States in the midst of the leaden night that broods over South America. At last we have said to each other in order to steel ourselves against present evils: "The Republic exists, strong and invincible, and its light will reach us when the South reflects the North." It is true, the Republic exists! However, on studying it at close range, one finds that in many respects it does not correspond to the abstract idea which we had formed of it. . . .

Why did the Saxon race happen upon this part of the world, so admirably suited to its industrial instincts? And why did South America, where there were gold and silver mines and gentle, submissive Indians, fall to the lot of the Spanish race—a region made to order for its proud laziness, backwardness, and industrial ineptitude? Is there not order and premeditation in all these cases? Is there not a Providence? . . .

I do not propose to make Providence an accomplice in all American usurpations, nor in its bad example which, in a more or less remote period, may attract to it politically, or annex to it, as the Americans say, Canada, Mexico, etc. Then the union of free men will begin at the North Pole and, for lack of further territory, end at the Isthmus of Panama. . . .

The American village . . . is a small edition of the whole country, with its civil government, its press, schools, banks, municipal organization, census, spirit, and appearance. Out of the primitive forests, the stagecoaches or railroad cars emerge into small clearings in the midst of which stand ten or twelve houses of machine-made bricks held together by mortar laid in very fine, straight lines, which gives their walls the smoothness of geometrical figures. The houses are two stories high and have painted, wooden roofs. Doors and windows, painted white, are fastened by patent locks. Green shades brighten and vary the regularity of the façade. I pay much attention to these details because they alone are sufficient to characterize a people and to give rise to a whole train of reflections. . . .

Westward, where civilization declines and in the far west where it is almost nonexistent because of the sparseness of the population, the aspect, of course, changes. Comfort is reduced to a bare minimum and houses become mere log cabins built in twenty-four hours out of logs set one on top of the other and crossed and dove-tailed at the corners. But even in those remote settlements, there is an appearance of perfect equality among the people in dress, manner, and even intelligence. The merchant, the doctor, the sheriff, and the farmer all look alike. . . . Gradations of civilization and wealth are not expressed, as among us, by special types of clothing. Americans wear no jacket or poncho, but a common type of clothes, and they have even a common bluntness of manner that preserves the appearance of equality in education. . . .

They have no kings, nobles, privileged classes, men born to command, or human machines born to obey. Is not this result consonant with the ideas of justice and equality which Christianity accepts in theory? Well-being is more widely distributed among them than among any other people. . . . They say that this prosperity is all due to the ease of taking up new land. But why, in South America, where it is even easier to take up new land, are neither population nor wealth on the increase, and cities and even capitals so static that not a hundred new houses have been built in them during the past ten years? . . .

The American male is a man with a home or with the certainty of owning one, beyond the reach of hunger and despair, able to hope for any future that his imagination is capable of conjuring up, and endowed with political feelings and needs. In short, he is a man who is his own master, and possessed of a mind elevated by education and a sense of his own dignity. . . .

God has at last permitted the concentration in a single nation of enough virgin territory to permit society to expand indefinitely without fear of poverty. He has given it iron to supplement human strength, coal to turn its machines, forests to provide material for naval construction, popular education to develop the productive capacity of every one of its citizens, religious freedom to attract hundreds of thousands of foreigners to its shores, and political liberty which views despotism and special privilege with abhorrence. It is the republic, in short—strong and ascendant like a new star in the firmament. . . .

The approach to New Orleans is marked by visible changes in the type of cultivation and the architecture of the buildings. . . . Alas slavery, the deep, incurable sore that threatens gangrene to the robust body of the Union! . . . A racial war of extermination will come within a century, or else a mean, black, backward nation will be found alongside a white one—the most powerful and cultivated on earth! . . .

NO. 11

1848

The Treaty of Guadalupe Hidalgo

The Governments of Mexico and the United States

The admission of Texas as a state in 1845 (see Document No. 7) led almost inevitably to war with Mexico, which continued to claim all of Texas as Mexican territory. After hostilities started on April 25, 1846, U.S. forces expanded the war by striking against California and New Mexico, and by marching inland from Veracruz to occupy Mexico City. President James Polk sent Nicholas Trist to Mexico City to negotiate a peace treaty, which was signed on February 2, 1848, in the town of Guadalupe Hidalgo outside the Mexican capital. The United States would acquire its last territory from Mexico in 1853, when a weak and impoverished government agreed to sell another 30,000 square miles of land, the Mesilla Valley, now part of southern Arizona and New Mexico. Known as the Gadsden Purchase in the United States, that agreement also annuled the provision of the Treaty of Guadalupe Hidalgo that made the United States responsible for Indian raids into Mexico.

In the name of Almighty God: The United States of America, and the United Mexican States, animated by a sincere desire to put an end to the calamities of the war which unhappily exists between the two Republics, and to establish upon a solid basis relations of peace and friendship, which shall confer reciprocal benefits upon the citizens of both, and assure the concord, harmony and mutual confidence, wherein the two Peoples should live, as good Neighbours, have for that purpose appointed their respective Plenipotentiaries . . . who . . . have, under the protection of Almighty God, the author of Peace, arranged, agreed upon, and signed the following treaty of peace, friendship, limits and settlement. . . .

ARTICLE 5. The Boundary line between the two Republics shall commence in the Gulf of Mexico, three leagues from land, opposite the mouth of the Rio Grande, otherwise called Rio Bravo del Norte, or opposite the mouth of it's deepest branch . . . thence, up the middle of that river, following the deepest

Source: U.S. Department of State. *Treaties and Other International Agreements of the United States of America 1776–1949.* Vol. 9, comp. Charles I. Bevans, pp. 791–806. Washington, D.C.: GPO, 1972.

channel, . . . to the point where it strikes the Southern boundary of New Mexico; thence, westwardly along the whole Southern Boundary of New Mexico (which runs north of the town called Paso) to it's western termination; thence, northward, along the western line of New Mexico, until it intersects the first branch of the river Gila; . . . until it empties into the Rio Colorado; thence, across the Rio Colorado, following the division line between Upper and Lower California, to the Pacific Ocean. . . .

In order to designate the Boundary line with due precision, upon authoritative maps, and to establish upon the ground landmarks which shall show the limits of both Republics, as described in the present Article, the two Governments shall each appoint a Commissioner and a Surveyor, who, before the expiration of one year from the date of the exchange of ratifications of this treaty, shall meet at the Port of San Diego, and proceed to run and mark the said Boundary in it's whole course to the mouth of the Rio Bravo del Norte. They shall keep journals and make out plans of their operations; and the result, agreed upon by them, shall be deemed a part of this treaty, and shall have the same force as if it were inserted therein. . . .

The Boundary line established by this Article shall be religiously respected by each of the two Republics, and no change shall ever be made therein, except by the express and free consent of both nations, lawfully given by the General Government of each, in conformity with it's own constitution.

ARTICLE 6. The vessels and citizens of the United States shall, in all time, have a free and uninterrupted passage by the Gulf of California, and by the river Colorado below it's confluence with the Gila, to and from their possessions situated north of the Boundary line defined in the preceding Article: it being understood that this passage is to be by navigating the Gulf of California and the river Colorado, and not by land, without the express consent of the Mexican Government. . . .

ARTICLE 8. Mexicans now established in territories previously belonging to Mexico, and which remain for the future within the limits of the United States, as defined by the present Treaty, shall be free to continue where they now reside, or to remove at any time to the Mexican Republic, retaining the property which they possess in the said territories, or disposing thereof and removing the proceeds wherever they please; without their being subjected, on this account, to any contribution, tax or charge whatever.

Those who shall prefer to remain in the said territories, may either retain the title and rights of Mexican citizens, or acquire those of citizens of the United States. But, they shall be under the obligation to make their election within one year from the date of the exchange of ratifications of this treaty: and those who shall remain in the said territories, after the expiration of that year, without having declared their intention to retain the character of Mexicans, shall be considered to have elected to become citizens of the United States.

In the said territories, property of every kind, now belonging to Mexicans not established there, shall be inviolably respected. The present owners, the heirs of these, and all Mexicans who may hereafter acquire said property by contract, shall enjoy with respect to it, guaranties [sic] equally ample as if the same belonged to citizens of the United States.

ARTICLE 9. The Mexicans who, in the territories aforesaid, shall not preserve the character of citizens of the Mexican Republic, conformably with what is stipulated in the preceding article, shall be incorporated into the Union of the United States and be admitted as soon as possible, according to the principles of the Federal Constitution, to the enjoyment of all the rights of citizens of the United States. . . .

ARTICLE 11. Considering that a great part of the territories which, by the present treaty, are to be comprehended for the future within the limits of the United States, is now occupied by savage tribes, who will hereafter be under the exclusive control of the Government of the United States, and whose incursions within the territory of Mexico would be prejudicial in the extreme; it is solemnly agreed that all such incursions shall be forcibly restrained by the Government of the United States, whensoever this may be necessary; and that when they cannot be prevented, they shall be punished by the said Government, and satisfaction for the same shall be exacted: all in the same way, and with equal diligence and energy, as if the same incursions were meditated or committed within it's own territory against it's own citizens.

It shall not be lawful, under any pretext whatever, for any inhabitant of the United States, to purchase or acquire any Mexican or any foreigner residing in Mexico, who may have been captured by Indians inhabiting the territory of either of the two Republics; nor to purchase or acquire horses, mules, cattle or property of any kind, stolen within Mexican territory by such Indians; . . .

And, in the event of any person or persons, captured within Mexican territory by Indians, being carried into the territory of the United States, the Government of the latter engages and binds itself, in the most solemn manner, so soon as it shall know of such captives being within it's territory, and shall be able so to do, through the faithful exercise of it's influence and power, to rescue them, and return them to their country, or deliver them to the agent or representative of the Mexican Government. . . . And finally, the sacredness of this obligation shall never be lost sight of by the said Government [of the United States], when providing for the removal of the Indians from any portion of the said territories, or for it's being settled by citizens of the United States; but on the contrary, special care shall then be taken not to place it's Indian occupants under the necessity of seeking new homes, by committing those invasions which the United States have solemnly obliged themselves to restrain.

ARTICLE 12. In consideration of the extension acquired by the boundaries of the United States, as defined in the fifth Article of the present treaty, the Government of the United States engages to pay to that of the Mexican Republic the sum of fifteen Millions of Dollars. . . .

NO. 12

1850

The Clayton–Bulwer Treaty

The Governments of the United States and Great Britain

With the conclusion of the Mexican-American War in 1848, a secure overland passageway between the Atlantic and Pacific Oceans was increasingly viewed by the United States as a strategic and economic imperative. A major obstacle to that objective was Great Britain, the world's greatest industrial and naval power and the foreign country with the biggest single commercial and financial interest in Latin America. Britian asserted political control over part of the Central American isthmus, having established protectorates on the Caribbean coasts of Mexico and Guatemala (in territory that in 1871 became the colony of British Honduras) and Nicaragua. As a result, the United States and Britain signed the "Convention as to Ship-Canal Connecting Atlantic and Pacific Oceans," on April 19, 1850. Known as the Clayton–Bulwer Treaty after Secretary of State John M. Clayton and Sir Henry Bulwer, the British minister in Washington, it was criticized by a nationalistic faction of the Democratic Party for violating the Monroe Doctrine by legitimizing the British presence in Central America. Yet the treaty also represented a diplomatic triumph for the young republic, which managed to curb British ambitions in the region while elevating itself to a status of equality with the world's superpower. Subsequently ratified by the U.S. Senate, the treaty remained in force until 1901, when it was superceded by the Hay-Pauncefote Treaty (Document No. 30).

The United States of America and Her Britannic Majesty, being desirous of consolidating the relations of amity which so happily subsist between them by setting forth and fixing in a convention their views and intentions with reference to any means of communication by ship-canal which may be constructed between the Atlantic and Pacific Oceans by the way of the river San Juan de Nicaragua, and either or both of the lakes of Nicaragua or Managua, to any port or place on the Pacific Ocean. . . .

Source: U.S. Congress. Senate. *Treaties, Conventions, International Acts, Protocols and Agreements Between the United States of America and Other Powers, 1776–1909.* Vol. 1. "Convention as to Ship-Canal Connecting Atlantic and Pacific Oceans." Pp. 659–664. 61st Congress, 2nd Session, Document No. 357. Washington, D.C.: GPO, 1910.

ARTICLE 1. The Governments of the United States and Great Britain hereby declare that neither the one nor the other will ever obtain or maintain for itself any exclusive control over the said ship-canal; agreeing that neither will ever erect or maintain any fortifications commanding the same, or in the vicinity thereof, or occupy, or fortify, or colonize, or assume or exercise any dominion over Nicaragua, Costa Rica, the Mosquito coast, or any part of Central America. . . .

ARTICLE 2. Vessels of the United States or Great Britain traversing the said canal shall, in case of war between the contracting parties, be exempted from blockade, detention, or capture by either of the belligerents. . . .

ARTICLE 3. In order to secure the construction of the said canal, the contracting parties engage that, if any such canal shall be undertaken upon fair and equitable terms by any parties having the authority of the local government or governments through whose territory the same may pass, then the persons employed in making the said canal, and their property used or to be used for that object, shall be protected, from the commencement of the said canal to its completion. . . .

ARTICLE 5. The contracting parties further engage that when the said canal shall have been completed they will protect it from interruption, seizure, or unjust confiscation, and that they will guarantee the neutrality thereof, so that the said canal may forever be open and free, and the capital invested therein secure. . . .

ARTICLE 6. The contracting parties in this convention engage to invite every State with which both or either have friendly intercourse to enter into stipulations with them similar to those which they have entered into with each other, to the end that all other States may share in the honor and advantage of having contributed to a work of such general interest and importance as the canal herein contemplated. . . .

ARTICLE 7. [T]he Governments of the United States and Great Britain determine to give their support and encouragement to such persons or company as may first offer to commence the same, with the necessary capital, the consent of the local authorities, and on such principles as accord with the spirit and intention of this convention. . . .

ARTICLE 8. The Governments of the United States and Great Britain having not only desired, in entering into this convention, to accomplish a particular object, but also to establish a general principle, they hereby agree to extend their protection, by treaty stipulations, to any other practicable communications, whether by canal or railway, across the isthmus which connects North and South America, and especially to the interoceanic communications, should the same prove to be practicable, whether by canal or railway, which are now proposed to be established by the way of Tehuantepec or Panama. . . .

NO. 13

1854

The Ostend Manifesto

James Buchanan, J. Y. Mason and Pierre Soulé

In 1854, when three U.S. diplomats wrote this letter to Secretary of State William L. Marcy, the United States had just completed its westward expansion as far as the Pacific Ocean. Intensifying sectional strife over slavery would lead to civil war in just six years. Proslavery expansionists demanded that the Spanish colony of Cuba—where African slavery continued to sustain the island's sugar plantation economy—be added to the Union. The nationalistic administration of Franklin Pierce (1853–57) made that cry its own. On April 3, 1854, Marcy instructed the U.S. minister in Spain, Pierre Soulé, to make yet another offer to Spain to buy Cuba, but Spain again declined to sell the island. In August, Marcy instructed Soulé; James Buchanan, the U.S. minister to Great Britain; and John Y. Mason, the U.S. minister to France, to confer and advise him on a course of action that would lead to the U.S. acquisition of Cuba. Although their report to Marcy was a secret letter sent by messenger, it became known as the Ostend Manifesto after the city in Belgium in which their meetings had commenced on October 9. The men adjourned their discussions to Aix-la-Chapelle, Prussia, on October 18. After their report was leaked to the press, unfavorable publicity and election defeats for the administration's candidates in the midterm congressional elections convinced Pierce to abandon the effort to acquire Cuba. Pierce's successor was none other than the principal author of the "Ostend Manifesto," James Buchanan, whose election platform called for the island's annexation.

Aix-la-Chapelle [Prussia], October 18th, 1854.
To the Hon. Wm. L. Marcy, Secretary of State.

SIR: The undersigned, in compliance with the wish expressed by the President [Franklin Pierce] in the several confidential despatches you have addressed to us respectively to that effect, have met in conference, first at Ostend, in Belgium, on the 9th, 10th, and 11th instant, and then at Aix-la-Chapelle, in Prussia, on the days next following, up to the date hereof. . . .

Source: John Bassett Moore, ed., *The Works of James Buchanan, Comprising His Speeches, State Papers, and Private Correspondence.* Vol. 9, 1853–1855, pp. 260–67. New York: Antiquarian Press Ltd., 1960.

We have arrived at the conclusion and are thoroughly convinced that an immediate and earnest effort ought to be made by the Government of the United States to purchase Cuba from Spain, at any price for which it can be obtained, not exceeding the sum of one hundred and twenty millions of dollars. . . .

We proceed to state some of the reasons which have brought us to this conclusion; and, for the sake of clearness, we shall specify them under two distinct heads:

1. The United States ought, if practicable, to purchase Cuba with as little delay as possible.

2. The probability is great that the Government and Cortes of Spain will prove willing to sell it, because this would essentially promote the highest and best interests of the Spanish people.

Then—1. It must be clear to every reflecting mind that, from the peculiarity of its geographical position and the considerations attendant on it, Cuba is as necessary to the North American Republic as any of its present members, and that it belongs naturally to that great family of States of which the Union is the Providential Nursery.

From its locality it commands the mouth of the Mississippi and the immense and annually increasing trade which must seek this avenue to the ocean.

On the numerous navigable streams, measuring an aggregate course of some thirty thousand miles, which disembogue themselves through this magnificent river into the Gulf of Mexico, the increase of the population, within the last ten years, amounts to more than that of the entire Union at the time Louisiana was annexed to it.

The natural and main outlet of the products of this entire population, the highway of their direct intercourse with the Atlantic and the Pacific States, can never be secure, but must ever be endangered whilst Cuba is a dependency of a distant Power, in whose possession it has proved to be a source of constant annoyance and embarrassment to their interests.

Indeed, the Union can never enjoy repose, nor possess reliable security, as long as Cuba is not embraced within its boundaries.

Its immediate acquisition by our Government is of paramount importance, and we cannot doubt but that it is a consummation devoutly wished for by its inhabitants.

The intercourse which its proximity to our coasts begets and encourages between them and the citizens of the United States has, in the progress of time, so united their interests and blended their fortunes, that they now look upon each other as if they were one people and had but one destiny.

Considerations exist which render delay in the acquisition of this Island exceedingly dangerous to the United States.

The system of emigration and labor lately organized within its limits, and the tyranny and oppression which characterize its immediate rulers, threaten an insurrection, at every moment, which may result in direful consequences to the American People.

Cuba has thus become to us an unceasing danger, and a permanent cause of anxiety and alarm. . . .

2. But if the United States and every commercial nation would be benefited by this transfer, the interests of Spain would also be greatly and essentially promoted.

She cannot but see that such a sum of money as we are willing to pay for the Island would effect in the development of her vast natural resources. . . .

But Spain is in imminent danger of losing Cuba without remuneration.

Extreme oppression, it is now universally admitted, justifies any people in endeavoring to relieve themselves from the yoke of their oppressors. The sufferings which the corrupt, arbitrary, and unrelenting local administration necessarily entails upon the inhabitants of Cuba cannot fail to stimulate and keep alive that spirit of resistance and revolution against Spain which has of late years been so often manifested. In this condition of affairs, it is vain to expect that the sympathies of the people of the United States will not be warmly enlisted in favor of their oppressed neighbors. . . .

But if Spain, deaf to the voice of her own interest, and actuated by stubborn pride and a false sense of honor, should refuse to sell Cuba to the United States, then the question will arise, what ought to be the course of the American Government under such circumstances? . . .

Our past history forbids that we should acquire the Island of Cuba without the consent of Spain, unless justified by the great law of self-preservation. We must in any event preserve our own conscious rectitude and our own self-respect. . . .

After we shall have offered Spain a price for Cuba, far beyond its present value, and this shall have been refused, it will then be time to consider the question, does Cuba in the possession of Spain seriously endanger our internal peace and the existence of our cherished Union?

Should this question be answered in the affirmative, then, by every law human and Divine, we shall be justified in wresting it from Spain, if we possess the power; and this, upon the very same principle that would justify an individual in tearing down the burning house of his neighbor, if there were no other means of preventing the flames from destroying his own home.

Under such circumstances, we ought neither to count the cost, nor regard the odds which Spain might enlist against us. We forbear to enter into the question, whether the present condition of the Island would justify such a measure. We should, however, be recreant to our duty, be unworthy of our gallant forefathers, and commit base treason against our posterity, should we permit Cuba to be Africanized and become a second St. Domingo, with all its attendant horrors to the white race, and suffer the flames to extend to our neighboring shores, seriously to endanger or actually to consume the fair fabric of our Union. . . .

❖

1860

Filibuster

William Walker

W illiam Walker was the best known of the filibusters (from the Spanish *fil-ibustero,* for freebooter or buccaneer), those North Americans who raided Mexico, Central America and the Caribbean in the mid–nineteenth century. Inspired by an ideology of Manifest Destiny and motivated by factors ranging from joblessness to the extension of Southern slavery, filibusters became imperialistic brigands to some and rebellious heroes to others. In 1853 at the age of twenty-nine, William Walker of Tennessee led his first expedition into northern Mexico, where he declared the states of Baja California and Sonora to be an "independent republic" before being ejected by the Mexican army. Nicaragua soon became the scene of Walker's most famous exploits, from 1855 to 1860. Initially backed by the Vanderbilt Steamship Company, Walker managed to briefly become the president of Nicaragua. He declared English the official language and legalized slavery. Holding tenuously to power, he soon confronted a Central American military alliance that defeated his government in April 1857 and drove him temporarily back to the United States. Walker wrote *The War in Nicaragua,* excerpted below, in part to convince Southerners to support his cause. His final attempt at Central American conquest ended when he was captured by the British and executed by a Honduran firing squad on September 12, 1860.

On the first of March, 1856, the regular American force in the service of Nicaragua was about six hundred men. It was organized in two battalions, one denominated the Rifle and the other the Light Infantry Battalion. . . .

During the four months which had elapsed since the establishment of the provisional government, the Americans had been, for the most part, stationed in [the declared capital of] Granada. But the sickness prevailing there, as well as the partial necessity for a force elsewhere, had caused small bodies to be sent in several directions through the Republic, thus familiarizing the people of the

Source: William Walker. *The War in Nicaragua,* pp. 177–78, 206–07, 213–14, 252, 254, 255–56, 259–60, 266, 280, 429–30. Mobile: S. H. Goetzel, 1860.

remote districts with the appearance of the Americans, and furnishing the latter with a knowledge of the roads and local prejudices of the inhabitants. . . .

After the return of the Americans to Granada an enemy fiercer and more malignant than the Costa Ricans [who led a Central American attack against Walker] began to ravage their thinned ranks. The fever which had before carried off many, re-appeared in an even aggravated form [sic]. . . .

New-comers, however, began to arrive to take the place of those cut off by battle and disease. . . . Upward of twenty men had come at their own expense to Granada, and they were enlisted for four months, and put into the rangers under Captain Davenport. This addition to the numbers of the army of course re-animated the old troops . . . and after the arrival of the new men all were as eager as ever to march against the enemy at [the town of] Rivas. . . .

. . . The common people, with their strong religious instinct, thought that Providence had sent the cholera in order to drive the Costa Ricans from the soil. The Americans with that faith in themselves which has carried them in a wonderfully short period from one ocean to another, regarded their establishment in Nicaragua as fixed beyond the control of casualties. But to him who knows that great changes in states and societies are not wrought without long and severe labor, the difficulties of the Americans in Nicaragua might appear to be only beginning. To destroy an old political organization is a comparatively easy task, and little besides force is requisite for its accomplishment; but to build up and re-constitute society—to gather the materials from the four quarters, and construct them into an harmonious whole, fitted for the uses of a new civilization—requires more than force, more than even genius for the work, and agents with which to complete it. Time and patience, as well as skill and labor, are needed for success; and they who undertake it, must be willing to devote a lifetime to the work. . . .

The difference of language between the members of the old society and that portion of the white race, necessarily dominant in the new, while it was a cause keeping the elements apart, afforded also a means of regulating the relations between the several races meeting on the same soil. In order that the laws of the Republic might be thoroughly published, it was decreed that they should be published in English as well as in Spanish. . . .

The general tendency of these several decrees was the same; they were intended to place a large proportion of the land in the hands of the white race. The military force of the State might, for a time, secure the Americans in the government of the Republic, but in order that their possession of government might be permanent, it was requisite for them to hold the land. But the natives who had held the lands for more than a generation admitted that the cultivated fields had diminished in number and extent every year since the independence, for the want of a proper system of labor; hence, according to the admission of all parties, the reorganization of labor was necessary for the development of the resources of the country.

In order to command the labor already in the country a decree was issued for enforcing contracts for terms of service. A stringent decree against vagrants was also published, and this was a measure of military caution as well as of political economy. . . .

One of the earliest acts of the Federal Constituent Assembly was the abolition of slavery in Central America; and as this, among other acts, was repealed by the [presidential] decree of the 22nd of September, it was generally supposed the latter re-established slavery in Nicaragua. Whether this be a strictly legal deduction may be doubted; but the repeal of the prohibition clearly prepared the way for the reintroduction of slavery. . . . By this act must the Walker administration be judged; for it is the key to its whole policy. In fact, the wisdom or folly of this decree involved the wisdom or folly of the American movement in Nicaragua; for on the re-establishment of African slavery there depended the permanent presence of the white race in that region. . . . Without such labor as the new decree gave the Americans could have played no other part in Central America that that of the praetorian guard at Rome or of the Janizaries of the East; and for such degrading service as this they were ill suited by the habits and traditions of their race. . . .

. . . The conservation of slavery . . . goes to the vital relations of capital toward labor, and by the firm footing it gives the former it enables the intellect of society to push boldly forward in the pursuit of new forms of civilization. At present it is the struggle of free labor with slave labor which prevents the energies of the former from being directed against the capital of the North through the ingenious machinery of the ballot box and universal suffrage; and it is difficult to conceive how capital can be secured from the attacks of the majority in a pure democracy unless with the aid of a force which gets its strength from slave labor. . . .

While the slavery decree was calculated to bind the Southern States [in the United States] to Nicaragua, as if she were one of themselves, it was also a disavowal of any desire for annexation to the Federal Union. And it was important, in every respect, to make it appear that the American movement in Nicaragua did not contemplate annexation. . . .

. . . The true field for the exertion of slavery is in tropical America; there it finds the natural seat of its empire and thither it can spread if it will but make the effort, regardless of conflicts with adverse interests. The way is open and it only requires courage and will to enter the path and reach the goal. Will the South be true to herself in this emergency? . . .

. . . That which you ignorantly call "Filibusterism" is not the offspring of hasty passion or ill-regulated desire; it is the fruit of the sure, unerring instincts which act in accordance with laws as old as the creation. They are but drivellers who speak of establishing fixed relations between the pure white American race, as it exists in the United States, and the mixed Hispano-Indian race, as it exists in Mexico and Central America, without the employment of force. The history of the world presents no such Utopian vision as that of an inferior race yielding meekly and peacefully to the controlling influence of a superior people. Whenever barbarism and civilization, or two distinct forms of civilization, meet face to face, the result must be war. Therefore, the struggle between the old and the new elements in Nicaraguan society was not passing or accidental, but natural and inevitable. By the bones of the mouldering dead at Masaya, at Rivas, and at Granada, I adjure you never to abandon the cause of Nicaragua. Let it be your waking and your sleeping thought to devise means for a return to the land whence we were unjustly brought. And, if we be but true to ourselves, all will yet end well.

❖

NO. 15

1866

Mexico Seeks Support Against a Foreign Aggressor

Matías Romero

After losing the War of the Reform (1858–61), Mexican conservatives persuaded Napoléon III, the emperor of France, to deploy the French army to drive the liberal government of President Benito Juárez out of office and replace him with a European monarch. Napoléon complied, and as a result Mexico was subjected to its second major foreign intervention in two decades. The invasion and occupation of Mexico by the French army prepared the way for the installation of Austrian Archduke Maximilian as Emperor Maximilian I of Mexico in 1864. Juárez continued to direct loyalist forces in a prolonged guerrilla war against Maximilian's French-backed conservative government. After Napoléon III began to withdraw the French occupation army, the liberal resistance forces defeated Maximilian's weakened and unpopular government. Maximilian was arrested and executed on May 14, 1867, and Benito Juárez resumed office as president in August. Throughout the war against the French, Juárez depended on Matías Romero, his official representative in Washington, to lobby Presidents Lincoln and Johnson, the members of their cabinet and the members of Congress for material and political support. Below are excerpts from Romero's dispatches to his government.

Source: Copyright © 1986 from *Mexican Lobby: Matías Romero in Washington, 1861–1867,* by Thomas Schoonover, pp. 123–27. Reprinted with permission of the University Press of Kentucky.

April 8, 1866.

At the designated hour [10 A.M.] I arrived and at eleven the president [Andrew Johnson] received me in his private library. . . . I explained that our country was exhausted after our long civil war and, as a consequence of the current war, commerce was paralyzed, agriculture suspended, and all sources of wealth closed. In addition, with the French in possession of the small national income, the totality permitted one to form an exact idea of our situation. Only the patriotism of the Mexican people, I observed, had prolonged the resistance for so long in such an unequal contest. Until now, I acknowledged, the expectation that either Napoleon would cease his effort to conquer Mexico after the United States Civil War or that the United States would intervene in the contest had sustained the patriotism of the Mexican people. These expectations led them to accept sacrifices which they believed would not last much longer. However, neither expectation is being realized. Instead of retiring, Napoleon is making a major drive to reduce all resistance and consolidate Maximilian's position. At the same time, the exhaustion of Mexico has reached a dangerous level. . . . [V]arious units of our forces have had to surrender because of complete lack of munitions. . . . I had spoken frequently about this matter with [General Ulysses S.] Grant [secretary of war], I added, who expressed great interest in giving us some arms, but until now all steps taken toward this objective have failed. On this occasion I limited myself to speaking of our need for arms and how, in my judgment, we could obtain them from this government without causing it to fail in its neutral duties.

I had thought deeply on this matter, I told him then, and there seemed two ways in which we could obtain arms. First, as commanding general of the United States Army, Grant could request a certain number of arms without specifying why he needed them. Given his antecedents, good services, and actual position, they would probably be given him without question. If, unexpectedly, the French should discover that these arms had fallen into our hands and protest, the government could then decide to approve or disapprove Grant's conduct and the matter would not go beyond that.

The second method was more frank and perhaps more decorous for this country. I would request to purchase 50,000 rifles for my country and to pay for them with a long-term note drawn on our treasury or with other acceptable financial obligations. If the French government wanted to buy arms from the United States, I assumed it certainly would be sold any quantity it desired. If this were legitimate treatment for the French I saw no reason why Mexico should not be treated the same way.

The president told me then, somewhat surprised, that he understood we already had received arms via Grant. I replied in the negative. Although the general had adopted the first plan indicated and was prepared to accept the responsibility that might fall on him for such conduct, the secretary of war had encountered some difficulties that prevented the plan's realization.

He positively desired us to receive arms, the president asserted then, which he would give us if it could be done in a manner honorable for the United States. He would accept in payment what we could offer for them. With the great abundance of arms, he found it strange that some had not already passed into our hands.

Grant, who I saw frequently and who was well aware of our situation, I informed him, had made a special effort on his own responsibility to give us some weapons. Up to this point, however, he had not succeeded. . . .

Expanding my remarks regarding our lack of arms and resources a little, I told the president that we had to prepare for a long war because, in my judgment, Napoleon was not considering leaving Mexico soon. Although he certainly ought to be satisfied that the intervention was a big mistake, this expedition so involved his honor and reputation as an able, clever man that he will prefer to continue spending money and spilling blood rather than recognize his error. . . .

At once, the president asked me with great interest for my opinion regarding the state of affairs in Mexico. With proper frankness and clarity, I responded that with or without United States assistance, I judged we would ultimately triumph over our invaders, but it would take time. If we continued in our present state, without resources to organize, arm, or sustain armies, I recognized we are at the mercy of our invaders, who could remain in our country as long as they wished. We hoped then to prolong our resistance indefinitely until they are convinced of the impossibility of consolidating Maximilian's position. . . .

After the president repeatedly said that he desired us to have arms and that he saw no major difficulty in the United States government supplying us with them, he concluded not to give me a definite answer today, bestowing marked emphasis on the word definite. He said that he would talk with Grant tomorrow to see what could be done. . . . I will make certain that Grant learns the details of this conversation before he sees the president tomorrow.

April 11, 1866.

This morning at nine Grant made a lengthy visit. After his interview yesterday with the president, he told me, Johnson had requested him to attend yesterday's cabinet meeting in which Mexican affairs were discussed. At that meeting, Grant reported, it was resolved that the United States could not sell arms to any belligerent without failing in its neutral obligations. Nevertheless, if arms were sold to private parties, clearly it would not be necessary to examine where the arms might end up, and the belligerents did have the right to take arms from this country, carrying them where they wished.

1871

Santo Domingo Seeks Annexation by the United States

Hamilton Fish

Since the administration of President Franklin Pierce (1853–57), the United States had made sporadic attempts to negotiate a treaty with the Dominican Republic that would give it a naval base in the Bay of Samaná. These efforts were revived immediately after the U.S. Civil War, starting with the Andrew Johnson administration (1865–69) and reaching their climax during that of Ulysses S. Grant (1869–77), the most enthusiastic supporter yet of the project. Now, however, the government of the Dominican Republic was offering to turn over more than just the bay; it eagerly sought annexation of the entire country by the United States, a proposition that President Grant considered irresistible. A treaty signed by diplomats from both countries set the terms of the annexation. The treaty was rejected by the U.S. Senate on June 30, 1870, by a vote of 28–28, well short of the two-thirds majority required for treaties. Opponents of annexation variously denounced the treaty as a corrupt, foolhardy and imperialistic scheme to enrich a small group of U.S. investors, while immorally making colonial subjects of a free people who had little in common with those of the United States. Furious, President Grant continued trying to revive the annexation project until October 1871, when he finally decided to drop it. In the meantime, in response to a request by the U.S. Senate, Secretary of State Hamilton Fish submitted the following report on the proposed annexation.

Department of State, January 16, 1871.

. . . A mass of correspondence in the archives of this Department from a variety of sources, much of which was unprejudiced, and some of which may have been biased by prejudice or interest, appeared to demonstrate the following points:

Source: U.S. Congress. Senate. Senate Executive Document No. 17. 41st Cong., 3d sess. "Message of the President of the United States, . . ." 16 January 1871. Washington, D.C.: GPO, 1871.

First. That the Spanish portion of the island of San Domingo was sparsely populated. The estimates varied from 150,000 to 300,000 persons. Those who would appear to have the best opportunities for correct information, fixed the number at less than 200,000.

Second. That the soil of that part of the island was rich, and capable of a productive power beyond any corresponding extent of the island of Cuba.

Third. That its actual production was greatly diminished by the disturbed state of its civil and political society, caused partly by the Spanish invasion, partly by the character of the population, and largely by the aggressive policy of the neighboring republic of Hayti.

Fourth. That all parties, with equal unanimity, sought refuge from these disturbances in a more intimate connection with the United States, which was regarded as the natural protector of republican institutions in the western hemisphere.

Fifth. That to this end all desired to lease the bay and peninsula of Samana to the United States for a naval station, as a first step toward ultimate annexation.

Sixth. That the bay of Samana was the key to the Mona channel, which was the *"gate"* to the Caribbean Sea and the Isthmus of Panama.

The policy which led several previous administrations to entertain the negotiations which have been referred to, was regarded as too well settled by a practice of nearly seventy years to be then questioned. It was supposed, in the striking language of a then recent speech in the Senate on the acquisition of Alaska, that "our city can be nothing less than the North American continent, *with its gates on all the surrounding seas."*

Nevertheless, it was thought best not to act without further information. . . . On the 13th of July [1869] Brevet Brigadier General Babcock, who was employed in the Executive office, and who enjoyed the full confidence of the Government, was . . . instructed to proceed to San Domingo. . . . Upon his return to Washington General Babcock made a favorable verbal report. . . . The results of General Babcock's examination were deemed favorable to the maintenance of the American policy. He was therefore directed to return to San Domingo, in order to aid Mr. Raymond H. Perry, the commercial agent of the United States, in negotiating for the annexation of the whole territory of the republic to the United States, and (as an alternative proposition) for a lease of the peninsula and bay of Samana to the United States. A treaty for the annexation of the territories of the republic, and a convention for the lease of the bay and the peninsula of Samana, were accordingly concluded. . . . The treaty did not receive the assent of the Senate. The convention is still pending. The terms of the treaty require that a popular vote should be taken upon the question of annexation. The almost unanimous affirmative vote, (the transcripts of which are in the Department of State,) to whose spontaneous character Mr. Perry bears repeated testimony, justified the opinion alike of the friends of General Cabral and of the friends of General Baez, (in other words, of all the political leaders of the republic,) that the whole people desire annexation to the United States. . . .

... All parties alike have seemed to seek annexation to the United States as the surest hope for the future of the republic. ... [A]ll the correspondence in the archives of the Department tends to show that, should President Baez fail in the effort to annex the republic to the United States, the popular disappointment may find vent in another revolution.

NO. 17

1888

A U.S. Official Interprets Latin America

William Eleroy Curtis

In 1884, President Chester A. Arthur appointed a special three-man commission to travel to Latin America in order to sound out the possibilities for increased trade and inter-American cooperation. One of the members of the commission was a young Chicago journalist, William Eleroy Curtis. While the commission's official report of its journey attracted little interest, Curtis wrote a book about his tour called *The Capitals of Spanish America.* Published in 1888 and aimed mainly at businessmen, the book was the largest (700 pages) and the most comprehensive on the region yet to appear in the United States. The book, along with a number of journalistic articles on Latin America, turned Curtis into one of the country's most quoted experts on the region. Despite the fact that he spoke neither Spanish nor Portuguese, in 1890 Curtis was appointed the first director of the Commercial Bureau of the American Republics, the forerunner of the Pan American Union. What follows are his observations on Chile and Argentina.

The Chillano [i.e., Chilean or Spanish *chileno*] is the Yankee of South America—the most active, enterprising, ingenious, and thrifty of the Spanish American race—aggressive, audacious, and arrogant, quick to perceive, quick to resent,

Source: *The Capitals of Spanish America* by William Eleroy Curtis, pp. 550–51. Copyright © 1888 by Harper & Brothers. Reproduced with permission of Greenwood Publishing Group, Inc., Westport, CT.

fierce in disposition, cold-blooded, and cruel as a cannibal. He dreams of conquest. He has only a strip of country along the Pacific coast, so narrow that there is scarcely room enough to write its name upon the map, hemmed in on the one side by the eternal snows that crown the Cordilleras, and on the other side by six thousand miles of sea. He has been stretching himself northward until he has stolen all the sea-coast of Bolivia, with her valuable nitrate deposits, all the guano that belonged to Peru, and contemplates soon taking actual possession of both those republics. He has been reaching southward by diplomacy as he did northward by war; and under a recent treaty with the Argentine Republic he has divided Patagonia with that nation, taking to himself the control of that valuable international highway, the Strait of Magellan, and the unexplored country between the Andes and the ocean, with thousands of islands along the Pacific coast whose resources are unknown. By securing the strait, Chili acquired control of steam navigation in the South Pacific, and has established a colony and fortress at Punta Arenas by which all vessels must pass.

Reposing tranquilly now in the enjoyment of the newly acquired territory along the Bolivian and Peruvian border, and deriving an enormous revenue from the export tax upon nitrate, the Chillano contemplates the internal dissensions of Peru, and waits anxiously for the time when he can step in as arbitrator and, like the lawyer, take the estate that the heirs are silly enough to quarrel over. It is but a question of years when not only Peru but Bolivia will become a part of Chili; when the aggressive nation will want to push her eastern boundary back of the Andes, and secure control of the sources of the Amazon, as she has of the navigation of the strait. . . .

[T]here is no doubt that at present, in all the conditions of modern civilization, Chili leads the Southern Continent, and is the most powerful of all the republics in America except our own. Her statesmen are wise and able, her people are industrious and progressive, and have that strength of mind and muscle which is given only to the men of temperate zones. . . . There has not been a successful revolution in Chili since 1839; and although there is nowhere a more unruly and discordant people, nowhere so much murder and other serious crimes, in their love of country the haughty don and the patient peon, the hunted bandit and the cruel soldier, are one. . . .

The Chillano is not only vain but cruel—as cruel as death. He carries a long curved knife, called a *curvo* as the Italian carries a stiletto and the negro a razor, and uses it to cut throats. He never fights with his fists, and knows not the use of the shillalah; he never carries a revolver, and is nothing of a thug; but as a robber or bandit, in a private quarrel or a public mob, he always uses this deadly knife, and springs at the throat of his enemy like a blood-hound. There is scarcely an issue of a daily paper without one or two throat-cutting incidents, and in the publications succeeding feast days or carnivals their bloody annals fill columns. . . .

Our knowledge of the Argentine Republic amounts to little more than we know of the Congo State, and the man who goes there from the United States is kept in a state of astonishment until he leaves. Then, as he sits on shipboard and reflects over what he has seen, he cannot find an exclamation point big enough to do justice to his description of the country. The Argentinians think it is wicked indifference on our part to know so little about them, for the surprise of the few American visitors wounds their self-esteem. They are a proud people, like all the rest of the Spanish race, and, unlike some nations, have many things to be proud of. They know all about us. There are many men in the Argentine Republic who can tell you the percentage of increase in population, industry, and progress in the United States, as shown by the latest statistics, but how many people in the United States are aware that that country is growing twice as fast as ours? . . .

The people are right when they assert that their country is the United States of South America, and there is nothing else that they are so proud of. They study and imitate our institutions and our methods, and in some cases improve upon them. You can buy the New York dailies and illustrated papers at any of the news-stands in Buenos Ayres, although they are six weeks old, and the people purchase and read them. They understand the significance of the cartoons in Puck, and read *Harper's Magazine* and the *Century*. Blaine's book and Grant's Memoirs are on sale, and the issues of our Presidential campaigns are as well understood as their own local squabbles.

The greatest benefit to be derived by a traveller in the countries of South America is to make him think well of his own; but, nevertheless, his vanity receives a severe shock when he comes to the Argentine Republic, and discovers how little he knows of what is going on in the world. . . .

Twenty-five years ago our knowledge of the continent was pretty good, but we have learned nothing since. Our geographies read as they did then, our histories have not been rewritten, and our maps remain unaltered. But in the meantime mighty changes have been taking place among our neighbors that have escaped our attention. They have been growing as we have grown, and instead of a few half-civilized, ill-governed people upon the pampas of the Argentine Republic, a great nation has sprung up, as enterprising, progressive, and intelligent as ours, with "all the modern improvements," as house agents say, and an ambition to stand beside the United States in the front rank of modern civilization. While we have been occupied with our own internal development, the European nations have gone in and taken the commerce to which we by the logic of political and geographical considerations are entitled. . . .

❖

1889

The First Inter-American Conference

James G. Blaine

James G. Blaine, secretary of state in the administration of James A. Garfield, proposed a conference of American states in 1881. Garfield's assassination that year, however, led to Blaine's resignation and the indefinite postponement of a congress, an idea that was subsequently opposed by both the Arthur and the Cleveland administrations. The U.S. Congress strongly supported it, however, and in May 1888 it authorized a conference of American states to take place in Washington under the sponsorship of the U.S. Department of State. Returning as secretary of state under President Benjamin Harrison (1889–93), Blaine got his chance to preside over the "First International Conference of American States" from October 2, 1889, to April 19, 1890; delegates attended from every Latin American country except the Dominican Republic. His welcoming address on October 2 is excerpted below. The conference achieved little beyond establishing a Commercial Bureau of American Republics, later renamed the Pan-American Union, with its headquarters in Washington, D.C. Future conferences, under the sponsorship of the Pan-American Union, increased in frequency over the years, and finally culminated in the founding of the Organization of American States (see Document No. 70).

Gentlemen of the International American Conference:

Speaking for the Government of the United States, I bid you welcome to this capital. Speaking for the people of the United States, I bid you welcome to every section and to every State of the Union. You come in response to an invitation extended by the President on the special authorization of Congress. Your presence here is no ordinary event. It signifies much to the people of all America to-day. It may signify far more in the days to come. . . .

The Delegates whom I am addressing can do much to establish permanent relations of confidence, respect, and friendship between the nations which they

Source: James Blaine. "Opening Address." *International American Conference. Reports of Committees and Discussions Thereon.* Vol. 3. Washington, D.C.: GPO, 1890.

represent. They can show to the world an honorable, peaceful conference of eighteen independent American Powers, in which all shall meet together on terms of absolute equality; a conference in which there can be no attempt to coerce a single delegate against his own conception of the interests of his nation; . . . a conference which will tolerate no spirit of conquest, but will aim to cultivate an American sympathy as broad as both continents; a conference which will form no selfish alliance against the older nations from which we are proud to claim inheritance—a conference, in fine, which will seek nothing, propose nothing, endure nothing that is not, in the general sense of all the delegates, timely and wise and peaceful.

And yet we can not be expected to forget that our common fate has made us inhabitants of the two continents which, at the close of four centuries, are still regarded beyond the seas as the New World. Like situations beget like sympathies and impose like duties. We meet in firm belief that the nations of America ought to be and can be more helpful, each to the other, than they now are, and that each will find advantage and profit from an enlarged intercourse with the others.

We believe that we should be drawn together more closely by the highways of the sea, and that at no distant day the railway systems of the North and South will meet upon the Isthmus and connect by land routes the political and commercial capitals of all America. . . .

We believe that a spirit of justice, of common and equal interest between the American states, will leave no room for an artificial balance of power like unto that which has led to wars abroad and drenched Europe in blood. . . .

We believe that standing armies, beyond those which are needful for public order and the safety of internal administration, should be unknown on both American continents.

We believe that friendship and not force, the spirit of just law and not the violence of the mob, should be the recognized rule of administration between American nations and in American nations. . . .

It will be the greatest gain when the personal and commercial relations of the American states, South and North, shall be so developed and so regulated that each shall acquire the highest possible advantage from the enlightened and enlarged intercourse of all. . . .

❖

II.

THE COLOSSUS OF THE NORTH

1890

The Lessons of History

Alfred Thayer Mahan

The publication in 1890 of Alfred Thayer Mahan's three-volume book, *The Influence of Sea Power Upon History: 1660–1783,* crowned a forty-two-year career as a U.S. naval officer. Still in print a century later, the book appeared just as the United States began to move dramatically onto the world stage as a great power. Its enormous popularity was owing to the fact that it seemed to justify, by its appeal to "history," the naval expansion that would have to accompany the U.S. transition to world-power status. Its publication, moreover, coincided with the Depression of 1890, which farming and manufacturing interests attributed to the lack of foreign markets for their excess production. Thus Mahan's argument helped bolster the case for an "outward-looking" foreign policy, one in which naval might would help secure access to distant markets. The logic of an expanding merchant marine and navy in turn necessitated control over a transisthmian canal route. The passage below is taken from the twenty-fifth edition of the book, published in 1915.

The first and most obvious light in which the sea presents itself from the political and social point of view is that of a great highway; or better, perhaps, of a wide common, over which men may pass in all directions, but on which some well-worn paths show that controlling reasons have led them to choose certain lines of travel rather than others. These lines of travel are called trade routes; and the reasons which have determined them are to be sought in the history of the world.

Notwithstanding all the familiar and unfamiliar dangers of the sea, both travel and traffic by water have always been easier and cheaper than by land. . . .

Under modern conditions . . . home trade is but a part of the business of a country bordering on the sea. Foreign necessaries or luxuries must be brought

Source: A. T. Mahan. *The Influence of Sea Power Upon History.* Ch. 1. 25th edition. Boston: Little Brown & Co., 1915.

to its ports, either in its own or in foreign ships, which will return, bearing in exchange the products of the country, whether they be the fruits of the earth or the works of men's hands; and it is the wish of every nation that this shipping business should be done by its own vessels. The ships that thus sail to and fro must have secure ports to which to return, and must, as far as possible, be followed by the protection of their country throughout the voyage. . . .

In these three things—production, with the necessity of exchanging products, shipping, whereby the exchange is carried on, and colonies, which facilitate and enlarge the operations of shipping and tend to protect it by multiplying points of safety—is to be found the key to much of the history, as well as of the policy, of nations bordering upon the sea. The policy has varied both with the spirit of the age and with the character and clear-sightedness of the rulers; but the history of the seaboard nations has been less determined by the shrewdness and foresight of governments than by conditions of position, extent, configuration, number and character of their people,—by what are called, in a word, natural conditions. It must however be admitted, and will be seen that the wise or unwise action of individual men has at certain periods had a great modifying influence upon the growth of sea power in the broad sense, which includes not only the military strength afloat, that rules the sea or any part of it by force of arms, but also the peaceful commerce and shipping from which alone a military fleet naturally and healthfully springs, and on which it securely rests. . . . Two remarks . . . are here appropriate.

Circumstances have caused the Mediterranean Sea to play a greater part in the history of the world, both in a commercial and a military point of view, than any other sheet of water of the same size. Nation after nation has striven to control it, and the strife still goes on. Therefore a study of the conditions upon which preponderance in its waters has rested, and now rests, and of the relative military values of different points upon its coasts, will be more instructive than the same amount of effort expended in another field. Furthermore, it has at the present time a very marked analogy in many respects to the Caribbean Sea—an analogy which will be still closer if a Panama canal-route ever be completed. A study of the strategic conditions of the Mediterranean, which have received ample illustration, will be an excellent prelude to a similar study of the Caribbean, which has comparatively little history.

The second remark bears upon the geographical position of the United States relatively to a Central-American canal. If one be made, and fulfill the hopes of its builders, the Caribbean will be changed from a terminus, and place of local traffic, or at best a broken and imperfect line of travel, as it now is, into one of the great highways of the world. Along this path a great commerce will travel, bringing the interests of other great nations, the European nations, close along our shores, as they have never been before. With this it will not be so easy as heretofore to stand aloof from international complications. The position of the United States with reference to this route will resemble that of England to the Channel, and of the Mediterranean countries to the Suez route. As regards influence and control over it, depending upon geographical position, it is of course plain that the centre of the national power, the permanent base, is much nearer than that of other great nations. The positions now or hereafter occupied by them on island or mainland, however strong, will be but outposts of their power; while in all the raw materials of military strength no nation is superior to the United States. She is, however, weak in a confessed unpreparedness for war; and her geographical nearness to the point of contention loses some of its value by the character of the Gulf coast, which is deficient in ports combining security from an enemy with facility for repairing war-ships of the first class, without which ships no country can pretend to control any part of the sea. In case of a contest for supremacy in the Caribbean, it seems evident from the depth of the South Pass of the Mississippi, the nearness of New Orleans, and the advantages of the Mississippi Valley for water transit, that the main effort of the country must pour down that valley, and its permanent base of operations be found there. The defence of the entrance to the Mississippi, however, presents peculiar difficulties; while the only two rival ports, Key West and Pensacola, have too little depth of water, and are much less advantageously placed with reference to the resources of the country. To get the full benefit of superior geographical position, these defects must be overcome. Furthermore, as her distance from the Isthmus, though relatively less, is still considerable, the United States will have to obtain in the Caribbean stations fit for contingent, or secondary, bases of operations; which by their natural advantages, susceptibility of defence, and nearness to the central strategic issue, will enable her fleets to remain as near the scene as any opponent. With ingress and egress from the Mississippi sufficiently protected, with such outposts in her hands, and with the communications between them and the home base secured, in short with proper military preparation, for which she has all necessary means, the preponderance of the United States on this field follows, from her geographical position and her power, with mathematical certainty. . . .

To turn now from the particular lessons drawn from the history of the past to the general question of the influence of government upon the sea career of its people, it is seen that that influence can work in two distinct but closely related ways.

First, in peace: The government by its policy can favor the natural growth of a people's industries and its tendencies to seek the adventure and gain by way of the sea; or it can try to develop such industries and such sea-going bent, when they do not naturally exist; or, on the other hand, the government may by mistaken action check and fetter the progress which the people left to themselves would make. In any one of these ways the influence of the government will be felt, making or marring the sea power of the country in the matter of peaceful commerce; upon which alone, it cannot be too often insisted, a thoroughly strong navy can be based.

Secondly, for war: The influence of the government will be felt in its most legitimate manner in maintaining an armed navy, of a size commensurate with the growth of its shipping and the importance of the interests connected with it. . . . Undoubtedly under this second head of warlike preparation must come the maintenance of suitable naval stations, in those distant parts of the world to which the armed shipping must follow the peaceful vessels of commerce. . . . Colonies attached to the mother-country afford . . . the surest means of supporting abroad the sea power of a country. . . . Such colonies the United States has not and is not likely to have. . . . Having therefore no foreign establishments, either colonial or military, the ships of war of the United States, in war, will be like land birds, unable to fly far from their own shores. To provide resting-places for them, where they can coal and repair, would be one of the first duties of a government proposing to itself the development of the power of the nation at sea.

As the practical object of this inquiry is to draw from the lessons of history inferences applicable to one's own country and service, it is proper now to ask how far the conditions of the United States involve serious danger, and call for action on the part of the government, in order to build again her sea power. It will not be too much to say that the action of the government since the Civil War, and up to this day, has been effectively directed solely to what has been called the first link in the chain which makes sea power. Internal development, great production, with the accompanying aim and boast of self-sufficingness, such has been the object, such to some extent the result. . . . However that may be, there is no doubt that, besides having no colonies, the intermediate link of a peaceful shipping, and the interests involved in it, are now likewise lacking. . . .

The question is eminently one in which the influence of the government should make itself felt, to build up for the nation a navy which, if not capable of reaching distant countries, shall at least be able to keep clear the chief approaches to its own. The eyes of the country have for a quarter of a century been turned from the sea; the results of such a policy and of its opposite will be shown in the instance of France and of England. Without asserting a narrow parallelism between the case of the United States and either of these, it may safely be said that it is essential to the welfare of the whole country that the conditions of trade and commerce should remain, as far as possible, unaffected by an external war. In order to do this, the enemy must be kept not only out of our ports, but far away from our coasts.

Can this navy be had without restoring the merchant shipping? It is doubtful. History has proved that such a purely military sea power can be built up by a despot, as was done by Louis XIV; but though so fair seeming, experience showed that his navy was like a growth which having no root soon withers away. But in a representative government any military expenditure must have a strongly represented interest behind it, convinced of its necessity. Such an interest in sea power does not exist, cannot exist here without action by the government. How such a merchant shipping should be built up, whether by subsidies or by free trade, by constant administration of tonics or by free movement in the open air, is not a military but an economical question. Even had the United States a great national shipping, it may be doubted whether a sufficient navy would follow; the distance which separates her from other great powers, in one way a protection, is also a snare. The motive, if any there be, which will give the United States a navy, is probably now quickening in the Central American Isthmus. Let us hope it will not come to the birth too late.

❖

NO. 20

1892

The Baltimore Affair

Benjamin Harrison

Relations between Chile and the United States began to deteriorate during the War of the Pacific (1879–83), in which Chile defeated Peru and Bolivia. An attempt by U.S. Secretary of State James G. Blaine to mediate the dispute in 1881 turned Chilean opinion against the United States. Blaine happened to be serving his second term as secretary of state (1889–92) when a civil war broke out in Chile and set the stage for a further decline in relations between the two countries. A Chilean naval vessel, the *Itata,* was detained by U.S. authorities in San Diego, California, in May 1891 and charged with violating U.S. neutrality laws for having attempted to purchase arms for one of the sides in the Chilean civil war. But the crew of the *Itata* managed to escape U.S. custody and sailed for Chile, chased by U.S. naval vessels. The *Itata* was duly surrendered to the United States after her arrival in Chile, and then released after a U.S. court ruled that in fact the *Itata* had not violated U.S. neutrality laws. In October 1891, with the war now firmly decided for the former rebel forces, who now governed the country, anti-U.S. feelings were stronger than ever. On October 16, the captain of the U.S.S. *Baltimore,* moored in the Chilean port of Valparaiso, allowed 117 of his men to go on shore leave. That night, a Chilean mob attacked the sailors, killing two and wounding some others. President Benjamin Harrison regarded the incident as a serious insult to the honor of the United States. Chile refused to apologize, and the two countries appeared to be headed toward war when Chile backed down, apologized and agreed to pay damages on January 26, 1892, the day after President Harrison sent the following special message to Congress.

Source: Benjamin Harrison. *Congressional Record.* Fifty-Second Congress, 1st sess. Vol. 23, 25 January 1892, pp. 517–20. Washington, D.C.: GPO, 1892.

To the Senate and House of Representatives:

... The evidences of the existence of animosity towards our sailors in the minds of the sailors of the Chilean navy and of the populace of Valparaiso are so abundant and various as to leave no doubt in the mind of anyone. ... It manifested itself in threatening and insulting gestures towards our men as they passed the Chilean men-of-war in their boats and in the derisive and abusive epithets with which they greeted every appearance of an American sailor on the evening of the riot. Capt. Schley reports that boats from the Chilean war ships several times went out of their course to cross the bows of his boats, compelling them to back water. ...

Several of our men sought security from the mob by such complete or partial changes in their dress as would conceal the fact of their being seamen of the *Baltimore,* and found it then possible to walk the streets without molestation. These incidents conclusively establish that the attack was upon the uniform—the nationality—and not upon the men. ...

We can not consent that these incidents [i.e., the *Itata* and others related to U.S. conduct during the Chilean civil war] ... shall be used to excite a murderous attack upon our unoffending sailors and the Government of Chile go acquit of responsibility. ...

As to the participation of the police, the evidence of our sailors shows that our men were struck and beaten by police officers before and after arrest, and that one, at least, was dragged with a lasso about his neck by a mounted policeman. ...

The communications of the Chilean Government in relation to this cruel and disastrous attack upon our men ... have not in any degree taken the form of a manly and satisfactory expression of regret, much less of apology. ...

On the 21st instant, I caused to be communicated to the Government of Chile [a request for] ... a suitable apology and for some adequate reparation for the injury done to this Government. ... I am of the opinion that the demands made of Chile by this Government should be adhered to and enforced. If the dignity as well as the prestige and influence of the United States are not to be wholly sacrificed, we must protect those who in foreign ports display the flag or wear the colors of the Government against insult, brutality and death, inflicted in resentment of the acts of their Government, and not for any fault of their own. ...

I have as yet received no reply to our note of the 21st instant, but in my opinion I ought not to delay longer to bring these matters to the attention of Congress for such action as may be deemed appropriate.

Benj. Harrison. Executive Mansion, January 25, 1892.

❖

1894

The Character of the United States

José Martí

José Martí (1853–95) was a Cuban-born journalist, essayist and leader of the independence movement against Spanish rule. Martí joined the first, unsuccessful war for Cuban independence, the Ten Years War of 1868–1878. Exiled to Spain in 1871, he later lived in France, the United States and Latin America, writing poetry and essays on Latin American and U.S. politics and culture. Settling in New York City in 1881, he was among the founders of the Partido Revolucionario Cubano (Cuban Revolutionary Party) in 1892, and he promoted its cause through his journal *Patria.* Joining the second war for independence that broke out in 1895, Martí returned to Cuba and died in combat on May 19, 1895. The day before his death, he had written a letter to his Mexican friend and confidant, Manuel Mercado. The first selection is from an essay published in *Patria* in 1894; the second is from the letter to Mercado.

THE TRUTH ABOUT THE UNITED STATES

In our America it is vital to know the truth about the United States. We should not exaggerate its faults purposely, out of a desire to deny it all virtue, nor should these faults be concealed or proclaimed as virtues. . . . A nation of strapping young men from the North, bred over the centuries to the sea and the snow and the virility aided by the perpetual defense of local freedom, cannot be like a tropical isle, docile and smiling, where the famished outgrowth of a backward and war-minded European people, descendants of a coarse and uncultured tribe, divided by hatred for an accommodating submission to rebellious virtue, work under contract for a government that practices political piracy. And also working under contract are those simple but vigorous

Sources: José Martí. "The Truth About the United States (1894)." In *Inside the Monster by José Martí: Writings on the United States and American Imperialism,* edited by Philip S. Foner and translated by Luis A. Baralt, Roslyn Held Foner, Juan de Onis and Elinor Randall, pp. 49–54. Copyright © 1975 by Monthly Review Press. Reprinted by permission of Monthly Review Foundation. "Carta a Manuel Mercado (18 May 1895)," in Jorge Quintana, ed., *José Martí. Obras Completas,* vol. 1 (part 2), pp. 271–73. Caracas: 1964. Translation by Robert H. Holden and Eric Zolov.

Africans, either vilified or rancorous, who from a frightful slavery and a sublime war [1868–78] have entered into citizenship with those who bought and sold them, and who, thanks to the dead of that sublime war, today greet as equals the ones who used to make them dance to the lash. . . .

With some people, an excessive love of the North is the unwise but easily explained expression of such a lively and vehement desire for progress that they are blind to the fact that ideas, like trees, must come from deep roots and compatible soil in order to develop a firm footing and prosper, and that a newborn babe is not given the wisdom and maturity of age merely because one glues on its smooth face a mustache and a pair of sideburns. Monsters are created that way, not nations. They have to live of themselves, and sweat through the heat. With other people, their Yankeemania is the innocent result of an occasional little leap of pleasure, much as a man judges the inner spirit of a home, and the souls who pray or die therein, by the smiles and luxury in the front parlor, or by the champagne and carnations on the banquet table. . . . With other posthumous weaklings of Second Empire literary dandyism, or the false skeptics under whose mask of indifference there generally beats a heart of gold, the fashion is to scorn the indigenous, and more so. They cannot imagine greater elegance than to drink to the foreigner's breeches and ideas, and to strut over the globe, proud as the pompom tail of the fondled lap dog. With still others it is like a subtle aristocracy which, publicly showing a preference for the fairskinned as a natural and proper thing to do, tries to conceal its own humble halfbreed origins, unaware that when one man brands another as a bastard, it is always a sign of his own illegitimacy. . . . It matters not whether the reason is impatience for freedom or the fear of it, moral sloth or a laughable aristocracy, political idealism or a recently acquired ingenuity—it is surely appropriate, and even urgent, to put before our America the entire American truth, about the Saxon as well as the Latin, so that too much faith in foreign virtue will not weaken us in our formative years with an unmotivated and baneful distrust of what is ours. . . . From the standpoint of justice and a legitimate social science it should be recognized that, in relation to the ready compliance of the one and the obstacles of the other, the North American character has gone downhill since the winning of independence, and is today less human and virile; whereas the Spanish American character today is in all ways superior, in spite of its confusion and fatigue, to what it was when it began to emerge from the disorganized mass of grasping clergy, unskilled ideologists, and ignorant or savage Indians. . . . [One must] demonstrate two useful truths to our America: the crude, uneven, and decadent character of the United States, and the continuous existence there of all the violence, discord, immorality, and disorder blamed upon the peoples of Spanish America.

LETTER TO MANUEL MERCADO, CAMPAMENTO DE DOS RÍOS, 18 MAY 1895

My dearest brother: Now I can write, now I can tell you the affection, appreciation and respect that I have for you; and for that house that is mine, my pride and obligation; every day I am now in danger of giving my life for my country, and for my duty—given that I understand it and am motivated to do so—to impede in time with the independence of Cuba the extension of the United States throughout the Antilles and to prevent its full weight from falling upon our American soil. All that I've done up to now and will do is for that purpose. This has had to be done silently and indirectly because, in order to achieve certain things, they must remain hidden for if one were to announce what they really are this would make it too difficult to achieve them.

The lesser and public duties of the peoples—like yours and mine—have kept them from joining us in this sacrifice, which we are doing for them and in their interest. These are the peoples most vitally interested in keeping those Imperialists up there and the Spaniards from annexing the peoples of our America to the savage and brutal North, which holds them in contempt; with our own blood we are blocking their path.

I lived in the monster and I know its entrails:—and my sling is that of David. It's been several days now that we achieved the victory of being welcomed by the Cubans after six of us walked for fourteen days in the Sierras. Now the correspondent for the *Herald* . . . tells me of the activities in favor of annexation. This doesn't worry me much because those who favor it do not seem to be in touch with reality, they are people of the same class as the priests, ignorant and poorly bred. While comfortably disguising themselves by their willingness to submit to Spain they faithlessly ask her for autonomy for Cuba, satisfied only that there is some master, a Yankee or a Spaniard, who maintains them, or who, as a reward for being their pimps, makes them bosses who are disdainful of the great masses—the mestiza masses of the country, capable and inspiring, the intelligent and creative masses of whites and blacks. . . .

I'm doing my duty here. The war in Cuba—overshadowing the vague and ephemeral wishes of the Cuban and Spanish annexationists, whose alliance with the Spanish government would only give them relative power—has arrived at the proper moment in America, to prevent—even against the open use of all those forces—the annexation of Cuba to the United States. The United States will never accept a country at war, nor can the United States make—given that the war will not allow for annexation—the odious and absurd commitment to subdue on their own and with their arms a war of American independence. . . .

❖

1895

The Olney Memorandum

Richard Olney

A longstanding dispute between Great Britain and Venezuela over the location of the boundary between Venezuela and the British colony of Guiana is the subject of this letter of instruction from Secretary of State Richard Olney to the U.S. ambassador in Great Britain, Thomas F. Bayard, on July 20, 1895. The note's belligerent and even insolent tone, its controversial claim that a boundary dispute properly fell within the reach of the Monroe Doctrine, and the timing of its release have made it a key indicator of the passage to hemispheric hegemony, at the expense of Great Britain, by the United States in the 1890s. Olney, like his predecessors in the State Department and the government of Venezuela, insisted that Britain submit the dispute to arbitration. The British government's blunt rejection of Olney's arguments and its refusal to arbitrate provoked an outraged response from President Grover Cleveland, who implied that his government was disposed to go to war with Britain to protect territory that was rightfully Venezuelan. Shocked by displays of popular support in the United States for war, and mindful of the risks of overextending itself militarily, the British agreed to cooperate with a Cleveland-appointed commission to investigate the boundary dispute. Representatives of Venezuela and Great Britain, acting under the good offices of the United States, agreed in 1897 to arbitrate all disputed areas except those that had been in the possession of either country for more than fifty years. The arbitrators issued their decision in 1899 and it was accepted by both parties.

His Excellency Thomas F. Bayard,

. . . To the territorial controversy between Great Britain and the Republic of Venezuela, . . . the United States has not been and, indeed, in view of its traditional policy, could not be indifferent. . . . Since the close of the negotiations initiated in 1893, Venezuela has repeatedly brought the controversy to the no-

Source: U.S. Department of State. *Papers Relating to the Foreign Relations of the United States,* . . . *1895,* Part I. Washington, D.C.: GPO, 1896.

tice of the United States, has insisted upon its importance to the United States as well as to Venezuela, has represented it to have reached an acute stage—making definite action by the United States imperative—and has not ceased to solicit the services and support of the United States in aid of its final adjustment. . . . [T]he Government of the United States has made it clear to Great Britain and to the world that the controversy is one in which both its honor and its interests are involved and the continuance of which it can not regard with indifference.

That there are circumstances under which a nation may justly interpose in a controversy to which two or more other nations are the direct and immediate parties is an admitted canon of international law. The doctrine is ordinarily expressed in terms of the most general character and is perhaps incapable of more specific statement. . . . President Monroe, in the celebrated Message of December 2, 1823, . . . declared that the American continents were fully occupied and were not the subjects for future colonization by European powers. . . . It was realized that it was futile to lay down such a rule unless its observance could be enforced. It was manifest that the United States was the only power in this hemisphere capable of enforcing it. It was therefore courageously declared not merely that Europe ought not to interfere in American affairs, but that any European power doing so would be regarded as antagonizing the interests and inviting the Opposition of the United States.

That America is in no part open to colonization, though the proposition was not universally admitted at the time of its first enunciation, has long been universally conceded. We are now concerned, therefore, only with that other practical application of the Monroe doctrine the disregard of which by any European power is to be deemed an act of unfriendliness towards the United States. The precise scope and limitations of this rule cannot be too clearly apprehended. It does not establish any general protectorate by the United States over other American states. . . . It does not contemplate any interference in the internal affairs of any American state or in the relations between it and other American states. It does not justify any attempt on our part to change the established form of government of any American state or to prevent the people of such state from altering that form according to their own will and pleasure. The rule in question has but a single purpose and object. It is that no European power or combination of European powers shall forcibly deprive an American state of the right and power of self-government and of shaping for itself its own political fortunes and destinies. . . .

If . . . for the reasons stated the forcible intrusion of European powers into American politics is to be deprecated—if, as it is to be deprecated, it should be resisted and prevented—such resistance and prevention must come from the United States. They would come from it, of course, were it made the point of attack. But, if they come at all, they must also come from it when any other American state is attacked, since only the United States has the strength adequate to the exigency.

Is it true, then, that the safety and welfare of the United States are so concerned with the maintenance of the independence of every American state as against any European power as to justify and require the interposition of the United States whenever that independence is endangered? The question can be candidly answered in but one way. The states of America, South as well as North, by geographical proximity, by natural sympathy, by similarity of governmental constitutions, are friends and allies, commercially and politically, of the United States. To allow the subjugation of any of them by an European power is, of course, to completely reverse that situation and signifies the loss of all the advantages incident to their natural relations to us. But that is not all. The people of the United States have a vital interest in the cause of popular self-government. They have secured the right for themselves and their posterity at the cost of infinite blood and treasure. They have realized and exemplified its beneficent operation by a career unexampled in point of national greatness or individual felicity. They believe it to be for the healing of all nations, and that civilization must either advance or retrograde accordingly as its supremacy is extended or curtailed. Imbued with these sentiments, the people of the United States might not impossibly be wrought up to an active propaganda in favor of a cause so highly valued both for themselves and for mankind. But the age of the Crusades has passed, and they are content with such assertion and defense of the right of popular government as their own security and welfare demand. It is in that view more than in any other that they believe it not to be tolerated that the political control of an American state shall be forcibly assumed by an European power.

. . . To-day the United States is practically sovereign on this continent, and its fiat is law upon the subjects to which it confines its interposition. Why? It is not because of the pure friendship or good will felt for it. It is not simply by reason of its high character as a civilized state, nor because wisdom and justice and equity are the invariable characteristics of the dealings of the United States. It is because, in addition to all other grounds, its infinite resources combined with its isolated position render it master of the situation and practically invulnerable as against any or all other powers.

All the advantages of this superiority are at once imperiled if the principle be admitted that European powers may convert American states into colonies or provinces of their own. . . .

There is, then, a doctrine of American public law, well founded in principle and abundantly sanctioned by precedent, which entitles and requires the United States to treat as an injury to itself the forcible assumption by an European power of political control over an American state. The application of the doctrine to the boundary dispute between Great Britain and Venezuela remains to be made and presents no real difficulty. Though the dispute relates to a boundary line, yet, as it is between states, it necessarily imports political control to be lost by one party and gained by the other. The political control at stake, too, is of no mean importance, but concerns a domain of great extent . . . and, if it also directly involves the command of the mouth of the Orinoco, is of immense consequence in connection with the whole river navigation of the interior of South America. . . .

. . . It being clear, therefore, that the United States may legitimately insist upon the merits of the boundary question being determined, it is equally clear that there is but one feasible mode of determining them, viz., peaceful arbitration. . . .

In these circumstances, the duty of the President appears to him unmistakable and imperative. Great Britain's assertion of title to the disputed territory combined with her refusal to have that title investigated being a substantial appropriation of the territory to her own use, not to protest and give warning that the transaction will be regarded as injurious to the interests of the people of the United States as well as oppressive in itself would be to ignore an established policy with which the honor and welfare of this country are closely identified. . . .

You are instructed, therefore, to present the foregoing views to Lord Salisbury by reading to him this communication (leaving with him a copy should he so desire). . . . They call for a definite decision upon the point whether Great Britain will consent or will decline to submit the Venezuelan boundary question in its entirety to impartial arbitration. It is the earnest hope of the President that the conclusion will be on the side of arbitration. . . . If he is to be disappointed in that hope, . . . it is his wish to be made acquainted with the fact at such early date as will enable him to lay the whole subject before Congress in his next annual message.

NO. 23

1896

The Calvo Clause

Carlos Calvo

B y the nineteenth century, the great powers were claiming an international legal right to protect their nationals and their nationals' property anywhere in the world, a right that could be pursued according to a variety of means, from diplomacy to armed force. The legality of intervention on these grounds was first challenged by the Argentine diplomat and scholar Carlos Calvo (1822–1906), who formulated what became known as the Calvo Doctrine. Its two core principles—the absolute right to freedom from intervention, and the absolute equality of foreigners and nationals—were never accepted as part of international law. Calvo's principles did live on, however, as the "Calvo Clause," an attempt to implement the doctrine by including it in contracts with foreigners. His doctrine was thus transformed from a general legal claim into a binding personal commitment, freely accepted by the signers of contracts, not to call on their own governments in cases of contractual disputes. In the form of a contractual "clause," Calvo's doctrine has been widely implemented in Latin America, and some constitutions, such as that of Mexico, even require it in contracts with foreigners. The excerpts that follow were Calvo's statement of his doctrine, taken from the fifth and final edition of his six-volume treatise on international law, whose first edition was published in 1868.

America as well as Europe is inhabited today by free and independent nations, whose sovereign existence has the right to the same respect, and whose internal public law does not admit of intervention of any sort on the part of foreign peoples, whoever they may be. . . . Aside from political motives these interventions have nearly always had as apparent pretexts, injuries to private interests, claims and demands for pecuniary indemnities in behalf of subjects. . . . According to strict international law, the recovery of debts and the pursuit of private claims does not justify *de plano* the armed intervention of governments,

Source: Carlos Calvo. *Le droit international théorique et pratique* (5th ed., Paris, 1896), I:350–51, 231, 140, 142, 138. Quoted in Donald R. Shea, *The Calvo Clause: A Problem in Inter-American and International Law and Diplomacy*, pp. 17–19. © Copyright 1955 by the University of Minnesota.

and, since European states invariably follow this rule in their reciprocal relations, there is no reason why they should not also impose it upon themselves in their relations with nations of the new world. . . .

It is certain that aliens who establish themselves in a country have the same right to protection as nationals, but they ought not to lay claim to a protection more extended. If they suffer any wrong, they ought to count on the government of the country prosecuting the delinquents, and not claim from the state to which the authors of the violence belong any pecuniary indemnity. . . .

The rule that in more than one case it has been attempted to impose on American states is that foreigners merit more regard and privileges more marked and extended than those accorded even to the nationals of the country where they reside. This principle is intrinsically contrary to the law of equality of nations. . . .

To admit in the present case governmental responsibility, that is the principle of an indemnity, is to create an exorbitant and fatal privilege, essentially favorable to the powerful states and injurious to the weaker nations, establishing an unjustifiable inequality between nationals and foreigners. From another standpoint, in sanctioning the doctrine that we are combating, one would deal, although indirectly, a strong blow to one of the constituent elements of the independence of nations, that of territorial jurisdiction; here is, in effect, the real extent, the true significance of such frequent recourse to diplomatic channels to resolve the questions which from their nature and the circumstances in the middle of which they arise come under the exclusive domain of the ordinary tribunals. The responsibility of governments toward foreigners cannot be greater than that which these governments have toward their own citizens.

1898

The Decision to Act Against Spain

William McKinley

President William McKinley (1897–1901) had sought to stay clear of war with Spain when he was elected in 1896. But a series of events, including the mysterious sinking of the battleship U.S.S. *Maine* in a Cuban harbor on February 15, 1898, as well as sensationalist newspaper reporting about Spanish atrocities against Cuban insurgents, increased the popular pressure for U.S. intervention to liberate Cuba from Spain. On April 11, 1898, in a speech excerpted below, McKinley asked Congress for authority to use force against Spain to defend U.S. interests. Congress complied, and on April 24, Spain declared war on the United States, which was followed by a congressional declaration of war against Spain the next day.

To the Congress of the United States:

. . . The present revolution [in Cuba] is but the successor of other similar insurrections which have occurred in Cuba against the dominion of Spain, extending over a period of nearly half a century, each of which, during its progress, has subjected the United States to great effort and expense in enforcing its neutrality laws, caused enormous losses to American trade and commerce, caused irritation, annoyance, and disturbance among our citizens, and, by the exercise of cruel, barbarous, and uncivilized practices of warfare, shocked the sensibilities and offended the humane sympathies of our people.

Since the present revolution began, in February, 1895, this country has seen the fertile domain at our threshold ravaged by fire and sword in the course of a struggle unequaled in the history of the island and rarely paralleled as to the numbers of the combatants and the bitterness of the contest by any revolution of modern times where a dependent people striving to be free have been opposed by the power of the sovereign state.

Our people have beheld a once prosperous community reduced to compar-

Source: U.S. Department of State. "Message." *Papers Relating to the Foreign Relations of the United States, . . . 1898.* pp. 750–60. Washington, D.C.: GPO, 1901.

ative want, its lucrative commerce virtually paralyzed, its exceptional productiveness diminished, its fields laid waste, its mills in ruins, and its people perishing by tens of thousands from hunger and destitution. We have found ourselves constrained, in the observance of that strict neutrality which our laws enjoin, and which the law of nations commands, to police our own waters and watch our own seaports in prevention of any unlawful act in aid of the Cubans. . . .

The war in Cuba is of such a nature that short of subjugation or extermination a final military victory for either side seems impracticable. The alternative lies in the physical exhaustion of the one or the other party, or perhaps of both—a condition which in effect ended the ten years' war by the truce of Zanjon. The prospect of such a protraction and conclusion of the present strife is a contingency hardly to be contemplated with equanimity by the civilized world, and least of all by the United States, affected and injured as we are, deeply and intimately, by its very existence. . . .

The spirit of all our acts hitherto has been an earnest, unselfish desire for peace and prosperity in Cuba, untarnished by differences between us and Spain, and unstained by the blood of American citizens.

The forcible intervention of the United States as a neutral to stop the war, according to the large dictates of humanity and following many historical precedents where neighboring States have interfered to check the hopeless sacrifices of life by internecine conflicts beyond their borders, is justifiable on rational grounds. . . .

The grounds for such intervention may be briefly summarized as follows:

First. In the cause of humanity and to put an end to the barbarities, bloodshed, starvation, and horrible miseries now existing there, and which the parties to the conflict are either unable or unwilling to stop or mitigate. It is no answer to say this is all in another country, belonging to another nation, and is therefore none of our business. It is specially our duty, for it is right at our door.

Second. We owe it to our citizens in Cuba to afford them that protection and indemnity for life and property which no government there can or will afford, and to that end to terminate the conditions that deprive them of legal protection.

Third. The right to intervene may be justified by the very serious injury to the commerce, trade, and business of our people, and by the wanton destruction of property and devastation of the island.

Fourth, and which is of the utmost importance. The present condition of affairs in Cuba is a constant menace to our peace, and entails upon this Government an enormous expense. . . .

In any event the destruction of the *Maine,* by whatever exterior cause, is a patent and impressive proof of a state of things in Cuba that is intolerable. That condition is thus shown to be such that the Spanish Government can not assure safety and security to a vessel of the American Navy in the harbor of Havana on a mission of peace, and rightfully there. . . .

The long trial has proved that the object for which Spain has waged the war can not be attained. The fire of insurrection may flame or may smolder with varying seasons, but it has not been and it is plain that it can not be extinguished by present methods. The only hope of relief and repose from a condition which can no longer be endured is the enforced pacification of Cuba. In the name of humanity, in the name of civilization, in behalf of endangered American interests which give us the right and the duty to speak and to act, the war in Cuba must stop.

In view of these facts and of these considerations, I ask the Congress to authorize and empower the President to take measures to secure a full and final termination of hostilities between the Government of Spain and the people of Cuba, and to secure in the island the establishment of a stable government, capable of maintaining order and observing its international obligations, insuring peace and tranquillity and the security of its citizens as well as our own, and to use the military and naval forces of the United States as may be necessary for these purposes. . . .

William McKinley Executive Mansion, April 11, 1898.

❖

NO. 25

1898

The Teller Amendment

The Congress of the United States

In response to President McKinley's message to Congress on April 11, 1898 (Document No. 24), debate ensued over what limits, if any, Congress should impose on McKinley's freedom to act against Spain. While there was strong support for U.S. military intervention to separate the island from Spain, some members of Congress feared that the McKinley administration might seize the

Source: U.S. Department of State. *Papers Relating to the Foreign Relations of the United States,* . . . "Public Resolution—No. 21," 763. Washington, D.C.: GPO, 1901.

opportunity to annex the island. The following Congressional resolution, adopted on April 20, gave McKinley what he asked for—the authority to use force against Spain to stop the fighting on the island. But the resolution also declared that the Cuban people "are, and of right ought to be, free and independent." And it went even further by accepting without dissent an amendment submitted by Senator Henry M. Teller, Republican of Colorado, which is the last paragraph of this document. While Teller's amendment posed an obstacle to annexation, it did not necessarily commit the United States to recognizing a fully independent Cuba, as the phrase "except for the pacification thereof" implied. This phrase became the loophole for Congressional approval of the Platt Amendment (Document No. 29) four years later.

Whereas the abhorrent conditions which have existed for more than three years in the island of Cuba, so near our own border, have shocked the moral sense of the people of the United States, have been a disgrace to civilization, culminating as they have in the destruction of a United States battle ship, with two hundred and sixty-six of its officers and crew, while on a friendly visit in the harbor of Havana, and can not longer be endured, as has been set forth by the President of the United States in his message to Congress of April eleventh, eighteen hundred and ninety-eight, upon which the action of Congress was invited: Therefore,

Resolved by the Senate and House of Representatives of the United States of America in Congress assembled,

First, that the people of the island of Cuba are, and of right ought to be, free and independent.

Second. That it is the duty of the United States to demand, and the Government of the United States does hereby demand, that the Government of Spain at once relinquish its authority and government in the island of Cuba, and withdraw its land and naval forces from Cuba and Cuban waters.

Third. That the President of the United States be, and he hereby is, directed and empowered to use the entire land and naval forces of the United States, and to call into the actual service of the United States the militia of the several States, to such extent as may be necessary to carry these resolutions into effect.

Fourth. That the United States hereby disclaims any disposition or intention to exercise sovereignty, jurisdiction, or control over said island, except for the pacification thereof, and asserts its determination, when that is accomplished, to leave the government and control of the island to its people.

NO. 26

1898

Anti-Imperialism in the United States

Andrew Carnegie

The acquisition of new territory that accompanied the U.S. victory in the war with Spain led to a nationwide debate over the propriety of this kind of expansion. An "anti-imperialist" movement that was nevertheless strongly nationalistic regarded U.S. expansionism—especially into the Pacific—as a threat to republican values. The issue was a prominent one in the 1900 presidential election, in which the Republican incumbent, William McKinley, defended the policies that had led to expansion, easily defeating the Democratic anti-imperialist candidate Williams Jennings Bryan. One of the leading figures in the anti-imperialist movement was the Scottish-born immigrant and industrialist Andrew Carnegie (1835–1919). Excerpted below is an article by Carnegie that was published just after the Spanish surrender in Cuba on July 17, 1898.

. . . Is the Republic, the apostle of Triumphant Democracy, of the rule of the people, to abandon her political creed and endeavor to establish in other lands the rule of the foreigner over the people, Triumphant Despotism?

Is the Republic to remain one homogeneous whole, one united people, or to become a scattered and disjointed aggregate of widely separated and alien races?

Is she to continue the task of developing her vast continent until it holds a population as great as that of Europe, all Americans, or to abandon that destiny to annex, and to attempt to govern, other far distant parts of the world as outlying possessions, which can never be integral parts of the Republic? . . .

There are two kinds of national possessions, one colonies, the other dependencies. In the former we establish and reproduce our own race. Thus Britain has peopled Canada and Australia with English-speaking people, who have naturally adopted our ideas of self-government. . . .

With "dependencies" it is otherwise. The most grievous burden which

Source: Carnegie, Andrew. "Distant Possessions: The Parting of Ways." *North American Review* 167 (August 1898), pp. 239–48. Reprinted from *North American Review* by permission of the University of Northern Iowa.

Britain has upon her shoulders is that of India, for there it is impossible for our race to grow. . . . India means death to our race. The characteristic feature of a "dependency" is that the acquiring power cannot reproduce its own race there. . . .

Some of the organs of manufacturing interests, we observe, favor foreign possessions as necessary or helpful markets for our products. But the exports of the United States this year are greater than those of any other nation in the world. Even Britain's exports are less, yet Britain "possesses," it is said, a hundred "colonies" and "dependencies" scattered all over the world. . . .

If we could establish colonies of Americans, and grow Americans in any part of the world now unpopulated and unclaimed by any of the great powers, and thus follow the example of Britain, heart and mind might tell us that we should have to think twice, yea, thrice, before deciding adversely. . . . What we have to face is the question whether we should embark upon the difficult and dangerous policy of undertaking the government of alien races in lands where it is impossible for our own race to be produced.

As long as we remain free from distant possessions we are impregnable against serious attack. . . . Up to this time we have disclaimed all intention to interfere with affairs beyond our own continent, and only claimed the right to watch over American interests according to the Monroe Doctrine, which is now firmly established. This carries with it serious responsibilities, no doubt, which we cannot escape. European nations must consult us upon territorial questions pertaining to our Continent, but this makes no tremendous demand upon our military or naval forces. We are at home, as it were, near our base, and sure of the support of the power in whose behalf and on whose request we may act. If it be found essential to possess a coaling station at Porto Rico for future possible, though not probable, contingencies, there is no insuperable objection. Neither would the control of the West Indies be alarming, if pressed upon us by Britain, since the islands are small and the populations must remain insignificant and without national aspirations. Besides, they are upon our own shores, American in every sense. Their defense by us would be easy. No protest need be entered against such legitimate and peaceful expansion in our own hemisphere, should events work in that direction. I am no "Little" American, afraid of growth, either in population or territory, provided always that the new territory be American and that it will produce Americans, and not foreign races bound in time to be false to the Republic in order to be true to themselves. . . .

The Philippines have about seven and a half millions of people, composed of races bitterly hostile to one another, alien races, ignorant of our language and institutions. Americans cannot be grown there. . . . With what face shall we hang in the school-houses of the Philippines the Declaration of our own Independence, and yet deny independence to them? What response will the heart of the Philippine Islander make, as he reads of Lincoln's Emancipation Proclamation? Are we to practice independence and preach subordination, to teach rebellion in our books, yet to stamp it out with our swords, to sow the seed of revolt and expect the harvest of loyalty? . . .

To be more powerful at home is the surest way to be more powerful abroad. To-day the Republic stands the friend of all nations, the ally of none; she has no ambitious designs upon the territory of any power upon another continent; she crosses none of their ambitious designs, evokes no jealousy of the bitter sort, inspires no fears; she is not one of them, scrambling for "possessions;" she stands apart, pursuing her own great mission, and teaching all nations by example. Let her become a power annexing foreign territory, and all is changed in a moment. . . .

The page which recites the resolve of the Republic to rid her neighbor Cuba from the foreign "possessor" will grow brighter with the passing centuries, which may dim many pages now deemed illustrious. . . .

We repeat there is no power in the world that could do more than inconvenience the United States by attacking its fringe, which is all that the world combined could do, so long as our country is not compelled to send its forces beyond its own compact shores to defend worthless "possessions." If our country were blockaded by the united powers of the world for years, she would emerge from the embargo richer and stronger, and with her own resources more completely developed. We have little to fear from external attack. . . .

❖

NO. 27

1898

The Treaty of Paris

The Governments of the United States and Spain

Ten days after declaring war on Spain, the United States ensured victory by destroying the Spanish fleet at Manila Bay on May 1, 1898. Spain surrendered on August 12, 1898, and the two sides signed a peace treaty in Paris on December 10, 1898. The Spanish-American-Cuban-Filipino War thus became simply the Spanish-American War. The Cuban independence forces, whose struggle had led to U.S. intervention against Spain, were not even invited to partici-

Source: U.S. Department of State. *Papers Relating to the Foreign Relations of the United States, . . . 1898*, pp. 831–40. Washington, D.C.: GPO, 1901.

pate in the peace negotiations. The U.S. Senate approved the treaty on February 6, 1899, by the margin of a single vote and it went into effect on April 11, 1899. With the defeat of Spain and the military occupation of Cuba, the Philippines and Puerto Rico, U.S. military and political strategists saw an opportunity for global expansion. At the very least, the U.S. occupation of Cuba and Puerto Rico seemed to guarantee future U.S. control over an isthmian canal route. Nevertheless, the outcome of the war generated a strident, if short-lived, debate over the costs of victory (see Document No. 26).

ARTICLE 1. Spain relinquishes all claim of sovereignty over and title to Cuba.

And as the island is, upon its evacuation by Spain, to be occupied by the United States, the United States will, so long as such occupation shall last, assume and discharge the obligations that may under international law result from the fact of its occupation, for the protection of life and property.

ARTICLE 2. Spain cedes to the United States the island of Porto Rico and other islands now under Spanish sovereignty in the West Indies, and the island of Guam in the Marianas or Ladrones.

ARTICLE 3. Spain cedes to the United States the archipelago known as the Philippine Islands . . .

The United States will pay to Spain the sum of twenty million dollars . . . within three months after the exchange of the ratifications of the present treaty. . . .

ARTICLE 9. Spanish subjects, natives of the Peninsula, residing in the territory over which Spain by the present treaty relinquishes or cedes her sovereignty, may remain in such territory or may remove therefrom, retaining in either event all their rights of property. . . . The civil rights and political status of the native inhabitants of the territories hereby ceded to the United States shall be determined by the Congress.

ARTICLE 10. The inhabitants of the territories over which Spain relinquishes or cedes her sovereignty shall be secured in the free exercise of their religion. . . .

ARTICLE 14. Spain shall have the power to establish consular officers in the ports and places of the territories, the sovereignty over which has been either relinquished or ceded by the present treaty. . . .

1900

"Ariel"

José Enrique Rodó

T he Uruguayan writer José Enrique Rodó (1871–1917) was twenty-nine years old when he wrote *Ariel,* a book titled after a character in William Shakespeare's play *The Tempest.* Concerned above all with identifying and analyzing a Latin American identity, Rodó inevitably compared what he regarded as Latin American values with others that he associated with that rising giant, the United States. Widely read in Latin America, *Ariel* helped shape the response to the turn-of-the-century surge in U.S. economic, cultural and military influence there, even though its author had never been in the United States.

North American life, in fact, perfectly describes the vicious circle identified by Pascal: the fervent pursuit of well-being that has no object beyond itself. North American prosperity is as great as its inability to satisfy even an average concept of human destiny. In spite of its titanic accomplishments and the great force of will that those accomplishments represent, and in spite of its incomparable triumphs in all spheres of material success, it is nevertheless true that as an entity this civilization creates a singular impression of insufficiency and emptiness. And when following the prerogative granted by centuries of evolution dominated by the dignity of classicism and Christianity we ask, what is its directing principle, what its ideal *substratum,* what the ultimate goal of the present Positivist interests surging through that formidable mass, we find nothing in the way of a formula for a definitive ideal but the same eternal preoccupation with material triumphs. Having drifted from the traditions that set their course, the peoples of this nation have not been able to replace the inspiring idealism of the past with a high and selfless concept of the future. They live for the immediate reality, for the present, and thereby subordinate all their activity to the egoism of personal and collective well-being. Of the sum of their riches and power could be said what Bourget said of the intelligence of the

Source: From *Ariel,* by José Enrique Rodó, translated by Margaret Sayers Peden, pp. 79–90. Copyright © 1988. By permission of the University of Texas Press.

Marquis de Norbert, a figure in one of his books: that it is like a well-laid fire to which no one has set a match. What is lacking is the kindling spark that causes the flame of a vivifying and exciting ideal to blaze from the abundant but unlighted wood. Not even national egoism, lacking a higher motivation, not even exclusiveness and pride of nationhood, which is what in antiquity transfigured and exalted the prosaic severity of Roman life, can engender glimmers of idealism and beauty in a people in whom cosmopolitan confusion and the atomism of a poorly understood democracy impede the formation of a true national consciousness. . . .

Sensibility, intelligence, customs—everything in that enormous land is characterized by a radical ineptitude for selectivity which, along with the mechanistic nature of its materialism and its politics, nurtures a profound disorder in anything having to do with idealism. It is all too easy to follow the manifestations of that ineptitude, beginning with the most external and apparent, then arriving at those that are more essential and internal. Prodigal with his riches—because in his appetites, as Bourget has astutely commented, there is no trace of Moliere's miserely Harpagon—the North American has with his wealth achieved all the satisfaction and vanity that come with sumptuous magnificence—but good taste has eluded him. In such an atmosphere, true art can exist only in the form of individual rebellion. . . . They ignore in art all that is selfless and selective. They ignore it, in spite of the munificence with which private fortunes are employed to stimulate an appreciation of beauty; in spite of the splendid museums and exhibitions their cities boast; in spite of the mountains of marble and bronze they have sculptured into statues for their public squares. And if a word may some day characterize their taste in art, it will be a word that negates art itself: the grossness of affectation, the ignorance of all that is subtle and exquisite, the cult of false grandeur, the *sensationalism* that excludes the serenity that is irreconcilable with the pace of a feverish life.

The idealism of beauty does not fire the soul of a descendant of austere Puritans. Nor does the idealism of truth. He scorns as vain and unproductive any exercise of thought that does not yield an immediate result. He does not bring to science a selfless thirst for truth, nor has he ever shown any sign of revering science for itself. For him, research is merely preparation for a utilitarian application. His grandiose plans to disseminate the benefits of popular education were inspired in the noble goal of communicating rudimentary knowledge to the masses; but although those plans promote the growth of education, we have seen no sign that they contain any imperative to enhance selective education, or any inclination to aid in allowing excellence to rise above general mediocrity. Thus the persistent North American war against ignorance has resulted in a universal *semi*-culture, accompanied by the diminution of high culture. To the same degree that basic ignorance has diminished in that gigantic democracy, wisdom and genius have correspondingly disappeared. This, then, is the reason that the trajectory of their intellectual activity is one of decreasing brilliance and originality. While in the period of independence and the formation of their nation many illustrious names emerged to expound both the thought and the will of that people, only a half century later de Tocqueville could write of them, *the gods have departed*. . . .

To the degree that the generic utilitarianism of that civilization assumes more defined, more open, and more limiting characteristics, the intoxication of material prosperity increases the impatience of its children to propagate that doctrine and enshrine it with the historical importance of a Rome. Today, North Americans openly aspire to preeminence in universal culture, to leadership in ideas; they consider themselves the forgers of a type of civilization that will endure forever. . . .

I want each of you to be aware that when in the name of the rights of the spirit I resist the mode of North American utilitarianism, which they want to impose on us as the summa and model of civilization, I do not imply that everything they have achieved in the sphere of what we might call *the interests of the soul* has been entirely negative. Without the arm that levels and constructs, the arm that serves the noble work of the mind would not be free to function. Without a certain material well-being, the realm of the spirit and the intellect could not exist. . . . Ultimately, the work of North American Positivism will serve the cause of Ariel. What that Cyclopean nation, with its sense of the useful and its admirable aptitude for mechanical invention, has achieved directly in the way of material well-being, other peoples, or they themselves in the future, will effectively incorporate into the process of selection. . . . [I]n the same way that motion is transformed into heat, elements of spiritual excellence may also be obtained from material benefits.

As yet, however, North American life has not offered us a new example of that incontestable relationship, nor even afforded a glimpse of a glorious future. Our confidence and our opinion must incline us to believe, however, that in an inferred future their civilization is destined for excellence. . . . Let us hope that the spirit of that titanic society, which has until today been characterized solely by Will and Unity, may one day be known for its intelligence, sentiment, and idealism. Let us hope that from that enormous crucible will ultimately emerge the exemplary human being, generous, balanced, and select, whom Spencer, . . . predicted would be the product of the costly work of the melting pot. But let us not expect to find such a person either in the present reality of that nation or in its immediate evolution. And let us refuse to see an exemplary civilization where there exists only a clumsy, though huge, working model that must still pass through many corrective revisions before it acquires the serenity and confidence with which a nation that has achieved its perfection crowns its work. . . .

❖

1901

The Platt Amendment

The Congress of the United States

A lthough the Teller Amendment appeared to promise that the United States would not block Cuba's full independence after the defeat of Spain, the U.S. government nevertheless refused to terminate the military occupation of Cuba until certain guarantees limiting Cuban sovereignty were written into the new Cuban constitution. When delegates to the Cuban constitutional convention refused to do so, Secretary of War Elihu Root urged the U.S. Congress to take action. An amendment to the army appropriation bill of March 2, 1901, the so-called Platt Amendment (named for Senator Orville H. Platt) effectively authorized the president to make Cuba a U.S. protectorate. The delegates to the Cuban constitutional convention were informed that unless they added the Platt Amendment to the new constitution, U.S. military occupation of the island would continue. After receiving assurances from Washington that the Platt Amendment was not intended to authorize any U.S. meddling in the operations of the Cuban government, the delegates complied in early June 1902, appending the Platt Amendment to the Cuban constitution by a margin of one vote. The U.S. military occupation ended and the Platt Amendment was incorporated into a treaty signed by both countries on May 22, 1903. The Cuban government unilaterally renounced the Platt Amendment in 1933, but it was not formally abrogated by both countries until May 29, 1934, when Cuba finally achieved full sovereignty.

. . . [I]n fulfillment of the declaration contained in the joint resolution approved April 20, 1898, . . . the President is hereby authorized to "leave the government and control of the island of Cuba to its people" as soon as a government shall have been established in said island under a constitution which, either as a part thereof or in an ordinance appended thereto, shall define the future relations of the United States with Cuba, substantially as follows:

   1. That the government of Cuba shall never enter into any treaty or other compact with any foreign power or powers which will impair or tend to im-

Source: U.S. Congress. *Statutes of the United States of America Passed at the Second Session of the Fifty-Sixth Congress, 1900–1901, . . .* Pp. 897–98. Washington, D.C.: GPO, 1902.

pair the independence of Cuba, nor in any manner authorize or permit any foreign power or powers to obtain by colonization or for military or naval purposes or otherwise, lodgment in or control over any portion of said island.

2. That said government shall not assume or contract any public debt, to pay the interest upon which, and to make reasonable sinking fund provision for the ultimate discharge of which, the ordinary revenues of the island, after defraying the current expenses of government shall be inadequate.

3. That the government of Cuba consents that the United States may exercise the right to intervene for the preservation of Cuban independence, the maintenance of a government adequate for the protection of life, property, and individual liberty, and for discharging the obligations with respect to Cuba imposed by the treaty of Paris on the United States, now to be assumed and undertaken by the government of Cuba.

4. That all Acts of the United States in Cuba during its military occupancy thereof are ratified and validated, and all lawful rights acquired thereunder shall be maintained and protected.

5. That the government of Cuba will execute, and as far as necessary extend, the plans already devised or other plans to be mutually agreed upon, for the sanitation of the cities of the island, to the end that a recurrence of epidemic and infectious diseases may be prevented thereby assuring protection to the people and commerce of Cuba, as well as to the commerce of the southern ports of the United States and the people residing therein.

6. That the Isle of Pines shall be omitted from the proposed constitutional boundaries of Cuba, the title thereto being left to future adjustment by treaty.

7. That to enable the United States to maintain the independence of Cuba, and to protect the people thereof, as well as for its own defense, the government of Cuba will sell or lease to the United States lands necessary for coaling or naval stations at certain specified points to be agreed upon with the President of the United States.

8. That by way of further assurance the government of Cuba will embody the foregoing provisions in a permanent treaty with the United States.

NO. 30

1901

The Hay-Pauncefote Treaty

The Governments of the United States and Great Britain

As pressure grew in the United States for the construction of a canal across the Central American isthmus, its proponents insisted it be under the exclusive control of the U.S. government. But exclusive U.S. control was prohibited by the Clayton-Bulwer Treaty of 1850 (Document No. 12). The British government, therefore, had to be persuaded to relinquish its right under the treaty to share with the United States the control of any future canal. The British yielded to U.S. pressure in 1900, agreeing to allow exclusive U.S. control yet nevertheless insisting on the preservation of the Clayton-Bulwer clause forbidding the future canal to be "fortified." However, 1900 was a presidential election year, and the nonfortification provision soon became the target of nationalist and anglophobic criticism. Britain eventually agreed to a new draft of the treaty that omitted any reference to fortifications. This second Hay-Pauncefote treaty was signed by John Hay, the U.S. secretary of state, and Sir Julian Pauncefote, the British ambassador, on November 18, 1901, in Washington, D.C. After its ratification in both countries in December and January, the treaty was formally proclaimed on February 22, 1902.

The United States of America and His Majesty Edward the Seventh, of the United Kingdom of Great Britain and Ireland, and of the British Dominions beyond the Seas, King, and Emperor of India, being desirous to facilitate the construction of a ship canal to connect the Atlantic and Pacific Oceans, by whatever route may be considered expedient, and to that end to remove any objection which may arise out of the Convention of the 19th April, 1850, commonly called the Clayton-Bulwer Treaty, to the construction of such canal under the auspices of the Government of the United States, without impairing the "general principle" of neutralization . . . have agreed upon the following. . . .

. . . [T]he present Treaty shall supercede the afore-mentioned Convention of the 19th April, 1850. It is agreed that the canal may be constructed under the

Source: U.S. Congress. *Statutes at Large of the United States of America, from December 1901 to March 1903,* . . . Vol. 32, Part 2, pp. 1903–05. Washington, D.C.: GPO, 1903.

auspices of the Government of the United States, either directly at its own cost, or by gift or loan of money to individuals or Corporations, or through subscription to or purchase of stock or shares and that, subject to the provisions of the present Treaty, the said Government shall have and enjoy all the rights incident to such construction, as well as the exclusive right of providing for the regulation and management of the canal. . . .

. . . The canal shall be free and open to the vessels of commerce and of war of all nations observing these Rules, on terms of entire equality, so that there shall be no discrimination against any such nation or its citizens or subjects, in respect of the conditions or charges of traffic or otherwise. Such conditions and charges of traffic shall be just and equitable. . . . The canal shall never be blockaded, nor shall any right of war be exercised nor any act of hostility be committed within it. The United States, however, shall be at liberty to maintain such military police along the canal as may be necessary to protect it against lawlessness and disorder. . . .

❖

NO. 31

1902

Vanity and Ambition on the Rio Grande

José María Roa Bárcena

This interpretation of the U.S.-Mexican war was published a half-century after the event, in 1902, at a time when Mexico had recovered from the terrible period of constant civil war and economic disintegration that had characterized it from independence from Spain in 1821 until the rise of the dictator Porfirio Díaz after 1880. The author, José María Roa Bárcena (1827–1908), was a well-known Mexican historian and writer, a political conservative and a traditionalist in the broadest sense who disliked the "Saxons" to the north as much as he despised the upstart Mexican politicians whom he believed shared responsibility

Source: "Memories of the North American Invasion, Vol. II," by José María Roa Bárcena from *The View from Chapultepec: Mexican Writers on the Mexican-American War*, translated and edited by Cecil Robinson, pp. 44–49. Copyright © 1989 The Arizona Board of Regents. Reprinted by permission of the University of Arizona Press.

for the loss of half of Mexico's national territory as a result of the U.S.-Mexican War. This passage reveals a mixture of shame and pride toward his own people, and of admiration and disgust for the Americans. In this sense, it is a sign of the ambivalence that many Mexicans continue to feel toward their northern neighbor.

Our war with the United States was the double result of inexperience and vanity about our own capacities, on the one hand; and of an ambition unconstrained by concepts of justice and of the abuse of force, on the other.

The rebellion of Texas, more due to the emancipation of the slaves in Mexico than to the fall of the federalist constitution of 1824, would have taken place without the one or the other. It was the result of a plan by the United States, calculated and executed calmly and coldbloodedly in a manner truly Saxon. It consisted in sending its nationals to colonize lands then belonging to Spain and later to ourselves and in inciting and aiding them to rebel against Mexico, repulsing any counterattack on our part and setting up an independent nation, obtaining in the process the recognition of some nations, and entering finally into the North American confederation as one of its states. Is there calumny or simply happenstance in this? Look at the extensive and illuminating information presented by General Don Manuel de Mier y Terán, who researched in our archives on the subject of the situation and dangers of Texas and of our northern frontier, long before the rebellion of the colonists; consider the initiatives of our Minister of Relations, Don Lucas Alamán, on April 6, 1830, and, most of all, the note of the North American envoy William Shannon of October 14, 1844, which said about the motion for the annexation of Texas then pending in Washington: "This has been a political measure that has been fostered for a long time and been considered indispensable to the security and well-being [of the United States], and consequently it has been an objective invariably pursued by all parties, and the acquisition of this territory [of Texas] has been a subject of negotiation by almost all the administrations in the last twenty years."

The rebellion of Texas found Mexico flushed with pride over the brilliant results of its war of independence and believing itself capable of any enterprise. With the presumption and boldness that come with youth and inexperience it sent its ill-equipped and ill-provisioned army across immense deserts to the Sabine River to severely punish the rebels, but in the bewilderment of its first defeat this army was forced to retreat to the Rio Grande, as though signaling in anticipation the entire area that we were going to lose, all the way down to this point. Mexico's later and futile shows and preparations aimed at the recovery of Texas, which took place before and during the act of annexation of that state to the American Union, provided that country with a pretext for bringing war upon us, by virtue of which it took over, in the end, the areas above the Rio Grande which remained to us, such as New Mexico and Upper California.

Mexico, if it were to have acted with prevision and wisdom, should have written off Texas in 1835 while fastening into itself and fortifying its new frontiers. It should have recognized as an accepted fact the independence of that colony and, by way of negotiations, should have resolved any differences and settled boundary questions with the United States. It was imprudence and madness not to have done either the one or the other, but one has to agree that such judicious conduct would not have prevented the new territorial losses suffered in 1848. The area between the Rio Grande and Nueces rivers, New Mexico and Upper California, all these too were indispensable to the security and well-being of the United States, as is demonstrated in its diplomatic correspondence, in various allusions in President Polk's messages to Congress, in Trist's note of September 7, 1847 to the Mexican commissioners, and above all by the armed invasions of New Mexico and Upper California, all carried out when the two nations were presumably in a state of peace. Thus the pretext might have been different but the appropriation of those territories would have been the same.

The war with the United States found us in disadvantageous conditions in all respects. To the physical inferiority of our races must be added the weakness of our social and political organization, the general demoralization, the weariness and poverty resulting from twenty-five years of civil war, and an army insufficient in number, composed of forced conscripts, with armaments which were in a large part castoffs sold to us by England, without means of transportation, without ambulances, and without depots. The federation, which in the enemy country was the bond by which the different states united to form one, was here the dismemberment of the old order to constitute many diverse states. In sum, we changed the monetary units of the peso to centavos while our neighbor combined its small change to make a stronger monetary unit. One of the more deplorable effects of this political organization, weakened and made even more complicated by our racial heterogeneity, could be seen in the indifference and egotism with which many states—while others such as San Luis Potosí made astounding contributions to the defense effort—entrenched themselves in their own sovereignty, deriving the resources of money and manpower to the general government which were needed both to face the foreign invasion and to contain and suppress the Indian uprisings. As for our army, its inferiority and deficiency could be seen from that first campaign on the other side of the Rio Grande, which signaled the beginning of the war in 1846. There a detachment of from three to four thousand men, who, because of a rapid and unexpected movement, called Taylor's attention to their advance, had to stop to cross the river in two launches. They were decimated by the artillery of the enemy while our cannon balls could not reach them, and they had to abandon on the field of battle their wounded to the humanity and mercy of the conqueror, while they retired in complete disorder to Matamoros to regroup and await replacements, only to be defeated again at Monterrey. . . .

And as for the commander-in-chief, Santa Anna, his errors and faults notwithstanding, when the fog of political passions and hatreds has cleared away, who will be able to deny his valor, his energetic vigor, his constancy, his fortitude in the face of the repeated strikes of an always adverse fortune, the marvelous energy with which he roused others to the defense and produced materials and provisions out of nothing and improvised and organized armies, raising himself up like Antaeus, strong and courageous after each reverse. What might not the defense of Mexico have been if there had been some years of interior peace, with an army better organized and armed, and under a political system which would have permitted the chief to dispose freely of all the resistant elements in the nation? One word more about the campaign in order to do proper justice to the enemy: his grave and phlegmatic temperament, his lack of hatred in an adventure embarked upon with the simple intention of extending territory, his discipline, vigorous and severe among the corps of the line, which even extended to the volunteers, with the exception of some of the detached forces that were a veritable scourge, and above all, the noble and kind characters of Scott and Taylor lessened to the extent possible the evils of warfare. And the second of those chiefs cited, who commanded the first of the invading armies, was, once the campaign in the Valley [Mexico City and environs] was ended, the most sincere and powerful of the friends of peace.

Not only was this not dishonorable, but it will figure in the diplomatic annals of the Hispanic American countries as having contributed to the result of a negotiation which only the patriotism and intelligence of Peña y Peña and Couto [Mexican president and Mexican peace commissioner] could have resumed on the agreed-upon conditions, when we were completely at the mercy of the conqueror.

❖

1902

The Drago Doctrine

Luis M. Drago

Venezuela, whose boundary dispute with Great Britain nearly led to war between the United States and Britain in 1895 (see Document No. 22), became the center of a second crisis involving Europe in 1902. Claims for damages submitted to the Venezuelan government by the citizens of various European countries were being rebuffed by the president, Cipriano Castro. In an attempt to force Castro's government to pay the claims, British, German and Italian warships blockaded and then bombarded Venezuelan ports in December 1902. Venezuela finally agreed to allow their claims to be submitted to arbitration and the crisis passed. On December 29, the government of Argentina instructed its minister in Washington to present its views on the matter to the government of President Theodore Roosevelt. The Argentine letter was written by Luis M. Drago (1859–1921), the foreign minister, and its argument that force cannot be used to collect a public debt was a restricted application of the broader Calvo Doctrine (Document No. 23). The United States shortly responded to the problem in a manner very different from that proposed by Drago. President Roosevelt announced what became known as the Roosevelt Corollary to the Monroe Doctrine, which asserted the right of the United States to use force unilaterally against other governments in the hemisphere, in part in order to prevent the use of force by nonhemispheric powers (see Document No. 37). The Venezuelan crisis of 1902 was the last time that any European power would attempt to use force against a Latin American country to collect debts.

Buenos Aires, December 29, 1902.

Mr. Minister: I have received your excellency's telegram of 20th instant concerning the events that have lately taken place between the Government of the Republic of Venezuela and the Governments of Great Britain and Germany.

Source: U.S. Department of State. *Papers Relating to the Foreign Relations of the United States, . . . 1903.* "'Monroe Doctrine' and Diplomatic Claims of European Powers." Pp. 1–5. Washington, D.C.: GPO, 1904.

According to your excellency's information the origin of the disagreement is, in part, the damages suffered by subjects of the claimant nations during the revolutions and wars that have recently occurred within the borders of [Venezuela] . . . and in part also the fact that certain payments on the external debt of the nation have not been met at the proper time. . . . [T]his Government has deemed it expedient to transmit to your excellency some considerations with reference to the forcible collection of the public debt suggested by the events that have taken place. . . .

Among the fundamental principles of public international law which humanity has consecrated, one of the most precious is that which decrees that all states, whatever be the force at their disposal, are entities in law, perfectly equal one to another, and mutually entitled by virtue thereof to the same consideration and respect.

The acknowledgment of the debt, the payment of it in its entirety, can and must be made by the nation without diminution of its inherent rights as a sovereign entity, but the summary and immediate collection at a given moment, by means of force, would occasion nothing less than the ruin of the weakest nations, and the absorption of their governments, together with all the functions inherent in them, by the mighty of the earth. . . .

This is in no wise a defense for bad faith, disorder, and deliberate and voluntary insolvency. It is intended merely to preserve the dignity of the public international entity which may not thus be dragged into war. . . . The fact that collection can not be accomplished by means of violence does not, on the other hand, render valueless the acknowledgment of the public debt, the definite obligation of paying it.

As these are the sentiments of justice, loyalty, and honor which animate the Argentine people and have always inspired its policy, your excellency will understand that it has felt alarmed at the knowledge that the failure of Venezuela to meet the payments of its public debt is given as one of the determining causes of the capture of its fleet, the bombardment of one of its ports, and the establishment of a rigorous blockade along its shores. If such proceedings were to be definitely adopted they would establish a precedent dangerous to the security and the peace of the nations of this part of America. The collection of loans by military means implies territorial occupation to make them effective, and territorial occupation signifies the suppression or subordination of the governments of the countries on which it is imposed.

Such a situation seems obviously at variance with the principles many times proclaimed by the nations of America, and particularly with the Monroe Doctrine, sustained and defended with so much zeal on all occasions by the United States, a doctrine to which the Argentine Republic has heretofore solemnly adhered. . . .

The only principle which the Argentine Republic maintains and which it would, with great satisfaction, see adopted, in view of the events in Venezuela, by a nation that enjoys such great authority and prestige as does the United States, is the principle, already accepted, that there can be no territorial expansion in America on the part of Europe, nor any oppression of the peoples of this continent, because an unfortunate financial situation may compel some one of them to the fulfillment of its promises. In a word, the principle which she would like to see recognized is: that the public debt can not occasion armed intervention nor even the actual occupation of the territory of American nations by a European power.

The loss of prestige and credit experienced by States which fail to satisfy the rightful claims of their lawful creditors brings with it difficulties of such magnitude as to render it unnecessary for foreign intervention to aggravate with its oppression the temporary misfortunes of insolvency. . . .

At this time, then, no selfish feeling animates us, nor do we seek our own advantage in manifesting our desire that the public debt of States should not serve as a reason for an armed attack on States. . . .

I address you, . . . that you may communicate to the Government of the United States our point of view regarding the events in the further development of which that Government is to take so important a part. . . .

Luis M. Drago.

❖

NO. 33

1903

Hay–Bunau-Varilla Treaty

The Governments of the United States and Panama

The United States chose the Isthmus of Panama, part of the national territory of Colombia, as the canal site over its closest competitor, Nicaragua. Washington and the government of Colombia subsequently negotiated the Hay–Herrán Treaty, under which the United States would receive a 100-year lease of Panamanian territory for a canal route. The U.S. Senate ratified the treaty on March 17, 1903, but the Colombian Senate unanimously rejected it on August

Source: U.S. Congress. *The Statutes At Large of the United States of America, from November 1903, to March 1905; . . .* Vol. 33, Part 2, pp. 2,234–241. Washington, D.C.: GPO, 1905.

12, on the grounds that the U.S. compensation ($10 million plus $250,000 a year) was too low. Denouncing the Colombians as "jack rabbits," President Theodore Roosevelt assured a group of Colombians interested in the canal route that the United States would support a Panamanian secessionist movement. Roosevelt kept his word. U.S. naval vessels and troops joined the insurgent forces and on November 4 Panama declared its independence. Fifteen days later, Secretary of State John Hay signed this treaty in Washington with the representative of the Panamanian government, Philippe Bunau-Varilla, a French citizen who was a major stockholder in a French company that had gone bankrupt in 1889 digging a canal across Panama under a concession from the Colombian government. The terms of the Hay–Bunau-Varilla Treaty were considerably more favorable to the United States than those of the Hay–Herrán Treaty; Bunau-Varilla's company received $40 million from the U.S. government for the rights and assets it held in Panama.

The President of the United States of America, John Hay, Secretary of State, and the Government of the Republic of Panama, Philippe Bunau-Varilla, Envoy Extraordinary and Minister Plenipotentiary of the Republic of Panama, . . . have agreed upon and concluded the following articles:

ARTICLE 1. The United States guarantees and will maintain the independence of the Republic of Panama.

ARTICLE 2. The Republic of Panama grants to the United States in perpetuity the use, occupation and control of a zone of land and land under water for the construction, maintenance, operation, sanitation and protection of said Canal of the width of ten miles extending to the distance of five miles on each side of the center line of the route of the Canal to be constructed. . . . The Republic of Panama further grants to the United States in perpetuity the use, occupation and control of any other lands and waters outside of the zone above described which may be necessary and convenient for the construction, maintenance, operation, sanitation and protection of the said Canal or of any auxiliary canals or other works necessary and convenient for the . . . said enterprise.

The Republic of Panama further grants in like manner to the United States in perpetuity all islands within the limits of the zone above described. . . .

ARTICLE 3. The Republic of Panama grants to the United States all the rights, power and authority within the zone mentioned and described in Article 2 of this agreement and within the limits of all auxiliary lands and waters . . . which the United States would possess and exercise if it were the sovereign of the territory . . . to the entire exclusion of the exercise by the Republic of Panama of any such sovereign rights, power or authority. . . .

ARTICLE 5. The Republic of Panama grants to the United States in perpetuity a monopoly for the construction, maintenance and operation of any system of communication by means of canal or railroad across its territory between the Caribbean Sea and the Pacific Ocean. . . .

ARTICLE 7. The Republic of Panama grants to the United States within the limits of the cities of Panama and Colon and their adjacent harbors . . . the right to acquire by purchase or by the exercise of the right of eminent domain, any lands, buildings, water rights or other properties. . . .

ARTICLE 10. The . . . Republic of Panama agrees that there shall not be imposed any taxes . . . upon the Canal, the railways and auxiliary works. . . .

ARTICLE 14. As the price or compensation for the rights, powers and privileges granted in this convention by the Republic of Panama to the United States, the Government of the United States agrees to pay to the Republic of Panama the sum of ten million dollars ($10,000,000) in gold coin of the United States . . . and also an annual payment during the life of this convention of two hundred and fifty thousand dollars ($250,000) in gold coin, beginning nine years after the date [of ratification]. . . .

ARTICLE 18. The Canal, when constructed, and the entrances thereto shall be neutral in perpetuity. . . .

ARTICLE 23. If it should become necessary at any time to employ armed forces for the safety or protection of the Canal, or of the ships that make use of the same, or the railways and auxiliary works, the United States shall have the right, at all times and in its discretion, to use its police and its land and naval forces or to establish fortifications for these purposes. . . .

❖

NO. 34

1903

"I Took Final Action in 1903"

Theodore Roosevelt

Former President Theodore Roosevelt's autobiography was published just after he was defeated in a final bid for reelection as a nominee of the Progressive Party in 1912. In the excerpts below he describes his role in the creation of Panama and the construction of the canal (see Document No. 33 for more background).

Source: Theodore Roosevelt. *Theodore Roosevelt: An Autobiography with Illustrations*, pp. 512–25. New York: Charles Scribner's Sons, 1920; N.Y.: Macmillan Company, 1913.

By far the most important action I took in foreign affairs during the time I was President related to the Panama Canal. Here again there was much accusation about my having acted in an "unconstitutional" manner . . . which meant, that when nobody else could or would exercise efficient authority, I exercised it. . . .

We had again and again been forced to intervene to protect the transit across the Isthmus, and the intervention was frequently at the request of Colombia herself. The effort to build a canal by private capital had been made under De Lesseps and had resulted in lamentable failure. Every serious proposal to build the canal in such manner had been abandoned. The United States had repeatedly announced that we would not permit it to be built or controlled by any old-world government. Colombia was utterly impotent to build it herself. Under these circumstances it had become a matter of imperative obligation that we should build it ourselves without further delay.

I took final action in 1903. During the preceding fifty-three years the Governments of New Granada and of its successor, Colombia, had been in a constant state of flux; and the State of Panama had sometimes been treated as almost independent, in a loose Federal league, and sometimes as the mere property of the Government at Bogota; and there had been innumerable appeals to arms, sometimes for adequate, sometimes for inadequate, reasons. . . .

In short, the experience of over half a century had shown Colombia to be utterly incapable of keeping order on the Isthmus. Only the active interference of the United States had enabled her to preserve so much as a semblance of sovereignty. Had it not been for the exercise by the United States of the police power in her interest, her connection with the Isthmus would have been sundered long before it was. . . .

When the people of Panama declared their independence in November, 1903, no Congress had sat in Colombia since the year 1898, except the special Congress called by [President] Maroquin [sic] to reject the canal treaty, and which did reject it by a unanimous vote, and adjourned without legislating on any other subject. The constitution of 1886 had taken away from Panama the power of self-government and vested it in Colombia. The *coup d'état* of Maroquin [in 1900] took away from Colombia herself the power of government and vested it in an irresponsible dictator. . . .

The Hay–Herrán Treaty, if it erred at all, erred in being overgenerous toward Colombia. The people of Panama were delighted with the treaty, and the President of Colombia, who embodied in his own person the entire government of Colombia, had authorized the treaty to be made. But after the treaty had been made the Colombia Government thought it had the matter in its own hands; and the further thought, equally wicked and foolish, came in to the heads of the people in control at Bogota that they would seize the French Company [of De Lesseps] at the end of another year and take for themselves the forty million dollars which the United States had agreed to pay the Panama Canal Company. . . .

On November 3 the revolution occurred. Practically everybody on the Isthmus, including all the Colombian troops that were already stationed there, joined in the revolution, and there was no bloodshed. . . . On the Pacific side a Colombian gunboat shelled the City of Panama, with the result of killing one Chinaman—the only life lost in the whole affair.

No one connected with the American Government had any part in preparing, inciting, or encouraging the revolution, and except for the reports of our military and naval officers, which I forwarded to Congress, no one connected with the Government had any previous knowledge concerning the proposed revolution, except such as was accessible to any person who read the newspapers and kept abreast of current questions and current affairs. By the unanimous action of its people, and without the firing of a shot, the state of Panama declared themselves an independent republic. The time for hesitation on our part had passed.

My belief then was, and the events that have occurred since have more than justified it, that from the standpoint of the United States it was imperative, not only for civil but for military reasons, that there should be the immediate establishment of easy and speedy communication by sea between the Atlantic and the Pacific. These reasons were not of convenience only, but of vital necessity, and did not admit of indefinite delay. . . . Every consideration of international morality and expediency, of duty to the Panama people, and of satisfaction of our own national interests and honor, bade us take immediate action. . . .

From the beginning to the end our course was straight-forward and in absolute accord with the highest of standards of international morality. Criticism of it can come only from misinformation, or else from a sentimentality which represents both mental weakness and a moral twist. To have acted otherwise than I did would have been on my part betrayal of the interests of the United States, indifference to the interests of Panama, and recreancy to the interests of the world at large. Colombia had forfeited every claim to consideration; indeed, this is not stating the case strongly enough: she had so acted that yielding to her would have meant on our part that culpable form of weakness which stands on a level with wickedness. . . . There had been fifty years of continuous bloodshed and civil strife in Panama; because of my action Panama has now known ten years of such peace and prosperity as she never before saw during the four centuries of her existence—for in Panama, as in Cuba and Santo Domingo, it was the action of the American people, against the outcries of the professed apostles of peace, which alone brought peace. We gave to the people of Panama self-government, and freed them from subjection to alien oppressors.

❖

1904

"To Roosevelt"

Rubén Darío

Félix Rubén García Sarmiento (1867–1916) adopted the pseudonym Rubén Darío when he began writing at the age of fourteen. In 1886 he abandoned his native Nicaragua to adopt a life of constant travel throughout Latin America and Europe. His first major collection of writings, *Azul,* was published in 1888 and established Darío as the founder and principal figure of *modernismo* (modernism) in Latin American literature. Cultivated in the relatively stable, cosmopolitan urban climate of the late nineteenth century, the modernists looked to France for literary inspiration, and in doing so radically transformed traditional Spanish verse. In 1898 the Argentine newspaper *La Nación* sent Darío to cover events in Spain in the aftermath of its war with the United States. That war affected the poet deeply. His poem "To Roosevelt" was first published in the Spanish literary journal *Helios* in February 1904.

To Roosevelt

The voice that would reach you, Hunter, must speak
in Biblical tones, or in the poetry of Walt Whitman.
You are primitive and modern, simple and complex;
you are one part George Washington and one part Nimrod.
   You are the United States,
future invader of our native America
with its Indian blood, an America
that still prays to Christ and still speaks Spanish.

You are a strong, proud model of your race;
you are cultured and able; you oppose Tolstoy.
You are an Alexander-Nebuchadnezzar,
breaking horses and murdering tigers.
(You are a Professor of Energy,
as the current lunatics say).

Source: From *Selected Poems of Rubén Darío* by Rubén Darío, translated by Lysander Kemp, pp. 69–70. Copyright © 1965, renewed 1993. Reprinted by permission of the University of Texas Press.

You think that life is a fire,
that progress is an irruption,
that the future is wherever
your bullet strikes.

No.

The United States is grand and powerful.
Whenever it trembles, a profound shudder
runs down the enormous backbone of the Andes.
If it shouts, the sound is like the roar of a lion.
And Hugo said to Grant: "The stars are yours."
(The dawning sun of the Argentine barely shines;
the star of Chile is rising . . .) A wealthy country,
joining the cult of Mammon to the cult of Hercules;
while Liberty, lighting the path
to easy conquest, raises her torch in New York.

But our own America, which has had poets
since the ancient times of Nezahualcóyotl;
which preserved the footprints of great Bacchus,
and learned the Punic alphabet once,
and consulted the stars; which also knew Atlantis
(whose name comes ringing down to us in Plato)
and has lived, since the earliest moments of its life,
in light, in fire, in fragrance, and in love —
the America of Moctezuma and Atahualpa,
the aromatic America of Columbus,
Catholic America, Spanish America,
the America where noble Cuauhtémoc said:
"I am not on a bed of roses"—our America,
trembling with hurricanes, trembling with Love:
O men with Saxon eyes and barbarous souls,
our America lives. And dreams. And loves.
And it is the daughter of the Sun. Be careful.
Long live Spanish America!
A thousand cubs of the Spanish lion are roaming free.
Roosevelt, you must become, by God's own will,
the deadly Rifleman and the dreadful Hunter
before you can clutch us in your iron claws.

And though you have everything, you are lacking one thing:
God!

1904

Banana Republics

O. Henry

O. Henry was the pseudonym of the popular fiction writer William Sydney Porter (1862–1910). *Cabbages and Kings,* published in 1904, was drawn from Porter's own experiences in Central America, where he briefly lived after he jumped bail in 1896 to escape charges of embezzlement stemming from his job as a bank clerk in Texas. Returning several months later to comfort his dying wife and to face the criminal charges, Porter spent the next three years in an Ohio prison where he began to write short stories under the pseudonym O. Henry in order to shield his outlaw past from public scrutiny. By the time he left prison in 1901, Porter had become a famous writer. *Cabbages and Kings* takes place in the fictional port city of Coralio, located in "Anchuria"—most likely Honduras, where Porter spent most of his time during his Central American adventure. In this chapter, titled "The Admiral," Porter refers to Anchuria as a "banana republic," establishing the term for the first time in print.

Spilled milk draws few tears from an Anchurian administration. Many are its lacteal sources; and the clocks' hands point forever to milking time. Even the rich cream skimmed from the treasury by the bewitched [ex-president] Miraflores did not cause the newly-installed patriots to waste time in unprofitable regrets. The government philosophically set about supplying the deficiency by increasing the import duties and by "suggesting" to wealthy private citizens that contributions according to their means would be considered patriotic and in order. Prosperity was expected to attend the reign of Losada, the new president. The ousted office-holders and military favourites organized a new "Liberal" party, and began to lay their plans for a re-succession. Thus the game of Anchurian politics began, like a Chinese comedy, to unwind slowly its serial length. Here and there Mirth peeps for an instant from the wings and illumines the florid lines.

A dozen quarts of champagne in conjunction with an informal sitting of the president and his cabinet led to the establishment of the navy and the appointment of Felipe Carrera as its admiral.

Source: O. Henry, *Cabbages and Kings,* pp. 130–43. New York: Doubleday, Page, 1917 (1904).

Next to the champagne the credit of the appointment belongs to Don Sabas Placido, the newly confirmed Minister of War.

The president had requested a convention of his cabinet for the discussion of questions politic and for the transaction of certain routine matters of state. The session had been signally tedious; the business and the wine prodigiously dry. A sudden, prankish humour of Don Sabas, impelling him to the deed, spiced the grave affairs of state with a whiff of agreeable playfulness.

In the dilatory order of business had come a bulletin from the coast department of Orilla del Mar reporting the seizure by the custom-house officers at the town of Coralio of the sloop *Estrella del Noche* [sic] and her cargo of dry goods, patent medicines, granulated sugar and three-star brandy. Also six Martini rifles and a barrel of American whisky. Caught in the act of smuggling, the sloop with its cargo was now, according to law, the property of the republic.

The Collector of Customs, in making his report, departed from the conventional forms so far as to suggest that the confiscated vessel be converted to the use of the government. The prize was the first capture to the credit of the department in ten years. The collector took opportunity to pat his department on the back.

It often happened that government officers required transportation from point to point along the coast, and means were usually lacking. Furthermore, the sloop could be manned by a loyal crew and employed as a coast guard to discourage the pernicious art of smuggling. The collector also ventured to nominate one to whom the charge of the boat could be safely intrusted—a young man of Coralio, Felipe Carrera—not, be it understood, one of extreme wisdom, but loyal and the best sailor along the coast.

It was upon this hint that the Minister of War acted, executing a rare piece of drollery that so enlivened the tedium of executive session.

In the constitution of this small, maritime banana republic was a forgotten section that provided for the maintenance of a navy. This provision—with many other wiser ones—had lain inert since the establishment of the republic. Anchuria had no navy and had no use for one. It was characteristic of Don Sabas—a man at once merry, learned, whimsical and audacious—that he should have disturbed the dust of this musty and sleeping statute to increase the humour of the world by so much as a smile from his indulgent colleagues.

With delightful mock seriousness the Minister of War proposed the creation of a navy. He argued its need and the glories it might achieve with such gay and witty zeal that the travesty overcame with its humour even the swart dignity of President Losada himself.

The champagne was bubbling trickily in the veins of the mercurial statesmen. It was not the custom of the grave governors of Anchuria to enliven their sessions with a beverage so apt to cast a veil of disparagement over sober affairs. The wine had been a thoughtful compliment tendered by the agent of the Vesuvius Fruit Company as a token of amicable relations—and certain consummated deals—between that company and the republic of Anchuria.

The jest was carried to its end. A formidable, official document was prepared, encrusted with chromatic seals and jaunty with fluttering ribbons, bearing the florid signatures of state. This commission conferred upon el Señor Don Felipe Carrera the title of Flag Admiral of the Republic of Anchuria. Thus within the space of a few minutes and the dominion of a dozen "extra dry," the country took its place among the naval powers of the world, and Felipe Carrera became entitled to a salute of nineteen guns whenever he might enter port. . . .

During the next few months the navy had its troubles. Even an admiral is perplexed to know what to do without any orders. But none came. Neither did any salaries. El Nacional swung idly at anchor.

When Felipe's little store of money was exhausted he went to the collector and raised the question of finances.

"Salaries!" exclaimed the collector, with hands raised; "Valgame Dios! [sic] not one centavo of my own pay have I received for the last seven months. The pay of an admiral, do you ask? Quién sabe? Should it be less than three thousand pesos? Mira! you will see a revolution in this country very soon. A good sign of it is when the government calls all the time for pesos, pesos, pesos, and pays none out."

Felipe left the collector's office with a look almost of content on his sombre face. A revolution would mean fighting, and then the government would need his services. It was rather humiliating to be an admiral without anything to do, and have a hungry crew at your heels begging for reales to buy plantains and tobacco with.

When he returned to where his happy-go-lucky Caribs were waiting they sprang up and saluted, as he had drilled them to do.

"Come, muchachos," said the admiral; "it seems that the government is poor. It has no money to give us. We will earn what we need to live upon. Thus will we serve our country. Soon"—his heavy eyes almost lighted up—"it may gladly call upon us for help."

Thereafter El Nacional turned out with the other coast craft and became a wage-earner. She worked with the lighters freighting bananas and oranges out to the fruit steamers that could not approach nearer than a mile from the shore. Surely a self-supporting navy deserves red letters in the budget of any nation.

After earning enough at freighting to keep himself and his crew in provisions for a week Felipe would anchor the navy and hang about the little telegraph office, looking like one of the chorus of an insolvent comic opera troupe besieging the manager's den. A hope for orders from the capital was always in his heart. That his services as admiral had never been called into requirement hurt his pride and patriotism. At every call he would inquire, gravely and expectantly, for despatches. The operator would pretend to make a search, and then reply:

"Not yet, it seems, Señor el Almirante—poco tiempo!"

Outside in the shade of the lime-trees the crew chewed sugar cane or slumbered, well content to serve a country that was contented with so little service.

One day in the early summer the revolution predicted by the collector flamed out suddenly. It had long been smouldering. At the first note of alarm the admiral of the navy force and fleet made all sail for a larger port on the coast of a neighboring republic, where he traded a hastily collected cargo of fruit for its value in cartridges for the five Martini rifles, the only guns that the navy could boast. Then to the telegraph office sped the admiral. Sprawling in his favourite corner, in his fast-decaying uniform, with his prodigious sabre distributed between his red legs, he waited for the long-delayed, but now soon expected, orders.

"Not yet, Señor el Almirante," the telegraph clerk would call to him—"poco tiempo!"

At the answer the admiral would plump himself down with a great rattling of scabbard to await the infrequent tick of the little instrument on the table.

"They will come," would be his unshaken reply; "I am the admiral."

❖

NO. 37

1904

The Roosevelt Corollary to the Monroe Doctrine

Theodore Roosevelt

In his annual message to Congress of December 6, 1904, President Theodore Roosevelt declared what became known as the Roosevelt Corollary. The president recognized the legal right of one state to use force against another to collect debts, a right that had just been sanctioned in February by the Hague Permanent Court of Arbitration in a case involving Venezuela (see Document No. 32). But Roosevelt feared the use of debt collection as a pretext for the expansion of Europe's presence in Latin America, and the possible creation of European protectorates in the New World. At the moment of Roosevelt's address, Germany—now considered the principal military threat to U.S. power—seemed poised to intervene against the Dominican Republic. Roosevelt's solution was to

Source: U.S. Department of State. *Papers Relating to the Foreign Relations of the United States, with the Annual Message of the President Transmitted to Congress, 6 December 1904*, pp. xli–xlii. Washington, D.C.: GPO, 1905.

impose U.S.-appointed customs collectors on financially delinquent governments, in effect guaranteeing that foreign debts were paid on time. The policy succeeded in preventing the kind of intervention that Roosevelt feared, and as U.S. banks took over European loans, the Roosevelt "Big Stick" policy became known as "Dollar Diplomacy" under President William H. Taft (1909–13).

To The Senate and House of Representatives:

. . . It is our duty to remember that a nation has no more right to do injustice to another nation, strong or weak, than an individual has to do injustice to another individual; that the same moral law applies in one case as in the other. But we must also remember that it is as much the duty of the Nation to guard its own rights and its own interests as it is the duty of the individual so to do. Within the Nation the individual has now delegated this right to the State, that is, to the representative of all the individuals, and it is a maxim of the law that for every wrong there is a remedy. But in international law we have not advanced by any means as far as we have advanced in municipal law. There is as yet no judicial way of enforcing a right in international law. . . . Therefore it follows that a self-respecting, just, and far-seeing nation should on the one hand endeavor by every means to aid in the development of the various movements which tend to provide substitutes for war, which tend to render nations in their actions toward one another, and indeed toward their own peoples, more responsive to the general sentiment of humane and civilized mankind; and on the other hand that it should keep prepared, while scrupulously avoiding wrongdoing itself, to repel any wrong, and in exceptional cases to take action which in a more advanced stage of international relations would come under the head of the exercise of the international police. A great free people owes it to itself and to all mankind not to sink into helplessness before the powers of evil. . . .

It is not true that the United States feels any land hunger or entertains any projects as regards the other nations of the Western Hemisphere save such as are for their welfare. All that this country desires is to see the neighboring countries stable, orderly, and prosperous. Any country whose people conduct themselves well can count upon our hearty friendship. If a nation shows that it knows how to act with reasonable efficiency and decency in social and political matters, if it keeps order and pays its obligations, it need fear no interference from the United States. Chronic wrong-doing, or an impotence which results in a general loosening of the ties of civilized society, may in America, as elsewhere, ultimately require intervention by some civilized nation, and in the Western Hemisphere the adherence of the United States to the Monroe Doctrine may force the United States, however reluctantly, in flagrant cases of such wrongdoing or impotence, to the exercise of an international police power. If every country washed by the Caribbean Sea would show the progress in stable and just civilization which with the aid of the Platt Amendment Cuba has shown since our troops left the island, and which so many of the republics in both Americas are constantly and brilliantly showing, all question of interference by this Nation with their affairs would be at an end. Our interests and those of our southern neighbors are in reality identical. They have great natural riches, and if within their borders the reign of law and justice obtains, prosperity is sure to come to them. While they thus obey the primary laws of civilized society they may rest assured that they will be treated by us in a spirit of cordial and helpful sympathy. We would interfere with them only in the last resort, and then only if it became evident that their inability or unwillingness to do justice at home and abroad had violated the rights of the United States or had invited foreign aggression to the detriment of the entire body of American nations. It is a mere truism to say that every nation, whether in America or anywhere else, which desires to maintain its freedom, its independence, must ultimately realize that the right of such independence can not be separated from the responsibility of making good use of it. . . .

There must be no effort made to remove the mote from our brother's eye if we refuse to remove the beam from our own. But in extreme cases action may be justifiable and proper. What form the action shall take must depend upon the circumstances of the case; that is, upon the degree of the atrocity and upon our power to remedy it. The cases in which we could interfere by force of arms as we interfered to put a stop to intolerable conditions in Cuba are necessarily very few. Yet it is not to be expected that a people like ours, which in spite of certain very obvious shortcomings, nevertheless as a whole shows by its consistent practice its belief in the principles of civil and religious liberty and of orderly freedom, a people among whom even the worst crime, like the crime of lynching, is never more than sporadic, so that individuals and not classes are molested in their fundamental rights. . . .

1904–05

The Dominican Republic Challenge

Theodore Roosevelt

The "international police power" that President Roosevelt pledged to use as part of what became known as the Roosevelt Corollary (Document No. 37) to the Monroe Doctrine was deployed almost immediately in the Dominican Republic. According to Roosevelt, the Dominicans themselves were begging him to intervene in order to stabilize the country's finances and protect it from European powers demanding the payment of defaulted loans. These excerpts from a letter to Joseph Bucklin Bishop (1847–1928), a New York journalist and Roosevelt's authorized biographer, and from a message to Congress, depict a president who was extremely reluctant to intervene yet convinced of his duty to do so. Roosevelt wanted the Senate to ratify an agreement that was negotiated with the Dominicans and already being implemented, under which Washington would control the country's finances. Roosevelt's request was ignored by the Senate until 1907, when it was finally approved.

LETTER FROM THEODORE ROOSEVELT TO
JOSEPH BUCKLIN BISHOP, FEBRUARY 23, 1904

I have been hoping and praying for three months that the Santo Domingans would behave so that I would not have to act in any way. I want to do nothing but what a policeman has to do in Santo Domingo. As for annexing the island, I have about the same desire to annex it as a gorged boa constrictor might have to swallow a porcupine wrong-end-to. Is that strong enough? I have asked some of our people to go there because, after having refused for three months to do anything, the attitude of the Santo Domingans has become one of half chaotic war towards us. If I possibly can I want to do nothing to them. If it is absolutely necessary to do something, then I want to do as little as possible. Their government has been bedeviling us to establish some kind of a protec-

Source: Reprinted with the permission of Scribner, a division of Simon & Schuster from *Theodore Roosevelt and His Time Shown In His Own Letters,* Vol. I by Joseph Bucklin Bishop. Pp. 431–32.

torate over the islands, and take charge of their finances. We have been answering them that we could not possibly go into the subject now at all. . . .

SPECIAL MESSAGE TO CONGRESS, FEBRUARY 15, 1905

. . . We on our part are simply performing in a peaceful manner, not only with the cordial acquiescence, but in accordance with the earnest request of the government concerned, part of that international duty which is necessarily involved in the assertion of the Monroe Doctrine. I call attention to the urgent need of prompt action on this matter. We now have a great opportunity to secure peace and stability in the island, without friction or bloodshed, by acting in accordance with the cordial invitation of the governmental authorities themselves. It will be unfortunate from every standpoint if we fail to grasp this opportunity; for such failure will probably mean increasing revolutionary violence in Santo Domingo, and very possibly embarrassing foreign complications in addition. This protocol affords a practical test of the efficiency of the United States Government in maintaining the Monroe Doctrine.

❖

NO. 39

1912

Managing Nicaragua

Adolfo Díaz and Philander C. Knox

In 1909, an armed revolt against the Nicaraguan government of José Santos Zelaya had broken out. The U.S. government, hostile to Zelaya's nationalistic policies, openly sided with the rebels and helped them take power in 1910. Adolfo Díaz, a former employee of a U.S. mining company in Nicaragua, welcomed the U.S. intervention and became president. When his government was threatened by an uprising in 1911–12, the Taft Administration deployed 2,500 U.S. Marines

Source: U.S. Department of State. *Papers Relating to the Foreign Relations of the United States, . . . 1912,* pp. 1112–17. Washington, D.C.: GPO, 1919.

to defend it. In the meantime, U.S. bankers had taken control of Nicaragua's finances and a U.S. army officer, appointed by President Taft, was collecting Nicaragua's customs revenue, the government's main source of income. The main purpose of these arrangements was to guarantee the repayment of Nicaragua's defaulted debts to U.S. and European bankers. In the midst of this turmoil, and sensitive to the hostility that U.S. policies in the Caribbean region were generating, U.S. Secretary of State Philander C. Knox arrived in Nicaragua on a goodwill tour. In these excerpts, Díaz's phrase "your famous note" refers to Knox's letter of Dec. 1, 1909 to Zelaya's government, condemning it as a dictatorship and breaking off diplomatic relations. Díaz also refers to the Knox–Castrillo Treaty, then pending before the U.S. Senate. That treaty, which was rejected by the Senate two months after Knox's visit, would have formalized the financial arrangements mentioned above.

SPEECH OF MR. KNOX AT THE RAILROAD STATION AT MANAGUA, NICARAGUA, MARCH 5, 1912

Mr. Mayor, Ladies, and Gentlemen:

My especial regret at this moment is that I have not an acquaintance with the beautiful language of your good people which will enable me to respond in fitting terms to your words of welcome. . . . I appreciate the honor that was done me by the citizens of Nicaragua in sending to the seashore so many of your distinguished men and beautiful women to greet us at the threshold of your country. . . .

SPEECH OF HIS EXCELLENCY DON ADOLFO DÍAZ, PRESIDENT OF NICARAGUA, WELCOMING MR. KNOX, MANAGUA, MARCH 6, 1912

Mr. Secretary:

You are in a country where your name has long been known, because on a memorable occasion for our liberty you linked it with the history of our struggles for advancement by an act of justice of the American Government. . . .

Unfortunate has been the existence of Central American democracy. A prolonged and bloody struggle has consumed the vigorous life of these nations during almost an entire century of sterile uprisings. To refer only to my own country; it has been a republic for almost a hundred years without having known republican methods in all that time, except at brief intervals. Our political struggles have unfortunately not been a luminous contest of ideas and principles; they have been a terrible duel between despotism, on one hand, and, on the other, the ill-directed efforts of the people in search of happiness never attained—a duel, a horrible duel, which has at length left the Republic, if not dead, at least almost utterly exhausted.

. . . We are weak and we need your strong help for the regeneration of our debilitated land. The hand which your Government generously and fraternally extends to us I accept without reserve or fear, for I know it belongs to a people which has made a religion of liberty and, educated in and for freedom, loves its independence above everything and respects the independence of others.

In this work for the welfare of Nicaragua, increasing the hope of its ultimate success, your name is pledged. It has been connected, to the joy of our people, with two of our principal events: With your famous note, in which, as the mouthpiece of civilization, you pronounced the doom of tyranny before the world, and with the treaty you signed in Washington with our Minister Castrillo. . . .

The name of your worthy President, William H. Taft, and your own name are pronounced by all Nicaraguans, from the statesman to the humblest countryman, as though they were names of personages of our fatherland, due to the fact that every day the bonds are becoming closer between your great and happy country and my own small country. . . .

REPLY OF MR. KNOX

Mr. President, Ladies, and Gentlemen:

. . . Although the interest of the people of the United States in the welfare of your country is keen there is not and never has been any desire either on the part of the American Government or people to mix unduly or unbidden in the internal affairs of Nicaragua, but to the request for assistance in the regeneration of Nicaragua, my Government was happy promptly to respond.

The political and economic situation that had arisen, due to many years of misrule, rendered the task of reorganization of your Government exceedingly difficult, and your leaders, because of the frank friendship and good faith of the United States toward the Nicaraguan people as a whole, naturally turned to the American Government for council [sic] and assistance in the arduous task before them. My Government was glad to send to Managua a special commissioner to aid in making a fixed program which the leaders pledged themselves to carry out and in which was contemplated loyal cooperation in the rehabilitation of Nicaragua.

. . . In the zone of the Caribbean the responsibilities of the United States are becoming increasingly great as the opening of the great waterway which is to change the trade routes of the world draws nearer and the desire of the United States to see order and prosperity becomes even more intensified. We are especially interested in the prosperity of all the people of Nicaragua. Their prosperity means contentment and contentment means repose. . . .

❖

1913

The Pact of the Embassy

Henry Lane Wilson

A popular revolt led by Mexican businessman Francisco Madero in 1911 over-threw the dictatorial government of General Porfirio Díaz, who had ruled for three decades. Although he won election as president that year after the old general resigned, Madero had to fend off constant challenges to the survival of his government. On February 9, 1913, a 2,000-man army led by General Félix Díaz, the ex-dictator's nephew, rebelled against Madero. For ten days, a period known as the "Decena Trágica," Félix Díaz's men held out in Mexico City against government troops commanded by General Victoriano Huerta. Thousands of civilians were dying in the crossfire and property damage was mounting when the Taft administration's ambassador to Mexico, Henry Lane Wilson, invited Díaz and Huerta to the embassy to work out a peaceful settlement of the conflict. The result was the Pact of the Embassy. In this excerpt from his memoirs, Wilson re-counts his controversial role in the pact, which led to the arrest of Madero and his vice president José María Pino Suárez by General Huerta, and the assassina-tion of both men on February 21.

Later in the day I determined that I must take a decisive step on my own re-sponsibility to bring about a restoration of order. This was the situation: Two hostile armies were in possession of the capital and all civil authority had dis-appeared; sinister bands of looters and robbers were beginning to appear in many of the streets of the capital; starving men, women, and children were parading in many public thoroughfares. Some 35,000 foreigners who, as de-veloped during the bombardment, seemed to rely upon the embassy for pro-tection, were at the mercy of the mob or exposed to indiscriminate firing which might at any moment begin between the forces of General Huerta and General Felix Diaz, thus reinvolving the lives and property of non-combatants. With-out having conferred with any one, I decided to ask Generals Huerta and Diaz to come to the embassy, which, as neutral ground, would guarantee good faith

Source: Henry Lane Wilson. *Diplomatic Episodes in Mexico, Belgium and Chile,* Chs. 41–42. Port Wash-ington, N.Y.: Kennikat Press, 1971. Reprint of 1927 edition.

and protection, for a consultation. My object was to have them enter into an agreement for the suspension of hostilities and for joint submission to the federal congress.

. . . I lost no time in bringing the two generals together in the embassy library. . . . [T]o force a decision, I said to them that unless they brought about peace the demand by European powers for intervention might become too strong to be resisted by the Washington government. This had the desired effect, and at one o'clock in the morning, the agreement was signed, deposited in the embassy safe, and a proclamation announcing the cessation of hostilities was issued. . . . When it was finally announced that by the agreement of all parties an arrangement had been reached, and that with the authority of Congress General Huerta was to be provisional president and General Diaz was to be free to pursue his candidacy for the presidency, the news ran like wildfire through the city and was welcomed with universal rejoicing. . . . President Wilson considered the part played by the embassy as an intrusion in the domestic affairs of Mexico; persons who rest pleasantly by the home fires sometimes have curious conceptions of what the conduct of a public officer should be under critical and dangerous conditions. . . . The consummation of this arrangement I regard as the most successful and far-reaching of the difficult work I was called upon to perform during the revolution. . . .

Soon after the overthrow of Madero the Washington government instructed me to take precautions to see that his life and that of the ex-Vice-president were preserved. Complying with these instructions I visited General Huerta with Admiral von Hintze and we jointly made representations in the sense of the department's instructions. . . . General Huerta then . . . asked me directly whether I thought it better to have Madero impeached by Congress for violation of the constitution or to incarcerate him in a lunatic asylum. I answered, with the concurrence of the German minister, that I had no authority to speak in the premises and could only express the hope that he would do what was right and best for the peace of Mexico. As we were closing the interview I requested Huerta to transfer the ex-President to more commodious quarters and to provide him with his customary food and other things essential to his always delicate state of health. . . .

On the morning of February 23d, I was informed at an early hour that during the preceding night the government had attempted to transfer Madero and Suarez from the national palace to the national penitentiary; that while en route the automobiles had been attacked and, in the struggle which followed, Madero and Suarez had been shot to death by their guards. Profoundly shocked by this unhappy event, I immediately requested a suspension of the diplomatic reception which Mr. De la Barra, the new Minister of Foreign Affairs, was about to give. . . .

While I was endeavouring to mark my course, Francisco De la Barra, whom I had known intimately for ten or twelve years, came to the embassy and in the most unequivocal terms informed me that neither the government nor General Huerta was in any way connected with the death of Mr. Madero; that his death had resulted from an organized conspiracy of people whose relatives had been killed during the Madero régime and who were, by reason of their close contact with the government, able to obtain information of the proposed transfer to the penitentiary. . . . His statement made a deep impression upon me, and as I was unable to secure reliable evidence of what had actually occurred, I adopted the only course which the unusual situation and the necessities of the moment seemed to warrant: I accepted the government's version. . . .

Profoundly as the violent death of Madero must be regretted by all right-thinking people, it should be remembered that he had resigned the office of President and at the time of his death was a simple Mexican citizen in no wise entitled through accepted international practice to the diplomatic intervention of any foreign government. . . . Certainly his death should not have excited greater sorrow than the death of scores of Americans who had been sacrificed during the Madero regime, unrequited of justice, with no idle sentimentalist to cry from the housetops the story of their wrongs.

Madero was a person of unsound intellect, of imperfect education and vision. He was a disciple of the French school in politics and economics, but never gathered for the uses of practical application its threads of philosophy or comprehended in the least the deep common sense which lies at the root of all French political opinion. He came into power as an apostle of liberty but he was simply a man of disordered intellect who happened to be in the public eye at the psychological moment. The responsibilities of office and the disappointments growing out of rivalries and intrigues shattered his reason completely, and in the last days of his government, during the bombardment of the capital, his mental qualities, always abnormal, developed into a homicidal, dangerous form of lunacy. Remote from the great position where his misguided ambition carried him he would doubtless have remained a quiet and simple country gentleman of benevolent ideals and blameless life; clothed with the chief power of the nation, dormant evil qualities in the blood or in the race came to the surface and wrought ruin to him and to thousands of the Mexican people. . . . Huerta, in my opinion, was not responsible for the death of Madero, unless he betrayed to others his intention of transferring Madero elsewhere, or was guilty of contributory negligence in furnishing such an inadequate escort to his new prison.

❖

1913

The Mobile Speech

Woodrow Wilson

I n his first year in office, President Woodrow Wilson (1913–21) pledged a sharp turn in U.S. policy toward Latin America, away from the armed interference and the dollar diplomacy associated with his Republican predecessors. This excerpt from one of his best-known statements of Latin American policy, to a businessmen's convention in Mobile, Alabama, is a classic expression of the soaring idealism of Wilsonian diplomacy—the faith in democracy, in the "spiritual" unity of the Americas, and in the emancipatory potential of U.S. investment capital. Wilson's subsequent actions in Latin America have often been held to contradict the noble words of the Mobile address; his administration accumulated a record of intervention in Mexico and the Caribbean that exceeded those of Presidents Roosevelt and Taft. However, a careful reading of this excerpt provides clues about a certain moralizing tendency that was not incompatible with intervention.

The future, ladies and gentlemen, is going to be very different for this hemisphere from the past. These States lying to the south of us, which have always been our neighbors, will now be drawn closer to us by innumerable ties, and, I hope, chief of all, by the tie of a common understanding of each other. Interest does not tie nations together; it sometimes separates them. But sympathy and understanding does unite them, and I believe that by the new route that is just about to be opened, while we physically cut two continents asunder, we spiritually unite them. It is a spiritual union which we seek.

. . . [T]hat opening gate at the Isthmus of Panama will open the world to a commerce that she has not known before, a commerce of intelligence, of thought and sympathy between North and South. The Latin American states, which, to their disadvantage, have been off the main lines, will now be on the main lines. . . . Do you realize that New York, for example, will be nearer the western coast of South America than she is now to the eastern coast of South America? . . .

Source: U.S. Senate. 63d Cong., 1st sess. Document No. 226. *Address of President Woodrow Wilson delivered before the Southern Commercial Congress Held at Mobile, Ala., October 27, 1913.* Washington, D.C.: GPO, 1913.

These things are significant, therefore, of this, that we are closing one chapter in the history of the world and are opening another, of great, unimaginable significance.

There is one peculiarity about the history of the Latin American States which I am sure they are keenly aware of. You hear of "concessions" to foreign capitalists in Latin America. You do not hear of concessions to foreign capitalists in the United States. They are not granted concessions. They are invited to make investments. . . . States that are obliged, because their territory does not lie within the main field of modern enterprise and action, to grant concessions are in this condition, that foreign interests are apt to dominate their domestic affairs, a condition of affairs always dangerous and apt to become intolerable. What these States are going to see, therefore, is an emancipation from the subordination, which has been inevitable, to foreign enterprise and an assertion of the splendid character which, in spite of these difficulties, they have again and again been able to demonstrate. The dignity, the courage, the self-possession, the self-respect, of the Latin American States, their achievements in the face of all these adverse circumstances, deserve nothing but the admiration and applause of the world. They have had harder bargains driven with them in the matter of loans than any other peoples in the world. . . . I rejoice in nothing so much as in the prospect that they will now be emancipated from these conditions, and we ought to be the first to take part in assisting in that emancipation. . . .

We must prove ourselves their friends and champions upon terms of equality and honor. You can not be friends upon any other terms than upon the terms of equality. You can not be friends at all except upon any other terms of honor. We must show ourselves friends by comprehending their interest whether it squares with our own interest or not. It is a very perilous thing to determine the foreign policy of a nation in the terms of material interest. It not only is unfair to those with whom you are dealing, but it is degrading as regards your own actions.

Comprehension must be the soil in which shall grow all the fruits of friendship, and there is a reason and a compulsion lying behind all this which is dearer than anything else to the thoughtful men of America. I mean the development of constitutional liberty in the world. Human rights, national integrity, and opportunity as against material interests—that, ladies and gentlemen, is the issue which we now have to face. I want to take this occasion to say that the United States will never again seek one additional foot of territory by conquest. She will devote herself to showing that she knows how to make honorable and fruitful use of the territory she has, and she must regard it as one of the duties of friendship to see that from no quarter are material interests made superior to human liberty and national opportunity. I say this, not with a single thought that anyone will gainsay it, but merely to fix in our consciousness what our real relationship with the rest of America is. It is the relationship of a family of mankind devoted to the development of true constitutional liberty. We know that that is the soil out of which the best enterprise springs. We know that this is a cause which we are making in common with our neighbors, because we have had to make it for ourselves.

. . . What is at the heart of all our national problems? It is that we have seen the hand of material interest sometimes about to close upon our dearest rights and possessions. We have seen material interests threaten constitutional freedoms in the United States. Therefore, we will now know how to sympathize with those in the rest of America who have to contend with such powers, not only within their borders, but from outside their borders also. . . .

In emphasizing the points which must unite us in sympathy and in spiritual interest with the Latin American peoples we are only emphasizing the points of our own life, and we should prove ourselves untrue to our own traditions if we proved ourselves untrue friends to them. Do not think, therefore, gentlemen, that the questions of the day are mere questions of policy and diplomacy. They are shot through with the principles of life. We dare not turn from the principle that morality and not expediency is the thing that must guide us and that we will never condone iniquity because it is most convenient to do so. It seems to me that this is a day of infinite hope, of confidence in a future greater than the past has been, for I am fain to believe that in spite of all the things that we wish to correct the nineteenth century that now lies behind us has brought us a long stage toward the time when, slowly ascending the tedious climb that leads to the final uplands, we shall get our ultimate view of the duties of mankind. We have breasted a considerable part of that climb and shall presently—it may be in a generation or two—come out upon those great heights where there shines unobstructed the light of the justice of God.

1914

The Bryan–Chamorro Treaty

The Governments of the United States and Nicaragua

Although the United States had just opened its newly built Panama Canal to interoceanic traffic on August 15, 1914, "canal diplomacy" had not ended. Ten days earlier, on August 5, U.S. Secretary of State William Jennings Bryan and Emiliano Chamorro, Nicaragua's representative in Washington, signed this treaty giving the United States the exclusive right to build a canal across Nicaragua. The purpose was to eliminate the possibility that a rival foreign power might compete with the Panama Canal by opening a second one in Nicaragua. Negotiations with Nicaragua over the treaty had already begun during the Taft administration. The Wilson administration not only decided to consummate the agreement, but even added language (which was agreed to by Nicaragua) similar to that of the Platt Amendment, authorizing U.S. military intervention. In response to opposition to that provision in the U.S. Senate, it was dropped and the Senate finally ratified the treaty on June 19, 1916. The treaty, along with all the rights and privileges accorded under it to the United States, was abrogated in a convention signed by the governments of both countries in Managua on July 14, 1970.

ARTICLE 1. The Government of Nicaragua grants in perpetuity to the Government of the United States, forever free from all taxation or other public charge, the exclusive proprietary rights necessary and convenient for the construction, operation and maintenance of an interoceanic canal by way of the San Juan River and the great Lake of Nicaragua or by way of any route over Nicaraguan territory, the details of the terms upon which such canal shall be constructed, operated and maintained to be agreed to by the two governments whenever the Government of the United States shall notify the Government of Nicaragua of its desire or intention to construct such canal.

ARTICLE 2. To enable the Government of the United States to protect the Panama Canal and the proprietary rights granted to the Government of the

Source: U.S. Department of State. *Treaties and Other International Agreements of the United States of America 1776–1949*. Vol. 10, comp. Charles I. Bevans, pp. 379–81. Washington, D.C.: GPO, 1968.

United States by the foregoing article, . . . the Government of Nicaragua hereby leases for a term of ninety-nine years to the Government of the United States the islands in the Caribbean Sea known as Great Corn Island and Little Corn Island; and the Government of Nicaragua further grants to the Government of the United States for a like period of ninety-nine years the right to establish, operate and maintain a naval base at such place on the territory of Nicaragua bordering upon the Gulf of Fonseca as the Government of the United States may select. The Government of the United States shall have the option of renewing for a further term of ninety-nine years the above leases and grants upon the expiration of their respective terms, it being expressly agreed that the territory hereby leased and the naval base which may be maintained under the grant aforesaid shall be subject exclusively to the laws and sovereign authority of the United States during the terms of such lease and grant and of any renewal or renewals thereof.

ARTICLE 3. In consideration of the foregoing stipulations and for the purposes contemplated by this Convention and for the purpose of reducing the present indebtedness of Nicaragua, the Government of the United States shall, upon the date of the exchange of ratification of this Convention, pay for the benefit of the Republic of Nicaragua the sum of three million dollars . . . to be deposited . . . in such bank . . . as the Government of the United States may determine, to be applied by Nicaragua upon its indebtedness or other public purposes . . . in a manner to be determined by the two High Contracting Parties, all such disbursements to be made by orders drawn by the Minister of Finance of the Republic of Nicaragua and approved by the Secretary of State of the United States or by such person as he may designate. . . .

1916

The State Department and Public Opinion

Robert Lansing

The Mexican revolutionary Francisco "Pancho" Villa attacked Columbus, New Mexico, on March 9, 1916, in a futile effort to revive his status against a rival revolutionary leader, Venustiano Carranza. Two days earlier the U.S. Congress had passed a resolution endorsing armed intervention to protect U.S. citizens. President Woodrow Wilson (1913–21) opposed intervention and was reluctant to commit unseasoned U.S. troops, but under the pressure of reelection Wilson, a Democrat, released an expeditionary force of 6,000 men against Villa within a week of the attack. Republicans, led by Senator Albert B. Fall of New Mexico, called for a full-scale invasion of Mexico. By midsummer, with 150,000 U.S. national guardsmen stationed along the U.S.–Mexican border, war seemed increasingly likely. Some of the political ramifications of the conflict with Mexico were the subject of this letter by Secretary of State Robert Lansing to President Wilson on June 21, 1916. Having failed in their mission, the U.S. expeditionary force completed its withdrawal on February 5, 1917, two days after the United States broke off relations with Germany. Lansing's reference to "the St. Louis platform" means the Democratic Party platform, adopted by the party's nominating convention in St. Louis on June 13, a week before Lansing wrote this letter. The platform declared that "Intervention, implying as it does, military subjugation, is revolting to the people of the United States," but defended the U.S. military occupation of northern Mexico as a necessary response to the lack of "law and order" there.

My Dear Mr. President: As there appears to be an increasing probability that the Mexican situation may develop into a state of war I desire to make a suggestion for your consideration.

It seems to me that we should avoid the use of the word 'Intervention' and deny that any invasion of Mexico is for the sake of intervention.

Source: Robert Lansing, Secretary of State, to President Wilson, 21 June 1916. *Papers Relating to the Foreign Relations of the United States: The Lansing Papers, 1914–1920.* Vol. 2, pp. 558–59. Washington, D.C.: GPO, 1940.

There are several reasons why this appears to me expedient:

First. We have all along denied any purpose to interfere in the internal affairs of Mexico and the St. Louis platform declares against it. Intervention conveys the idea of such interference.

Second. Intervention would be humiliating to many Mexicans whose pride and sense of national honor would not resent severe terms of peace in case of being defeated in a war.

Third. American intervention in Mexico is extremely distasteful to all Latin America and might have a very bad effect upon our pan-American program.

Fourth. Intervention, which suggests a definite purpose to "clean up" the country, would bind us to certain accomplishments which circumstances might make extremely difficult or inadvisable, and, on the other hand, it would impose conditions which might be found to be serious restraints upon us as the situation develops.

Fifth. Intervention also implies that the war would be made primarily in the interest of the Mexican people, while the fact is it would be a war forced on us by the Mexican Government, and, if we term it intervention, we will have considerable difficulty in explaining why we had not intervened before but waited until attacked.

It seems to me that the real attitude is that the *de facto* Government having attacked our forces engaged in a rightful enterprise or invaded our borders (as the case may be) we had no recourse but to defend ourselves and to do so it has become necessary to prevent future attacks by forcing the Mexican Government to perform its obligations. That is, it is simply a state of international war without purpose on our part other than to end the conditions which menace our national peace and the safety of our citizens, and that it is *not* intervention with all that the word implies.

I offer the foregoing suggestion, because I feel that we should have constantly in view the attitude we intend to take if worse comes to worse, so that we may regulate our present policy and future correspondence with Mexico and other American Republics with that attitude.

In case this suggestion meets with your approval I further suggest that we send to each diplomatic representative of a Latin American Republic in Washington a communication stating briefly our attitude and denying any intention to intervene. . . . If this is to be done at all, it seems to me that it should be done at once, otherwise we will lose the chief benefit, namely, a right understanding by Latin America at the very outset.

Faithfully yours, Robert Lansing.

1916

Dollar Diplomacy and Social Darwinism

F. M. Huntington Wilson

As an assistant secretary of state for Latin America during the administration of President William Howard Taft (1909–13), Francis Mairs Huntington Wilson (1875–1946) helped to shape what came to be known by defenders and detractors alike as Dollar Diplomacy, which sought to substitute financial control for Theodore Roosevelt's Big Stick. The method was a simple one: Take over the European loan obligations of some of the poorest countries in the hemisphere while imposing U.S. government control of their customs offices to guarantee payments to the U.S. lenders. Excerpted below is an article by Wilson that was published in 1916.

The relation of government to foreign investment by its citizens is one of correlative obligation and authority, general obligation to protect the citizens' rights, and authority to control the citizens' course by giving great or little protection, or none at all. In the discharge of its obligation the duty of government is to measure the protection to be given any investment first of all by the advantage of that investment to the nation; and secondarily to mete out that protection in proportion to the right of the investor to expect protection. . . .

This theme and its illustration by example lead to an exposition of what has been called "Dollar Diplomacy." It might better be described as common sense diplomacy, in contradistinction from the diplomacy of perfunctoriness or that of whimsical sentimentality from which the United States has suffered so much. It is submitted, moreover, that one who will carefully study the so-called "Dollar Diplomacy" will be fully convinced that it was a diplomacy of common sense in the highest sense of that term, that is, a diplomacy determined by the application of scientific principles and sound thinking to plain facts studied and understood as they really are; a diplomacy preferring to build for the long future, rather than to dogmatize for the moment's expediency; preferring the truth to a beautiful idealization not resting upon truth.

Source: F. M. Huntington Wilson. "The Relation of Government to Foreign Investment," *The Annals of the American Academy of Political and Social Science* 68 (1916): 298–311.

Now the national advantage of a foreign investment may consist in (1) political advantage or (2) economic advantage. Service to humanity is not mentioned separately because charity begins at home; because it is America's first duty to serve America. . . . Those who dissent from this view and yield to our national foible for grandiloquent sentimentality ought to reflect that a trustee, however admirable his private charities, would be put in jail if he used funds for benefactions; and that exactly so the American executive defrauds the nation if he uses its prestige and power in a diplomacy directed by sentimentality to the service of humanity in general, instead of a diplomacy seeking the political and economic advantage of the American taxpayer, the American nation. . . .

Every great power has some "doctrines" that it conceives to be as vital to it as the Monroe Doctrine is considered here. Korea and Manchuria, Persia and Siam, come to mind as examples of territory where, while conducting ordinary trade, we should be wasting our energies to attempt intensive developments. In return we should gradually crowd out from our own sphere of special interest foreign interests wherever they are predominant to an uncomfortable extent and quite beyond the requirements of an ordinary trade outside the spheres of special interest of the foreign governments concerned.

Quite aside from the common sense circumscribing of our spheres of greatest effort to make them comport with the facts of world politics, it is still true that there is not enough American capital yet available for foreign investment thoroughly to cover the duty of consolidating our economic position in the spheres where that necessity is most obvious. Also, there is a lack of men trained for this work and willing to reside under tropical rain, amidst mountain peaks, on broad savannas, and in ancient cities of manners and ideas quite alien to our own, in order to carry it on. "God gives a man his relatives; he chooses his friends." A nation is less fortunate. The hazards of history have made us a sphere of vital interest which we have to cultivate, however difficult it be. . . .

Suffice it to say that the object of the Central American policy was "to substitute dollars for bullets," to create a material prosperity which should wean the Central Americans from their usual preoccupation of revolution. Those countries have great natural wealth. Lack of capital, lack of skill, and still more the absence of any guarantee against confiscation and destruction due to the frequent revolutions when law and order are thrown overboard, prevent the development of their natural wealth by the people themselves. The same conditions throttle their export trade and destroy their purchasing power. Attacks upon American interests, and even upon the personal safety of American planters and others engaged in those countries, call for our government's protection. . . . To cite a case where the political and economic advantages are both of the first rank and where, therefore, the measure of governmental support should be at its highest, I will refer to the policy toward Nicaragua, which illustrates only more completely what should be the spirit of our policy throughout the zone of the Caribbean. Indeed as now implemented our policy in effect is the same in principle in Panama, Cuba, Santo Domingo and Haiti. . . .

The public revenues, especially the customs dues, must be placed out of reach of the revolutionary robber or the dictator. Capital must be brought in to establish peaceful husbandry and unmolested industry. Education and civilization must bring justice. A guiding hand must prevent foreign entanglements, which, under the Monroe Doctrine, straightway involve us. Even if the Monroe Doctrine had never been announced, common prudence would today force upon us the same policy from our southern border throughout the zone of the Caribbean. . . .

There are so many analogies between biology and international evolution that one may invoke a sort of "international biology." The march of civilization brooks no violation of the law of the survival of the fittest. Neighboring countries comprise an environment. The strongest will dominate that environment. Sentimental phrases about the sovereignty of weaker countries will no more permit them to run amuck with impunity than ranting about individual rights will permit an outrageous citizen to annoy a municipality and escape the police. The biological law of the tendency to revert to the lower type as the higher attributes are disused is at work among nations; and nature, in its rough method of uplift, gives sick nations strong neighbors and takes its inexorable course with private enterprise and diplomacy as its instruments. And this course is the best in the long run, for all concerned and for the world. . . .

❖

NO. 45

1917

The Zimmermann Telegram

Alfred Zimmermann

As U.S. troops withdrew from Mexico in January 1917 after an unsuccessful attempt to capture the revolutionary leader Francisco "Pancho" Villa, Germany turned to Mexico with a plan for a secret military alliance. Germany's proposal took the form of an encrypted note by German Foreign Secretary Alfred

Source: U.S. Department of State. *Papers Relating to the Foreign Relations of the United States, 1917, Supplement 1, The World War,* "The Ambassador in Great Britain (Page) to the Secretary of State, 24 February 1917." Pp. 147–48. Washington, D.C.: GPO, 1931.

Zimmermann, sent on January 16, 1917, to Count Johann von Bernstorff, the German ambassador in Washington, who forwarded it to Heinrich von Eckhardt, the German minister in Mexico. On February 20, Eckhardt proposed the alliance to the Mexican government. Unknown to the Germans, Great Britain had broken the German cipher and gave a copy of the telegram to the U.S. ambassador, whose report to President Woodrow Wilson and Secretary of State Robert Lansing is excerpted below. President Wilson, hoping to use the note to gain support for a U.S. declaration of war against Germany, leaked it to the press for publication on March 1; two days later Zimmermann admitted the telegram was authentic and on April 6 the United States declared war on Germany. President Carranza showed little interest in Zimmermann's proposal, but along with Chile and Argentina, Mexico remained neutral during World War I.

For the President and the Secretary of State. [Foreign Secretary of Great Britain] Balfour has handed me the text of a cipher telegram from Zimmermann, German Secretary of State for Foreign Affairs, to the German Minister to Mexico, which was sent via Washington and relayed by Bernstorff on January 19. . . . I shall send you by mail a copy of the cipher text and of the decode into German and meanwhile I give you the English translation as follows:

> We intend to begin on the 1st of February unrestricted submarine warfare. We shall endeavor in spite of this to keep the United States of America neutral. In the event of this not succeeding, we make Mexico a proposal of alliance on the following basis: make war together, make peace together, generous financial support and an understanding on our part that Mexico is to reconquer the lost territory in Texas, New Mexico, and Arizona. The settlement in detail is left to you. You will inform the President of the above most secretly as soon as the outbreak of war with the United States of America is certain and add the suggestion that he should, on his own initiative, invite Japan to immediate adherence and at the same time mediate between Japan and ourselves. Please call the President's attention to the fact that the ruthless employment of our submarines now offers the prospect of compelling England in a few months to make peace. Signed, Zimmermann.

The receipt of this information has so greatly exercised the British Government that they have lost no time in communicating it to me to transmit to you, in order that our Government may be able without delay to make such disposition as may be necessary in view of the threatened invasion of our territory.

Early in the war, the British Government obtained possession of a copy of the German cipher code used in the above message and have made it their business to obtain copies of Bernstorff's cipher telegrams to Mexico, amongst others, which are sent back to London and deciphered here. This accounts for their being able to decipher this telegram from the German Government to their representative in Mexico and also for the delay from January 19 until now

[February 24] in their receiving the information. This system has hitherto been a jealously guarded secret and is only divulged now to you by the British Government in view of the extraordinary circumstances and their friendly feeling toward the United States. They earnestly request that you will keep the source of your information and the British Government's method of obtaining it profoundly secret, but they put no prohibition on the publication of Zimmermann's telegram itself. . . .

❖

NO. 46

1917

The Jones Act

The Congress of the United States

Pressure by Puerto Ricans for greater self-government led to the passage of the Jones Act by the Congress of the United States on March 2, 1917. This law, which amended the Foraker Act of 1900, made all Puerto Ricans citizens of the United States, except for those who specifically renounced that citizenship. The Jones Act also established the form of government that would control relations between the United States and Puerto Rico until 1947, when Congress voted to allow Puerto Rico to elect its own governor. Further changes in the direction of self-government, including the establishment in 1952 of "commonwealth" status for Puerto Rico, took place with the passage of Public Law 600 in 1950.

Be it enacted by the Senate and House of Representatives of the United States of America, in Congress assembled, . . .

That all citizens of Porto Rico . . . are hereby declared, and shall be deemed and held to be, citizens of the United States: *Provided,* That any person hereinbefore described may retain his present political status by making a declaration of his decision to do so within six months. . . .

Source: U.S. Congress. *The Statutes at Large of the United States of America from December, 1915 to March, 1917,* Vol. 39, Part 1, pp. 951–68. Washington, D.C.: GPO, 1917.

That the supreme executive power shall be vested in an executive officer, whose official title shall be "The Governor of Porto Rico." He shall be appointed by the President, by and with the advice and consent of the Senate, and hold his office at the pleasure of the President. . . . The governor . . . shall have general supervision and control of all the departments and bureaus of the government in Porto Rico, . . . and shall be commander in chief of the militia. He may grant pardons and reprieves . . . and may veto any legislation enacted. . . . He shall be responsible for the faithful execution of the laws of Porto Rico and the United States applicable in Porto Rico, and whenever it becomes necessary he may call upon the commanders of the military and naval forces of the United States in the island, or summon the posse comitatus, or call out the militia to prevent or suppress lawless violence, invasion, insurrection, or rebellion, and he may, in case of rebellion or invasion, or imminent danger thereof, when the public safety requires it, suspend the privilege of the writ of habeas corpus, or place the island, or any part thereof, under martial law. . . . [A]nd he shall perform such additional duties and functions as may in pursuance of law be delegated to him by the President.

The attorney general and commissioner of education shall be appointed by the President, by and with the consent of the Senate of the United States. . . .

That all local legislative powers in Porto Rico, except as herein otherwise provided, shall be vested in a legislature which shall consist of two houses, one the senate and the other the house of representatives. . . .

All laws enacted by the Legislature of Porto Rico shall be reported to the Congress of the United States, . . . which hereby reserves the power and authority to annul the same. . . .

That the qualified electors of Porto Rico shall at the next general election choose a Resident Commissioner to the United States, . . . whose term of office shall be four years. . . .

That the chief justice and associate justices of the supreme court shall be appointed by the President, by and with the advice and consent of the Senate of the United States. . . .

1922

An Argentine Denunciation of Imperialism

José Ingenieros

José Ingenieros (1877–1925), a prominent Argentine writer and intellectual, was invited to speak at a dinner in Mexico City on October 11, 1922, in honor of Mexico's minister of education, José Vasconcelos. At the time, Mexico was seeking to rebuild itself politically as well as materially after a ten-year revolutionary civil war. The Mexican government's nationalistic policies were interpreted by the United States as a potential threat to U.S. economic and military hegemony in the region, and as a result, Washington was still withholding diplomatic recognition of the government of President Alvaro Obregón. In his speech, Ingenieros proposed the formation of a "Unión Latino Americana," aimed at forging a confederation of Latin nations allied in self-defense against the United States. The Unión was created in 1925 in Buenos Aires, joining intellectuals and political leaders to support a program that pledged, among other things, to "orient the nations of Latin America toward a Confederation that guarantees its independence and freedom against the imperialism of foreign capitalist States, . . . "

We must recognize that in the few years of this century, events have occurred in Latin America which demand serious, even gloomy reflection. And we hope that these words, spoken to this warm fraternal gathering of Argentine writers in honor of a Mexican colleague, will be echoed among the intellectuals of the continent, so that an insistent concern for the future will be awakened in all.

We are not, we no longer wish to be, we no longer can be pan-Americanists. The famous Monroe Doctrine, which for a century seemed to be the guarantee of our political independence against the threat of European conquests, has gradually proved to be a declaration of the American right to protect us and to intervene in our affairs. Our powerful neighbor and meddlesome friend, having developed to its highest level the capitalist mode of production, during the past war has attained world financial hegemony. This development has

Source: Jose Ingenieros. "Por la Unión Latino Americana." *Revista de Filosofía* 8 (November 1922) 6: 438–449. Translation reprinted by permission of Scholarly Resources Inc.

been accompanied by the growth in voracity of the American privileged caste, which has increasingly pressed for an imperialist policy, and has converted the government into an instrument of its corporations, with no principles other than the capture of sources of wealth and exploitation of the labor of a population already enslaved by an amoral, nationless, inflexible financial elite. Among the ruling classes of this great state, the urge to expand and conquer has grown to the point where the classic "America for the Americans" actually means "America—our Latin America—for the North Americans." . . .

This at least is the implication of recent American imperialist policy, the course of which is alarming for all of Latin America. Since the war with Spain, the United States has taken possession of Puerto Rico and imposed upon Cuba the vexatious conditions of the shameful Platt Amendment. It lost little time in amputating from Colombia the Isthmus of Panama, through which the country would join its Atlantic and Pacific coasts. Later, the United States intervened in Nicaragua to secure for itself the route of another possible interoceanic canal. It threatened the sovereignty of Mexico in the unfortunate Veracruz adventure. Under puerile pretexts, it militarily occupied Haiti. Soon afterwards, the United States shamefully occupied Santo Domingo, offering the usual excuse of pacifying the country and restoring its finances. . . .

Only yesterday, and now, as I speak, the United States cripples and dissolves the Central American Federation, knowing that its prey is easy to devour if it is first divided into small bites. Only yesterday, and now, as I speak, it refuses to recognize the constitutional government of Mexico unless it first signs treaties which favor foreign capitalism over national interests. Only yesterday, and now, as I speak, it insults Cuba by imposing on it General Crowder as titular governor.

I see on many faces the old objection: Panama is the natural limit of expansion, and capitalist imperialism will stop there. Until a few years ago, many of us believed this; we should admit it, even though this feeling of collective egotism does not honor us. The most distant nations—Brazil, Uruguay, Argentina, and Chile—felt safe from the clutches of the eagle, thinking the torrid zone would arrest its flight.

Lately, some of us have admitted that we were wrong. . . . We know that some governments—we will spare feelings by not naming them—live under a de facto tutelage, quite similar to the disgrace sanctioned by law in the Platt Amendment. We know that certain recent loans contain clauses which assure American financial control and imply to some extent the right of intervention. And finally, we know that during the past few years American influence has been felt with increasing intensity in all political, economic, and social activities in South America. . . .

The danger does not begin with annexation, as in Puerto Rico, nor with intervention, as in Cuba, not with a military expedition, as in Mexico, nor with tutelage, as in Nicaragua, nor with territorial secession, as in Colombia, nor with armed occupation, as in Haiti, nor with purchase, as in the Guianas. In its first phase, the danger begins with the progressive mortgaging of national independence through loans destined to grow and to be renewed endlessly, under conditions which are progressively detrimental to the sovereignty of the beneficiaries. . . .

For the peoples of Latin America, the issue is quite simply national defense, although many of our rulers often ignore or hide it. American capitalism seeks to capture the sources of our wealth, with the right to intervene in order to protect its investments and to assure returns on them. In the meantime, we are allowed only an illusion of political independence. As long as a foreign state expressly or surreptitiously possesses the right to intervene, political independence is not effective; as long as it refuses to recognize any government which does not support its policy of privilege and monopoly, it threatens national sovereignty; as long as it does not clearly show that it renounces such policies, it cannot be considered a friendly country. . . .

❖

NO. 48

1923

The Bucareli Accords

The Governments of Mexico and the United States

A s a result of the revolutionary upheaval in Mexico that began in 1910, a new constitution was adopted by the victorious rebels in 1917. Its Article 27 gave the government the right to expropriate, in the public interest, privately owned land and water as long as the owners were compensated. It made all subsurface minerals the property of the nation, prohibiting their removal without specific concessions issued by the federal government, and stipulated that such concessions could be extended to foreigners only if they accepted a "Calvo Clause" (see Document No. 23). Intended to restore control of the Mexican economy to the Mexican government, Article 27 became an immediate obstacle to full diplomatic recognition by the United States, which sought to shield U.S. land owners and oil investors from a possible confiscation of their properties. To settle their

Source: U.S. *Proceedings of the United States–Mexican Commission in Mexico City, Mexico, 14 May 1923*, pp. 47–49. Washington, D.C.: GPO, 1925.

differences, both governments agreed to send representatives to a conference to discuss the rights of U.S. property owners, including oil companies. The commissioners met from May 14 to August 15, 1923, at 85 Bucareli Street in Mexico City. They produced two draft treaties covering claims by property owners dating from 1868; the most controversial decision was not really an agreement at all but consisted of the signed minutes of the meetings. Those portions of the minutes concerning the status of the U.S.-owned oil companies are excerpted below. *Amparo* is roughly equivalent to a writ of habeas corpus in the U.S. legal system. Washington announced the resumption of full diplomatic relations on August 31.

A meeting of the Conferences was held at 10 o'clock a.m., August 2, 1923, at No. 85 Bucareli Street. Present: American Commissioners Charles Beecher Warren and John Barton Payne; Mexican Commissioners Ramón Ross and Fernando González Roa.

The Mexican Commissioners stated that the following are natural consequences of the political and administrative program which the Mexican Government has been carrying out, and that they state them in behalf of their Government in connection with the representations relating to the rights of the citizens of the United States of America in respect to the subsoil.

1. It is the duty of the federal executive power, under the constitution, to respect and enforce the decisions of the judicial power. In accordance with such a duty, the Executive has respected and enforced, and will continue to do so, the principles of the decisions of the Supreme Court of Justice in the "Texas Oil Company" case and the four other similar *amparo* cases, declaring that paragraph 4 of Article 27 of the Constitution of 1917 is not retroactive in respect to all persons who have performed, prior to the promulgation of said Constitution, some positive act which would manifest the intention of the owner of the surface or of the persons entitled to exercise his rights to the oil under the surface to make use of or obtain the oil under the surface: such as drilling, leasing, entering into any contract relative to the subsoil, making investments of capital in lands for the purpose of obtaining the oil in the subsoil, carrying out works of exploitation and exploration of the subsoil . . . and, in general, performing or doing any other positive act, or manifesting an intention of a character similar to those heretofore described. According to these decisions of the Supreme Court, the same rights enjoyed by those owners of the surface who have performed a positive act or manifested an intention such as has been mentioned above, will be enjoyed also by their legal assignees or those persons entitled to the rights to the oil. The protection of the Supreme Court extends to all the land or subsoil concerning which any of the above intentions have been manifested, or upon which any of the above specified acts have been performed. . . .

The above statement has constituted and will constitute in the future the policy of the Mexican Government, in respect to lands and the subsoil upon which or in relation to which any of the above specified acts have been performed, or in relation to which any of the above specified intentions have been manifested; and the Mexican Government will grant to the owners, assignees or other persons entitled to the rights to the oil, drilling permits on such lands. . . .

2. The [Mexican] Government, from the time that these decisions of the Supreme Court were rendered, has recognized and will continue to recognize the same rights for all those owners or lessees of land or subsoil or other persons entitled to the rights to the oil who are in a similar situation as those who obtained *amparo*; that is, those owners or lessees of land or subsoil or other persons entitled to the rights to the oil who have performed any positive act of the character already described or manifested any intention such as above specified.

3. The Mexican Government . . . has granted and grants preferential rights to all owners of the surface or persons entitled to exercise their preferential rights to the oil in the subsoil, who have not performed a positive act such as already mentioned. . . .

5. The American Commissioners have stated in behalf of their Government that the Government of the United States now reserves, and reserves should diplomatic relations between the countries be resumed, all the rights of the citizens of the United States in respect to the subsoil under the surface of lands in Mexico owned by citizens of the United States, or in which they have an interest in whatever form owned or held, under the laws and Constitution of Mexico in force prior to the promulgation of the Constitution, May 1, 1917, and under the principles of international law and equity. . . .

At 2 o'clock p. m. the Commissioners adjourned until 10 o'clock a. m. the following day, August 3, 1923.

1926

A Latin American Doctrine
of Anti-Imperialism

Victor Haya de la Torre

A fter World War I, which wrecked the economies of Europe, the financial and economic power of the United States expanded throughout Latin America. In Peru, where the oligarchy had long welcomed foreign (especially British) investors, U.S. capital flowed into the major export sectors—mining, oil and agriculture—during the 1910s and 1920s. Peru's labor movement increasingly found itself confronting U.S.-owned businesses. One of the organizers of that movement was Victor Haya de la Torre (1895–1979), destined to become Peru's most prominent twentieth-century political leader. Like many other labor leaders and intellectuals, in Peru and elsewhere in Latin America, Haya de la Torre saw a connection between the poverty of the masses and the prominent role that foreign capital often played in the economy of Latin America. In 1924, while exiled in Mexico City, Haya de la Torre organized the A.P.R.A. Although intended to be a continental alliance of like-minded political parties, the populist A.P.R.A. was strongest in Peru, where it began to compete in elections in the 1930s and remained a major force in politics.

The struggle organised in Latin America against Yankee Imperialism, by means of an international united front of manual and intellectual workers with a programme of common action, that is the A.P.R.A., the four initial letters of the following words: Alianza Popular Revolucionaria Americana (Popular Revolutionary American Alliance).

The programme of international action of the A.P.R.A. has five general points which serve as a basis for the national sections:

1. Action of the countries of Latin America against Yankee Imperialism.
2. The political unity of Latin America.

Source: Victor Haya de la Torre. "What is the APRA?" *The Labour Monthly* 8 (December 1926): 756–59.

3. The nationalisation of land and industry.

4. The internationalisation of the Panama Canal.

5. The solidarity of all the oppressed people and classes of the world. . . .

The A.P.R.A. organises the great Latin American Anti-Imperialist united front and works to include in its ranks all those who in one way or another have struggled and are still struggling against the North American danger in Latin America. Until 1923 this danger was regarded as a possible struggle of races—the Saxon and the Latin races—as a "conflict of cultures" or as a question of nationalism. From the "Gonzalez Prada" Popular Universities of Peru a new conception of the problem has arisen: the economic conception. . . .

The history of the political and economic relations between Latin America and the United States, especially the experience of the Mexican Revolution, lead to the following conclusions:

1. The governing classes of the Latin American countries—landowners, middle class or merchants—are allies of North American Imperialism.

2. These classes have the political power in our countries, in exchange for a policy of concessions, of loans, of great operations which they—the capitalists, landowners or merchants and politicians of the Latin American dominant classes—share with Imperialism.

3. As a result of this alliance the natural resources which form the riches of our countries are mortgaged or sold, and the working and agricultural classes are subjected to the most brutal servitude. Again, this alliance produces political events which result in the loss of national sovereignty: Panama, Nicaragua, Cuba, Santo Domingo, are really protectorates of the United States. . . .

The experience of history, especially that of Mexico, shows that the immense power of American Imperialism cannot be overthrown without the unity of the Latin American countries. Against this unity the national dominant classes, middle class, landowners, &c., whose political power is almost always buttressed by the agitation of nationalism or patriotism of countries hostile to their neighbours, are ranged. Consequently the overthrow of the governing classes is indispensable, political power must be captured by the workers, and Latin America must be united in a Federation of States. This is one of the great political objects of the A.P.R.A.

1928

A Defense of Intervention

Charles E. Hughes

When the Sixth International Conference of American States convened in Havana from January 16 to February 20, 1928, U.S. troops were occupying Haiti and fighting a guerrilla war in Nicaragua against the peasant army led by Augusto C. Sandino. Charles Evans Hughes, who had been secretary of state from 1921 to 1925, was appointed by the Coolidge administration to head the U.S. delegation to the conference. Resentment was building in Latin America against the U.S. interventions in the region, and Washington was expecting a barrage of criticism. During a debate over a motion condemning intervention, excerpted below, Hughes defended the U.S. position and the delegates decided to defer the question until the Seventh Conference, which took place in Montevideo in 1933. The controversy at the Havana meeting helped to inspire a gradual trend in the U.S. government away from direct intervention, as reflected first in the Clark Memorandum (see Document No. 52) and later in the U.S. response at Montevideo (see Document No. 55).

. . . There are no desires or ambitions which my country entertains which are opposed to the desires and aspirations of our sister republics. I merely recognized that this was a question which needed time and further study to resolve in principles which all could accept, and that was the view which I supposed that all my colleagues on the subcommittee, and on the full committee [Committee on Public International Law] as well, entertained. I gladly acquiesced in their decision. Now what is the situation when we come to the actual facts of the case? There is no one here who does not have enjoyment in the free air of independence. My country was nurtured in the desire for independence. One hundred years ago we declared the policy that all the American Republics should be recognized in their independence. We have given our arms and our blood for the independence of the American Republics and are always ready

Source: International Conference of American States. *Report of the Delegates of the United States of America to the Sixth International Conference of American States, Held at Habana, Cuba, 16 January to 20 February 1928*, pp. 13–15. Washington, D.C.: GPO, 1928.

to do so. We yield to none in the establishment of the ideal of sovereignty and independence for every one of the American Republics from the greatest to the smallest. And I have the right, speaking here on behalf of the delegation of the United States, to declare the policy of my country. I joined readily in the resolution of the delegation of Mexico against aggression. We want no aggression. We want no aggression against ourselves. We cherish no thought of aggression against anybody else. We desire to respect the rights of every country and to have the rights of our own country equally respected. We do not wish the territory of any American Republic. We do not wish to govern any American Republic. We do not wish to intervene in the affairs of any American Republic. We simply wish peace and order and stability and recognition of honest rights properly acquired so that this hemisphere may not only be the hemisphere of peace but the hemisphere of international justice. Much has been said of late with regard to Nicaragua. There sits the Foreign Minister of Nicaragua, a delegate of his country to this Conference. He can tell you the situation in Nicaragua and I can tell you that we desire nothing more than the independence and peace of his country and that we are there simply to aid them in obtaining free elections, in order that they may have a sovereign and independent government. I mention that merely because I speak in a spirit of entire frankness.

Now what is the real difficulty? Let us face the facts. The difficulty, if there is any, in any one of the American Republics, is not of any external aggression. It is an internal difficulty, if is exists at all. From time to time there arises a situation most deplorable and regrettable in which sovereignty is not at work, in which for a time in certain areas there is no government at all, in which for a time and within a limited sphere there is no possibility of performing the functions of sovereignty and independence. Those are the conditions that create the difficulty with which at times we find ourselves confronted. What are we to do when government breaks down and American citizens are in danger of their lives? Are we to stand by and see them killed because a government in circumstances which it cannot control and for which it may not be responsible can no longer afford reasonable protection? I am not speaking of sporadic acts of violence, or of the rising of mobs, or of those distressing incidents which may occur in any country however well administered. I am speaking of the occasion where government itself is unable to function for a time because of difficulties which confront it and which it is impossible for it to surmount.

Now it is a principle of international law that in such a case a government is fully justified in taking action—I would call it interposition of a temporary character—for the purpose of protecting the lives and property of its nationals. . . .

Of course the United States cannot forego its right to protect its citizens. No country should forego its right to protect its citizens. International law cannot be changed by the resolutions of this Conference. International law remains. The rights of nations remain, but nations have duties as well as rights. We all recognize that. This very formula, here proposed, is a proposal of duty on the part of a nation. But it is not the only duty. There are other obligations which courts, and tribunals declaring international law, have frequently set forth; and we cannot codify international law and ignore the duties of states, by setting up the impossible reign of self-will without any recognition upon the part of a state of its obligations to its neighbors. . . .

I have made this statement merely to avoid any possible misunderstanding. I am too proud of my country to stand before you as in any way suggesting a defense of aggression or of assault upon the sovereignty or independence of any state. I stand before you to tell you that we unite with you in the aspiration for complete sovereignty and the realization of complete independence. I stand here with you ready to cooperate in every way in establishing the ideals of justice by institutions in every land which will promote fairness of dealing between man and man and nation and nation.

I cannot sacrifice the rights of my country but I will join with you in declaring the law. I will try to help you in coming to a just conclusion as to the law; but it must be the law of justice infused with the spirit which has given us from the days of Grotius this wonderful development of the law of nation by which we find ourselves bound.

❖

NO. 51

1928

With Sandino in Nicaragua

Carleton Beals

A civil war between armies aligned with the Liberal Party and the Conservative Party in Nicaragua led to a U.S.-mediated peace agreement between the two sides in May 1927. One of the generals fighting on the side of the Liberals, Augusto C. Sandino (1895–1934), refused to accept the terms of the agreement and continued to fight against the Nicaraguan government and its most important ally, the U.S. Marines who were occupying the country. The marines, under

Source: "With Sandino in Nicaragua" by Carleton Beals. Reprinted with permission from the February 22, February 29, March 7, and March 14, 1928 issues of *The Nation*.

the terms of the peace agreement, began to organize and train a National Guard. In February 1928 *The Nation* assigned journalist Carleton Beals to report on Sandino's insurgency and interview the general, whose movement was characterized as "banditry" by the U.S. government. Beals's chronicle, published in weekly installments from February 22 to April 18, 1928, embarrassed the U.S. government and generated worldwide support for Sandino's cause. What follows are excerpts from the first four installments of Beals's report. Sandino's guerrilla army survived the combined efforts of the marines and the new National Guard to defeat it. After the marines withdrew from Nicaragua in January 1933, Sandino negotiated a peace settlement with the Nicaraguan government. He was assassinated by members of the National Guard on February 21, 1934.

Several days ago I rode out of the camp of General Augusto C. Sandino, the terrible "bandit" of Nicaragua who is holding the marines at bay. Not a single hair of my blond, Anglo-Saxon head had been injured. On the contrary, I had been shown every possible kindness. I went, free to take any route I might choose, with permission to relate to anybody I encountered any and every thing I had seen and heard. Perhaps my case is unique. I am the first and only American since Sandino began fighting the marines who has been granted an official interview, and I am the first bona fide correspondent of any nationality to talk to him face to face.

"Do you still think us bandits?" was his last query as I bade him goodbye.

"You are as much a bandit as Mr. Coolidge is a bolshevik," was my reply.

"Tell your people," he returned, "there may be bandits in Nicaragua, but they are not necessarily Nicaraguans." . . .

[Beals goes on to recount his quest to interview Sandino.] Our Odyssey had begun. From the San Pedro ranch, the point where our connections with the next Sandino outpost were broken and we lost track of the route taken by General Sandino after his evacuation of El Chipote, our way led us even deeper into the mountains in an ever-widening inland circle about the scene of operations of the American marines. On every hand loomed height after height, crags and ridges, profound valleys, enormous precipices, all blanketed with the most dense tropical vegetation. On some days the earth simmered under a hot, tropical sky; at other times it was almost invisible while tropical storms deluged it. These would have been difficult mountains to cross even if we had known the exact direction of the trail we had to follow in order to reach Sandino. . . .

The few people we met were all loyal Sandinistas, fleeing ever deeper into the wilderness in order to escape the dreaded *macho,* the hated American marine. Their homes were burned, their crops destroyed, their possessions smashed, but one and all vowed never to give up the struggle. . . .

We dropped into a clearing where there were barracks harboring about thirty soldiers and a dozen camp *juana,* women who had attended to the cooking and washing at El Chipote. One of them, Theresa, a vivacious, slender girl with a little boy about five, was also bound for the camp and promptly offered me two packs of Camel cigarettes which she had taken from the body of a marine—rather a gruesome gift. She had been wounded in the forehead by shrapnel during an American airplane bombardment on January 14, and lifted the towel from her head to show me an ugly star-shaped scar over her left eye. She declared that Sandino in that attack had lost one man killed and another and herself wounded—a decidedly different story from the marines' report. . . .

From the depths of the forest, mountain lions roar. Huge macaws wing across the sky, crying hoarsely and flashing crimson. We ford and reford the north-flowing tributary, for endless hours we toil across the Yali range, and finally drop down near Jinotega in another night of driving rain over a road where the horses roll pitifully, up to their bellies in mud.

A few miles from Jinotega, where a hundred marines were stationed, our little group of thirty men swung boldly, in broad daylight, out through the smiling open country of farms and meadows filled with cattle and wild horses; but occasionally the men scanned the sky apprehensively for airplanes. Here the soldiers singled out the farms of *Cachurecos* (Conservatives) and confiscated horses and saddles. This was the only instance of forced requisitioning I observed on the entire trip. . . .

Soon we were at the first sentry outpost.

"Quien viva?"

"Viva Nicaragua!"

"Give the countersign."

"Don't sell out the fatherland."

"Advance one by one to be recognized."

A short, youngish soldier with a dark-green uniform and smoked glasses took me in tow, saying in perfect English, "You are the American," and "A warm welcome, sir." . . .

After describing the manner in which several American airplanes were brought down, Sandino in rapid fire gave me the basis of his demands in the present struggle: first, evacuation of Nicaraguan territory by the marines; second, the appointment of an impartial civilian President chosen by the notables of the three parties—one who has never been President and never a candidate for the Presidency; third, supervision of the elections by Latin America.

"The day these conditions are carried out," declared Sandino, "I will immediately cease all hostilities and disband my forces. In addition I shall never accept a government position, elective or otherwise. No position, no salary— this I swear. I will not accept any personal reward either today or tomorrow, or at any time in the future."

He left his chair and paced to and fro to emphasize this point. He stated vehemently: "Never, never will I accept public office. I am fully capable of gaining a livelihood for myself and my wife in a some humble, happy pursuit. By trade I am a mechanic and if necessary I will return to my trade. Nor will I ever take up arms again in any struggle between the Liberals and the Conservatives, nor, indeed, in any other domestic struggle—only in case of a new foreign invasion. We have taken up arms from the love of our country because all other leaders have betrayed it and have sold themselves out to the foreigner or have bent the neck in cowardice. We, in our own house, are fighting for our inalienable rights. What right have foreign troops to call us outlaws and bandits, and to say that we are the aggressors? I repeat that we are in our own house. We declare that we will never live in cowardly peace under a government installed by a foreign Power. Is this patriotism or is it not? And when the invader is vanquished, as some day he must be, my men will be content with their plots of ground, their tools, their mules, and their families."

❖

NO. 52

1928

The Clark Memorandum

J. Reuben Clark

By the 1920s, the justification for aggression that President Theodore Roosevelt had claimed for the Monroe Doctrine in his famous "corollary" (Document No. 37) was being questioned within the State Department. In Latin America and even in the United States, the unilateralism of U.S. policy was harshly criticized. In the first of a series of moves that would eventually lead to a categorical renunciation by the United States of the right to intervene, the State Department sought to separate the Monroe Doctrine from the right of intervention presumed in Roosevelt's Corollary. In November 1928, Secretary of State Frank B. Kellogg asked Undersecretary of State J. Reuben Clark to undertake a legal study of the Corollary. Clark's reply the following month, excerpted below, was not made public until 1930.

Source: U.S. Department of State. *Memorandum on the Monroe Doctrine prepared by J. Reuben Clark, Undersecretary of State, 17 December 1928*. Washington, D.C.: GPO, 1930.

The Secretary:

Herewith I transmit a Memorandum on the Monroe Doctrine, prepared by your direction, given a little over two months ago.

The Doctrine . . . declared by Monroe, when reduced to its lowest terms, covers—

(1) Future *colonization by any European powers* of the *American continents.*

(2) Any attempt by the *allied powers* to extend their political system *to any portion of this hemisphere. . . .*

(3) Any interposition, *by any European power,* for the purpose of oppressing or controlling in any other manner the destinies of the Latin American Governments "who have declared their independence and maintained it, and whose independence we have on great consideration and just principles acknowledged."

(4) Noninterference by the United States with the existing colonies or dependencies of any European power.

(5) Policy of leaving Spanish American colonies and Spain to themselves in the hope that other powers will pursue the same course. . . .

It is of first importance to have in mind that Monroe's declaration in its terms, relates solely to the relationships between European states on the one side, and, on the other side, the American continents, the Western Hemisphere, and the Latin American Governments which on December 2, 1823, had declared and maintained their independence which we had acknowledged.

It is of equal importance to note, on the other hand, that the declaration does not apply to purely inter-American relations.

Nor does the declaration purport to lay down any principles that are to govern the interrelationship of the states of this Western Hemisphere as among themselves.

The Doctrine states a case of United States *vs.* Europe, not of United States *vs.* Latin America.

Such arrangements as the United States has made, for example, with Cuba, Santo Domingo, Haiti, and Nicaragua, are not within the Doctrine as it was announced by Monroe. They may be accounted for as the expression of a national policy which, like the Doctrine itself, originates in the necessities of security or self-preservation . . . but such arrangements are not covered by the terms of the Doctrine itself.

Should it become necessary to apply a sanction for a violation of the Doctrine as declared by Monroe, that sanction would run against the European power offending the policy, and not against the Latin American country which was the object of the European aggression, unless a conspiracy existed between the European and the American states involved.

In the normal case, the Latin American state against which aggression was aimed by a European power, would be the beneficiary of the Doctrine not its victim. This has been the history of its application. The Doctrine makes the United States a guarantor, in effect, of the independence of Latin American states. . . .

The so-called "Roosevelt corollary" was to the effect, as generally understood, that in case of financial or other difficulties in weak Latin American countries, the United States should attempt an adjustment thereof lest European Governments should intervene, and intervening should occupy territory—an act which would be contrary to the principles of the Monroe Doctrine. . . . As has already been indicated above, it is not believed that this corollary is justified by the terms of the Monroe Doctrine, however much it may be justified by the application of the doctrine of self-preservation. . . .

So far as Latin America is concerned, the Doctrine is now, and always has been, not an instrument of violence and oppression, but an unbought, freely bestowed, and wholly effective guaranty of their freedom, independence, and territorial integrity against the imperialistic designs of Europe.

III.
BURYING THE BIG STICK

1933

The Good Neighbor Policy

Franklin Delano Roosevelt

The roots of that transformation in U.S. policy toward Latin America that became known as the Good Neighbor Policy can be detected in the Republican administrations of Presidents Calvin Coolidge and Herbert Hoover. Indeed, the phrase *good neighbor* was used by President Hoover during a ten-country tour of Latin America between his election in 1928 and his inauguration in 1929. But the new direction that Hoover seemed to be promising was officially launched and firmly implemented by President Franklin D. Roosevelt, a Democrat, who occupied the White House from 1933 until 1945. As early as 1928, Roosevelt had publicly criticized the Coolidge and Harding administrations for their failure to do more to create good will in Latin America. He denounced the habit of intervention, though as assistant secretary of the navy in the Wilson administration, Roosevelt had played a key role in the U.S. occupations of Haiti, the Dominican Republic and the Mexican port of Veracruz. In his inaugural address on March 4, 1933, Roosevelt declared that his "world policy" would be that of "the good neighbor—the neighbor who resolutely respects himself and, because he does so, respects the rights of others. . . ." He used the term expressly in connection with Latin America in this speech before the Governing Board of the Pan American Union, in Washington, on April 12, 1933, "Pan-American Day."

I rejoice in this opportunity to participate in the celebration of "Pan-American Day" and to extend on behalf of the people of the United States a fraternal greeting to our sister American Republics. . . .

This celebration commemorates a movement based upon the policy of fraternal cooperation. In my Inaugural Address I stated that I would "dedicate this Nation to the policy of the good neighbor—the neighbor who resolutely respects himself and, because he does so, respects the rights of others—the neighbor who respects his obligations and respects the sanctity of his agreements in and with a world of neighbors." Never before has the significance of

Source: Franklin D. Roosevelt. *The Public Papers and Addresses of Franklin D. Roosevelt.* Vol. 2, *The Year of Crisis 1933,* pp. 129–33. New York: Random House, 1938.

the words "good neighbor" been so manifest in international relations. Never have the need and benefit of neighborly cooperation in every form of human activity been so evident as they are today. . . .

The essential qualities of a true pan Americanism must be the same as those which constitute a good neighbor, namely, mutual understanding, and, through such understanding, a sympathetic appreciation of the other's point of view. . . . In this spirit the people of every Republic on our continent are coming to a deep understanding of the fact that the Monroe Doctrine, of which so much has been written and spoken for more than a century, was and is directed at the maintenance of independence by the peoples of the continent. It was aimed and is aimed against the acquisition in any manner of the control of additional territory in this hemisphere by any non-American power.

Hand in hand with this pan-American doctrine of continental self-defense, the peoples of the American Republics understand more clearly, with the passing years, that the independence of each Republic must recognize the independence of every other Republic. Each one of us must grow by an advancement of civilization and social well-being and not by the acquisition of territory at the expense of any neighbor.

In this spirit of mutual understanding and of cooperation on this continent you and I cannot fail to be disturbed by any armed strife between neighbors. I do not hesitate to say to you, the distinguished members of the Governing Board of the Pan-American Union, that I regard existing conflicts between four of our sister Republics as a backward step.

Your Americanism and mine must be a structure built of confidence, cemented by a sympathy which recognizes only equality and fraternity. It finds its source and being in the hearts of men and dwells in the temple of the intellect.

We all of us have peculiar problems, and, to speak frankly, the interest of our own citizens must, in each instance, come first. But it is equally true that it is of vital importance to every Nation of this Continent that the American Governments, individually, take, without further delay, such action as may be possible to abolish all unnecessary and artificial barriers and restrictions which now hamper the healthy flow of trade between the peoples of the American Republics. . . .

❖

1933

Mission to Havana

Sumner Welles

President Franklin D. Roosevelt's Good Neighbor Policy met its first serious test in Cuba, where open warfare had erupted against the dictatorial government of Gerardo Machado. Opponents of Machado seemed to be leading the country toward a social revolution. In May 1933, Roosevelt appointed his assistant secretary of state, Sumner Welles (1892–1961), as the U.S. ambassador to Cuba, with orders to resolve the crisis through mediation. Machado resisted Welles's persistent efforts to convince him to resign until the Cuban army turned against him in August and forced Machado to leave. Welles's efforts were frustrated, however, by his inability to control subsequent events. In September, Welles's choice for president, Carlos Manuel de Céspedes, was overthrown and a left-leaning university professor, Ramón Grau San Martín, took power with the support of a group of army sergeants, corporals and enlisted men led by Sergeant Fulgencio Batista. Refusing to recognize Grau San Martín's reform-oriented government, the United States continued to seek an acceptable alternative, which it finally achieved in January 1934 when Fulgencio Batista, now promoted to colonel, switched his support from Grau San Martín to Carlos Mendieta. Excerpts from Welles's memoirs follow.

It happened that I had the opportunity of carrying out the policy of the good neighbor in its first major application to inter-American relations. For some time prior to 1933 the situation which had arisen in Cuba had created a maximum amount of embarrassment to the government in Washington. General Machado, the President of Cuba, had been elected in 1925 for the constitutional four-year term. In 1928, by methods which were generally regarded as questionable, and unconstitutional, he had secured a revision of the Cuban Constitution which not only extended the term of office for which he had been elected, but likewise provided for a second term of six years rather than of the original four.

The world depression had hit Cuba very hard indeed. Eighty-five per cent of her national income was derived from the sale of sugar in the world market, and her ability to prosper depended on her ability to sell to the United States with some reasonable margin of profit. Consequently, the material increase in the tariff on sugar, imposed by the Smoot–Hawley Tariff Act, had rapidly brought the Cuban people to a condition of abject destitution which had never previously been equaled in the history of their independence. . . .

Like many others of his domineering type in positions of authority, President Machado had deluded himself into the conviction that his government still had popular support. He was sure that the opposition to him, now daily becoming more vocal and more violent, was stimulated by what he termed "communistic" agitators and professional oppositionists, who would soon cease to give trouble if they were repressed with a strong hand. The violence and cold-blooded cruelty of the repressive measures which he understood were immediately answered by equally violent outbursts on the part of the opposition.

By the winter of 1933 the situation had reached such a point that the processes of constitutional government were halted, business was at a standstill, the universities and high schools could no longer function. The atrocities perpetrated by the federal police employed by the Machado government—atrocities quite similar to those later carried on by the Nazi Gestapo—had aroused indignation throughout the Americas. . . .

The original treaty between the United States and Cuba, granting the United States the right to intervene by force if in its judgment the Cuban authorities were unable to render due protection to life and property, was still in existence. The Hoover Administration closed its eyes to a situation which was fast degenerating into anarchy, and was shocking the conscience of the Western world. . . .

To President Roosevelt two facts were clear. First, that, while the existing treaty with Cuba gave this country the right to intervene, any such intervention would be entirely contrary to the general line of inter-American policy which he had set for himself. Second, that a state of affairs where governmental murder and clandestine assassination had become matters of daily occurrence must be ended. Such a condition at the front door of the United States could not be allowed to continue indefinitely, particularly in a country bound to this nation by peculiarly close treaty ties, and for which the people of this country had a very special regard. . . .

[I]n the early days of August [1933] a spontaneous mutiny of the Cuban Army took the matter out of [Machado's] hands and he was forced to flee from Cuba. . . . In the meantime, however, by the free designation of the heads of the opposition parties, Dr. Carlos Manuel de Cespedes, only son of the great Cuban patriot of the same name, became Provisional President. . . .

During the brief anarchic period through which Cuba passed in August of

1933, there were, of course, innumerable demands for American armed intervention, especially from certain people representing commercial interests. Every request was rejected flatly. As a precautionary measure, however, President Roosevelt directed that certain vessels of the United States Navy be sent to Cuban waters, to take away any American citizens or other foreigners whose lives might be endangered and who were unable to find any other safe means of avoiding mob violence. At the same time the President created the precedent for what was to become the studied policy of his Administration: consultation with the other American republics whenever the United States should find itself in a position where it might be obliged to take action affecting any other people of the Americas. . . . The President did not request or suggest any action on the part of the inter-American family, but limited himself to a frank exposition of the circumstances in order that the other American governments might be fully and officially informed of what had taken place, and of the reasons why American men-of-war had been sent to Cuban ports. . . .

At the beginning of September, however, the constructive efforts of the Cespedes government to relieve the appalling distress of the Cuban people were suddenly arrested by a second mutiny in the Cuban Army . . . led, and to a very considerable extent planned, by that extraordinarily brilliant and able figure, Fulgencio Batista, now President of Cuba. . . .

For a brief period the direction of Cuban affairs was undertaken by a committee, largely inspired and controlled by the student council of the University of Havana. After some disorderly and sterile weeks, one of the members of the original committee, a well-known Havana physician, Dr. Ramón Grau San Martín, emerged as the sole head of the civilian branch of what was then termed a new provisional government.

. . . The new provisional government, while proclaiming its intention of helping the common man and while promulgating a series of decrees providing for better condition for the working classes, appeared to be completely incapable of maintaining even a semblance of public order. Property after property was seized by groups of workers, and industry generally was forced to close down. . . . By the end of November a seriously anarchic condition had once more arisen. . . .

None of the established political parties, none of the commercial or business interests, no responsible labor organization, and only a few of the members of the professional classes supported the government.

The failure of this government to recognize the provisional Cuban regime headed by Dr. Grau San Martín called forth the most violent complaints from his adherents, directed in particular against myself. I have always felt that, in view of the existence at that time of the Treaty of 1901, which granted this government the right of intervention in Cuba, and only because of that fact, the United States would have been derelict in its obligations to the Cuban people themselves had it given official support to a de facto regime which, in its considered judgment, was not approved by the great majority of the Cuban people, and which had shown itself so disastrously incompetent in every branch

of public administration. . . . The overthrow of the Grau San Martín government the following winter as a result of the determined attitude displayed
by Colonel Batista . . . was unquestionably welcomed by an overwhelming
majority of the people. It was the first step in the long process of Cuba's return to constitutional government, economic prosperity, and normal social
stability. . . .

❖

NO. 55

1933

The United States Accepts
the Non-Intervention Principle

The Delegates to the Seventh International Conference
of American States

As the Hoover and Roosevelt administrations moved closer and closer toward
pledging Washington to a policy of nonintervention, Latin Americans insisted
that Washington make it official. A legally binding promise renouncing the right
to intervene under any circumstances was, they believed, the most effective way
for the United States to prove its commitment to nonintervention. Such a promise
had been asked of Washington at Havana in 1928 (see Document No. 50), and
denied. By the time that the delegates to the Seventh International Conference
of American States gathered in Montevideo in December 1933, they had reason
to expect that Washington might finally take the pledge. In this they were not
disappointed, although Secretary of State Cordell Hull still insisted on adding a
"reservation" that left the door open to intervention under certain circumstances,
as dictated by "the law of nations as generally recognized and accepted."

Source: *The International Conferences of American States.* First Supplement, 1933–1940. Collected and
edited in the Division of International Law of the Carnegie Endowment for International Peace,
pp. 121–24. Washington, D.C.: Carnegie Endowment for International Peace, 1940.

Convention on Rights and Duties of States

ARTICLE 1. The state as a person of international law should possess the following qualifications: a) a permanent population; b) a defined territory; c) government; and d) capacity to enter into relations with the other states.

ARTICLE 2. The federal state shall constitute a sole person in the eyes of international law.

ARTICLE 3. The political existence of the state is independent of recognition by the other states. Even before recognition the state has the right to defend its integrity and independence, to provide for its conservation and prosperity, and consequently to organize itself as it sees fit, to legislate upon its interests, administer its services, and to define the jurisdiction and competence of its courts. The exercise of these rights has no other limitation than the exercise of the rights of other states according to international law.

ARTICLE 4. States are juridically equal, enjoy the same rights, and have equal capacity in their exercise. The rights of each one do not depend upon the power which it possesses to assure its exercise, but upon the simple fact of its existence as a person under international law.

ARTICLE 5. The fundamental rights of states are not susceptible of being affected in any manner whatsoever.

ARTICLE 6. The recognition of a state merely signifies that the state which recognizes it accepts the personality of the other with all the rights and duties determined by international law. Recognition is unconditional and irrevocable.

ARTICLE 7. The recognition of a state may be express or tacit. The latter results from any act which implies the intention of recognizing the new state.

ARTICLE 8. No state has the right to intervene in the internal or external affairs of another.

ARTICLE 9. The jurisdiction of states within the limits of national territory applies to all the inhabitants. Nationals and foreigners are under the same protection of the law and the national authorities and the foreigners may not claim rights other or more extensive than those of the nationals.

ARTICLE 10. The primary interest of states is the conservation of peace. Differences of any nature which arise between them should be settled by recognized pacific methods.

ARTICLE 11. The contracting states definitely establish as the rule of their conduct the precise obligation not to recognize territorial acquisitions or special advantages which have been obtained by force whether this consists in the employment of arms, in threatening diplomatic representations, or in any other effective coercive measure. The territory of a state is inviolable and may not be the object of military occupation nor of other measures of force imposed by another state directly or indirectly or for any motive whatever even temporarily. . . .

[Here follow the signatures of the delegates of Argentina, Brazil, Chile, Colombia, Cuba, the Dominican Republic, Ecuador, El Salvador, Guatemala, Haiti, Honduras, Mexico, Nicaragua, Panama, Paraguay, Peru, the United States of America, Uruguay, and Venezuela.]

Reservations Made at Signature [by the United States of America]

. . . The policy and attitude of the United States Government toward every important phase of international relationships in this hemisphere could scarcely be made more clear and definite than they have been made by both word and action especially since March 4. . . . Every observing person must by this time thoroughly understand that under the Roosevelt Administration the United States Government is as much opposed as any other government to interference with the freedom, the sovereignty, or other internal affairs or processes of the governments of other nations. . . . I feel safe in undertaking to say that under our support of the general principle of non-intervention as has been suggested, no government need fear any intervention on the part of the United States under the Roosevelt Administration. I think it unfortunate that during the brief period of this Conference there is apparently not time within which to prepare interpretations and definitions of these fundamental terms that are embraced in the report. . . . In the meantime in case of differences of interpretations and also until they (the proposed doctrines and principles) can be worked out and codified for the common use of every government, I desire to say that the United States Government in all of its international associations and relationships and conduct will follow scrupulously the doctrines and policies which it has pursued since March 4 which are embodied in . . . the law of nations as generally recognized and accepted.

NO. 56

1936

Hemispheric Security and Non-Intervention

The Delegates to the Inter-American Conference
for the Maintenance of Peace

I n letters sent to the presidents of the Latin American republics on January 30, 1936, U.S. President Franklin D. Roosevelt proposed a special conference to consider measures to prevent war among the countries of the Western Hemisphere while heading off any threat that might emanate from outside the hemisphere. The United States was maintaining an official policy of neutrality in respect to German and Italian aggression, and it hoped to win Latin American support for that policy. Held in Buenos Aires from December 1 to 23, 1936, the conference opened with an address by Roosevelt himself, who traveled there by battleship immediately after winning election to his second term. Roosevelt's speech marked the first time since the pan-American conferences had begun in 1889 that the delegates were asked to take steps against a possible attack from a nonhemispheric aggressor. The delegates complied by adopting the Convention for the Maintenance, Preservation and Reestablishment of Peace. But they also insisted on taking further action against intervention, seeking to go beyond the declaration agreed on at the Montevideo conference in 1933 (see Document No. 55). As a result, the Buenos Aires declaration of nonintervention, adopted as an "additional protocol," broadened the meaning of nonintervention, and this time the United States did not respond by attaching reservations to the declaration, as it had at Montevideo.

Convention for the Maintenance, Preservation
and Reestablishment of Peace

ARTICLE 1. In the event that the peace of the American Republics is menaced, and in order to coordinate efforts to prevent war, any of the Governments of the American Republics signatory to the Treaty of Paris of 1928 or to the Treaty of Non-Aggression and Conciliation of 1933, or to both, whether or not a mem-

Source: *The International Conferences of American States: First Supplement, 1933–1940.* Collected and edited in the Division of International Law of the Carnegie Endowment for International Peace, pp. 188–92. Washington,D.C.: Carnegie Endowment for International Peace, 1940.

ber of other peace organizations, shall consult with the other Governments of the American Republics, which, in such event, shall consult together for the purpose of finding and adopting methods of peaceful cooperation.

ARTICLE 2. In the event of war, or a virtual state of war between American States, the Governments of the American Republics represented at this Conference shall undertake without delay the necessary mutual consultations, in order to exchange views and to seek, within the obligations resulting from the pacts above mentioned and from the standards of international morality, a method of peaceful collaboration; and, in the event of an international war outside America which might menace the peace of the American Republics, such consultation shall also take place to determine the proper time and manner in which the signatory states, if they so desire, may eventually cooperate in some action tending to preserve the peace of the American Continent. . . .

Additional Protocol Relative to Non-Intervention

ARTICLE 1. The High Contracting Parties declare inadmissible the intervention of any one of them, directly or indirectly, and for whatever reason, in the internal or external affairs of any other of the Parties. The violation of the provisions of this Article shall give rise to mutual consultation, with the object of exchanging views and seeking methods of peaceful adjustment. . . .

❖

NO. 57

1938

Just Compensation for the Good Neighbor

Cordell Hull

In response to a labor dispute between petroleum producers and unions representing oilfield employees, the government of Mexico nationalized foreign-owned oil properties on March 18, 1938. U.S. oil firms demanded $200 million in compensation. As a result, the Roosevelt administration had to defend the in-

Source: "The Secretary of State to the Mexican Ambassador (Castillo Nájera)," 21 July 1938. *Foreign Relations of the United States: Diplomatic Papers 1938*. Vol. 5, The American Republics, pp. 674–78. Washington, D.C.: GPO, 1956.

ternational legal principle of just compensation while upholding its Good Neighbor commitment to nonintervention. Without mentioning the oil dispute directly, Secretary of State Cordell Hull addressed the issue of other outstanding claims against the Mexican government in a letter to the Mexican ambassador to the United States, Francisco Castillo Nájera, on July 21, 1938, excerpted below. The two countries agreed in 1941 to appoint a joint commission to decide the value of all the U.S. property that had been expropriated by Mexico. The commission's recommendation of $29 million for the oil companies, and the Roosevelt administration's decision not to continue supporting the companies in their dispute with Mexico, led the oil companies to accept a negotiated settlement of $30 million from Mexico in 1943.

Excellency:

During the recent years the Government of the United States has upon repeated occasions made representations to the Government of Mexico with regard to the continuing expropriation by Your Excellency's Government of agrarian properties owned by American citizens, without adequate, effective and prompt compensation being made therefor.

In extenuation of such action, the Mexican Government both in its official correspondence and in its public pronouncements has adverted to the fact that it is earnestly endeavoring to carry forward a program for the social betterment of the masses of its people.

The purposes of this program, however desirable they may be, are entirely unrelated to and apart from the real issue under discussion between our two Governments. The issue is not whether Mexico should pursue social and economic policies designed to improve the standard of living of its people. The issue is whether in pursuing them the property of American nationals may be taken by the Mexican Government without making prompt payment of just compensation to the owner in accordance with the universally recognized rules of law and equity.

My Government has frequently asserted the right of all countries freely to determine their own social, agrarian and industrial problems. This right includes the sovereign right of any government to expropriate private property within its borders in furtherance of public purposes. The Government of the United States has itself been very actively pursuing a program of social betterment. . . . Under this program it has expropriated from foreigners as well as its own citizens properties of various kinds. . . . In each and every case the Government of the United States has scrupulously observed the universally recognized principle of compensation and has reimbursed promptly and in cash the owners of the properties that have been expropriated. . . .

We have been mutually helpful to each other, and this Government is most desirous, in keeping with the good neighbor policy which it has been carrying forward during the last five years, to continue to cooperate with the Mexican Government in every mutually desirable and advantageous way.

One of the greatest services we can render is to pursue, and to urge others to pursue, a policy of fair dealing and fair play based on law and justice. Just as within our own borders we strive to prevent exploitation of debtors by powerful creditors and to protect the common man in making an honest living, so we are justified in accordance with recognized international law in striving to prevent unfair or oppressive treatment of our own people in other countries. . . .

In its negotiations with the Mexican Government for compensation for the lands of American citizens that have been expropriated, my Government has consistently maintained the principle of compensation. . . .

Up to August 30, 1927, 161 moderate sized properties of American citizens had been taken. The claims arising therefrom were after much discussion referred to the General Claims Commission established by agreement between the two Governments. It is appropriate to point out, however, that, as yet, and for whatever the reasons may be, not a single claim has been adjusted and none has been paid. . . . Subsequent to 1927, additional properties, chiefly farms of a moderate size, with a value claimed by their owners of $10,132,388, have been expropriated by the Mexican Government. This figure does not include the large land grants frequently mentioned in the press. . . . None of them as yet has been paid for. . . .

The taking of property without compensation is not expropriation. It is confiscation. It is no less confiscation because there may be an expressed intent to pay at some time in the future. . . .

We cannot question the right of a foreign government to treat its own nationals in this fashion if it so desires. This is a matter of domestic concern. But we cannot admit that a foreign government may take the property of American nationals in disregard of the rule of compensation under international law. Nor can we admit that any government unilaterally and through its municipal legislation can, as in this instant case, nullify this universally accepted principle of international law, based as it is on reason, equity and justice. . . .

We are entirely sympathetic to the desires of the Mexican Government for the social betterment of its people. We cannot accept the idea, however, that these plans can be carried forward at the expense of our citizens, any more than we would feel justified in carrying forward our plans for our own social betterment at the expense of citizens of Mexico. . . .

The Government of Mexico from the standpoint of the long run and healthy progress of the Mexican people should be just as vitally interested in maintaining the integrity of the good neighbor policy as any other country. The surest way of breaking up the good neighbor policy would be to allow the impression that it permits the disregard of the just rights of the nationals of one country owning property in another country. . . .

❖

1938

Populist Diplomacy in Mexico

Josephus Daniels

As secretary of the navy under President Woodrow Wilson, Josephus Daniels (1862–1948) ordered the occupation of Veracruz in an ultimately futile effort to control the outcome of the Mexican revolution. Franklin D. Roosevelt, who had served as assistant secretary of the navy under Daniels, appointed him ambassador to Mexico, where he served from 1933 to 1941. In his memoirs, excerpted below, Daniels described the popular response to President Lázaro Cárdenas's nationalization of foreign-owned oil companies (see Documents No. 48 and 57), and his own reaction to Cárdenas's decision. Daniels delayed delivering a sharply worded State Department note in order to keep relations between the two countries from deterioriating further. Under pressure from the Roosevelt administration, the U.S. oil companies agreed to accept the amount of compensation that would be decided on by a joint commission; Daniels also refers to an agreement on other outstanding claims by U.S. citizens that was reached on November 19, 1941.

I was sitting in my study in the Embassy on the evening of March 18, 1938 when representatives of the American and Mexican press came to the Embassy and asked to see me. They were excited and surprised, and I was surprised also when they told me that earlier in the evening President Cárdenas had announced on the radio that he issued a decree expropriating the properties of American and British oil companies in the republic, accusing them of "a conspiracy" against Mexico. . . .

The expropriation decree rattled the windows of the British Parliament, where government was in partnership with the oil interests affected. There were reverberations in the editorial rooms of some newspapers, whose columns, under scare headlines, blistered the Mexicans as "thieves and bandits." In the oil world there was unrestrained wrath as executives of the oil industry in the United States demanded that Uncle Sam "do something" to

Source: From *Shirt-Sleeve Diplomat* by Josephus Daniels. Chapters 20–22, 24. Copyright © 1947 by the University of North Carolina Press. Used by permission of the publisher.

compel restoration of the property to the owners at once or else—meaning that force should be employed and war with Mexico, if necessary, to "teach the Greasers 'Thou Shalt Not Steal.'" . . .

In Mexico, after sending the information to the State Department, without waiting for instructions I called on President Cárdenas and discussed the acute situation which the expropriation had brought about, expressing surprise and regret at the action, and stressing that my government would insist upon payment by Mexico for the properties expropriated. It was then, before I could go further, that President Cárdenas gave me his assurance that his government would take the necessary steps to make payment to the companies and requested me to ask them to confer with him to negotiate as to the valuation and the terms of payment. . . .

I found when I reached Washington that some of the oil officials had already started to build propaganda fires under the government to compel a return of the properties. They praised Secretary Hull's strong declarations and opined that when Mexico could not be warned by tufts of grass that Hull would soon be throwing stones. But, though Hull was irritated by the expropriation and the manner of it and wrote condemnatory notes to Mexico and never receded from his thesis that "universally recognized rules of law and equity" required "prompt and adequate payment," he never could be moved from his position that Mexico had the right—though he did not approve its exercise—to expropriate with "prompt and adequate payment." This caused the oil companies to say, "The Government let us down." . . .

With the expropriation of foreign oil properties, a wave of delirious enthusiasm swept over Mexico, heightened by bitter denunciations from other countries, as the people felt that a day of deliverance had come. On March 22, upon the call of the Confederation of Mexican Workers, some two hundred thousand people passed in compact files before the National Palace acclaiming President Cárdenas and carrying banners such as: "They shall not scoff at Mexican laws." Old inhabitants said there had never been such manifestations of the unity of the Mexican people in the history of Mexico as followed the appeals to the people to uphold the Constitution and the sovereignty of Mexico. It was shared by people who lost sight of oil in their belief that Mexicans must present a united and solid front. . . .

Noticeable was the enthusiasm of Catholics, many of whom had been critical of the Cárdenas government, in raising funds to support his expropriation move. On Sunday, April 30, the Archbishop of Guadalajara advised from the pulpit that it was a "patriotic duty to contribute to this national fund." It was announced (April 3) that Archbishop Martínez had promised a "letter on the oil controversy during Holy Week." On May 3, a circular, approved by archbishops and bishops, was published, exhorting Catholics to send contributions. All over the country in churches collections were taken to help pay for the seized oil properties. . . .

Women in Mexico have generally followed an old slogan: "The place of women is in the home." That was the attitude of women in the early part of

April, 1938. Then, as by a miracle, suddenly they became vocal in their patriotism. Cárdenas had made approval of the expropriation of oil a sort of national religion. The people believed—and had grounds for their opinion—that their patrimony had been given for a song to foreigners who refused to pay living wages to the men who worked in the oil fields. When the men gathered by the hundred thousands to show allegiance to Cárdenas after the oil expropriation, the women poured out of their homes by the thousands to voice their ardent support of the leaders who had somehow made the people feel that the oil exploiters were the enemies of their country. . . .

Something the like of which has rarely been seen in any country occurred on the twelfth day of April. By the thousands, women crowded the Zócalo and other parks and in companies marched to the Palace of Fine Arts to give of their all to the call of their country's honor. It was a scene never to be forgotten. Led by Señora Amalia Solórzano de Cárdenas, the President's young and handsome wife, old and young, well-to-do and poor—mainly the latter—as at a religious festival gathered to make, what was to many, an unheard-of sacrifice. They took off wedding rings, bracelets, earrings, and put them, as it seemed to them, on a national altar. All day long, until the receptacles were full and running over, these Mexican women gave and gave. When night came crowds still waited to deposit their offerings, which comprised everything from gold and silver to animals and corn. . . .

November 19, 1941, might go down in the annals of Mexico and the United States as the Day of Deliverance. On that date final agreement was reached, just before I retired from office. . . . Within five months (April 17, 1942) by diligence and justice the two representatives [of the joint commission] agreed that the amount Mexico should pay to oil companies was $23,995,991. In the early days after the expropriation, spokesmen of some of the companies had put a valuation of from three to four hundred million dollars on the properties expropriated. . . .

The day after the settlement had been signed by Secretary Cordell Hull for the United States and Ambassador Castillo Nájera for Mexico, Lombardo Toledano, labor leader of Mexico, said: "Bonfires should be lighted throughout Latin America because for the first time a small country (Mexico) and a big country (U.S.A.) have sat down at the Council Table and ironed things out without the use of force."

❖

1938

A Skeptic Views the Good Neighbor Policy

Carleton Beals

B y the time Carleton Beals (1893–1979) wrote *The Coming Struggle for Latin America* (1938), he was the well-known author of articles and books about Latin America, Western Europe and Africa. While his criticism of the Good Neighbor policy represented a minority view in the United States, it nevertheless touched on certain underlying truths that the State Department preferred not to acknowledge. Defying political labels, Beals remained an independent critic of authoritarian rule and an activist against imperialism in all of its manifestations. *The Coming Struggle for Latin America* was translated into Spanish and published in Chile in 1942.

Our good-neighbor policy rests in great part upon certain falsehoods, misconceptions, and non-existent conditions. Some of these are:

1. *The belief that the Western Hemisphere is a unity, that all countries in it have identical interests, merely because they are in the same part of the world.* Does France have the same policy as Germany? They have different policies, in part, precisely because they are neighbors. . . .

2. *The belief that the Western Hemisphere is a brotherhood of democracies in contrast to the evil dictatorships of Europe.* Governments to the south have rarely represented the people less than at present. Some are worse tyrannies than any in Europe, their danger limited merely by their relative weakness in the world scene. . . . The complexion of the various governments differs widely. But it is pure cocaine-dope to argue that democracy exists in the Western Hemisphere or even the larger part of it. Few of its governments have the slightest basis in democracy. . . .

3. *The belief that the Western nations are peace-loving as opposed to the war-thirsty nations of Europe.* Recent wars and recent international injustices have shaken the southern continent time and again. . . . Even while Roosevelt was uttering these wrong platitudes, Dictator Trujillo, in the Dominican Republic, was

Source: Carleton Beals. *The Coming Struggle for Latin America*, pp. 299–316. New York: Halcyon House, 1938.

butchering 12,000 peaceable Haitians—men, women, children and babes. Nicaragua and Honduras almost went to war over a postage stamp. Other troubles were brewing and are still brewing along with new ones. Never before have the southern countries put out so much on armaments. . . .

4. *We are showing friendship to the governments, not to the people of Latin America.* We are helping to support tyrannies of the same brutal sort as those we cry out against in Europe. It is perhaps no business of the United States, though we have often made it our business, what kind of governments South America may have. But certainly we do not need to scrape and bow to governments which are the shame of the continents, to send them money, offer to lend them battleships, sell them armaments, send them naval missions to help them keep down the people. We are playing the game with petty brutal minorities temporarily in power rather than with the people of Latin America. . . . If the oppressed people of Latin America could speak at this moment—their newspapers, their political rights, their means of expression are everywhere suppressed—they would cry out a mighty protest at the falseness of our good-will protestations; a mighty curse against us would rise up from many parts of the two continents.

5. *Our belief Latin America loves us because we are now friendly instead of aggressive, that whenever we wish it, Latin America should be glad to love us.* Latin America's interests are today varied and international. Only by force or political and economic pressure does she bow specifically to our will. The southern folk consider us, as we do them in our more sober moments, as foreigners to whom they owe nothing except for value received. . . .

Latin Americans feel that since their countries gained independence, they have been more endangered by the United States than any other power. . . .

The Latin-American countries are under no obligation to be "democratic," to trade exclusively with us, to follow our political pattern, to follow our foreign policy rather than their own. They are not obliged to think of any interests except their own. It is for them to decide whether they want Japanese or German goods instead of ours. In fact the competition of the various powers greatly benefits them. . . .

6. *The belief that, as Admiral Leahy stated, we have to have a navy to protect the whole continent and uphold the Monroe Doctrine. . . .* The Monroe Doctrine has never been accepted in principle by Latin-American nations. For us it is a totem pole to dance around. In Hispanic America it is considered a collar of servitude. . . . The nations of the south, on the way to standing on their own feet, resent our paternalism, resent our acting as spokesman for two continents. . . .

1. *Our government should at once get out of the propaganda business in foreign lands.* The Latin-American countries, to the extent that they restrict foreign government propaganda, should also restrict ours. . . .

2. *Our government should quit helping out in the dirty armament business.* The arms thus sold are likely, one of these fair days, to kill our own citizens. We

have no assurances that the battleships we have sold to Brazil, the planes we have sold to Argentina, the munitions we have sold to Perú, will not eventually be turned against us. . . .

3. *We should at once recall our naval and army missions home from Brazil and Perú and Guatemala, our air mission home from Argentina.* They have no proper business there. They are helping unpopular governments, which means that they stand against the people. They are helping our munitions venders. They are helping oppress the peoples of those countries.

4. *We should get rid of our official language of patronizing condescension and superiority.* . . . Mr. Roosevelt recently spoke in the name of all the twenty-one countries of the Western Hemisphere. By what right? By what authorization? However lofty his sentiments, he should know that Latin-American countries secretly or openly resent such paternalism. . . .

The only possibility for sound American influence in Latin America is to stand squarely with the democratic and progressive forces of those countries. We can gain nothing by imitating the political tactics of the Fascist powers, though we might learn something in the field of economics. . . .

In the long run we will gain by the downfall of feudal regimes in Latin America, whatever the temporary loss to American property. We will gain by such economic strengthening of the Latin-American countries. We will gain by progressive measures to raise the standards of the people, the large majority of whom are not now purchasers of world goods but who can be converted into one of the largest mass markets in the world. . . .

In Latin America we are not supporting the forces of democracy and freedom any more than we are in Spain. We are actively supporting Fascist trends, under the noble cloak of brave words about freedom, democracy and international justice. Those sleek words no longer have meaning in connection with our actual policy. We are merely playing a conventional game of power politics on the southern continent. Would we play it better if we weren't such arrant hypocrites?

1940

Marketing Pan-Americanism

The U.S. Office of the Coordinator of Inter-American Affairs

After the start of the war in Europe in 1939, the Roosevelt administration began taking steps to counter Axis propaganda and subversion in Latin America. On August 1, 1940, President Roosevelt created the Office for Coordination of Commercial and Cultural Relations between the American Republics and appointed thirty-two-year-old Nelson A. Rockefeller to direct it. It was shortly renamed the Office of Coordinator of Inter-American Affairs (OCIAA, or CIAA), and in the first two years of its existence its annual budget rose tenfold, from $3.5 million to $38 million. The purpose of the OCIAA was to foster Pan-American sentiment in Latin America while countering the growth of the Axis countries' cultural and commercial ties with the region. Among the initiatives of the OCIAA were a commodities purchase program; public works, health and sanitation projects; training and educational exchanges; media subsidies and news dissemination; and the development of closer ties between Hollywood and the nascent film industries in Mexico and Brazil. The following excerpt from the agency's official history deals with its Motion Picture Division, which was headed by John Hay Whitney (1904–82), a major movie-industry investor. The OCIAA was abolished on May 20, 1946, but many of its cultural and propaganda activities were later assumed by the United States Information Agency, established in 1953.

The Motion Picture Division of CIAA was organized to employ motion pictures as one of the three main media in its information program. In all probability motion pictures, particularly those originating in the United States, provided the most direct approach to the widest audience in the hemisphere, with this being particularly true in the other American republics because of the high rate of illiteracy. In addition, motion picture activities were in a favorable position from the start, for while Axis films presented some competition, in general the technical excellence of those prepared in the United States gave them a definite advantage. Motion picture operations of the agency were to be

Source: U.S. Office of Inter-American Affairs. *History of the Office of the Coordinator of Inter-American Affairs*, pp. 67–82. Washington, D.C.: GPO, 1947.

likewise exceptionally successful because of a high degree of cooperation on the part of the industry. It was also to be a medium very useful in furthering other aspects of the CIAA program, for films dealing with health and sanitation activities were widely used both as a means of popular education and for training purposes. The education divisions of CIAA also utilized motion pictures as a tool. Finally, it was just as successful in the propaganda field. . . .

The first need of the Division upon its inception in 1940 was the establishment of a plan of operation and Mr. Whitney, like Mr. Francisco for radio, made a trip to the field to survey possibilities. By January 1941, the agency had organized its program. . . . A number of Hollywood committees representative of the producers, stars, writers, and directors, who had agreed to cooperate in carrying out the program, were listed; those mentioned were an Executive Committee, one on Visits to South America, another on South American Film Facilities, another on Short Subjects, another on Art Direction, one on Story Material, and one representing the Academy of Motion Picture Arts and Sciences. Plans which were being developed at the time covered such activities as the encouragement of feature films involving Central and South American themes, such as "The Life of Simon Bolivar," "The Road to Rio," and "Blood and Sand." It was hoped also that certain pictures scheduled for production in the near future might be photographed at least in part in Latin America. It was also the plan of the industry to send a number of its leading performers to the other American republics to appear personally at premieres. Another part of the plan involved increased newsreel coverage of events of significance in Latin America. . . .

The Motion Picture Division continued with its orderly plan for increased production of materials dealing with Latin America, and with the coming of war, in common with the other information divisions, laid great emphasis upon subjects connected with the war effort. A summary of objectives as they had developed by 1943 is of interest. The most important specific objectives named were the following:

1. An increase in United States production of feature pictures, short subjects and newsreels about the United States and the other Americas for distribution throughout the Hemisphere;

2. Producing and stimulating the production of pictures in the other Americas, particularly short subjects and newsreels, that could be exhibited effectively in the United States;

3. Eliminating Axis-sponsored and produced pictures from exhibition throughout the Hemisphere;

4. Inducing the motion picture industry voluntarily to refrain from producing and/or distributing in the other Americas pictures that are objectionable in whole or in part; and

5. Persuading producers that it is unwise to distribute in the other Americas pictures that create a bad impression of the United States and our way of life.

. . . The Motion Picture Division also claimed credit for a great increase in the number of feature pictures based on Latin American themes or of particular interest to Latin Americans; in 1943 it was noted that since the inception of the Division in October 1940, about thirty feature pictures on Latin American subjects had been released. These and many other pictures contained Latin American sequences for which CIAA had responsibility. Another area in which the Division was active was the attempt to drive Axis-produced and sponsored pictures from possible distribution and exhibition throughout the hemisphere. This was carried out through the cooperation of United States distributors operating in the other Americas, and by aid from the producers of film and equipment. . . .

An additional field in which the Motion Picture Division was interested was the production of short subjects, prepared on Latin American themes, or those of particular value in regard to United States relations with the other American republics. As early as November 1941, "all major companies accepted commitments to produce a minimum of 24 hemisphere shorts for theatrical release in addition to specially designed travelogues." By 1943 some 61 such shorts had been produced and released at the request of CIAA, without cost to it. Included in the group were such films as "Viva Mexico," "Highway to Friendship," "Gaucho Sports," "Madero of Mexico," "Der Fuehrer's Face," "Cuba, Land of Romance and Adventure," and "Price of Victory."

The Motion Picture Division supplied ideas and story material on Latin American themes to the industry whenever possible. In addition, they were behind many more ambitious projects designed to produce important features and short subjects for distribution. . . .

The Motion Picture Division also worked in close cooperation with the Walt Disney Studios, since the cartoon medium utilized by Mr. Disney was held to be one of the most effective in the field. In 1941 CIAA financed a trip by Mr. Disney and a staff of assistants to the other American republics, with the purpose of affording an opportunity to gain background for a picture or pictures later on. In addition, it served as a good-will tour since the Disney cartoons were extremely popular in the other American republics. Following his return, Mr. Disney completed one feature and several short subjects inspired by the trip. In succeeding years, to further augment its program and to take advantage of the Disney method of visual presentation, CIAA entered into additional contracts with the Walt Disney Studios, Inc., for research on and the production of a series of educational and propaganda films to be distributed throughout the hemisphere. Several of these were designed to further the programs of other divisions of the Office, particularly in the fields of health and sanitation, food supply, and education. . . .

❖

NO. 61

1942

Confronting the Fascist Threat

The Delegates to the Third Meeting of Ministers of Foreign Affairs of the American Republics

Two days after Japan attacked the U.S. Pacific fleet at Pearl Harbor, Hawaii, the United States called for a meeting of foreign ministers of the American republics. By the time the meeting took place in Rio de Janeiro from January 15 to 28, 1942, nine Central American and Caribbean countries (in addition to the United States) had declared war on the Axis powers (Germany, Japan and Italy). Of the eleven other hemispheric republics that had not yet become belligerents, three of them—Colombia, Mexico and Venezuela—had broken diplomatic relations with the Axis. The U.S. objective at the Rio meeting was to persuade the foreign ministers to adopt a resolution requiring all the American republics to sever diplomatic relations with the Axis. The resistance of Argentina and Chile led to a compromise resolution that merely recommended a break in relations. A number of other resolutions encouraged inter-American economic and military collaboration against fascism, foreshadowing similar measures that would be directed against communism during the Cold War.

As a result of its deliberations the Third Meeting of Ministers of Foreign Affairs of the American Republics approved the following conclusions:

1. Breaking of Diplomatic Relations

The American Republics reaffirm their declaration to consider any act of aggression on the part of a non-American State against one of them as an act of aggression against all of them, constituting as it does an immediate threat to the liberty and independence of America.

The American Republics reaffirm their complete solidarity and their deter-

Source: *The Department of State Bulletin.* Vol. 6, No. 137 (Publication 1696), 7 February 1942. Third Meeting of Ministers of Foreign Affairs of the American Republics, pp. 117–41. Washington, D.C.: GPO, 1942.

mination to cooperate jointly for their mutual protection until the effects of the present aggression against the Continent have disappeared.

The American Republics, in accordance with the procedures established by their own laws and in conformity with the position and circumstances obtaining in each country in the existing continental conflict, recommend the breaking of their diplomatic relations with Japan, Germany and Italy, since the first-mentioned State attacked and the other two declared war on an American country.

Finally, the American Republics declare that, prior to the reestablishment of the relations referred to in the preceding paragraph, they will consult among themselves in order that their action may have a solidary character. . . .

2. Production of Strategic Materials

The . . . Meeting . . . recommends:

1. That, as a practical expression of continental solidarity, an economic mobilization of the American Republics be effected, with a view to assuring to the countries of this Hemisphere, and particularly to those at war, an adequate supply of basic and strategic materials in the shortest possible time.

2. That such mobilization include mining, agricultural, industrial and commercial activities related to the supply not only of materials for strictly military use but also of products essential for civilian needs.

3. That full recognition be given to the imperative character and extreme urgency of the existing situation when formulating measures necessary to effect economic mobilization.

4. That the mobilization include measures to stimulate production and other measures designed to eliminate or minimize administrative formalities and the regulations and restrictions which impede the production and free flow of basic and strategic materials. . . .

3. Maintenance of the Internal Economy of the American Countries

The . . . Meeting . . . resolves:

1. To recommend to the nations which produce raw materials, industrial machinery and articles essential for the maintenance of the domestic economies of the consuming countries that they do everything possible to supply articles and products in quantities sufficient to prevent a scarcity thereof. . . .

2. To recommend that all the nations of this continent have access, with the greatest possible degree of equality, to inter-American commerce and to the raw materials which they require for satisfactory and prosperous development of their respective economies, provided, however, that they shall give preferential treatment to the nations at war for equal access to materials essential to their defense. . . .

4. Mobilization of Transportation Facilities

The . . . Meeting . . . resolves:

1. To recommend to the Governments of the American Republics:

(a) That they adopt immediately, in so far as possible, adequate measures to expand and improve all the communications systems of importance to continental defense and to the development of commerce between the American nations;

(b) That they make every effort consistent with national or continental defense fully to utilize and develop their respective internal transportation facilities in order to assure the rapid delivery of those goods which are essential to the maintenance of their respective economies. . . .

5. Severance of Commercial and Financial Relations

The . . . Meeting . . . recommends:

That the Governments of the American Republics, in a manner consistent with the usual practices and the legislation of the respective countries, adopt immediately:

(a) Any additional measures necessary to cut off for the duration of the present Hemispheric emergency all commercial and financial intercourse, direct or indirect, between the Western Hemisphere and the nations signatory to the Tripartite Pact and the territories dominated by them;

(b) Measures to eliminate all other financial and commercial activities prejudicial to the welfare and security of the American Republics, measures which shall have, among others, the following purposes: . . .

To supervise and control all commercial and financial transactions within the American Republics by nationals of the states signatory to the Tripartite Pact, or of the territories dominated by them, who are resident within the American Republics, and prevent all transactions of whatsoever nature which are inimical to the security of Western Hemisphere.

Whenever a government of an American republic considers it desirable . . . the properties, interests, and enterprises of such states and nationals which exist within its jurisdiction, may be placed in trust or subjected to permanent administrative intervention for purposes of control; moreover, such government of an American Republic may resort to sales to its nationals. . . .

17. Subversive Activities

The . . . Meeting . . . resolves . . . .

To recommend to the Governments of American Republics the adoption of . . . legislative measures tending to prevent or punish as crimes, acts against the democratic institutions of the States of the Continent in the same manner as attempts against the integrity, independence or sovereignty of any one of them; and that the Governments of the American Republics maintain and expand their systems of surveillance designed to prevent subversive activities of nationals of non-American countries, as individuals or groups of individuals, that originate in or are directed from a foreign country and are intended to interfere with or limit the efforts of the American Republics individually or collectively to preserve their integrity and independence. . . .

19. Coordination of the Systems of Investigation

The . . . Meeting . . . resolves:

That the Governments of the American Republics shall coordinate their national intelligence and investigation services, providing adequate personnel for the inter-American interchange of information, investigations and suggestions for the prevention, repression, punishment and elimination of such activities as espionage, sabotage and subversive incitement which endanger the safety of the American Nations. . . .

❖

NO. 62

1942

The Bracero Program

The Governments of Mexico and the United States

A shortage of unskilled labor during World War II prompted the United States to negotiate an agreement with Mexico under which Mexican workers and their families would be admitted to work temporarily in the United States, mainly on farms and railroads. The purpose was to free U.S. workers for military service. The first of a series of "bracero" (laborer) agreements was signed on July 23, 1942, and led to the employment of tens of thousands of Mexicans. Discriminatory treatment and acts of violence against Mexicans increased during the war, however, leading the Mexican government to prohibit braceros from work-

Source: U.S. Department of State. *Treaties and Other International Agreements of the United States of America 1776–1949*. Vol. 9, compiled by Charles I. Bevans, pp. 1069–75. Department of State Publication 8615. Washington, D.C.: GPO, 1972.

ing in Texas from 1943 to 1947. After the war, the program was extended and its original provisions amended under a variety of official arrangments until it was finally terminated in 1964.

In order to effect a satisfactory arrangement whereby Mexican agricultural labor may be made available for use in the United States and at the same time provide means whereby this labor will be adequately protected while out of Mexico, the following general provisions are suggested:

1) It is understood that Mexicans contracting to work in the United States shall not be engaged in any military service.

2) Mexicans entering the United States as a result of this understanding shall not suffer discriminatory acts of any kind in accordance with the Executive Order No. 8802 issued at the White House June 25, 1941.

3) Mexicans entering the United States under this understanding shall enjoy the guarantees of transportation, living expenses and repatriation established in Article 29 of the Mexican Labor Law.

4) Mexicans entering the United States under this understanding shall not be employed to displace other workers, or for the purpose of reducing rates of pay previously established.

In order to implement the application of the general principles mentioned above the following specific clauses are established.

(When the word "employer" is used hereinafter it shall be understood to mean the Farm Security Administration of the Department of Agriculture of the United States of America; the word "sub-employer" shall mean the owner or operator of the farm or farms in the United States on which the Mexican will be employed; the word "worker" hereinafter used shall refer to the Mexican farm laborer entering the United States under this understanding.)

Contracts

a. Contracts will be made between the employer and the worker under the supervision of the Mexican Government. (Contracts must be written in Spanish.)

b. The employer shall enter into a contract with the sub-employer, with a view to proper observance of the principles embodied in this understanding. . . .

Transportation

All transportation and living expenses from the place of origin to destination, and return, as well as expenses incurred in the fulfillment of any requirements of a migratory nature shall be met by the employer. . . .

Wages and Employment

a. (1) Wages to be paid the worker shall be the same as those for similar work to other agricultural laborers in the respective regions of destination; but in no case shall this wage be less than 30 cents per hour (U.S. currency); piece rates shall be so set as to enable the worker of average ability to earn the prevailing wage.

a. (2) On the basis of prior authorization from the Mexican Government salaries lower than those established in the previous clause may be paid those emigrants admitted into the United States as members of the family of the worker under contract and who, when they are in the field, are able also to become agricultural laborers but who, by their condition of age or sex, cannot carry out the average amount of ordinary work. . . .

d. Work for minors under 14 years shall be strictly prohibited, and they shall have the same schooling opportunities as those enjoyed by children of other agricultural laborers. . . .

f. Housing conditions, sanitary and medical services enjoyed by workers admitted under this understanding shall be identical to those enjoyed by the other agricultural workers in the same localities.

g. Workers admitted under this understanding shall enjoy as regards occupational diseases and accidents the same guarantees enjoyed by other agricultural workers under United States legislation. . . .

i. For such time as they are unemployed under a period equal to 75% of the period (exclusive of Sundays) for which the workers have been contracted they shall receive a subsistence allowance at the rate of $3.00 per day. For the remaining 25% of the period for which the workers have been contracted during which the workers may be unemployed they shall receive subsistence on the same bases that are established for farm laborers in the United States. . . .

k. At the expiration of the contract under this understanding, and if the same is not renewed, the authorities of the United States shall consider illegal, from an immigration point of view, the continued stay of the worker in the territory of the United States, exception made of cases of physical impossibility. . . .

Mexico City, the 23rd of July 1942. [Entered into force August 4, 1942]

1943

A Historian Defends U.S. Policy

Samuel Flagg Bemis

Often referred to as the "dean" of diplomatic historians and particularly of the history of U.S.-Latin American relations, Samuel Flagg Bemis (1891–1973) was a professor at Yale University from 1935 until his retirement in 1960. Though he was considered a pioneer in the methodology of multiarchival research, his work was later criticized for being overly nationalistic. As an isolationist until the United States entered World War II, Bemis later became a strong partisan of the U.S. policy of containment and was resolutely hostile to the Cuban Revolution of 1959. Excerpted below are the conclusions of his *The Latin American Policy of the United States* (1943), perhaps Bemis's most widely known work. The book was reprinted in four editions and served as a standard textbook for undergraduate courses on U.S.–Latin American relations for many years.

From the Era of Emancipation to the Second World War, the Latin American policy of the United States has reflected constantly the vital necessities of national security and idealism of the American people. Of these two elements, national security has always been uppermost. It is natural and understandable that this should be so, for without national security there could be no American idealism, no so-called "American mission." . . .

The very existence of the Continental Republic created a bulwark against imperialism in the Western Hemisphere. It made possible a power capable of protecting the republican New World against the imperialism of the Old in today's great time of trial. Had it not been for the development of the Continental Republic and the preservation of its united nationhood, North America would have been South-Americanized, so to speak, divided up into a number of small and feeble independent states that would be easy prey to any aggression from Europe or Asia. . . .

That the United States has been an imperialistic power since 1898 there is

Source: Excerpt from *The Latin American Policy of the United States: An Historical Interpretation*, pp. 384–393. Copyright 1943 and renewed 1973 by Samuel Flagg Bemis, reprinted by permission of Harcourt Brace & Company.

no doubt, although that comparatively mild imperialism was tapered off after 1921 and is fully liquidated now. A careful and conscientious appraisal of United States imperialism shows, I am convinced, that it was never deep-rooted in the character of the people, that it was essentially a protective imperialism, designed to protect, first the security of the Continental Republic, next the security of the entire New World, against intervention by the imperialistic powers of the Old World. It was, if you will, an imperialism against imperialism. It did not last long and it was not really bad. . . .

On the Isthmian question, on the Panama Canal, was based the strategic imperialism of the first two decades of the twentieth century. Without the existence of the Panama Canal under the unchallengeable control of the United States there would be no strength in the solidarity of the Union of American Republics. It would be a limp and flaccid organization. . . . Any President who had frustrated the Manifest Destiny of continental expansion, any President who had permitted an intrusion of European power in the Caribbean to neutralize the effectiveness of the Panama Canal, would not have deserved well of his country, indeed would not have deserved well of the New World, or of humanity today.

This picture does not justify the methods by which Theodore Roosevelt "took" the Canal Zone. . . . It was an act for which reparation has since been paid, and we may hope that the rancor that it caused lies wholly buried today in the grave of the rough-riding statesman who was responsible for it. The canal itself was and is an indispensable necessity to the defense and liberty of the New World as well as of the United States, and to the liberation of the United Nations today. . . .

Today the gyroscope of Pan Americanism is the Good Neighbor Policy. The fundamentals of that policy are the Doctrine of Nonintervention and the Monroe Doctrine, including the No-Transfer principle. Thus developed and formulated, the Latin American policy of the United States has become identified in our times with the security of the whole Western Hemisphere. It has built up the policy of one for all and all for one which so promptly met its supreme test in the Second World War. It has been further baptized and galvanized by the American mission.

Although national and continental (in the hemispheric sense of the word) security is the real watchword of the Latin American policy of the United States today, there is more to it than that. From the beginning it has had an ideological and missionary background, originally derived from Protestant Christianity, now resting also on the gospel of progress. The political reflection of this was popular sovereignty and republican government as opposed to monarchy and totalitarianism. It has received a missionary impulse to save peoples not only from political tyranny, but also from political instability, from ignorance, from disease, from poverty, all of which the Latin American countries have possessed in varying measure. In the past missionary endeavor has not served to curb imperialism or political intervention; on the contrary. Today it has inspired the Good Neighbor of the North, working loyally within the diplomatic framework of Pan American collaboration, to fortify the political independence and territorial integrity of the nations of the New World by increasing their economic and sociological *well-being* in order to further a *general advance in civilization.* . . .

❖

NO. 64

1944

"Rum and Coca-Cola"

Lionel Belasco and others

During the Second World War, the Andrews Sisters (Laverne, Maxene and Patti) were ubiquitous on Armed Forces Radio and often joined with Bing Crosby and Bob Hope to perform at U.S. military bases around the globe. They also appeared in several Hollywood films, including *Argentine Nights* (1940) and *Hollywood Canteen* (1944). On October 18, 1944, the Andrews Sisters recorded the song "Rum and Coca-Cola," an immediate hit that sold 200,000 records and credited three Americans as the composers: the comedian Morey Amsterdam, the singer Jeri Sullavan and Paul Baron, an executive at the Columbia Broadcasting Co. In 1947, a U.S. District Court judge ruled that the three had plagiarized the music from a song actually written by Lionel Belasco of Trinidad as "L'Année Passée" in 1906. Lord Invader, a Trinidadian calypso singer, won a separate suit against the publisher of "Rum & Coca Cola" in 1950 on the grounds that the three Americans had stolen the words of the song, including its title, from him. The Andrews Sisters' plagiarized version is reprinted below, followed by Lord Invader's version.

Source: *Rum and Coca-Cola*, by Jeri Sullavan, Paul Baron, Morey Amsterdam, with additional lyrics by Al Stillman. © 1944 (Renewed) EMI Feist Catalog Inc. All rights reserved. Used by permission Warner Bros. Publications U.S. Inc., Miami FL 33014. Lyrics by Lord Invader are from a private tape recorded by John Bessor of Washington, D.C., tape number 3C1, Library of Congress, AFS 12,303 LW0-4395, recorded in Invader's Calypso Club, Port of Spain, Trinidad, March 16, 1950, cited by Donald R. Hill, *Calypso Calaloo: Early Carnival Music in Trinidad*, pp. 239–40. Gainesville: University Press of Florida, 1993.

ANDREWS SISTERS' VERSION

If you ever go down Trinidad
They make you feel so very glad
Calypso sing and make up rhyme
Guarantee you one real good fine time

[Chorus:]
Drinkin' rum and Coca-Cola
Go down Point Koomahnah
Both mother and daughter
Workin' for the Yankee dollar

Oh, beat it man, beat it

If a Yankee comes to Trinidad
They got the young girls all goin' mad
Young girls say they treat 'em nice
Make Trinidad like paradise

[Chorus]

Oh, you vex me, you vex me

From Chicachicaree to Mona's Isle
Native girls all dance and smile
Help soldier celebrate his leave
Makes every day like New Year's Eve

[Chorus]

It's a fact, man, it's a fact

In old Trinidad, I also fear
The situation is mighty queer
Like the Yankee girls, and native swoon
When she hear der Bingo croon

[Chorus]

Out on Manzanella Beach
G.I. romance with native peach
All night long, make tropic love
Next day, sit in hot sun and cool off

[Chorus]

It's a fact, man, it's a fact

Rum and Coca-Cola
Rum and Coca-Cola
Workin' for the Yankee dollar

LORD INVADER'S VERSION

When the Yankees first came to Trinidad
Some of the young girls were more than glad
They said that the Yankees treat them nice
And they give them a better price
[Spoken:] "They buy"

[Chorus:]
Rum and Coca cola
Go down Point Cumana
Both mothers and daughters
Working for the Yankee dollar

I had a little girlfriend the other day
But her mother came and took her away
Self, her mother, and her sisters
Went in a cab with some soldiers
[Spoken:] "They bought"

I know a couple who got married one afternoon
And was to fly to Miami on their honeymoon
But the bride run away with a soldier lad
And the stupid husband went staring mad
[Spoken:] "They bought"

They have some aristos in Port of Spain
I know a lot but I wouldn't call name
And indicate, they wouldn't give you a ride
Well you can see them with the foreigners in the night
[Spoken:] "Drinking"

Mr. Hal Morrow I want you to know
And if you do appreciate this calypso
You have some people there in your company
I sure they appreciate the melody
[Spoken:] "Singing"

I wonder what is your interested opinion
We haven't got no bad speaking Trinidadian
We never said, "Caca cola" [refers to Amsterdam's song
    as recorded by the Andrews Sisters]
Neither did we say, "Yankee dallah"
[Spoken:] "We sang"

[The following verse is extemporaneous, by Lord Invader in 1950.]
Now gentleman I want you to know
It seem as you love this calypso
But I tell you very flat
You look like an American diplomat
[Spoken:] "Singing"

❖

NO. 65

1945

The Act of Chapultepec

The Delegates to the Inter-American Conference on Problems of War and Peace

As World War II slowly drew to a close in 1944 and 1945, and the threat of a common enemy to the Americas receded, tensions between the United States and the Latin American governments rose closer to the surface. The Latin Americans were increasingly concerned about the shape of postwar economic relations with the United States and the implications for the region of the U.S. commitment to founding a new world organization, the United Nations. Under pressure from the Latin American nations, Washington agreed in December 1944 to consult with them in Mexico City, from February 21 to March 8, 1945. The

Source: U.S. Department of State. *Treaties and Other International Agreements of the United States of America 1776–1949.* Compiled by Charles I. Bevans. Vol. 3, Multilateral, 1931–45, pp. 1024–27. Department of State Publication No. 8484. Washington, D.C.: GPO, 1969.

single most important resolution adopted at the meeting was known as the Act of Chapultepec, after the building that housed the meeting, a historic castle of the same name. The act was the first major step toward a regional security system, and called for the negotiation of a formal security treaty after World War II. Part 3 of the act was intended to reconcile the potential conflict that these security measures and recommendations might have posed with the plans for the United Nations.

Inter-American Reciprocal Assistance and Solidarity (Act of Chapultepec)

Whereas:

. . . The new situation in the world makes more imperative than ever the union and solidarity of the American peoples, for the defense of their rights and the maintenance of international peace. . . .

The security and solidarity of the Continent are affected to the same extent by an act of aggression against any of the American States by a non-American State, as by an act of aggression of an American State against one or more American States;

Part 1

The Governments Represented at the Inter-American Conference on Problems of War and Peace

Declare:

1. That all sovereign States are juridically equal among themselves.

2. That every State has the right to the respect of its individuality and independence, on the part of the other members of the international community.

3. That every attack of a State against the integrity or the inviolability of the territory, or against the sovereignty or political independence of an American State, shall, conformably to Part 3 hereof, be considered as an act of aggression against the other States which sign this Act. In any case invasion by armed forces of one State into the territory of another trespassing boundaries established by treaty and demarcated in accordance therewith shall constitute an act of aggression.

4. That in case acts of aggression occur or there are reasons to believe that an aggression is being prepared by any other State against the integrity or inviolability of the territory, or against the sovereignty or political independence of an American State, the States signatory to this Act will consult among themselves in order to agree upon the measures it may be advisable to take. . . .

Part 2

The Inter-American Conference on Problems of War and Peace Recommends:

That for the purpose of meeting threats or acts of aggression against any American Republic following the establishment of peace, the Governments of the American Republics consider the conclusion, in accordance with their constitutional processes, of a treaty establishing procedures whereby such threats or acts may be met by the use, by all or some of the signatories of said treaty, of any one or more of the following measures: recall of chiefs of diplomatic missions; breaking of diplomatic relations; breaking of consular relations; breaking of postal, telegraphic, telephonic, radio-telephonic relations; interruption of economic, commercial and financial relations; use of armed force to prevent or repel aggression.

Part 3

The above Declaration and Recommendation constitute a regional arrangement for dealing with such matters relating to the maintenance of international peace and security as are appropriate for regional action in this Hemisphere. The said arrangement, and the pertinent activities and procedures, shall be consistent with the purposes and principles of the general international organization, when established.

This agreement shall be known as the "Act of Chapultepec." [The final act of the Inter-American Conference on Problems of War and Peace was signed on March 8, 1945, by delegates representing Argentina, Bolivia, Brazil, Chile, Colombia, Costa Rica, Cuba, the Dominican Republic, Ecuador, El Salvador, Guatemala, Haiti, Honduras, Mexico, Nicaragua, Panama, Paraguay, Peru, the United States, Uruguay and Venezuela.]

1946

The Blue Book on Argentina (Braden Report)

Spruille Braden and the U.S. State Department

Argentina's neutrality during most of World War II infuriated Washington. Under pressure from the United States, Argentina finally broke relations with Germany and Japan in January 1944. When the Argentine military sought to increase its control of the government a month later by appointing Gen. Edelmiro J. Farrell as president, Washington refused to recognize the regime and froze Argentine assets in the United States. Despite Argentina's belated declaration of war on Germany and Japan in March 1945, the United States and its ambassdor, Spruille Braden, continued to try to force a change in government. The strongest figure in that government was Colonel Juan Perón, who used his power as Argentina's labor minister to consolidate his position, making him the likely winner of the presidential elections scheduled for February 1946. Braden, who was promoted to assistant secretary of state for Latin America in August 1945, was a bitter opponent of Perón. In order to weaken Perón and the military junta, Braden initiated the publication of a State Department "Blue Book" or formal policy statement denouncing Argentina's role during the war. The booklet, excerpted below, was released just two weeks before the Argentine elections. Despite its title (*Consultation Among the American Republics with Respect to the Argentine Situation*), there had been no "consultation" with the other governments of the hemisphere. Adopting the campaign slogan "Braden or Perón?" Perón won the election and handed the United States a stinging diplomatic defeat.

On October 3, 1945 the Department of State initiated consultation among the American republics with respect to the Argentine situation. All of the other American republics agreed to participate in this consultation.

During the intervening period, this Government has made a careful study and evaluation of all the information in its possession with regard to Argentina. An enormous volume of documents of the defeated enemy, in many cases

Source: U.S. Department of State. *Consultation Among the American Republics with Respect to the Argentine Situation; Memorandum of the United States Government, February 11, 1946.* Publication 2473, Inter-American Series 29. Washington, D.C.: GPO, 1946.

found only with much difficulty and after prolonged search, have now been studied and verified. German and Italian officials charged with responsibility for activities in and with Argentina have been interrogated. Although this work of investigation continues, the Government of the United States at present has information which establishes that:

1. Members of the military government collaborated with enemy agents for important espionage and other purposes damaging to the war effort of the United Nations.

2. Nazi leaders, groups and organization have combined with Argentine totalitarian groups to create a Nazi-Fascist state.

3. Members of the military regime who have controlled the government since June, 1943 conspired with the enemy to undermine governments in neighboring countries in order to destroy their collaboration with the Allies and in an effort to align them in a pro-Axis bloc.

4. Successive Argentine governments protected the enemy in economic matters in order to preserve Axis industrial and commercial power in Argentina.

5. Successive Argentine governments conspired with the enemy to obtain arms from Germany.

This information warrants the following conclusions:

1. The Castillo Government and still more the present military regime pursued a policy of positive aid to the enemy.

2. Solemn pledges to cooperate with the other American republics were completely breached and are proved to have been designed to protect and maintain Axis interests in Argentina.

3. The policies and actions of the recent regimes in Argentina were aimed at undermining the Inter-American System.

4. The totalitarian individuals and groups, both military and civilian, who control the present government in Argentina, have, with their Nazi collaborators, pursued a common aim: The creation in this Hemisphere of a totalitarian state. This aim has already been partly accomplished.

5. Increasingly since the invasion of Normandy, and most obviously since the failure of the last German counteroffensive in January, 1945, the military regime has had to resort to a defensive strategy of camouflage. The assumption of the obligations of the Inter-American Conference on Problems of War and Peace to wipe out Nazi influence and the repeated avowals of pro-democratic intentions proceeded from this strategy of deception.

6. By its brutal use of force and terrorist methods to strike down all opposition from the Argentine people the military regime has made a mockery of its pledge to the United Nations to "reaffirm faith in human rights, in the dignity and worth of the human person." . . .

The information in support of these charges is respectfully submitted to the Governments of the American republics for their consideration in relation to the Treaty of Mutual Assistance to be negotiated at the forthcoming conference at Rio de Janeiro.

By its terms the Act of Chapultepec lays the basis for a mutual assistance pact which will obligate the member governments to assist one another to meet an attack or a threat of aggression from any source whatsoever. . . . This implementation would require a close cooperation in the development of security plans of vital importance to every American republic. It would also require cooperation in the maintenance of adequate military establishments for the defense of the continent.

Such a defense structure can be built only on a foundation of absolute trust and confidence. Because the Government of the United States did not have such trust and confidence in the present Argentine regime, it took the position in October, 1945 that it could not properly sign a military assistance treaty with that regime.

It is submitted that the information transmitted to the Governments of the American republics in this memorandum makes abundantly clear a pattern which includes aid to the enemy, deliberate misrepresentation and deception in promises of Hemisphere cooperation, subversive activity against neighboring republics, and a vicious partnership of Nazi and native totalitarian forces. This pattern raises a deeper and more fundamental question than that of the adequacy of decrees and administrative measures allegedly enacted in compliance with Argentina's obligations under Resolution LIX of the Mexico Conference [at Chapultepec]. The question is whether the military regime, or any Argentine government controlled by the same elements, can merit the confidence and trust which is expressed in a treaty of mutual military assistance among the American republics.

❖

1946

Chilean Labor and U.S. Capital

U.S. Department of State

As the worldwide demand for copper wire and related products rose spectacularly with the growth of electrification in the early twentieth century, Chile's immense deposits of copper ore came under the control of two U.S. companies, the Anaconda Copper Co. and the Braden Copper Co.; the latter became part of Kennecott Copper Co. in 1915. At the same time, the Chilean economy's dependence on copper intensified markedly; after the 1920s, copper accounted for two-thirds or more of Chilean exports. In 1946, the companies and the U.S. government considered the miners' unions and the Chilean Communist Party's leading role in those unions to be the principal threats to U.S. security and economic interests in Chile. After the miners struck Kennecott's El Teniente mine in September 1946, the U.S. State Department and Kennecott pressured the Chilean government to curb the power of the unions and to eliminate communist influence in the government as well as in the unions. President Gabriel González Videla promised Kennecott a favorable decision on the issues dividing the company and the miners if the company agreed to let a Chilean court arbitrate the dispute. The court's procompany decision was rejected by the miners and led to further unrest at El Teniente. In 1947, González Videla sent the army into the copper mining districts, arresting union leaders and prominent Communists; the Communist Party was outlawed in 1948. As a result, Anaconda and Kennecott announced expansion plans, while the U.S. government and the World Bank offered Chile new loans. During this period, the U.S. assistant secretary of state for Latin America was Spruille Braden, whose father, William, had founded the Braden Copper Co. in 1904. Because the first document reprinted below is a cable, the sender used abbreviations and omitted some words.

Source: U.S. Department of State. *Foreign Relations of the United States 1946*. XI, *The American Republics*, pp. 604–09. Washington, D.C.: GPO, 1960.

ACTING SECRETARY OF STATE DEAN ACHESON TO AMBASSADOR BOWERS IN CHILE, 9 NOVEMBER 1946

[The State] Dept. has already informally pointed out to Chilean Chargé [in Chilean embassy in Washington] the embarrassing even untenable position in which this Govt. would be placed in considering Chile's request for further Eximbank loans and credits on Naval vessels at very time when proposed arbitrary settlement strike (described by [the Chilean foreign minister] himself as a Communist plot, which would have grave consequences Chilean economy unless challenged) was jeopardizing highly important US investment copper industry. It was made clear to Chargé Rodríguez that with all good will in world for Chile this Govt. might be bitterly criticized by press and Congress if it were alleged that at time when interests of thousands of Kennecott stock holders were endangered American Govt. had made additional loans to Chile. . . .

MEMORANDUM OF CONVERSATION. E. T. STANNARD, PRESIDENT, KENNECOTT COPPER CORP. AND SPRUILLE BRADEN, ASSISTANT SECRETARY OF STATE, AMONG OTHERS, AT THE STATE DEPARTMENT, WASHINGTON, 12 NOVEMBER 1946

President of Kennecott feels that cumulative concessions to Chilean Government's endeavoring to extricate itself from difficult political positions at the expense of the copper companies have placed Braden Copper Company in a tenuous economic position necessitating a clear-cut answer as to whether that Company will continue to be subject to such pressures; and inquires what further assistance can be expected from the Department, particularly in the event of intervention or expropriation by Chilean Government. In latter event, the Department will be requested to persuade European consumers that due consideration must be given the legitimate American interests in the producing company.

The purpose of Stannard's visit was to review the strike situation up to the moment; and to inquire what further advice and assistance the Department could offer, particularly in the event of Chilean Government intervention or expropriation. The great concern of the Company has to do with broad principles and long-range prospects. In terms of dollars and cents, their best estimate is that settlement of all 14 points on union terms would just about equal the $2–3,000,000 profit anticipated on this year's operations. . . . The whole history of the Company's relations with the Government in Chile has been one of continuous appeasement, one concession after another on taxes and special exchange rates, and of government pressure for political convenience on one issue after another. He feels strongly that the time has come to end appeasement and to face the issue squarely on its economic merits.

The present situation . . . is that President González Videla has given the

Company until 12 noon, today, to accept arbitration on all points. . . . Stannard is of the firm opinion that the Company should accept arbitration only on the wage demands, leaving the other demands, which the Company deems unconstitutional, for subsequent discussion, if necessary. He feels the Company is faced with a crisis, and he would like to know (1) what further advice the State Department can offer, and (2) what the Department proposes to do if the Chilean Government intervenes or expropriates. . . . Mr. Stannard inquired whether, if the Company agreed to arbitrate on all points and if the arbitration award substantially met the demands of the Communist union, the Department would use its influence to prevent the Chilean Government from drawing on credits established by the Eximbank.

MEMORANDUM OF CONVERSATION. MARIO RODRÍGUEZ, CHILEAN CHARGÉ D'ÁFFAIRES, AND SPRUILLE BRADEN, ASSISTANT SECRETARY OF STATE, AT THE STATE DEPARTMENT, WASHINGTON, 12 NOVEMBER 1946

Mr. Braden took advantage of the Chargé's call . . . to reiterate the Department's very serious concern with the El Teniente (Braden Copper Company) strike situation. . . . Mr. Braden impressed upon Señor Rodríguez the possible adverse effects on public opinion and Congress of precipitate action and subsequent settlement on terms that might prove tantamount to government intervention. In this connection, he mentioned that Kennecott's 90,000 stockholders are not without influence. Should the situation develop to the point of irrevocably damaging this U.S. private investment in Chile, the Department, the Eximbank, and the Government as a whole would be in a most embarrassing position for having simultaneously extended large loans to Chile.

We had taken great pains to demonstrate good will toward President Gonzalez Videla, this in spite of a feeling of uneasiness in certain quarters at the inclusion of Communists in the Chilean cabinet. Admittedly, the strike is Communist-directed, and is aimed at an American enterprise.

IV.
THE COLD WAR

NO. 68

1947 and 1954

A Charter for Covert Action?

The Congress of the United States and the Doolittle Committee

D uring the Cold War, covert action by the U.S. Central Intelligence Agency, both for and against foreign governments, political parties, labor unions and other groups and individuals, became an important instrument of U.S. foreign policy in Latin America. As many of the CIA's covert operations gradually were exposed to public knowledge in the 1970s, questions were asked about the authority of the agency to carry them out. Was the CIA limited merely to collecting, analyzing and distributing foreign intelligence? Or was it also empowered to undertake secret operations abroad? The debate over these questions often began by quoting what has served as the "charter" of the CIA: that section of the National Security Act, approved by Congress on July 26, 1947, that established the agency. The so-called "Fifth Function," as Sec. 102 (d)(5) became known, was interpreted by successive administrations as authorizing covert action. Further support for covert action was provided in 1954 by the Special Study Group, also known as the Doolittle Committee after its chairman, General James H. Doolittle. President Eisenhower appointed the four-man panel to study the covert activities of the CIA; the committee submitted its report, classified top secret, directly to the president on September 30, 1954. Declassified excerpts are reprinted below.

NATIONAL SECURITY ACT OF 1947

Central Intelligence Agency

Sec. 102.

(a) There is hereby established under the National Security Council a Central Intelligence Agency with a Director of Central Intelligence, who shall be

Sources: (1) U.S. *Statutes At Large . . . 1947 . . .* Vol. 61, Part I. Ch. 343, Section 102. Pp. 497–98. Washington, D.C.: GPO, 1948. (2) National Archives of the United States. Record Group 263, 190/24/34/5, "History Source Collection, Records Relating to the Doolittle & Hoover Investigation of the CIA, 1954–56, Box 1."

the head thereof. The Director shall be appointed by the President, by and with the advice and consent of the Senate, from among the commissioned officers of the armed services or from among individuals in civilian life. . . .

(d) For the purpose of coordinating the intelligence activities of the several Government departments and agencies in the interest of national security, it shall be the duty of the Agency, under the direction of the National Security Council—

(1) to advise the National Security Council in matters concerning such intelligence activities of the Government departments and agencies as relate to national security; (2) to make recommendations to the National Security Council for the coordination of such intelligence activities of the departments and agencies of the Government as relate to the national security; (3) to correlate and evaluate intelligence relating to the national security, and provide for the appropriate dissemination of such intelligence within the Government using where appropriate existing agencies and facilities: Provided, That the Agency shall have no police, subpoena, law-enforcement powers, or internal-security functions: . . . (4) to perform, for the benefit of the existing intelligence agencies, such additional services of common concern as the National Security Council determines can be more efficiently accomplished centrally; (5) to perform such other functions and duties related to intelligence affecting the national security as the National Security Council may from time to time direct. . . .

THE DOOLITTLE COMMITTEE REPORT OF 1954

The acquisition and proper evaluation of adequate and reliable intelligence on the capabilities and intentions of Soviet Russia is today's most important military and political requirement. Several agencies of Government and many thousands of capable and dedicated people are engaged in the accomplishment of this task. Because the United States is relatively new at the game, and because we are opposed by a police state enemy whose social discipline and whose security measures have been built up and maintained at a high level for many years, the usable information we are obtaining is still far short of our needs.

As long as it remains national policy, another important requirement is an aggressive covert psychological, political and paramilitary organization more effective, more unique and, if necessary, more ruthless than that employed by the enemy. No one should be permitted to stand in the way of the prompt, efficient and secure accomplishment of this mission.

In the carrying out of this policy and in order to reach minimal standards for national safety under present world conditions, two things must be done. First, the agencies charged by law with the collection, evaluation and distribution of intelligence must be strengthened and coordinated to the greatest practicable degree. This is a primary concern of the National Security Council and must be accomplished at the national policy level. Those elements of the problem that fall within the scope of our directive are dealt with in the report which follows. The second consideration is less tangible but equally important. It is now clear that we are facing an implacable enemy whose avowed objective is world domination by whatever means and at whatever cost. There are no rules in such a game. Hitherto acceptable norms of human conduct do not apply. If the United States is to survive, long-standing American concepts of "fair play" must be reconsidered. We must develop effective espionage and counterespionage services and must learn to subvert, sabotage and destroy our enemies by more clever, more sophisticated and more effective methods than those used against us. It may become necessary that the American people be made acquainted with, understand and support this fundamentally repugnant philosophy. . . .

❖

NO. 69

1947

The Rio Treaty

The Governments of the United States and Latin America

The Act of Chapultepec of 1945 (Document No. 65) committed the American states to negotiate a mutual security treaty, a task that was carried out two years later by delegates from the United States and nineteen Latin American countries at the Inter-American Conference for the Maintenance of Continental Peace and Security in Petropolis, Brazil, forty miles from Rio de Janeiro, from August 15 to September 2, 1947. The result was the Inter-American Treaty of Reciprocal Assistance, better known as the Rio Treaty. While it committed all the American states to share responsibility for the defense of the Western Hemisphere, the overwhelming military and industrial superiority of the United States made its government the principal influence in the maintenance of the treaty system and in determining what constituted aggression.

Source: U.S. Department of State. "Inter-American Treaty of Reciprocal Assistance," 2 September 1947. *Treaties and Other International Agreements of the United States of America 1776–1949*, vol. 4, pp. 559–66. Washington, D.C.: GPO, 1970.

In the name of their Peoples, the Governments represented at the Inter-American Conference for the Maintenance of Continental Peace and Security, desirous of consolidating and strengthening their relations of friendship and good neighborliness, and

Considering:

. . . That the High Contracting Parties reaffirm their adherence to the principles of inter-American solidarity and cooperation, and especially to those set forth in the preamble and declarations of the Act of Chapultepec, all of which should be understood to be accepted as standards of their mutual relations and as the juridical basis of the Inter-American System. . . .

That the American regional community affirms as a manifest truth that juridical organization is a necessary prerequisite of security and peace, and that peace is founded on justice and moral order and, consequently, on the international recognition and protection of human rights and freedoms, on the indispensable well-being of the people, and on the effectiveness of democracy for the international realization of justice and security,

Have resolved, in conformity with the objectives stated above, to conclude the following Treaty, in order to assure peace, through adequate means, to provide for effective reciprocal assistance to meet armed attacks against any American State, and in order to deal with threats of aggression against any of them:

ARTICLE 1. The High Contracting Parties formally condemn war and undertake in their international relations not to resort to the threat or the use of force in any manner inconsistent with the provisions of the Charter of the United Nations or of this Treaty.

ARTICLE 2. . . . [T]he High Contracting Parties undertake to submit every controversy which may arise between them to methods of peaceful settlement and to endeavor to settle any such controversy among themselves by means of the procedures in force in the Inter-American System before referring it to the General Assembly or the Security Council of the United Nations.

ARTICLE 3. The High Contracting Parties agree that an armed attack by any State against an American State shall be considered as an attack against all the American States and, consequently, each one of the said Contracting Parties undertakes to assist in meeting the attack in the exercise of the inherent right of individual or collective self-defense recognized by Article 51 of the Charter of the United Nations. . . .

ARTICLE 6. If the inviolability or the integrity of the territory or the sovereignty or political independence of any American State should be affected by an aggression which is not an armed attack or by an extra-continental or intra-continental conflict, or by any other fact or situation that might endanger the peace of America, the Organ of Consultation shall meet immediately in order to agree on the measures which must be taken in case of aggression to assist the victim of the aggression or, in any case, the measures which should be taken for the common defense and for the maintenance of the peace and security of the Continent.

ARTICLE 7. In the case of a conflict between two or more American States, without prejudice to the right of self-defense in conformity with Article 51 of the Charter of the United Nations, the High Contracting Parties, meeting in consultation shall call upon the contending States to suspend hostilities and re-store matters to the *status quo ante bellum,* and shall take in addition all other necessary measures to reestablish or maintain inter-American peace and secu-rity and for the solution of the conflict by peaceful means. . . .

ARTICLE 8. For the purposes of this Treaty, the measures on which the Organ of Consultation may agree will comprise one or more of the following: recall of chiefs of diplomatic missions; breaking of diplomatic relations; breaking of consular relations; partial or complete interruption of economic relations or of rail, sea, air, postal, telegraphic, telephonic, and radiotelephonic or radiotele-graphic communications; and use of armed force.

ARTICLE 9. In addition to other acts which the Organ of Consultation may characterize as aggression, the following shall be considered as such:

a. Unprovoked armed attack by a State against the territory, the people, or the land, sea or air forces of another State;

b. Invasion, by the armed forces of a State, of the territory of an American State, through the trespassing of boundaries demarcated in accordance with a treaty, judicial decision, or arbitral award, or, in the absence of frontiers thus demarcated, invasion affecting a region which is under the effective jurisdic-tion of another State. . . .

NO. 70

1948

The Charter of the Organization of American States

The Delegates to the Ninth International Conference
of American States

D elegates to the Chapultepec conference in Mexico City in 1945 approved a
resolution directing the Governing Board of the Pan American Union to draft
a charter "for the improvement and strengthening of the pan-American system."
In compliance with this directive, delegates at the Ninth International Conference of American States meeting at Bogotá from March to May 1948 approved
the charter of the Organization of American States (OAS), which replaced what
had been known since 1910 as the Union of American Republics, whose staff
organization was the Pan American Union.

In the name of their peoples, the states represented at the Ninth International
Conference of American States,

Convinced that the historic mission of America is to offer to man a land of
liberty, and a favorable environment for the development of his personality
and the realization of his just aspirations;

Conscious that that mission has already inspired numerous agreements,
whose essential value lies in the desire of the American peoples to live together
in peace, and, through their mutual understanding and respect for the sovereignty of each one, to provide for the betterment of all, in independence, in
equality and under law;

Confident that the true significance of American solidarity and good neighborliness can only mean the consolidation on this continent, within the framework of democratic institutions, of a system of individual liberty and social
justice based on respect for the essential rights of man;

Persuaded that their welfare and their contribution to the progress and the

Source: U.S. Department of State. Ninth International Conference of American States, in Bogotá,
Colombia, 30 March–2 May 1948, Report of the Delegation of the United States of America with
Related Documents, pp. 166–85. Department of State Publication 3263. Washington, D.C.: GPO,
1948.

civilization of the world will increasingly require intensive continental cooperation;

Resolved to persevere in the noble undertaking that humanity has conferred upon the United Nations, whose principles and purposes they solemnly reaffirm;

Convinced that juridical organization is a necessary condition for security and peace founded on moral order and on justice; . . . have agreed upon the following charter of the Organization of American States.

Part One
Chapter I: Nature and Purposes

ARTICLE 1. The American States establish by this Charter the international organization that they have developed to achieve an order of peace and justice, to promote their solidarity, to strengthen their collaboration, and to defend their sovereignty, their territorial integrity and their independence. Within the United Nations, the Organization of American States is a regional agency.

ARTICLE 2. All American States that ratify the present Charter are Members of the Organization. . . .

ARTICLE 4. The Organization of American States, in order to put into practice the principles on which it is founded and to fulfill its regional obligations under the Charter of the United Nations, proclaims the following essential purposes:

a) To strengthen the peace and security of the continent;

b) To prevent possible causes of difficulties and to ensure the pacific settlement of disputes that may arise among the Member States;

c) To provide for common action on the part of those States in the event of aggression;

d) To seek the solution of political, juridical and economic problems that may arise among them; and

e) To promote, by cooperative action, their economic, social and cultural development.

Chapter II: Principles

ARTICLE 5. The American States reaffirm the following principles:

a) International law is the standard of conduct of States in their reciprocal relations;

b) International order consists essentially of respect for the personality, sovereignty and independence of States, and the faithful fulfillment of obligations derived from treaties and other sources of international law;

c) Good faith shall govern the relations between States;

d) The solidarity of the American States and the high aims which are sought through it require the political organization of those States on the basis of the effective exercise of representative democracy;

e) The American States condemn war of aggression: victory does not give rights;

f) An act of aggression against one American State is an act of aggression against all the other American States;

g) Controversies of an international character arising between two or more American States shall be settled by peaceful procedures;

h) Social justice and social security are bases of lasting peace;

i) Economic cooperation is essential to the common welfare and prosperity of the peoples of the continent;

j) The American States proclaim the fundamental rights of the individual without distinction as to race, nationality, creed or sex;

k) The spiritual unity of the continent is based on respect for the cultural values of the American countries and requires their close cooperation for the high purposes of civilization;

l) The education of peoples should be directed toward justice, freedom and peace.

Chapter III: Fundamental Rights And Duties Of States

ARTICLE 6. States are juridically equal, enjoy equal rights and equal capacity to exercise these rights, and have equal duties. The rights of each State depend not upon its power to ensure the exercise thereof, but upon the mere fact of its existence as a person under international law. . . .

ARTICLE 15. No State or group of States has the right to intervene, directly or indirectly, for any reason whatever, in the internal or external affairs of any other State. The foregoing principle prohibits not only armed force but also any other form of interference or attempted threat against the personality of the State or against its political, economic and cultural elements.

ARTICLE 16. No State may use or encourage the use of coercive measures of an economic or political character in order to force the sovereign will of another State and obtain from it advantages of any kind.

ARTICLE 17. The territory of a State is inviolable; it may not be the object, even temporarily, of military occupation or of other measures of force taken by another State, directly or indirectly, on any grounds whatever. No territorial acquisitions or special advantages obtained either by force or by other means of coercion shall be recognized.

ARTICLE 18. The American States bind themselves in their international relations not to have recourse to the use of force except in the case of self-defense in accordance with existing treaties or in fulfillment thereof.

ARTICLE 19. Measures adopted for the maintenance of peace and security in accordance with existing treaties do not constitute a violation of the principles set forth in Articles 15 and 17. . . .

1948

The Menace of Communism

The Delegates to the Ninth International Conference of American States

While the main achievement of the Ninth International Conference of American States in Bogotá in 1948 was the adoption of the charter of the new Organization of American States (Document No. 70), one of the most important documents to emerge from that meeting reflected the growing concern of the United States with the spread of communism. The security threat attributed to Soviet and later Chinese aggression increasingly shaped U.S. foreign policy interests as the Cold War got under way in the late 1940s. Resolution 32, reprinted in full below, was the first official U.S.–Latin American expression of anticommunism. The first, U.S.-sponsored draft was amended by Latin American delegates to include a condemnation not just of communism but also of "any other totalitarian doctrine."

Resolution 32. The Preservation and Defense of Democracy in America

Whereas:

In order to safeguard peace and maintain mutual respect among states, the present world situation requires that urgent measures be taken, to proscribe the tactics of totalitarian domination that are irreconcilable with the tradition of the American Nations, and to prevent serving international communism or any other totalitarian doctrine from seeking to distort the true and the free will of the peoples of this continent,

The Republics Represented at the Ninth International Conference of American States

Declare:

That, by its anti-democratic nature and its interventionist tendency, the political activity of international communism or any other totalitarian doctrine is incompatible with the concept of American freedom, which rests upon two un-

Source: U.S. Department of State. *Ninth International Conference of American States, in Bogotá, Colombia, 30 March–2 May 1948, Report of the Delegation of the United States of America with Related Documents.* Department of State Publication 3263. Released November 1948.

deniable postulates: the dignity of man as an individual and the sovereignty of the nation as a state,

Reiterate:

The faith that the peoples of the New World have placed in the ideal and in the reality of democracy, under the protection of which they shall achieve social justice, offering to all increasingly broader opportunities to enjoy the spiritual and material benefits that are the guarantee of civilization and the heritage of mankind;

Condemn:

In the name of international law, interference by any foreign power, or by any political organization serving the interests of a foreign power, in the public life of the nations of the American continent,

And resolve:

1. To reaffirm their decision to maintain and further an effective social and economic policy for the purpose of raising the standard of living of their peoples; and their conviction that only under a system founded upon a guarantee of the essential freedoms and rights of the individual is it possible to attain this goal.

2. To condemn the methods of every system tending to suppress political and civil rights and liberties, and in particular the action of international communism or any other totalitarian doctrine.

3. To adopt, within their respective territories and in accordance with their respective constitutional provisions the measures necessary to eradicate and prevent activities directed, assisted or instigated by foreign governments, organizations or individuals tending to overthrow their institutions by violence, to foment disorder in their domestic political life or to disturb, by means of pressure, subversive propaganda, threats or by any other means, the free and sovereign right of their peoples to govern themselves in accordance with their democratic aspirations.

4. To proceed with a full exchange of information concerning any of the aforementioned activities that are carried on within their respective jurisdictions.

1950

A Realist Views Latin America

George F. Kennan

G eorge F. Kennan was the U.S. State Department's leading expert on the Soviet Union when he sent his famous "long telegram" to the State Department
from his post in the U.S. embassy in Moscow in February 1946. Kennan warned
that Washington's wartime ally was power-hungry and insecure, and that the
United States would have to be ready to firmly resist the Kremlin's expansionis-
tic impulses. In an unsigned article in *Foreign Affairs* the following year, Kennan
publicly presented his so-called "realist" view of U.S.–Soviet relations; his pre-
scription for a "long-term, patient but firm and vigilant containment of Russian
expansive tendencies" became the U.S. Cold War policy of containment. Just before resigning from the State Department in 1950 to join the Institute for Advanced
Study at Princeton University, Kennan made his first and only trip to Latin America for the State Department. Excerpted below is the secret, thirty-five page report
he submitted to Secretary of State Dean G. Acheson on March 29, 1950.

Mr. Secretary:

Below are some views about Latin America as a problem in United States foreign policy, as these things appear to me at the conclusion of a visit to some of
the Latin American countries. . . . Our relationship to Latin America occupies a
vitally important place in our effort to achieve, within the non-communist world
in general, a system of international relationships, political and economic, reasonably adequate to the demands of this post-war era, and henceforth qualified
to serve as a rebuttal of the Russian challenge to our right to exist as a great and
leading world power. . . .

   If the countries of Latin America should come to be generally dominated by
an outlook which views our country as the root of all evil and sees salvation
only in the destruction of our national power, I doubt very much whether our

Source: U.S. Department of State. *Foreign Relations of the United States, 1950, 2: The United Nations,
The Western Hemisphere,* "Memorandum by the Counselor of the Department (Kennan) to the Secretary of State," 29 March 1950, pp. 598–624. Washington, D.C.: GPO, 1976.

general political program in other parts of the non-communist world could be successful. . . .

While there are some fairly common and serious misunderstandings as to the *nature* of the importance to us of Latin America in the event of war with the Soviet Union, there is no question of that importance itself.

This is only in minor degree a question of bases, since Latin America offers little in this respect which could be of serious interest to the Russian adversary in the light of existing military realities. It is also no longer, to the degree that it once was, a problem of the defense of the Panama Canal and of assuring the fusion of our naval power in the two oceans, although that is still important. Finally, it is definitely not a question of the possible mobilization of Latin American military strength against us. In these days, when apprehensions of Soviet military expansion assume such fantastic forms, we could do well to remember that not even the Russians can create military strength where the essential components of that strength, in manpower, in industrial background and in native leadership are lacking.

The military significance to us of the Latin American countries lies today rather in the extent to which we may be dependent upon them for materials essential to the prosecution of a war, and more importantly in the extent to which the attitudes of the Latin American peoples may influence the general political trend in the international community. . . .

It seems to me unlikely that there could be any other region of the earth in which nature and human behavior could have combined to produce a more unhappy and hopeless background for the conduct of human life than in Latin America.

As for nature, one is struck at once with the way in which South America is the reverse of our own North American continent from the standpoint of its merits as a human habitat. . . .

Against this unfavorable geographical background, which would have yielded only to the most progressive and happy of human approaches, humanity superimposed a series of events unfortunate and tragic almost beyond anything ever known in human history. . . . To those portions of the New World where an Indian civilization was already in existence, [the Spaniards] came like men from Mars: terrible, merciless conquerors . . . to whom the only possible relationship was one of tragic and total submission, involving the abandonment of all prior attachments and customs. . . .

Elsewhere in Latin America, the large scale importation of Negro slave elements into considerable parts of the Spanish and other colonial empires, and the extensive intermarriage of all these elements, produced other unfortunate results which seemed to have weighed scarcely less heavily on the chances for human progress.

In these circumstances, the shadow of a tremendous helplessness and impotence falls today over most of the Latin American world. The handicaps to progress are written in human blood and in the tracings of geography; and in neither case are they readily susceptible of obliteration. . . .

And, in the realm of individual personality, this subconscious recognition of the failure of group effort finds its expression in an exaggerated self-centeredness and egotism—in a pathetic urge to create the illusion of desperate courage, supreme cleverness, and a limitless virility where the more constructive virtues are so conspicuously lacking. . . .

It is true that most of the people who go by the name of "communist" in Latin America are a somewhat different species than in Europe. Their bond with Moscow is tenuous and indirect. . . . Many of them are little aware of its reality. For this reason, and because their Latin American character inclines them to individualism, to indiscipline and to a personalized, rather than doctrinaire, approach to their responsibilities as communists, they sometimes have little resemblance to the highly disciplined communists of Europe, and are less conscious of their status as the tools of Moscow. The Moscow leaders, we may be sure, must view them with a mixture of amusement, contempt, and anxiety. . . .

Our problem then, is to create, where such do not already exist, incentives which will impel the governments and societies of the Latin American countries to resist communist pressures, and to assist them and spur them on in their efforts, where the incentives are already present. . . .

[W]here the concepts and traditions of popular government are too weak to absorb successfully the intensity of the communist attack, then we must concede that harsh governmental measures of repression may be the only answer; that these measures may have to proceed from regimes whose origins and methods would not stand the test of American concepts of democratic procedure; and that such regimes and such methods may be preferable alternatives, and indeed the only alternatives, to further communist successes.

I am not saying that this will be the case everywhere; but I think it may well be the case in certain places. And I would submit that it is very difficult for us, as outsiders, to pass moral judgement on these necessities and to constitute ourselves the arbiters of where one approach is suitable, and where the other should be used. . . . For us, it should be sufficient if there is a recognition of communist penetration for the danger that it is, a will to repel that penetration and to throw off communist influence, and effective action in response to that will. . . .

[A]s of today, the protection of U.S. investments in Latin America rests predominantly on the self-interest of the governing groups in the Latin American countries and on the ability of the American owners to enlist that self-interest through the judicious use of their financial power, where it does not exist from other causes. In many instances, bribery may be said to have replaced diplomatic intervention as the main protection of private capital; and the best sanction for its continued operation lies in the corruptibility, rather than the enlightenment, of the local regimes. . . .

It is important for us to keep before ourselves and the Latin American peoples at all times the reality of the thesis that we are a great power; that we are by and large much less in need of them than they are in need of us; that we are entirely prepared to leave to themselves those who evince no particular desire for the forms of collaboration that we have to offer; that the danger of a failure to exhaust the possibilities of our mutual relationship is always greater to them than to us; that we can afford to wait, patiently and good naturedly; and that we are more concerned to be respected than to be liked or understood. . . .

❖

NO. 73

1950

A New Economic Model for Latin America

Raúl Prebisch

Over the opposition of the United States, the United Nations Economic Commission for Latin America (ECLA) was created in February 1948. The ECLA (or CEPAL, according to its Spanish acronym) undertook the first regular collection, by Latin Americans, of economic and social data on the countries of the region. But its main contribution was a systematic critique of the economic policies that were being advocated by the United States and global financial institutions such as the International Monetary Fund. Raúl Prebisch (1901–86), the director of Argentina's Central Bank from 1935 to 1943, was ECLA's executive secretary from 1949 to 1963. In this 1950 defense of ECLA doctrine, Prebisch argued that the global trade system worked against the economic "peripheries," which export raw materials in exchange for high-cost processed goods from industrialized "centers." In addition to arguing for increased economic assistance to Latin America, ECLA advocated import-substitution industrialization and Keynesian policies of state-fostered growth as strategies for Latin American development. This approach, which included calls for an Inter-American Development Bank, would challenge the "trade, not aid" philosophy of the Eisenhower administration.

Source: Raúl Prebisch. *The Economic Development of Latin America and its Principal Problems*. Economic Commission for Latin America. 27 April 1950. Lake Success, NY: U.N. Department of Economic Affairs, 1950.

In Latin America, reality is undermining the out-dated schema of the international division of labour, which achieved great importance in the nineteenth century and, as a theoretical concept, continued to exert considerable influence until very recently.

Under that schema, the specific task that fell to Latin America, as part of the periphery of the world economic system, was that of producing food and raw materials for the great industrial centres.

There was no place within it for the industrialization of the new countries. It is nevertheless being forced upon them by events. Two world wars in a single generation and a great economic crisis between them have shown the Latin-American countries their opportunities, clearly pointing the way to industrial activity.

The academic discussion, however, is far from ended. In economics, ideologies usually tend either to lag behind events or to outlive them. It is true that the reasoning on the economic advantages of the international division of labour is theoretically sound, but it is usually forgotten that it is based upon an assumption which has been conclusively proved false by facts. According to this assumption, the benefits of technical progress tend to be distributed alike over the whole community, either by the lowering of prices or the corresponding raising of incomes. The countries producing raw materials obtain their share of these benefits through international exchange, and therefore have no need to industrialize. If they were to do so, their lesser efficiency would result in their losing the conventional advantages of such exchange.

The flaw in this assumption is that of generalizing from the particular. If by "the community" only the great industrial countries are meant, it is indeed true that the benefits of technical progress are gradually distributed among all social groups and classes. If, however, the concept of the community is extended to include the periphery of the world economy, a serious error is implicit in the generalization. The enormous benefits that derive from increased productivity have not reached the periphery in a measure comparable to that obtained by the peoples of the great industrial countries. Hence, the outstanding differences between the standards of living of the masses of the former and the latter and the manifest discrepancies between their respective abilities to accumulate capital, since the margin of savings depends primarily on increased productivity.

Thus there exists an obvious disequilibrium, a fact which, whatever its explanation or justification, destroys the basic premise underlying the schema of the international division of labour.

Hence, the fundamental significance of the industrialization of the new countries. Industrialization is not an end in itself, but the principal means at the disposal of those countries of obtaining a share of the benefits of technical progress and of progressively raising the standard of living of the masses. . . .

Admittedly much remains to be done in the Latin-American countries, both in learning the facts and in their proper theoretical interpretation. Though many of the problems of these countries are similar, no common effort has ever been made even to examine and elucidate them. It is not surprising, therefore, that the studies published on the economy of Latin-American countries often reflect the points of view or the experience of the great centres of world economy. Those studies cannot be expected to solve problems of direct concern to Latin America. The case of the Latin-American countries must therefore be presented clearly, so that their interests, aspirations and opportunities, bearing in mind, of course, the individual differences and characteristics, may be adequately integrated within the general framework of international economic cooperation. . . .

The industrialization of Latin America is not incompatible with the efficient development of primary production. On the contrary, the availability of the best capital equipment and the prompt adoption of new techniques are essential if the development of industry is to fulfill the social objective of raising the standard of living. The same is true of the mechanization of agriculture. Primary products must be exported to allow for the importation of the considerable quantity of capital goods needed.

The more active Latin America's foreign trade, the greater the possibility of increasing productivity by means of intensive capital formation. The solution does not lie in growth at the expense of foreign trade, but in knowing how to extract, from continually growing foreign trade, the elements that will promote economic development. . . .

❖

1954

Terminating a Revolution in Guatemala— A View from Washington

John C. Dreier

U.S. government opposition to the policies of reformist President Jacobo Arbenz of Guatemala (1951–54) proceeded on two tracks (see Document No. 75). The first was a covert operation organized by the Central Intelligence Agency to forcibly overthrow Arbenz and replace him with a president more acceptable to Washington. The second was a public campaign to isolate and weaken Arbenz politically and economically, a strategy in which the Organization of American States played a role. The United States made frequent reference to anticommunist resolutions adopted by the OAS (see Document No. 71), and sought to use the Rio Treaty procedures for OAS-sponsored "consultation" in the event of a collective security threat (see Document No. 69). On Sunday night, June 27, 1954, the CIA-sponsored invasion succeeded in forcing Arbenz to resign his office. The following day, John C. Dreier, the U.S. government's representative to the council of the OAS, made the following appeal for a vote to convoke a meeting of foreign ministers to consider the Guatemalan situation. The council immediately complied with Dreier's request, but Arbenz's resignation resulted in the indefinite postponement of the meeting called for by Dreier.

I speak today as the representative of one of 10 American countries who have joined in a request that a Meeting of Ministers of Foreign Affairs be convoked to act as Organ of Consultation under articles 6 and 11 of the Inter-American Treaty of Reciprocal Assistance. On behalf of the United States I wish to support this request with all the force and conviction that I can express, feeling profoundly as I and my countrymen do that this is a critical hour in which a strong and positive note of inter-American solidarity must be sounded.

The Republics of America are faced at this time with a serious threat to their

Source: U.S. Department of State. "The Guatemalan Problem Before the OAS Council." In *Intervention of International Communism in Guatemala*. Department of State Publication 5556, Inter-American Series 48. Released August 1954, pp. 25–30. Washington, D.C.: GPO, 1954.

peace and independence. Throughout the world the aggressive forces of Soviet Communist imperialism are exerting a relentless pressure upon all free nations. Since 1939, 15 once free nations have fallen prey to the forces directed by the Kremlin. Hundreds of millions of people in Europe and Asia have been pressed into the slavery of the Communist totalitarian state. Subversion, civil violence, and open warfare are the proven methods of this aggressive force in its ruthless striving for world domination. . . . The first objectives of this new drive for domination were the countries of Eastern Europe and the Balkans. . . . Communist forces then turned their attention to Asia. . . .

And now comes the attack on America.

There is no doubt . . . that it is the declared policy of the American States that the establishment of a government dominated by the international Communist movement in America would constitute a grave danger to all our American Republics and that steps must be taken to prevent any such eventuality. . . .

I should like to affirm the fact that there is already abundant evidence that the international Communist movement has achieved an extensive penetration of the political institutions of one American State, namely the Republic of Guatemala, and now seeks to exploit that country for its own ends. This assertion, which my Government is prepared to support with convincing detail at the right time, is clearly warranted by the open opposition of the Guatemalan Government to any form of inter-American action that might check or restrain the progress of the international Communist movement in this continent; by the open association of that Government with the policies and objectives of the Soviet Union in international affairs; by the evidences of close collaboration of the authorities in Guatemala and authorities in Soviet-dominated states of Europe for the purpose of obtaining under secret and illegal arrangements the large shipment of arms which arrived on board the HMS *Alfhem* on May 15, 1954; by the efforts of Guatemala in the United Nations Security Council, in collaboration with the Soviet Union, to prevent the Organization of American States, the appropriate regional organization, from dealing with her recent allegations of aggression, and finally by the vigorous and sustained propaganda campaign of the Soviet press and radio, echoed by the international Communist propaganda machine throughout the world in support of Guatemalan action in the present crisis.

The recent outbreak of violence in Guatemala adds a further sense of urgency to the matter. We well know from experience in other areas into which the international Communist movement has penetrated the tragic proportions to which this inevitable violent conflict may ultimately extend. . . .

Within the last 24 hours it appears that there has been a change in the Government of Guatemala. It is not possible, however, in the opinion of my Government, to arrive at any considered judgment of how this change may affect the problem with which we are concerned. Under the circumstances, it would appear to be essential that we do not relax our efforts at this moment, but proceed with our plans in order to be ready for any eventuality. . . .

I should like to emphasize the fact that the object of our concern, and the force against which we must take defensive measures, is an alien, non-American force. It is the international Communist organization controlled in the Kremlin which has created the present danger. That it is rapidly making a victim of one American State increases our concern for that country and our determination to unite in a defense of all 21 of our American nations. We are confident that the international Communist movement holds no real appeal for the peoples of America and can only subdue them if allowed to pursue its violent and deceitful methods unchecked. Having read the tragic history of other nations seduced by Communist promises into a slavery from which they later could not escape, we wish to leave no stone unturned, no effort unexerted, to prevent the complete subordination of one of our member states to Soviet Communist imperialism. For when one state has fallen history shows that another will soon come under attack. . . .

❖

NO. 75

1954

Terminating a Revolution in Guatemala— A View from Guatemala

Luis Cardoza y Aragón

A popular revolt that succeeded in overthrowing the Guatemalan dictator Jorge Ubico in 1944 led to the election of President Juan José Arévalo Guzmán on December 19, 1944. Arévalo initiated a series of reforms aimed at modernizing Guatemala's export-oriented economy, raising living standards and democratizing its political system. In Guatemala's first peaceful political transition, Arévalo's former minister of defense, Colonel Jacobo Arbenz Guzmán Bermejo, succeeded to the presidency in 1951 with 60 percent of the vote. Convinced of the need to deepen the process of change initiated by Arévalo, President Arbenz

Source: Luis Cardoza y Aragón, "Interview: The Revolution of '44–'54: A Reappraisal." In *Guatemala*, eds. Susanne Jonas and David Tobis, pp. 55–56. Copyright 1974 by the North American Congress on Latin America, 475 Riverside Dr., 454, New York, N.Y. 10115-0122.

encouraged labor organizing and decreed an agrarian reform law that resulted in the expropriation of 71 percent of the land of the U.S.-owned banana producer, the United Fruit Company. These measures, along with his appointment of Communist Party members to his government, led Arbenz into conflict with the United States (See Document No. 74). The Eisenhower administration considered Arbenz a tool of international communism, and authorized the Central Intelligence Agency to organize a secret invasion force of exiled Guatemalans. With CIA support, the invasion force overthrew Arbenz and replaced him with Colonel Carlos Castillo Armas, the leader of the insurgency. Luis Cardoza y Aragón (1904–92) was a poet and essayist who served in various ambassadorial posts under the Arévalo and Arbenz administrations. Excerpts from an interview with him in 1974 follow.

With respect to my Guatemala, the key factor, decisively and definitively, is summed up totally in *North American Imperialism.* This is the paramount fact: the rest is very relative, secondary, although necessary to recognize. I am just beginning to understand it completely. Given the backwardness of Guatemala (imperialism and its classical local mechanism, using its internal allies), the immense backwardness of Guatemala, it was civil progress rather than revolution (a serious word: Revolution) that commenced with Arévalo and his labor laws, social security, something (not much) in education, public health. A large, unified labor organization, the General Confederation of Guatemalan Laborers (CGTG), survived until the time of Arbenz. . . .

The politicization of the masses was in its initial stages, very rudimentary and without doctrine and was more concerned with labor demands, salaries, work conditions. The formation of the PGT [Guatemalan Labor Party, i.e., Communist Party] leadership was itself improvised, made up of manual workers; the truth is, there were no communists among them. It was a petty bourgeoisie that became radicalized and founded a party that never knew where it stood, or what time it was in the world; it was full of subjectivism, of excellent desires, of self-denial, of ignorance, of petulance, of yearnings to learn, to know, to serve its people with utmost honesty. But they were on the moon.

And even if there had been a real Communist Party, or if Arbenz' government had been communist (both impossible in 1944–54), they would never have posed the least threat to the United States. Apart from the right of a people to have the government it wishes, etc., the fact is that Arbenz' government was a soft nationalist model (none of the laws, including the agrarian reform, were more than moderate). But to people like Nixon and McCarthy, it was still a bad example on the continent. The U.S. (North American imperialism) squashed a little butterfly that wished to fly a little more freely within the capitalist system, and to emerge from a barbaric, inhumane situation to better living conditions for its people, of all classes.

The same climate of liberty, the possibility of forming labor unions, superficially politicized the labor masses and a few artisans and professionals. All was varnish, superficial, even among the leadership. The colossal political backwardness partly explains many things, but it does not excuse the imperialist crime. . . .

As for the Indians, the ingenuous, mistakenly called Revolution of October [1944] was beginning to discover them. Since the country is Indian, they had become invisible. Since racism is secular and daily, familiar, part of the environment, it had gone on undiscovered. The newly-arrived in the country (my case) or the foreigner was astonished by the treatment of the Indian, the native Guatemalan, and by his wretched poverty, his illiteracy, etc.

When it came to governmental decisions, I supposed they were made by Arbenz in consultation with his cabinet and the heads of the political parties that supported him. One of these was the PGT. I do not think there was a fixed strategy or political analysis on the part of Arbenz or the PGT. Had there been real, influential Communists, things would have been oriented differently, and there would have been intense struggle. Arbenz's resignation speech (lamentable) was written by a high functionary of the PGT who had recently stepped down from the Party leadership.

As is the case now, Latin America was submerged, backward, except for the existence of Cuba and combative, politicized groups throughout the continent. With its liberty, its nationalism, Guatemala set a "bad example." Keep in mind what sort of beasts Dulles and Eisenhower had to be to destroy a stammer of freedom in a very small, very backward country, which in no way could endanger anyone. That bestiality has to be seen in the clearest perspective, above all else. . . .

The upper middle class also took part in Arbenz' government. . . . The middle class provided the leadership; this was true also in the PGT. We hardly even had a proletariat! To recount the errors of the Revolution it would be necessary to write at great length. The chief one is geographical: to be in the zone where North American imperialism exercises its greatest influence.

1955

On the Road to Mexico

Jack Kerouac

J ack (Jean-Louis) Kerouac (1922–69) was one of the best known of the "beat" generation of U.S. writers of the 1950s. Unconventional in literary style and iconoclastic in their cultural outlook, they formed the literary counterpart to abstract expressionism in art and the bebop style of jazz music. Excerpted below is Kerouac's *On the Road,* an autobiographical narrative chronicling the adventures of the writer ("Sal Paradise") and his companion Neal Cassady ("Dean Moriarty") as they traveled across the United States and Mexico. The book, written in 1950 in three weeks on a single roll of teletype paper, made Kerouac famous after its publication in 1957, and influenced the 1960s counterculture. A Spanish-language edition of *On the Road* was published in Argentina in 1969.

. . . And now we were ready for the last hundred and fifty miles to the magic border. We leaped into the car and off. I was so exhausted by now I slept all the way through Dilley and Encinal to Laredo and didn't wake up till they were parking the car in front of the lunchroom at two o'clock in the morning. "Ah," sighed Dean, "the end of Texas, the end of America, we don't know no more." It was tremendously hot: we were all sweating buckets. There was no night dew, not a breath of air, nothing except billions of moths smashing at bulbs everywhere and the low, rank smell of a hot river in the night nearby— the Rio Grande, that begins in cool Rocky Mountain dales and ends up fashioning world-valleys to mingle its heats with the Mississippi muds in the great Gulf.

Laredo was a sinister town that morning. All kinds of cabdrivers and border rats wandered around, looking for opportunities. There weren't many; it was too late. It was the bottom and dregs of America where all the heavy villains sink, where disoriented people have to go to be near a specific elsewhere they can slip into unnoticed. Contraband brooded in the heavy syrup air. Cops were red-faced and sullen and sweaty, no swagger. Waitresses were dirty and disgusted. Just beyond, you could feel the enormous presence of whole great Mexico and almost smell the billion tortillas frying and smoking in the night. We had no idea what Mexico would really be like. We were at sea level again, and when we tried to eat a snack we could hardly swallow it. I wrapped it up in napkins for the trip anyway. We felt awful and sad. But everything changed when we crossed the mysterious bridge over the river and our wheels rolled on official Mexican soil, though it wasn't anything but carway for border inspection. Just across the street Mexico began. We looked with wonder. To our amazement, it looked exactly like Mexico. It was three in the morning, and fellows in straw hats and white pants were lounging by the dozen against battered pocky storefronts.

"Look-at-those-cats!" whispered Dean, "Oo," he breathed softly, "wait, wait." The Mexican officials came out, grinning, and asked please if we would take out our baggage. We did. We couldn't take our eyes from across the street. We were longing to rush right up there and get lost in those mysterious Spanish streets. It was only Nuevo Laredo but it looked like Holy Lhasa to us. "Man those guys are up all night," whispered Dean. We hurried to get our papers straightened. We were warned not to drink tapwater now we were over the border. The Mexicans looked at our baggage in a desultory way. They weren't like officials at all. They were lazy and tender. Dean couldn't stop staring at them. He turned to me. "See how the *cops* are in this country. I can't believe it!" He rubbed his eyes. "I'm dreaming." Then it was time to change our money. We saw great stacks of pesos on a table and learned that eight of them made an American buck, or thereabouts. We changed most of our money and stuffed the big rolls in our pockets with delight.

Then we turned our faces to Mexico with bashfulness and wonder as those dozens of Mexican cats watched us from under their secret hatbrims in the night. Beyond were music and all-night restaurants with smoke pouring out of the door. "Whee," whispered Dean very softly.

"Thassall!" A Mexican official grinned. "You boys all set. Go ahead. Welcome Mehico. I say this to you personal, I'm Red, everybody call me Red. Ask for Red. Eat good. Don't worry. Everything fine. Is not hard enjoin yourself in Mehico."

"*Yes!*" shuddered Dean and off we went across the street into Mexico on soft feet. We left the car parked, and all three of us abreast went down the Spanish street into the middle of the dull brown lights. Old men sat on chairs in the night and looked like Oriental junkies and oracles. No one was actually looking at us, yet everybody was aware of everything we did. We turned sharp left into the smoky lunchroom and went in to music of campo guitars on an American 'thirties jukebox. Shirt-sleeved Mexican cabdrivers and straw-hatted Mexican hipsters sat at stools, devouring shapeless messes of tortillas, beans, tacos, whatnot. We bought three bottles of cold beer—*cerveza* was the name for beer—for about thirty Mexican cents or ten American cents each. We bought packs of Mexican cigarettes for six cents each. We gazed and gazed at our wonderful Mexican money that went so far, and played with it and looked around and smiled at everyone. Behind us lay the whole of America and everything Dean and I had previously known about life and life on the road. We had finally found the magic land at the end of the road and we never dreamed the extent of the magic. "*Think* of these cats staying up all hours of the night," whispered Dean. "And think of this big continent ahead of us with those enormous Sierra Madre mountains we saw in the movies, and the jungles all the way down and a whole desert plateau as big as ours and reaching clear down to Guatemala and God knows where, whoo! What'll we do? What'll we do? Let's move!" We got out and went back to the car. One last glimpse of America across the hot lights of the Rio Grande bridge, and we turned our back and fender to it and roared off. . . .

❖

NO. 77

1956

Taming a Revolution in Bolivia

George Jackson Eder

The U.S. government responded to the Bolivian Revolution of 1952 with an extraordinary outpouring of economic assistance. Although one of the smallest and weakest countries in Latin America, Bolivia was, by the end of the 1950s, the largest recipient of U.S. aid in Latin America. By 1958, one-third of the Bolivian national budget was contributed by the U.S. government, which funded highway construction, food imports, health and educational services and the country's military forces. In exchange, the United States sought, and gained, Bolivia's cooperation in blocking or moderating some of the social and economic reforms proposed by the radical wing of the successful revolutionary movement. Another U.S. demand was the adoption of economic stabilization measures to

Source: George Jackson Eder. *Inflation and Development in Latin America: A Case History of Inflation and Stabilization in Bolivia.* Michigan International Business Studies No. 8. Appendix 6, "Report on the Progress and Problems of the Stabilization Program." Ann Arbor: Program in International Business, Graduate School of Business Administration, University of Michigan, 1968. Copyright The University of Michigan, 1968. Reprinted by permission.

control inflation; further U.S. aid was conditioned on their success. At the request of the United States, therefore, the Bolivian government put U.S. lawyer George Jackson Eder in charge of developing a stabilization program, which was put into effect under his direction in December 1956. A staunch monetarist, Eder believed that the only cure for inflation was to cut government spending. What follows are excerpts from a report by Eder, in his position as executive director of the National Monetary Stabilization Council, to Bolivian president Hernán Siles Zuazo on April 17, 1957.

In the present report I propose to outline the results to date of the stabilization measures taken last December [1956], pointing out the problems we now face and solutions for them, as I am convinced that there is no problem without a solution. . . . During his visit in August, 1956, Henry Holland [Assistant Secretary of State for Inter-American Affairs] pointed out specifically, in conversations with the President of the Republic and the President of the Senate (Juan Lechín) that it would be extremely difficult to get the American Congress to continue U.S. aid unless Bolivia put its house in order, as Holland phrased it, by carrying out a monetary and financial stabilization program and reestablishing its world credit through bilateral agreements with the bondholders and the former mine owners. He concluded by saying, nevertheless, that Bolivia had more than eight months in which to fulfill these conditions.

Now, on his recent visit, Holland repeated this warning, with this difference—that Bolivia no longer has eight months to fulfill these conditions, since the U.S. Congress will be studying the question of foreign aid this month and in the month of May. . . . All that I can do is to warn, with the utmost respect, the honorable representatives of the Bolivian government that the best and most carefully laid financial plans are bound to fail if they are put aside because of political or labor union pressure, or because of other self-seeking demands of the moment, and that it is not possible to give way here and there in matters which of themselves might not be of major importance, but which in sum must inevitably lead to the failure of the entire monetary and economic structure of the country. . . .

Thus, as a consequence of the *interferences*, departures from the program, and the delays to which I have referred, not only the monetary stabilization program but the entire economic future of Bolivia has been jeopardized. *We cannot assume that the political and labor leaders who have interfered with, and who are continuing to attack the stabilization program, have no desire to understand it, or that they wish to sabotage it, or that they have any ulterior or subversive motives. Instead, I may say that the fault is ours for not having explained the program with the necessary clarity. But the fact remains that the attacks on the program, and the interferences with it, on the part of those who should cooperate, have in actual fact sabotaged President Siles' program, for I repeat and shall continue to repeat that the Stabilization Program is not an "Eder Plan," as it is called by those who do not dare to attack the Chief Executive in person, but the program of the government of Bolivia, presented by that government as the basis for its request for financial aid. . . .*

The purpose of the stabilization measures is to improve the standard of living of the entire population. They are already beginning to show results for the farmers, and they will show results for the workers and middle class as prices go down and production goes up. Thus, time will provide its own remedy, although I admit that nowhere are workers inclined to consider a drop in prices as the equivalent of an increase in wages, so that there will always be pressure, in part demagogic, for a general increase in wages notwithstanding the fact that, unless there is increased production, a wage increase can only be illusory and inflationary. . . .

Inasmuch as, in readjusting wages and salaries between the various occupations, it will be impossible to reduce wages in any sector, this means, as a practical matter, that a readjustment process will result in an increase of the total wage bill. Probably no sector, no matter how well paid, can be left without some increase.

Now, inasmuch as any increase of wages and salaries without a prior increase in productivity inevitably means the issuance of bank notes and a renewal of the inflationary spiral, two other indispensable steps are necessary, namely, a simultaneous cut in the contributions to the National Social Security Administration and other similar funds, and the right of freedom to hire and fire. . . .

Of course, under present circumstances, freedom to fire cannot be granted without a comprehensive program to avoid unemployment. Such a program is being drawn up in Point IV [a U.S. economic assistance program], following the suggestions of the President of the Republic and of the Planning Commission. . . .

These measures, that is, the reduction of social security taxes, the freedom to hire and fire, and the unemployment program, are essential and urgent. I can see no alternative which would permit Bolivia to maintain a sound currency since without these measures the stabilization program must inevitably fail in view of the departures from the original plan. In that event, the continuation of U.S. aid would be endangered, together with any possibility of interesting foreign or domestic capital in the development of the national economy.

As another equally essential and urgent point, *Ross Moore, Director of Point IV, points out* the necessity of putting a definitive and early end to the agricultural reform, since the large estates have already been eliminated and small and medium farmers are now afraid to sow crops or cultivate their lands, under the menace of possible or probable expropriation.

As Bolivia has millions of hectares of vacant land, it is hard to understand why it continues to expropriate private property, particularly as this does not increase production and on the contrary diminishes it to a marked extent. . . .

[T]he people [of Bolivia] can decide whether they wish to listen to the advice of those who brought the country to the utter ruination of 1956, and who continue to proffer advice that is incompatible with reality, or whether they prefer to accept the new course laid out by the government of President Siles with the stabilization program, living within their resources and understanding that there can be no real increase in wages or salaries that does not correspond to an equivalent increase in production. . . .

The future lies in the hands of the Bolivians themselves; and, with the greater productivity resulting from human effort, private capital, and the enormous wealth of the soil and subsoil, Bolivia can look forward to an era of prosperity such as it has never had in its history. This does not mean sacrificing the enduring conquests of the Revolution—namely, universal suffrage, the distribution of the large estates, elimination of a mining empire more powerful than the state itself, and, now, monetary stabilization—but rather preserving those conquests under a regime of monetary and financial integrity.

❖

NO. 78

1957

With Castro in the Sierra Maestra

Herbert L. Matthews

Fidel Castro's insurgent army of eighty-two guerrilla fighters landed in Cuba on board the yacht *Granma* from Mexico on December 2, 1956. Nearly annihilated by a Cuban army patrol three days later, the insurgent force was reduced to just sixteen survivors and Batista boasted that Castro's insurrection had been totally extinguished. Then on February 24, 1957, *The New York Times* published a series of articles by veteran staff writer Herbert L. Matthews, who had been secretly led to Castro's camp in the Sierra Maestra mountains to interview the Cuban revolutionary leader. A photo of an armed Castro, including his signature and the date (February 17) was published with Matthews's first article on the front page of the *Times* in order to demonstrate that Castro was still alive and fighting. The stories were a sensational journalistic coup for the *Times,* and a stunning publicity achievement for Castro and his movement. Castro boasted in 1979 that he had fooled Matthews into believing that his forces were much larger than

Source: Herbert L. Matthews, "Cuban Rebel is Visited in Hideout." *The New York Times,* 24 February, 1957, p. 1ff. Copyright © 1957 by *The New York Times.* Reprinted by permission.

they were. While Matthews evidently exaggerated the strength of Castro's rebel army, which at the time of his visit consisted of just eighteen men, the reporter's conclusion that "General Batista cannot possibly hope to suppress the Castro revolt" turned out to be correct.

Fidel Castro, the rebel leader of Cuba's youth, is alive and fighting hard and successfully in the rugged, almost impenetrable fastnesses of the Sierra Maestra, at the southern tip of the island.

President Fulgencio Batista has the cream of his Army around the area, but the Army men are fighting a thus-far losing battle to destroy the most dangerous enemy General Batista has yet faced in a long and adventurous career as a Cuban leader and dictator.

This is the first sure news that Fidel Castro is still alive and still in Cuba. No one connected with the outside world, let alone with the press, has seen Señor Castro except this writer. No one in Havana, not even at the United States Embassy with all its resources for getting information, will know until this report is published that Fidel Castro is really in the Sierra Maestra. . . .

Havana does not and cannot know that thousands of men and women are heart and soul with Fidel Castro and the new deal for which they think he stands. It does not know that hundreds of highly respected citizens are helping Señor Castro, that bombs and sabotage are constant (eighteen bombs were exploded in Santiago on Feb. 15), that a fierce Government counter-terrorism has aroused the populace even more against President Batista. . . .

Fidel Castro and his 26th of July Movement are the flaming symbol of this opposition to the regime. The organization, which is apart from the university students' opposition, is formed of youths of all kinds. It is a revolutionary movement that calls itself socialistic. It is also nationalistic, which generally in Latin America means anti-Yankee.

The program is vague and couched in generalities, but it amounts to a new deal for Cuba, radical, democratic and therefore anti-Communist. The real core of its strength is that it is fighting against the military dictatorship of President Batista. . . . From the looks of things, General Batista cannot possibly hope to suppress the Castro revolt. . . .

The plan worked out to get through the Army's road blocks to Oriente was as simple as it was effective. We took my wife along in the car as "camouflage." Cuba is at the height of the tourist season and nothing could have looked more innocent than a middle-aged couple of American tourists driving down to Cuba's most beautiful and fertile province with some young friends. . . .

It was then midnight, the time we were to meet Castro's scouts; but we had to walk some first and it was hard going. At last we turned off the road and slid down a hillside to where a stream, dark brown under the nearly full moon, rushed its muddy way. . . . I waded through with the water almost to my knees and that was hard enough to do without falling. . . . The dripping leaves and boughs, the dense vegetation, the mud underfoot, the moonlight—all gave the impression of a tropical forest, more like Brazil than Cuba. . . .

We spoke in the lowest possible whispers. One man told me how he had seen his brother's store wrecked and burned by Government troops and his brother dragged out and executed. "I'd rather be here, fighting for Fidel, than anywhere in the world now," he said. . . .

With the light [of morning] I could see how young they all were. Señor Castro, according to his followers, is 30, and that is old for the 26th of July Movement. It has a motley array of arms and uniforms, and even a few civilian suits. The rifles and the one machine gun I saw were all American-discarded models. . . .

Several of the youths had lived in the United States and spoke English; others had learned it at school. One had been a professional baseball player in a minor league and his wife is still in the United States. . . .

Raul Castro, Fidel's younger brother, slight and pleasant, came into the camp with others of the staff, and a few minutes later Fidel himself strode in. Taking him, as one would at first, by physique and personality, this was quite a man—a powerful six-footer, olive-skinned, full-faced, with a straggly beard. He was dressed in an olive gray fatigue uniform and carried a rifle with a telescopic sight, of which he was very proud. It seems his men have something more than fifty of these and he said the soldiers feared them. . . .

The personality of the man is overpowering. It was easy to see that his men adored him and also to see why he has caught the imagination of the youth of Cuba all over the island. Here was an educated, dedicated fanatic, a man of ideals, of courage and of remarkable qualities of leadership.

As the story unfolded of how he had at first gathered the few remnants of the Eighty-two [from the Granma] around him; kept the Government troops at bay while youths came in from other parts of Oriente as General Batista's counter-terrorism aroused them; got arms and supplies and then began the series of raids and counter-attacks of guerrilla warfare, one got a feeling that he is now invincible. Perhaps he isn't, but that is the faith he inspires in his followers. . . .

Señor Castro speaks some English, but he preferred to talk in Spanish, which he did with extraordinary eloquence. His is a political mind rather than a military one. He has strong ideas of liberty, democracy, social justice, the need to restore the Constitution, to hold elections. He has strong ideas on economy, too, but an economist would consider them weak.

The 26th of July Movement talks of nationalism, anti-colonialism, anti-imperialism. I asked Señor Castro about that. He answered, "You can be sure we have no animosity toward the United States and the American people. . . . Batista has 3,000 men in the field against us. I will not tell you how many we have, for obvious reasons. He works in columns of 200; we in groups of ten to forty, and we are winning. It is a battle against time and time is on our side." . . .

1958

Operation Pan America

Juscelino Kubitschek

When Vice President Richard M. Nixon and his wife Patricia made a two-and-a-half-week "goodwill" tour of eight Latin American countries in April 1958, increasingly defiant public demonstrations against the U.S. government greeted him at every stop. Stoned and spat upon in Lima and Caracas, where his limousine was nearly overturned by an enraged crowd, Nixon blamed the demonstrations on communists. But in a letter to President Dwight D. Eisenhower on May 28, Brazilian president Juscelino Kubitschek (1956–61) tried to place the anger against Nixon in historical context. His letter's proposal for a massive U.S. commitment to Latin American development was later dubbed "Operation Pan America." The White House released Kubitschek's letter and Eisenhower's noncommital reply in June. Encouraged by the president's brother Milton to do more (see Document No. 89), and concerned about the success of Fidel Castro's revolution in Cuba, the Eisenhower administration eventually initiated the Act of Bogotá (see Document No. 80), an agreement for a hemispheric development program along the lines first proposed by Kubitschek.

Mr. President: I want to convey to Your Excellency, on behalf of the Brazilian people as well as for myself, an expression of sentiments of solidarity and esteem, the affirmation of which is become necessary in view of the aggressions and vexations undergone by Vice President Nixon during his recent visit to countries in Latin America.

The widespread reaction of aversion on the part of the governments and of public opinion in the very nations in which occurred those reprovable acts against the serene and courageous person of the Vice President, constitutes proof that such demonstrations proceeded from a factious minority.

Nonetheless, it would be hardly feasible to conceal the fact that, before world public opinion, the ideal of pan American unity has suffered serious impairment. Those disagreeable events, which we deplore so much, have nevertheless

Source: "U.S. and Brazilian Presidents Reaffirm Inter-American Solidarity, President Kubitschek to President Eisenhower," *Department of State Bulletin,* 38 (June 30, 1958): 1090–91.

imparted an inescapable impression that we misunderstand each other on this Continent. The propaganda disseminated by the tools of anti-Americanism is apparently now directed toward presenting such supposed misunderstandings as actual incompatibility and even enmity between the free countries of the American community. Fortunately, this is far from being the truth.

It appears to me, Mr. President, that it would be utterly inconvenient and unfair to allow this false impression to prevail, morally weakening the cause of democracy, to the defense of which we are pledged.

In addressing these words to Your Excellency, my sole purpose is to acquaint you with my deep-seated conviction that something must be done to restore composure to the continental unity. I have no definite and detailed plans to that effect, but rather ideas and thoughts which I could confide to Your Excellency should an early opportunity to do so arise.

I might venture at this juncture, however, that the hour has come for us to undertake jointly a thorough review of the policy of mutual understanding on this Hemisphere and to conduct a comprehensive reappraisal of the proceedings already in motion for the furtherance of pan American ideals in all their aspects and implications. The time has come for us to ask ourselves the pertinent question as to whether or not all of us are doing our utmost to weld the indestructible union of sentiments, aspirations and interests called for by the graveness of the world situation.

As a soldier who led democracy to victory, as an experienced statesman and, above all as a man sensitive to the ways of truth, Your Excellency is in an unique position to evaluate the seriousness of the question which I postulate with the exclusive purpose of defining and subsequently eliminating an entire range of misunderstandings that are easily capable of being removed at this moment but which may perhaps suffer a malignant growth should we fail to give it proper and timely attention.

It is hoped that the unpleasant memory of the ordeal undergone by Vice President Nixon will be effaced by the results of earnest efforts towards creating something deeper and more durable for the defense and preservation of our common destiny.

As I have already said to Your Excellency, it is advisable that we correct the false impression that we are not behaving in a fraternal way in the Americas; but besides this corrective effort, and in order that it be durable and perfect, we must search our consciences to find out if we are following the right path in regard to pan Americanism.

It is my earnest hope that Your Excellency will feel that this letter was written under the impulse of a desire to reaffirm the warm and sincere fraternal sentiments which have always bound my Country to the United States of America. . . .

May God guard Your Excellency and the people of the United States of America.

❖

NO. 80

1960

The Act of Bogotá

The Committee of 21

In the late 1950s, the United States was intensifying its search for new and bolder ways to cooperate with Latin America in overcoming some of the region's obstacles to economic and social development. Brazil's President Kubitschek proposed an "Operation Pan America" to President Eisenhower in May 1958 (Document No. 79). In September, as the result of a meeting in Washington at which Latin American foreign ministers highlighted their countries' economic problems, the Council of the Organization of American States established a special committee to study measures for economic cooperation. At its second meeting in Buenos Aires in April and May 1959, the Committee of 21, as it became known, was addressed by Fidel Castro, the Cuban prime minister and the leader of the popular revolt that had just overthrown the dictatorship of Fulgencio Batista. At that meeting, Castro proposed a ten-year, $30 billion, U.S.-funded economic development program for Latin America. The Eisenhower administration, meanwhile, announced its support for the creation of an Inter-American Development Bank, and a $500 million commitment to spending on economic and social development. The Committee of 21 met for the third and last time in September 1960 in Bogotá, where it adopted a series of recommendations, known as the Act of Bogotá, to be presented to the Council of the OAS.

I. Measures for Social Improvements

An inter-American program for social development should be established which should be directed to the carrying out of the following measures of social improvement in Latin America, as considered appropriate in each country:

A. MEASURES FOR THE IMPROVEMENT OF CONDITIONS OF RURAL LIVING AND LAND USE

1. The examination of existing legal and institutional systems with respect to:

Source: *Act of Bogotá: Measures for Social Improvement and Economic Development Within the Framework of Operation Pan America*. Washington, D.C.: Pan American Union, 1961.

   a. land tenure legislation and facilities with a view to ensuring a wider and more equitable distribution of the ownership of land, in a manner consistent with the objectives of employment, productivity and economic growth;

   b. agricultural credit institutions with a view to providing adequate financing to individual farmers or groups of farmers;

   c. tax systems and procedures and fiscal policies with a view to assuring equity of taxation and encouraging improved use of land, especially of privately-owned land which is idle.

2. The initiation or acceleration of appropriate programs to modernize and improve the existing legal and institutional framework to ensure better conditions of land tenure, extend more adequate credit facilities and provide increased incentives in the land tax structure.

3. The acceleration of the preparation of projects and programs for:

   a. land reclamation and land settlement, with a view to promoting more widespread ownership, and efficient use of land, particularly of unutilized or underutilized land;

   b. the increase of the productivity of land already in use; and

   c. the construction of farm-to-market and access roads.

4. The adoption or acceleration of other government service programs designed particularly to assist the small farmer, such as new or improved marketing organizations; extension services; research and basic surveys; and demonstration, education, and training facilities.

B. MEASURES FOR THE IMPROVEMENT OF HOUSING AND COMMUNITY FACILITIES

1. The examination of existing policies in the field of housing and community facilities, including urban and regional planning, with a view to improving such policies, strengthening public institutions and promoting private initiative and participation in programs in these fields. Special consideration should be given to encouraging financial institutions to invest in low-cost housing on a long-term basis and in building and construction industries.

2. The strengthening of the existing legal and institutional framework for mobilizing financial resources to provide better housing and related facilities for the people and to create new institutions for this purpose when necessary. . . .

C. MEASURES FOR THE IMPROVEMENT OF EDUCATIONAL SYSTEMS AND TRAINING FACILITIES

1. The re-examination of educational systems, giving particular attention to:

   a. the development of modern methods of mass education for the eradication of illiteracy;

   b. the adequacy of training in the industrial arts and sciences with due emphasis on laboratory and work experience and on the practical application of knowledge for the solution of social and economic problems;

c. the need to provide instruction in rural schools not only in basic subjects but also in agriculture, health, sanitation, nutrition, and in methods of home and community improvement;

d. the broadening of courses of study in secondary schools to provide the training necessary for clerical and executive personnel in industry, commerce, public administration, and community service;

e. specialized trade and industrial education related to the commercial and industrial needs of the community;

f. vocational agricultural instruction;

g. advanced education of administrators, engineers, economists, and other professional personnel of key importance to economic development.

D. MEASURES FOR THE IMPROVEMENT OF PUBLIC HEALTH

1. The re-examination of programs and policies of public health, giving particular attention to:

a. strengthening the expansion of national and local health services, especially those directed to the reduction of infant mortality;

b. the progressive development of health insurance systems, including those providing for maternity, accident and disability insurance, in urban and rural areas;

c. the provision of hospital and health service in areas located away from main centers of population;

d. the extension of public medical services to areas of exceptional need;

e. the strengthening of campaigns for the control or elimination of communicable diseases with special attention to the eradication of malaria;

f. the provision of water supply facilities for purposes of health and economic development;

g. the training of public health officials and technicians;

h. the strengthening of programs of nutrition for low-income groups.

E. MEASURES FOR THE MOBILIZATION OF DOMESTIC RESOURCES

1. This program shall be carried out within the framework of the maximum creation of domestic savings and of the improvement of fiscal and financial practices;

2. The equity and effectiveness of existing tax schedules, assessment practices and collection procedures shall be examined with a view to providing additional revenue for the purpose of this program;

3. The allocation of tax revenues shall be reviewed, having in mind an adequate provision of such revenues to the areas of social development mentioned in the foregoing paragraphs.

II. Creation of a Special Fund for Social Development

1. The delegations of the governments of the Latin American republics welcome the decision of the Government of the United States to establish a special inter-American fund for social development, with the Inter-American Development Bank to become the primary mechanism for the administration of the fund. . . .

III. Measures for Economic Development

The Special Committee. . . . expresses its conviction:

1. That within the framework of Operation Pan America the economic development of Latin America requires prompt action of exceptional breadth in the field of international cooperation and domestic effort comprising:
   a. additional public and private financial assistance on the part of capital exporting countries of America, Western Europe, and international lending agencies within the framework of their charters . . .
   b. mobilization of additional domestic capital, both public and private;
   c. technical assistance by the appropriate international agencies in the preparation and implementation of national and regional Latin American development projects and plans;
   d. the necessity for developing and strengthening credit facilities for small and medium private business, agriculture and industry.

[The Special Committee] recommends. . . that special attention be given to an expansion of long-term lending. . . .

In approving the Act of Bogotá the Delegations to the Special Committee, convinced that the people of the Americas can achieve a better life only within the democratic system, renew their faith in the essential values which lie at the base of Western civilization, and re-affirm their determination to assure the fullest measure of well-being to the people of the Americas under conditions of freedom and respect for the supreme dignity of the individual.

NO. 81

1960

Debating Cuba and Castro

Richard M. Nixon and John F. Kennedy

Relations between the governments of Cuba and the United States deteriorated rapidly after Fidel Castro's July 26th Movement seized power in January 1959. The Castro government's sweeping economic reforms, including the redistribution of agricultural land and a variety of other measures aimed at raising the standard of living of ordinary Cubans, were interpreted by Washington as signs of a communist takeover in Cuba. In early 1960, Cuba resumed diplomatic relations with the Soviet Union and signed trade agreements with it and other socialist countries. In March, President Dwight D. Eisenhower secretly authorized the Central Intelligence Agency to create an invasion force composed of anti-Castro Cuban exiles. As the Cuban government expropriated more property owned by U.S. investors, Washington responded with an economic embargo on October 13, two weeks before the U.S. presidential election. The two principal candidates, Senator John F. Kennedy, the Democratic nominee, and Vice President Richard M. Nixon, the Republican nominee, met in their fourth and final televised debate on the evening of October 21. That morning's newspapers had reported a Kennedy statement favoring U.S. government support for an exile invasion force. Since both candidates had already been fully briefed by the CIA on the secret plans for the invasion, Nixon was furious with Kennedy and responded forcefully in that night's debate. Neither candidate, of course, was free to reveal what he knew about the covert operation.

Mr. Kennedy. The question is: Are we moving in the direction of peace and security? Is our relative strength growing? Is—as Mr. Nixon says—our prestige at an all-time high, as he said a week ago, and that of the Communists at an all-time low? I don't believe it is. I don't believe that our relative strength is increasing, and I say that, not as a Democratic standard bearer, but as a citizen of the United States who is concerned about the United States.

Source: U.S. Congress. Senate. *Freedom of Communications. Final Report of the Committee on Commerce . . .* Part III, *The Joint Appearances of Senator John F. Kennedy and Vice President Richard M. Nixon . . .* 11 December 1961, 87th Cong., 1st session., pp. 260–68. Senate Report 994 Part 3. Washington, D.C.: GPO, 1961.

I look at Cuba, 90 miles off the coast of the United States. In 1957 I was in Havana. I talked to the American Ambassador there. He said that he was the second most powerful man in Cuba and yet even though Ambassador Smith and Ambassador Gardner, both Republican Ambassadors, both warned of Castro, the Marxist influences around Castro, the Communist influences around Castro, both of them have testified in the last 6 weeks that in spite of their warnings to the American Government, nothing was done.

Our security depends upon Latin America. Can any American, looking at the situation in Latin America, feel contented with what's happening today, when a candidate for the Presidency of Brazil feels it necessary to call, not on Washington during the campaign, but on Castro in Havana, in order to pick up the support of the Castro supporters in Brazil? . . .

Mr. [Frank] Singiser [Mutual Broadcasting System]. Mr. Vice President, I'd like to pin down the difference between the way you would handle Castro's regime and prevent the establishment of Communist governments in the Western Hemisphere and the way that Senator Kennedy would proceed. . . .

Mr. Nixon. Our policies are very different. I think that Senator Kennedy's policies and recommendations for the handling of the Castro regime are probably the most dangerously irresponsible recommendations that he's made during the course of this campaign. In effect, what Senator Kennedy recommends is that the United States Government should give help to the exiles and to those within Cuba who opposed the Castro regime, provided they are anti-Batista.

Now let's just see what this means. We have five treaties with Latin America, including the one setting up the Organization of American States in Bogotá in 1948, in which we've agreed not to intervene in the international affairs of any other American country, and they as well have agreed to do likewise.

The Charter of the United Nations, its preamble, Article 1 and Article 2 also provide that there shall be no intervention by one nation in the internal affairs of another. Now I don't know what Senator Kennedy suggests when he says that we should help those who oppose the Castro regime both in Cuba and without. But I do know this, that if we were to follow that recommendation that we would lose all of our friends in Latin America, we would probably be condemned in the United Nations, and we would not accomplish our objective. I know something else. It would be an open invitation for Mr. Khrushchev to come in, to come into Latin America and to engage us in what would be a civil war and possibly even worse than that.

This is the major recommendation that he's made. Now what can we do? We can do what we did with Guatemala. There was a Communist dictator that we inherited from the previous administration. We quarantined Mr. Arbenz. The result was that the Guatemalan people themselves eventually rose up and they threw him out. We are quarantining Mr. Castro today. We are quarantining him diplomatically by bringing back our Ambassador, economically by cutting off trade—and Senator Kennedy's suggestion that the trade that we cut off is not significant is just 100 percent wrong. We are cutting off the significant items that the Cuban regime needs in order to survive. By cutting off trade, by cutting off our diplomatic relations as we have, we will quarantine this regime so that the people of Cuba themselves will take care of Mr. Castro. But for us to do what Senator Kennedy has suggested, would bring results which I know he would not want and certainly which the American people would not want.

Mr. Kennedy. MR. Nixon shows himself misinformed. He surely must be aware that most of the equipment and arms and resources for Castro came from the United States, flowed out of Florida and other parts of the United States to Castro in the mountains. There isn't any doubt about that, No. 1.

No. 2, I believe that if any economic sanctions against Latin America are going to be successful, they have to be multilateral, they have to include the other countries of Latin America. The very minute effect of the action which has been taken this week on Cuba's economy, I believe Castro can replace those markets very easily through Latin America, through Europe, and through Eastern Europe. If the United States had stronger prestige and influence in Latin America it could persuade, as Franklin Roosevelt did in 1940, the countries of Latin America to join in an economic quarantine of Castro. That's the only way you can bring real economic pressure on the Castro regime and also the countries of Western Europe, Canada, Japan, and the others.

No. 3, Castro is only the beginning of our difficulties throughout Latin America. The big struggle will be to prevent the influence of Castro spreading to other countries—Mexico, Panama, Brazil, Bolivia, Colombia. We're going to have to try to provide closer ties to associate ourselves with the great desire of these people for a better life if we're going to prevent Castro's influence from spreading throughout all of Latin America. His influence is strong enough today to prevent us from getting the other countries of Latin America to join with us in economic quarantine. His influence is growing, mostly because this administration has ignored Latin America. You yourself said, Mr. Vice President, a month ago, that if we had provided the kind of economic aid five years ago that we are now providing, we might never have had Castro. Why didn't we? . . .

Mr. Nixon. I would like to point out that when we look at our programs in Latin America, we find that we have appropriated five times as much for Latin America as was appropriated by the previous administration. We find that we have $2 billion more for the Export-Import Bank. We have a new bank for Latin America alone of a billion dollars. We have the new program which was submitted at the Bogotá Conference, this new program that President Eisenhower submitted, approved by the last Congress for $500 million. . . .

1960

Listen, Yankee

C. Wright Mills

When the distinguished U.S. sociologist C. Wright Mills (1916–62) wrote *Listen, Yankee: The Revolution in Cuba,* his research on what he called the "power elite" had already won him a reputation as an outspoken, left-wing critic of U.S. society. An activist at a time in U.S. history when campus radicalism was both unfashionable and likely to damage one's career, Mills traveled to Cuba in August 1960, as revolutionary fervor on the island and U.S. hostility toward its government were mounting. He met with Fidel Castro and toured the island, interviewing officials and average citizens. Hastily published that fall, *Listen, Yankee* offered readers in the United States a highly sympathetic interpretation of the Cuban Revolution. Relying on tape-recorded interviews and his own poetic license, Mills wrote in the "voice" of Cubans themselves. *Listen, Yankee* sold more than 400,000 copies and immediately became a key text in the debate over policy toward Cuba and the "Third World" more generally. Despised by conservatives and regarded as suspect by traditional Marxists, Mills was eagerly embraced by the emerging generation of student radicals that would become known as the New Left.

. . . We Cubans know that you believe we are all led by a bunch of Communists, that the Russians are soon going to set up a rocket base, or something like that, here in Cuba, aimed at you; that we have killed thousands of people—out of hand—and are still doing it; that we have no democracy or freedom; that we have no respect for private property.

What you believe about us, after all, is your business: we don't really care. Anyway, much of what you believe—true or false—doesn't matter as much to us as it does to you. But we, too, have beliefs—and fears. . . .

Some of you came down to Havana—tens of thousands of you, in fact, during the fifties. Some of you came down just to lie in the sun or on the beaches we Cubans were not allowed to use. But some of you came down to gamble and to whore. We stood on our street corners and watched you in your holiday place in the sun, away from your bleak, Yankee winter. Some of us have begged from you; we were hungry, you see. But know this: that's over; we are not going to do that sort of thing again, ever. . . .

We suppose that off and on you've been hearing about Latin America since you were in high school, and we can imagine how boring it must have been for you. What you've heard, mainly, is about how one dictator has replaced another, and about bits and pieces of ancient history, and then those crowds rioting in the sultry streets. You haven't paid much attention to it, except to the violence now and then; and we can hardly blame you for it. But you can't afford to ignore us any longer.

For now our history is part of your present.

And now some of the American future is ours, too, as well as yours.

What is happening in Cuba today is not boring; it is not just another episode; it is not merely, as you might think, local stuff; it is not just another palace revolution; it is not something way off somewhere else. And you cannot understand it without understanding the history it is coming out of. . . .

If you can understand the things we are now going to tell you, we think you'll be able to make up your own mind about what is going on in Cuba and what it might mean for you, as well as for us.

First of all, we Cubans are part of Latin America—not of North America. We speak Spanish, we are mainly rural, and we are poor. Our history is not like your history; it is part of Latin American history. And Latin America is 180,000,000 people, growing faster than you are growing, and scattered over a territory more than twice as large as the U.S.A.

Like much of Latin America, but more so, we're fed up with what your corporations and what your governments do down here. They've dominated us long enough, we've said it to ourselves now. Your Government supported Batista right up to the last minute of his gangster regime. But now Cuba is not just another island in the Caribbean. The Caribbean is not a North American lake. All that—that's over. . . .

We've got others with us too. All over the world people, especially the young ones and the students, those who can read and who can talk and write and who are hungry enough to read well, they are beginning to react against your policies and the warrior establishments of your cold war and of your monopoly economy.

So this is who we Cubans are:

We're part of Latin America.

We're fed up with Yankee corporations and governments.

We've done something about it.

Your corporations and your Government don't like it.

We are not alone.

Today the revolution is going on in Cuba. Tomorrow—not next year—it is going to be going on elsewhere. A revolution like ours does not come about just because anyone wants it—although it takes that, too. Revolutions in our time, we Cubans believe, come out of misery, out of conditions like those of the old Cuba. Where such conditions continue and there's a mountain nearby, there'll be revolutions. And in Latin America and elsewhere there are many such countries still today in the old sloth. That is why this continent is going to become the scene of convulsions you've never dreamed of. . . . We're talking sense to you, Yankee; listen to us, please. . . .

Ours will be a simple, practical, flexible [political] system, we are sure of that. And it will take fully into itself the opinions of the people. Of course, we believe that minorities should have the means of expressing their opinions. For what is a political system but a way of protecting minority opinions? Otherwise, it is a dictatorship. We Cuban revolutionaries certainly know that! . . .

We want an absolutely free manifestation of the human spirit. That is our goal. We want a great and absolutely free intelligentsia. Up in the Sierra, nobody told us in which style we must act. Just so, men must write and paint freely. That liberty we revolutionaries have breathed; it is not some abstraction to us. It is what we have breathed in the streets, in the mountains, it is everywhere here in Cuba, everywhere that there is revolution. . . .

It was the U.S. pressure, it was the U.S. propaganda, it was what the U.S. has failed to do in connection with our revolution that has forced us, finally, to see that maybe we do *belong* in the Soviet political alliance. But whether we "belonged" with them at first, and whether we "belong" with them now—what choice has your Government *ever* given us about this? And that's one thing "Yankee" means to us: no choices given. . . .

So it seems to us, you're up against this: You've got to make your Government change its whole line of policy; you've got to argue for a completely new United States approach to the problems of the hungry world.

But to do that you've got to change drastically the whole economic system of your big corporations, at least as they operate outside the U.S.A.

You've got to smash Yankee imperialism from inside the United States. For you can't hope to make your Government—if it is your Government—change its line of policy unless you do smash that system. . . .

NO. 83

1961

The Alliance for Progress

John F. Kennedy

L ess than two months after he took office in 1961, President John F. Kennedy
pledged $20 billion in public and private funding to help Latin America carry
out the social changes that his administration considered necessary for the region's progress. Kennedy announced his plan for an Alliance for Progress to the
Latin American diplomatic corps on March 13, 1961, only a month before the
disastrous U.S.-sponsored invasion of Cuba at the Bay of Pigs. The timing of
the two events highlighted the close relationship between the U.S. government's
support for the Alliance and its fear of social revolution in the region. The Alliance for Progress built upon a commitment, extracted by Latin American leaders from President Dwight D. Eisenhower, for $500 million for development
projects (see Document No. 80).

It is a great pleasure for Mrs. Kennedy and for me, for the Vice President and
Mrs. Johnson, and for the Members of Congress, to welcome the Ambassadorial Corps of our Hemisphere, our long time friends, to the White House today.
One hundred and thirty-nine years ago this week the United States, stirred by
the heroic struggle of its fellow Americans, urged the independence and recognition of the new Latin American Republics. It was then, at the dawn of freedom throughout this hemisphere, that Bolívar spoke of his desire to see the
Americas fashioned into the greatest region in the world, "greatest," he said,
"not so much by virtue of her area and her wealth, as by her freedom and her
glory."

Never in the long history of our hemisphere has this dream been nearer to
fulfillment, and never has it been in greater danger.

The genius of our scientists has given us the tools to bring abundance to our
land, strength to our industry, and knowledge to our people. For the first time
we have the capacity to strike off the remaining bonds of poverty and igno-

Source: U.S. President. *Public Papers of the Presidents of the United States.* "Address at a White House
Reception for Members of Congress and for the Diplomatic Corps of the Latin American Republics,"
pp. 170–75. Washington, D.C.: GPO, 1962.

rance—to free our people for the spiritual and intellectual fulfillment which has always been the goal of our civilization.

Yet at this very moment of maximum opportunity, we confront the same forces which have imperiled America throughout its history—the alien forces which once again seek to impose the despotisms of the Old World on the people of the New. . . .

We meet together as firm and ancient friends, united by history and experience and by our determination to advance the values of American civilization. For this New World of ours is not a mere accident of geography. Our continents are bound together by a common history, the endless exploration of new frontiers. Our nations are the product of a common struggle, the revolt from colonial rule. And our people share a common heritage, the quest for the dignity and the freedom of man. . . .

But as we welcome the spread of the American revolution to other lands, we must also remember that our own struggle—the revolution which began in Philadelphia in 1776, and in Caracas in 1811—is not yet finished. Our hemisphere's mission is not yet completed. For our unfulfilled task is to demonstrate to the entire world that man's unsatisfied aspiration for economic progress and social justice can best be achieved by free men working within a framework of democratic institutions. If we can do this in our own hemisphere, and for our own people, we may yet realize the prophecy of the great Mexican patriot, Benito Juarez, that "democracy is the destiny of future humanity."

As a citizen of the United States let me be the first to admit that we North Americans have not always grasped the significance of this common mission, just as it is also true that many in your own countries have not fully understood the urgency of the need to lift people from poverty and ignorance and despair. But we must turn from these mistakes—from the failures and the misunderstandings of the past to a future full of peril, but bright with hope.

Throughout Latin America, a continent rich in resources and in the spiritual and cultural achievements of its people, millions of men and women suffer the daily degradations of poverty and hunger. They lack decent shelter or protection from disease. Their children are deprived of the education or the jobs which are the gateway to a better life. And each day the problems grow more urgent. . . .

If we are to meet a problem so staggering in its dimensions, our approach must itself be equally bold—an approach consistent with the majestic concept of Operation Pan America. Therefore I have called on all people of the hemisphere to join in a new Alliance for Progress—*Alianza para Progreso* [sic]—a vast cooperative effort, unparalleled in magnitude and nobility of purpose, to satisfy the basic needs of the American people for homes, work and land, health and schools—*techo, trabajo y tierra, salud y escuela.* . . .

With steps such as these, we propose to complete the revolution of the Americas, to build a hemisphere where all men can hope for a suitable standard of living, and all can live out their lives in dignity and in freedom.

To achieve this goal political freedom must accompany material progress.

Our Alliance for Progress is an alliance of free governments, and it must work to eliminate tyranny from a hemisphere in which it has no rightful place. Therefore let us express our special friendship to the people of Cuba and the Dominican Republic—and the hope they will soon rejoin the society of free men, uniting with us in common effort.

This political freedom must be accompanied by social change. For unless necessary social reforms, including land and tax reform, are freely made—unless we broaden the opportunity for all of our people—unless the great mass of Americans share in increasing prosperity—then our alliance, our revolution, our dream, and our freedom will fail. But we call for social change by free men . . . not change which seeks to impose on men tyrannies which we cast out a century and a half ago. Our motto is what it has always been—progress, yes, tyranny no—*progreso sí, tiranía no!* . . .

The completion of our task will, of course, require the efforts of all governments of our hemisphere. But the efforts of governments alone will never be enough. In the end, the people must choose and the people must help themselves.

And so I say to the men and women of the Americas—to the *campesino* in the fields, to the *obrero* in the cities, to the *estudiante* in the schools—prepare your mind and heart for the task ahead—call forth your strength and let each devote his energies to the betterment of all, so that your children and our children in this hemisphere can find an ever richer and a freer life.

Let us once again transform the American continent into a vast crucible of revolutionary ideas and efforts—a tribute to the power of the creative energies of free men and women—an example to all the world that liberty and progress walk hand in hand. Let us once again awaken our American revolution until it guides the struggle of people everywhere—not with an imperialism of force or fear—but the rule of courage and freedom and hope for the future of man.

1961

Lessons of the Bay of Pigs

John F. Kennedy

Code-named "Operation Zapata," the U.S.-sponsored invasion of Cuba at the Bay of Pigs was one of many covert U.S. operations against the Cuban government and its leader, Fidel Castro (see Document No. 102). Planning for the invasion began on March 17, 1960, when President Dwight D. Eisenhower authorized the Central Intelligence Agency to organize an expeditionary force of Cuban exiles. Some 1,300 Cubans were subsequently trained by the CIA in secret camps in Guatemala and Nicaragua. President John F. Kennedy continued to support the planning for the operation after he replaced Eisenhower, and on April 17, 1961, barely three months into his presidency, the exile force invaded the island, confident that its arrival would ignite a nationwide insurrection against Castro's government. Instead, the invasion was easily turned back by the Cubans, many of whom rallied to the defense of their government. The failure of Operation Zapata only seemed to strengthen Castro's control while giving his government a priceless claim to legitimacy and the right to boast that it had handed the United States a rare and humiliating military defeat. Although his administration initially denied any connection with the invasion, Kennedy was soon forced to acknowledge that Operation Zapata had been forged in Washington. The president talked about the fiasco in a speech to the American Society of Newspaper Editors in Washington, D.C., on April 20, five weeks after he announced the Alliance for Progress (Document No. 83).

The President of a great democracy such as ours, and the editors of great newspapers such as yours, owe a common obligation to the people: an obligation to present the facts, to present them with candor, and to present them in perspective. It is with that obligation in mind that I have decided in the last 24 hours to discuss briefly at this time the recent events in Cuba.

On that unhappy island, as in so many other arenas of the contest for free-

Source: U.S. President. *Public Papers of the Presidents of the United States; John F. Kennedy . . . January 20 to December 31, 1961.* (Address Before the American Society of Newspaper Editors, April 20, 1961) pp. 304–306. Washington, D.C.: GPO 1962.

dom, the news has grown worse instead of better. I have emphasized before that this was a struggle of Cuban patriots against a Cuban dictator. While we could not be expected to hide our sympathies, we made it repeatedly clear that the armed forces of this country would not intervene in any way.

Any unilateral American intervention, in the absence of an external attack upon ourselves or an ally, would have been contrary to our traditions and to our international obligations. But let the record show that our restraint is not inexhaustible. Should it ever appear that the inter-American doctrine of non-interference merely conceals or excuses a policy of nonaction—if the nations or this Hemisphere should fail to meet their commitments against outside Communist penetration—then I want it clearly understood that this Government will not hesitate in meeting its primary obligations which are to the security of our Nation! . . .

But Cuba is not an island unto itself; and our concern is not ended by mere expressions of nonintervention or regret. This is not the first time in either ancient or recent history that a small band of freedom fighters has engaged the armor of totalitarianism. . . .

Mr. Castro has said that these were mercenaries. According to press reports, the final message to be relayed from the refugee forces on the beach came from the rebel commander when asked if he wished to be evacuated. His answer was: "I will never leave this country." That is not the reply of a mercenary. He has gone now to join in the mountains countless other guerrilla fighters, who are equally determined that the dedication of those who gave their lives shall not be forgotten, and that Cuba must not be abandoned to the Communists. And we do not intend to abandon it either! . . .

Meanwhile we will not accept Mr. Castro's attempts to blame this nation for the hatred which his onetime supporters now regard his repression. But there are from this sobering episode useful lessons for us all to learn. Some may be still obscure, and await further information. Some are clear today.

First, it is clear that the forces of communism are not to be underestimated in Cuba or anywhere else in the world. . . .

Secondly, it is clear that this Nation, in concert with all the free nations of this hemisphere, must take an ever closer and more realistic look at the menace of external Communist intervention and domination in Cuba. The American people are not complacent about Iron Curtain tanks and planes less than 90 miles from their shore. But a nation of Cuba's size is less a threat to our survival than it is a base for subverting the survival of other free nations throughout the hemisphere. It is not primarily our interest or our security but theirs which is now, today, in the greater peril. It is for their sake as well as our own that we must show our will. . . .

Third, and finally, it is clearer than ever that we face a relentless struggle in every corner of the globe that goes far beyond the clash of armies or even nuclear armaments. . . .

Power is the hallmark of this offensive—power and discipline and deceit. The legitimate discontent of yearning people is exploited. The legitimate trappings of self-determination are employed. But once in power, all talk of discontent is repressed, all self-determination disappears, and the promise of a revolution of hope is betrayed, as in Cuba, into a reign of terror. . . .

We dare not fail to see the insidious nature of this new and deeper struggle. We dare not fail to grasp the new concepts, the new tools, the new sense of urgency we will need to combat it—whether in Cuba or South Viet-Nam. And we dare not fail to realize that this struggle is taking place every day, without fanfare, in thousands of villages and markets—day and night—and in classrooms all over the globe.

The message of Cuba, of Laos, of the rising din of Communist voices in Asia and Latin America—these messages are all the same. The complacent, the self-indulgent, the soft societies are about to be swept away with the debris of history. Only the strong, only the industrious, only the determined, only the courageous, only the visionary who determines the real nature of our struggle can possibly survive.

No greater task faces this country or this administration. No other challenge is more deserving of our every effort and energy. Too long we have fixed our eyes on traditional military needs, on armies prepared to cross borders, on missiles poised for flight. Now it should be clear that this is no longer enough—that our security may be lost piece by piece, country by country, without the firing of a single missile or the crossing of a single border.

We intend to profit from this lesson. We intend to reexamine and reorient our forces of all kinds—our tactics and our institutions here in this community. We intend to intensify our efforts for a struggle in many ways more difficult than war, where disappointment will often accompany us.

For I am convinced that we in this country and in the free world possess the necessary resource, and the skill, and the added strength that comes from a belief in the freedom of man. And I am equally convinced that this bitter struggle reached its climax in the late 1950's and the early 1960's. Let me then make clear as the President of the United States that I am determined upon our system's survival and success, regardless of the cost and regardless of the peril!

NO. 85

1961

The Charter of Punta del Este

The Delegates to the Special Meeting of the Inter-American Economic and Social Council

Following up his proposal on March 13, 1961, for the creation of an Alliance for Progress (Document No. 83), President John F. Kennedy asked the Organization of American States to convene a special meeting, at the ministerial level, of its Inter-American Economic and Social Council to draft concrete plans for the Alliance. Meeting in Punta del Este, Uruguay, from August 5 to 17, 1961, the council approved Kennedy's proposal. It adopted a charter establishing the alliance and setting up its organizational and administrative framework. The charter was signed by all the members of the OAS except Cuba, the leader of whose delegation, Ernesto "Che" Guevara, denounced it as an "instrument of economic imperialism."

We, the American Republics, hereby proclaim our decision to unite in a common effort to bring our people accelerated economic progress and broader social justice within the framework of personal dignity and political liberty. . . . Inspired by . . . the principles of Operation Pan America and the Act of Bogotá, the American Republics hereby resolve to adopt the following program of action to establish and carry forward an Alliance for Progress.

It is the purpose of the Alliance for Progress to enlist the full energies of the peoples and governments of the American republics in a great cooperative effort to accelerate the economic and social development of the participating countries of Latin America, so that they may achieve maximum levels of well-being, with equal opportunities for all, in democratic societies adapted to their own needs and desires.

The American republics agree to work toward the achievement of the following fundamental goals in the present decade:

1. To achieve in the participating Latin American countries a substantial and sustained growth of per capita incomes at a rate designed to attain, at the ear-

Source: "Charter of Punta del Este." *The Department of State Bulletin* 45, no. 1159 (September 1961): 463–69.

liest possible date, levels of income capable of assuring self-sustaining development, and sufficient to make Latin American income levels constantly larger in relation to the levels of the more industrialized nations. In this way the gap between the living standards of Latin America and those of the more developed countries can be narrowed. Similarly, presently existing differences in income levels among the Latin American countries will be reduced by accelerating the development of the relatively less developed countries and granting them maximum priority in the distribution of resources and in international cooperation in general. In evaluating the degree of relative development, account will be taken not only of average levels of real income and gross product per capita, but also of indices of infant mortality, illiteracy, and per capita daily caloric intake.

It is recognized that, in order to reach these objectives within a reasonable time, the rate of economic growth in any country of Latin America should be not less than 2.5 per cent per capita per year, and that each participating country should determine its own growth target in the light of its stage of social and economic evolution, resource endowment, and ability to mobilize national efforts for development.

2. To make the benefits of economic progress available to all citizens of all economic and social groups through a more equitable distribution of national income, raising more rapidly the income and standard of living of the needier sectors of the population, at the same time that a higher proportion of the national product is devoted to investment.

3. To achieve balanced diversification in national economic structures, both regional and functional, making them increasingly free from dependence on the export of a limited number of primary products and the importation of capital goods while seeking to attain stability in the prices of exports or in income derived from exports.

4. To accelerate the process of rational industrialization so as to increase the productivity of the economy as a whole, taking full advantage of the talents and energies of both the private and public sectors, utilizing the natural resources of the country and providing productive and remunerative employment for unemployed or part-time workers. Within this process of industrialization, special attention should be given to the establishment and development of capital-goods industries.

5. To raise greatly the level of agricultural productivity and output and to improve related storage, transportation, and marketing services.

6. To encourage, in accordance with the characteristics of each country, programs of comprehensive agrarian reform leading to the effective transformation, where required, of unjust structures and systems of land tenure and use, with a view to replacing latifundia and dwarf-holdings by an equitable system of land tenure so that, with the help of timely and adequate credit, technical assistance and facilities for the marketing and distribution of products, the land will become for the man who works it the basis of his economic stability, the foundation of his increasing welfare, and the guarantee of his freedom and dignity.

7. To eliminate adult illiteracy and by 1970 to assure, as a minimum, access to six years of primary education for each school-age child in Latin America; to modernize and expand vocational, secondary and higher educational and training facilities, to strengthen the capacity for basic and applied research, and to provide the competent personnel required in rapidly-growing societies.

8. To increase life expectancy at birth by a minimum of five years, and to increase the ability to learn and produce, by improving individual and public health. To attain this goal it will be necessary, among other measures, to provide adequate potable water supply and drainage to not less than 70 per cent of the urban and 50 per cent of the rural population; to reduce the mortality rate of children less than five years of age to at least one-half of the present rate; to control the more serious transmissible diseases, according to their importance as a cause of sickness and death; to eradicate those illnesses, especially malaria, for which effective cures are known; to improve nutrition; to train medical and health personnel to meet at least minimum standards of competence; to improve basic health services at national and local levels; to intensify scientific research and apply its results more fully and effectively to the prevention and cure of illness.

9. To increase the construction of low-cost houses for low-income families in order to replace inadequate and deficient housing and to reduce housing shortages; and to provide necessary public services to both urban and rural centers of population.

10. To maintain stable price levels, avoiding inflation or deflation and the consequent social hardships and maldistribution of resources, bearing always in mind the necessity of maintaining an adequate rate of economic growth.

11. To strengthen existing agreements on economic integration, with a view to the ultimate fulfillment of aspirations for a Latin American common market that will expand and diversify trade among the Latin American countries and thus contribute to the economic growth of the region.

12. To develop cooperative programs designed to prevent the harmful effects of excessive fluctuations in the foreign exchange earnings derived from exports of primary products, which are of vital importance to economic and social development; and to adopt the measures necessary to facilitate the access of Latin American exports to international markets. . . .

1961

The Shark and the Sardines

Juan José Arévalo

After surviving more than twenty coup attempts during his tenure as Guatemala's first democratically elected president, Juan José Arévalo (1904–90) stepped down at the end of his six-year term in 1951 to become an ambassador-at-large in the administration of his successor, Jacobo Arbenz. Arbenz's land reform program, his independent foreign policy and his appointment of members of the Communist Party to government posts contributed to a decision by the Eisenhower administration to force Arbenz out of office. An invasion of Guatemala by a small force of exiles, organized and financed by the Central Intelligence Agency, led to Arbenz's resignation on June 27, 1954 (see Document Nos. 74 and 75). The reforms initiated under Arévalo and Arbenz were overturned by the military government of Col. Carlos Castillo Armas, the exile leader chosen by the CIA to lead the invasion force and the CIA's choice for president of Guatemala. Arévalo's interpretation of U.S.–Latin American relations, *The Shark and the Sardines,* was first published in Chile in 1956 and appeared in English (with the preface excerpted below) in 1961.

In your hands you hold a controversial book—a book that speaks out against your State Department's dealings with the peoples of Latin America during the Twentieth Century. In it there is intended no insult to, nor offense to, the United States as a nation. The future of your country is identified with the future of contemporary democracy. Neither does this book seek to cast blame on the North American people—who, like us, are victims of an imperialist policy of promoting business, multiplying markets and hoarding money.

Very different was the ideology of the men who first governed your country. It was as thirteen widely varying former colonies inspired by ideals of individual freedom, collective well-being, and national sovereignty that the United States came into existence in the world. Protestants, Catholics and Masons alike, those men of the Eighteenth Century were moved by an ardent sense

Source: From *The Shark and the Sardines* by Juan José Arévalo. pp. 9–13. Copyright © 1961 by Lyle Stuart. Published by arrangement with Carol Publishing Group. A Lyle Stuart Book.

of dignity that won for them and for their cause the sympathy and the admiration of the entire world. They recognized worth in all kinds of work, they welcomed to their shores foreigners of every origin, and when their crops and their homes were threatened, they defended their crops and their homes just as they defended the privacy of the individual conscience. They went to church with their heads held high and they founded colleges so that their children might advance along the road to self-improvement.

Moral values served as a motivating force in the days of the Independence. Those same values, confirmed by the civilian populace of the young republic, figured among the norms of government. The nation was characterized by its grandeur of spirit and indeed great were the military accomplishments and the thesis of the new law. Amazed, the world applauded.

But as the Twentieth Century was dawning, the White House adopted a different policy. To North America as a nation were transferred the know-how, sentiments and appetites of a financial genius named Rockefeller. Grandeur of spirit was replaced by greed.

The government descended to become simple entrepreneur for business and protector of illicit commercial profits. . . . The new instrument of persuasion was the cannon. Now the United States had become different. It was neither a religious state nor a juridic state but, rather, a mercantile state—a gigantic mercantile society with all the apparatus of a great world power. The European juridic tradition was abandoned and North American morality was forgotten. The United States thenceforth was to be a Phoenician enterprise, a Carthaginian republic. Washington and Lincoln must have wept in shame in their graves.

The immediate victim was Latin America. To the North American millionaires converted into government, Latin America appeared as easy prey, a "big business." The inhabitants of this part of the world came to be looked upon as international *braceros*. The multiple-faceted exploitation was carried out with intelligence, with shrewdness, with the precision of clockwork, with "scientific" coldness, with harshness and with great arrogance. From the South the river of millions began to flow Northward and every year it increased.

The United States became great while progress in Latin America was brought to a halt. And when anything or anyone tried to interfere with the bankers or the companies, use was made of the Marines. Panama, 1903. Nicaragua, 1909. Mexico and Haiti, 1914. Santo Domingo, 1916. Along with the military apparatus, a new system of local "revolutions" was manipulated—financed by the White House or by Wall Street—which were now the same. This procedure continued right up to the international scandal of the assault on Guatemala in 1954, an assault directed by Mr. Foster Dulles, with the O.K. of Mr. Eisenhower who was your President at that time.

North American friends, this is history, true history, the briefest possible sketch of history.

We Latin Americans, who, more than anybody else, suffered from this change in political philosophy and its consequences, could no longer be friends of the government of the United States. The friendship certainly could be reestablished. But to do so, it would be necessary for the White House to alter its opinion of us and it would be necessary for conduct to change. We expect a new political treatment. We do not want to continue down this decline that takes us straight to colonial status, however it be disguised. Neither do we want to be republics of traders. Nor do we want to be African *factories.*

We Latin-Americans are struggling to prevent the businessman mentality from being confused with or merged into statesmanship. The North American example has been disastrous to us and has horrified us. We know that a government intimately linked to business and receiving favors from business loses its capacity to strive for the greatest possible happiness for the greatest number of its people. When businessmen are converted into governors, it is no longer possible to speak of social justice; and even the minimum and superficial "justice" of the common courts is corrupted. . . .

If you want to be our friends, you will have to accept us as we are. Do not attempt to remodel us after your image. Mechanical civilization, material progress, industrial techniques, fiduciary wealth, comfort, hobbies—all these figure in our programs of work and enjoyment of life. But, for us, the essence of human life does not lie in such things.

These lines, my North American friends, are meant to explain why I wrote the Fable of the Shark and the Sardines. This book was written with indignation—indignation wrapped from time to time in the silk of irony. It declares that international treaties are a farce when they are pacted between a Shark and a sardine. It denounces the pan-American system of diplomacy—valuable instrument at the service of the Shark. It denounces the Pan-American idea of "allegiance to the hemisphere"—juridic device that will inevitably lead to the establishing of an empire from Pole to Pole. It denounces the relentless and immense siphoning-off of wealth from South to North. It denounces the existence of the terrible syndicate of millionaires, whose interests lie even outside the United States.

It denounces the subordination of the White House to this syndicate. It denounces the conversion of your military into vulgar policemen for the big syndicates. . . .

This book, friends of the North, has been read all over Latin America. Read it now, yourselves, and accept it as a voice of alarm addressed to the great North American people who are still unaware of how many crimes have been committed in their name.

1962

The Hickenlooper Amendment

The Congress of the United States

In 1962, Senator Bourke B. Hickenlooper, Republican of Iowa, one of the Senate's leading experts on Latin America, sponsored an amendment to the Foreign Assistance Act of 1961 that was designed to discourage uncompensated nationalizations of U.S. corporate property. Although it was sponsored by Hickenlooper, the amendment was actually written by Monroe Leigh, a Washington lawyer whose firm had been hired to protect the property of the United Fruit Co. from a possible expropriation by the Honduran government. The Kennedy administration fought hard to prevent the passage of the amendment, which it considered a hindrance to its implementation of the Alliance for Progress. In 1994, the Hickenlooper Amendment was expanded when Congress required U.S. government representatives serving on the boards of directors of multilateral development banks and international financial institutions to vote against providing funds to countries whose U.S. government assistance would be suspended under the original 1962 legislation. The only exception allowed under the 1994 expansion was for assistance directed to serve the "basic human needs of the citizens of that country."

[T]he Foreign Assistance Act of 1961 . . . is amended as follows: . . .

The President shall suspend assistance to the government of any country to which assistance is provided under this Act when the government of such country or any governmental agency or subdivision within such country on or after January 1, 1962—

(1) has nationalized or expropriated or seized ownership or control of property owned by any United States citizen or by any corporation, partnership, or association not less than 50 per centum beneficially owned by United States citizens, or

(2) has imposed or enforced discriminatory taxes or other exactions, or restrictive maintenance or operational conditions, which have the effect of na-

Source: *United States Statutes at Large.* Vol. 76, pp. 260–61. Washington, D.C.: GPO, 1963.

tionalizing, expropriating, or otherwise seizing ownership or control of property so owned,

and such country, government agency or government subdivision fails within a reasonable time (not more than six months after such action or after the date of enactment of this subsection, whichever is later) to take appropriate steps, which may include arbitration, to discharge its obligations under international law toward such citizen or entity, including equitable and speedy compensation for such property in convertible foreign exchange, as required by international law, or fails to take steps designed to provide relief from such taxes, exactions, or conditions, as the case may be, and such suspension shall continue until he is satisfied that appropriate steps are being taken. . . .

❖

NO. 88

1962

The Principles of Economic Development— According to Washington

Thomas C. Mann

Thomas C. Mann was the U.S. ambassador to Mexico when he made this speech to the Confederación Patronal de la República Mexicana, a business organization, on September 25, 1962, in Mexico City. Mann, who grew up in the border town of Laredo, Texas, served as assistant secretary of state for inter-American affairs from 1960 to 1961, and again in 1964, when he was appointed by President Lyndon B. Johnson to simultaneously coordinate the Alliance for Progress. His views were shortly embodied in what became known as the Mann Doctrine—a turn away from measures aimed at instilling democracy and social reform in Latin America, a more tolerant attitude toward military rule, and a renewed emphasis on the protection of U.S. investments. Mann, whose doctrine was widely interpreted as a retreat from the founding principles of the Alliance for Progress, resigned from the State Department in May 1966.

Source: Thomas C. Mann, "The Experience of the United States in Economic Development: Its Relevance for Latin America." *The Department of State Bulletin* 47, no. 1221 (November 1962): 772–76.

In speaking of the experience of the United States in economic development, I shall refer to certain broad economic principles which I consider basic to our economic system. These same principles are also basic to other successful economies in the free world. However, it is not my intention to imply that every nation could or should apply these general principles or guidelines in the same general way that we have done. Cultures, situations, and problems differ from country to country and exact conformity is neither practical nor desirable. . . .

The first which I would like to mention is economic freedom. . . . We believe that freedom of choice by the individual unleashes individual ingenuity and inventiveness which in turn gives a vitality and dynamism to our economy that it could not otherwise have. . . . We are reluctant in the United States to stray too far from economic freedom in search of easy solutions to short-term problems. We would, for example, consider it against our own interest to deal with a temporary balance-of-payments problem in such a way as to diminish the prospects for a steady, long-term economic growth; or to force industrialization in a discriminatory manner and at a pace which would tie our economy, perhaps permanently, to a group of inefficient industries with dubious prospects of ever being able to compete and earn foreign exchange in the outside world. . . .

And now I turn to a second principal tenet of the United States economic system: High standards of living for the people can best be achieved in a competitive economy.

Let us first consider the protectionist, the one who does not wish to compete. . . . To be sure there are cases where protection is justified and desirable, as, for example, in the case of an infant industry which has good prospects of becoming efficient and competitive if, for a limited period of time, it is given a reasonable degree of protection. There are other exceptions. . . . But my point is that the national economy and the people pay a high price for excessive protection. Protection to a small group of individuals who own a particular factory is, in economic terms, a subsidy to the owners no matter what form it takes—whether it is a tariff, a quota, a licensing arrangement, or a cash subsidy.

The subsidy, if in the form of cash, is paid by the taxpayer. If it takes other forms, it is paid by the consuming public through higher prices, usually for an inferior product, hence lowering the real income of the people.

Precisely the same thing occurs when the industry is state-owned, with the difference that in this case the higher prices for consumer goods can be considered as an indirect tax. In any case the result is the same—a lowering of the real income of the individual.

So in these days when we are all talking so much about raising the real income of the masses the question may well be asked on social as well as economic grounds: Who receives the subsidy? Who pays the subsidy? Will the protected industry really be able, within a reasonable period of time, to pay the people back by efficiently producing goods of high quality at low cost? . . .

There are still other prices that are paid for excessive protectionism. National industries which cannot compete abroad cannot earn foreign exchange in the markets of the world. If too many industries are unable to compete, there will obviously be a problem of how the country can pay for its imports. . . .

Whether we consumers are employers or employees, whether we work in a factory, on a farm, or in an office, the quantity and quality of the things our money will buy is at least as important to our standard of living and our *real* income as the number of dollars we earn. . . .

This brings me to a third tenet of our economic system—the value of individual incentive.

There may be a few people in the world who have no interest in improving their material well-being. But most people do not consider it a virtue to content themselves with what they already have. Most of us want to have a better life for ourselves and our children.

It is this aspiration, plus the activity which it generates, that has ever been the mainspring of progress. For progress and economic growth require human effort. And the rate of progress and growth is related to the degree of human effort which people are willing to put into the job. . . .

And this brings me to the fourth and final tenet which I shall mention today: Capital and the capitalist are essential and useful elements in a free economic society. . . .

If one looks about the free world today, he must come to the conclusion that the single most important missing component in most economic development problems is risk capital. Those countries which have created internal conditions which attract the largest amounts of risk capital are those which will have the highest sustained rates of economic growth. Conversely, those which discourage risk capital, and which must then necessarily depend in the long run on their limited tax revenues, will have lower rates of economic growth. . . .

Some will disagree with the economic tenets I have referred to. But no one can dispute that these principles have worked well for the United States and for other countries too.

Since 1870 the gross national production of the United States has increased between 3 and 4 percent per annum. This is not a rate which is as spectacularly high as has been achieved for short periods of time in other countries, but no one can match this record of sustained growth and achievement over a long period of time. . . .

All of this has been accomplished because we have a climate of freedom and of competition; because we recognize the value of both the capitalist and the worker and the absolute importance of teamwork between them and with the entrepreneur and the technologist; because we recognize the value of individual incentive and the individual initiative which it produces; and because equal rights of every person, whether he is a citizen or a foreigner, are guaranteed by law.

1963

The Wine is Bitter

Milton Eisenhower

Milton Eisenhower (1899–1982) was President Dwight D. Eisenhower's younger brother and his intellectual confidant on matters of policy, especially affecting Latin America. The younger Eisenhower was president of Pennsylvania State University when the president appointed him special roving ambassador to Latin America, which he visited in 1953, 1958 and 1960. As a result of these trips, Milton Eisenhower advocated more U.S. government financial aid to Latin American governments; his support for more aid helped spur the establishment of the Social Progress Trust Fund by President Eisenhower on July 11, 1960. The fund would become the basis for President John F. Kennedy's Alliance for Progress (Document No. 83). Milton Eisenhower's widely read *The Wine is Bitter* (1963) lent credibility and support to the Alliance for Progress in its early years.

There is absolutely no doubt in my mind that revolution is inevitable in Latin America. The people are angry. They are shackled to the past with bonds of ignorance, injustice, and poverty. And they no longer accept as universal or inevitable the oppressive prevailing order which has filled their lives with toil, want, and pain. The terrible realization has dawned upon them that the futility of their lives and of their parents' lives need not have been, that it is the bitter fruit of an evil system of injustice. And so they are filled with a fury and a determination to change the future.

How will they change it? The enlightened among them—the good leaders, most intellectuals—call for a peaceful revolution, a series of sweeping reforms to topple the oligarchists, the corrupt, the dictators. But there are loud and insistent voices demanding violent revolution. The Communists and their fellow travelers feed the fury of the underprivileged with half-truths and false promises. They nourish a lust for revenge and a cynical conviction that only blood will wash away injustice.

The choice between these two courses is awesome. Cuba has succumbed to the lust for blood and violence. The remainder of the hemisphere teeters precariously on the verge of revolution—peaceful or violent.

For eight years I traveled and studied in seventeen of the twenty Latin-American countries. When I began, the voice of revolution was muted; the pleas of the privileged and the underprivileged alike were for massive economic assistance similar to that which we had extended to Europe under the Marshall Plan. The suddenly the mood changed and the quiet rumble of discontent became a strident drumbeat. Decades of sullen frustration suddenly crystallized into a wedge of anger which split Latin America asunder.

Architects of our Latin American foreign policy were jolted into a perplexing dilemma. They quickly realized that orthodox methods of helping our southern neighbors achieve a better life were not sufficient—indeed, orthodoxy seemed to be abetting the growing anger and discontent. They recognized that swift social change had to be part of economic growth. But the problem was to stimulate social change without violating the sacred hemispheric policy of nonintervention in the internal affairs of other nations. . . .

Optimistically, one may assert that the Act of Bogotá, the Charter of Punta del Este, and the Alliance for Progress constitute a modern Magna Carta of the Americas: land for the landless, tax systems that are fair and honestly administered, self-help projects to provide low-cost housing and better health facilities, concerted attacks on illiteracy, determined efforts to reduce economic instability that has long plagued the Latin American countries, and democratic institutions that protect freedom and the human spirit.

Pessimistically, many contend that this noble effort is doomed to failure because it is too late and because the oligarchists and Communists alike will not permit it to succeed, albeit for different reasons.

The United States has a crucial role in this drama. Our aid can be decisive in helping Latin Americans build better institutions, increase income, and purge injustice from their society. We must be swift and generous.

No one could spend a great deal of time with Latin Americans—political leaders, intellectuals, laborers, farmers, Indians, mestizos, whites, rich, poor, and dispossessed—as I have done without developing a genuine and abiding affection for them. They are the most engaging persons I have met in a lifetime of travel to most parts of the world. They are not, as too many believe, concerned mainly with the siesta and the serenade. They are a hard-working people who cherish individualism and human dignity. . . .

Knowing Latin Americans as I do, I believe that they will choose peaceful revolution, and that they will, in most of the republics, win the future without civil wars. I do not say this glibly, for I realize that the slightest spark could touch off flaming conflicts in a dozen different places in the hemisphere. I am aware of the harsh resistance that any effort for change will meet. I know the awesome dimensions of the problem that confronts the moderate Latin-American leader and the perils which he must negotiate to survive and triumph. But these things notwithstanding, I have a faith in the peoples of Latin

America and their cause. They have demonstrated a monumental patience in the face of abuse, and now that they are so close to a just and peaceful future, I think and pray that they will work for it rather than kill for it.

❖

NO. 90

1963

The Foco Theory

Ernesto "Che" Guevara

Born in Argentina in 1928, Che Guevara graduated from medical school in 1953 and immediately left for Guatemala. A supporter of the leftist government of Jacobo Arbenz, Guevara took refuge in the Argentine embassy when Arbenz's government was overthrown in June 1954 (See Document Nos. 74 and 75). Guevara was granted safe passage to Mexico, where he met Fidel Castro and joined the guerrilla army that Castro was organizing to overthrow the Batista government in Cuba. After the seizure of power by Castro's July 26th Movement on January 1, 1959, Guevara became an increasingly prominent theoretician and advocate of guerrilla war as a strategy for socialist revolution not only in Latin America but in Asia and Africa as well. His name soon became associated with the *foco* or "focus" theory of guerrilla warfare, which claimed that a national revolution could be launched and led by a small but dedicated band of combatants who would gradually attract a mass following of peasants and workers. Guevara personally applied his theory by leading a guerrilla column in Bolivia, where he was captured and put to death on October 9, 1967. The article from which this excerpt is taken was originally published in *Cuba Socialista* in September 1963, when Guevara was minister of industry in the Cuban government.

Source: "Guerrilla Warfare: A Method." In Rolando E. Bonachea and Nelson P. Valdes, eds. *Che: Selected Works of Ernesto Guevara*, pp. 89–103. Cambridge, Mass.: MIT Press, 1969. Original Spanish article appeared in *Cuba Socialista* in September 1963, pages 1–17.

"Guerrilla Warfare: A Method"

Guerrilla warfare has been employed on innumerable occasions throughout history in different circumstances to obtain different objectives. Lately it has been employed in various popular wars of liberation when the vanguard of the people chose the road of irregular armed struggle against enemies of superior military power. Asia, Africa, and Latin America have been the scene of such actions in attempts to obtain power in the struggle against feudal, neo-colonial, or colonial exploitation. In Europe, guerrilla units were used as a supplement to native or allied regular armies. . . .

This article will express our views on guerrilla warfare and its correct utilization. Above all, we must emphasize at the outset that this form of struggle is a means to an end. That end, essential and inevitable for any revolutionary, is the conquest of political power. Therefore, in the analysis of specific situations in different countries of America, we must use the concept of guerrilla warfare in the limited sense of a method of struggle in order to gain that end. . . .

The guerrilla is the combat vanguard of the people, situated in a specified place in a certain region, armed and willing to carry out a series of warlike actions for the one possible strategic end—the seizure of power. The guerrilla is supported by the peasant and worker masses of the region and of the whole territory in which it acts. Without these prerequisites, guerrilla warfare is not possible. . . .

Generally on this continent there exist objective conditions which propel the masses to violent actions against their bourgeois and landlord governments. In many countries there exist crises of power and also some subjective conditions for revolution. It is clear, of course, that in those countries where all of these conditions are found, it would be criminal not to act to seize power. In other countries where these conditions do not occur, it is right that different alternatives will appear and out of theoretical discussions the tactic proper to each country should emerge. The only thing which history does not admit is that the analysts and executors of proletarian policy be mistaken. . . .

The Yankees will intervene due to solidarity of interest and because the struggle in Latin America is decisive. As a matter of fact, they are intervening already as they prepare the forces of repression and the organization of a continental apparatus of struggle. But, from now on, they will do so with all their energies; they will punish the popular forces with all the destructive weapons at their disposal. They will not allow a revolutionary power to consolidate; and, if it ever happens, they will attack again, will not recognize it, and will try to divide the revolutionary forces. Moreover, they will infiltrate saboteurs, create border problems, will force other reactionary states to oppose it, and will impose economic sanctions attempting, in one word, to annihilate the new state. . . .

Let us think how a guerrilla focus can start. Nuclei with relatively few persons choose places favorable for guerrilla warfare, with the intention of unleashing a counterattack or to weather the storm, and there they start taking action. However, what follows must be very clear: At the beginning the relative weakness of the guerrilla is such that they should work only toward becoming acquainted with the terrain and its surroundings while establishing connections with the population and fortifying the places which eventually will be converted into bases.

A guerrilla force which has just begun its development must follow three conditions in order to survive: constant mobility, constant vigilance, constant distrust. Without the adequate use of these three conditions of military tactics, the guerrilla will find it hard to survive. . . .

Perhaps the guerrillas will be punished heavily by the enemy, divided at times into groups with those who are captured to be tortured. They will be pursued as hunted animals in areas where they have chosen to operate; the constant anxiety of having the enemy on their track will be with them. They must distrust everyone, for the terrorized peasants in some cases will give them away to the repressive troops in order to save themselves. Their only alternatives are life or death, at times when death is a concept a thousand times present and victory only a myth for a revolutionary to dream of.

This is the guerrilla's heroism. This is why it is said that walking is a form of fighting and to avoid combat at a given moment is also another form. Facing the general superiority of the enemy at a given place, one must find a form of tactics with which to gain a relative superiority at that moment either by being capable of concentrating more troops than the enemy or by using fully and well the terrain in order to secure advantages that unbalance the correlation of forces. In these conditions, tactical victory is assured; if relative superiority is not clear, it is better not to act. As long as the guerrilla is in the position of deciding the "how" and the "when," no combat should be fought that will not end in victory. . . .

We have predicted that the war will be continental. This means that it will be a protracted war; it will have many fronts; and it will cost much blood and countless lives for a long period of time. But another phenomenon occurring in Latin America is the polarization of forces, that is, the clear division between exploiters and exploited. Thus when the armed vanguard of the people achieves power, both the imperialists and the national exploiting class will be liquidated at one stroke. The first stage of the socialist revolution will have crystallized, and the people will be ready to heal their wounds and initiate the construction of socialism. . . .

In fact, the eruption of the Latin American struggle has begun. Will its storm center be in Venezuela, Guatemala, Colombia, Peru, Ecuador? Are today's skirmishes only manifestations of a restlessness that has not come to fruition? The outcome of today's struggles does not matter. It does not matter in the final count that one or two movements were temporarily defeated because what is definite is the decision to struggle which matures every day, the consciousness of the need for revolutionary change, and the certainty that it is possible.

❖

1965

Intervention in the Dominican Republic

J. William Fulbright

A s chairman of the Senate Foreign Relations Committee from 1959 to 1974, J. William Fulbright of Arkansas was a persistent critic of U.S. foreign policy. An early advocate of economic assistance for Latin America who frequently questioned U.S. support for dictatorial regimes, Fulbright opposed the Bay of Pigs invasion and denounced U.S. policy in Vietnam. In spring 1966, he delivered a series of lectures on U.S. foreign policy at the Johns Hopkins University. The lectures were expanded and published in book form as *The Arrogance of Power*. In the excerpt that follows, Fulbright addresses the U.S. invasion of the Dominican Republic on April 28, 1965. Within ten days, nearly 23,000 U.S. troops had occupied the country. Nominally carried out under the auspices of the Organization of American States, the invasion was the first of its kind in Latin America since 1934, when the United States terminated its military occupation of Haiti. The reason for the intervention was President Lyndon B. Johnson's fear that a military coup on April 24 in support of Juan Bosch, who had been deposed as president in 1963, could lead to "another Cuba."

Nowhere has the ambivalence in the American attitude toward revolution been more apparent and more troublesome than in the relations of the United Sates with Latin America. In Latin America as in Asia the United States, a profoundly unrevolutionary nation, is required to make choices between accepting revolution and trying to suppress it.

Caught between genuine sympathy for social reform on the one hand and an intense fear of revolution on the Cuban model on the other, we have thus far been unwilling, or unable, to follow a consistent course. On the one hand, we have made ourselves the friend of certain progressive democratic governments and have joined with Latin America in the Alliance for Progress, the purpose of which is social revolution by peaceful means. On the other hand, we have allowed our fear of communism to drive us into supporting a num-

Source: From *The Arrogance of Power* by J. William Fulbright, pp. 82–92. Copyright © 1966 by J. William Fulbright. Reprinted by permission of Random House, Inc.

ber of governments whose policies, to put it charitably, are inconsistent with the aims of the Alliance, and on three occasions—Guatemala in 1954, Cuba in 1961, and the Dominican Republic in 1965—we resorted to force, illegally, unwisely, and inasmuch as each of these interventions almost certainly strengthened the appeal of communism to the younger generation of educated Latin Americans, unsuccessfully as well.

The United States thus pursues two largely incompatible policies in Latin America—discriminating support for social reform and an undiscriminating anti-communism that often makes us the friend of military dictatorships and reactionary oligarchies. Anti-communism is increasingly being given precedence over support for reform. . . .

Guided by a reflex bred into them by Fidel Castro, American policymakers have developed a tendency to identify revolution with communism, assuming, because they have something to do with each other, as indeed they do, that they are one and the same thing, as indeed they are not. The pervading suspicion of social revolutionary movements on the part of United States policymakers is unfortunate indeed because there is the strong possibility of more explosions in Latin America and, insofar as the United States makes itself the enemy of revolutionary movements, communism is enabled to make itself their friend. The anti-revolutionary bias in United States policy, which is rooted in the fear of communism on the Cuban model, can only have the effect of strengthening communism.

The Alliance for Progress encouraged the hope in Latin America that the United States would not only tolerate but actively support domestic social revolution. The Dominican intervention at least temporarily destroyed that hope. . . .

The facts remain that the United States engaged in a unilateral military intervention in violation of inter-American law, the "good neighbor" policy of thirty years' standing, and the spirit of the Charter of Punta del Este; that the Organization of American States was gravely weakened as the result of its use—with its own consent—as an instrument of the policy of the United States; that the power of the reactionary military oligarchy in the Dominican Republic remains substantially unimpaired; that the intervention alienated from the United States the confidence and good opinion of reformers and young people throughout Latin American, the very people, that is, whose efforts are essential to the success of peaceful revolution through the Alliance for Progress; and that confidence in the word and in the intentions of the United States Government has been severely shaken, not only in Latin America but in Europe and Asia and even in our own country. . . .

The central fact about the intervention of the United States in the Dominican Republic was that we had closed our minds to the causes and to the essential legitimacy of revolution in a country in which democratic procedures had failed. The involvement of an undetermined number of communists in the Dominican Revolution was judged to discredit the entire reformist movement, like poison in a well, and rather than use our considerable resources to compete with the communists for influence with the democratic forces who actively solicited our support, we intervened militarily on the side of a corrupt and reactionary military oligarchy. We thus lent credence to the idea that the United States is the enemy of social revolution, and therefore the enemy of social justice, in Latin America. . . .

Intervention on the basis of communist participation as distinguished from control of the Dominican Revolution was a mistake of panic and timidity which also reflects a grievous misreading of the temper of contemporary Latin American politics. Communists are present in all Latin American countries, and they are going to inject themselves into almost any Latin American revolution and try to seize control of it. If any group or any movement with which the communists associate themselves is going to be automatically condemned in the eyes of the United States, then we have indeed given up all hope of influencing even to a marginal degree the revolutionary movements and the demands for social change which are sweeping Latin America. Worse, if that is our view, then we have made ourselves the prisoners of the Latin American oligarchs who are engaged in a vain attempt to preserve the status quo—reactionaries who habitually use the term "communist" very loosely, in part out of emotional predilection and in part in a calculated effort to scare the United States into supporting their selfish and discredited aims.

The movement of the future in Latin America is social revolution. The question is whether it is to be communist or democratic revolution and the choice which the Latin Americans make will depend in part on how the United States uses its great influence. It should be very clear that the choice is not between social revolution and conservative oligarchy but whether, by supporting reform, we bolster the popular non-communist left, or, by supporting unpopular oligarchies, we drive the rising generation of educated and patriotic young Latin Americans to an embittered and hostile form of communism like that of Fidel Castro in Cuba.

We simply cannot have it both ways; we must choose between the objectives of the Alliance for Progress and a foredoomed effort to sustain the status quo in Latin America. The choice which we are to make is the principal unanswered question arising out of the unhappy events in the Dominican Republic and, indeed, the principal unanswered question for the future of our relations with Latin America.

1966

Two, Three, Many Vietnams

Ernesto "Che" Guevara

In October 1966 Ernesto "Che" Guevara, after traveling in Africa and resigning as the Cuban government's minister of industry, secretly left the island to personally apply his *foco* theory of revolutionary warfare (Document No. 90) in Bolivia, where he took command of a guerrilla column. Guevara was captured by the Bolivian army and put to death on October 9, 1967. Following are excerpts from a message he sent to the founding conference of the Organization of Solidarity with the Peoples of Asia, Africa and Latin America (also known as the Tricontinental) in Havana in January 1966. The message was first published in Havana in April 1967 under Guevara's title, "Create two, three, many Vietnams, that is the watchword."

. . . The fundamental field of imperialist exploitation comprises the three underdeveloped continents: America, Asia, and Africa. Every country also has its own characteristics, but each continent, as a whole, also presents a certain unity. Our America is integrated by a group of more or less homogeneous countries, and in most parts of its territory U.S. monopoly capital maintains an absolute supremacy. Puppet governments, or, in the best of cases, weak and fearful local rulers, are incapable of contradicting orders from their Yankee master. The United States has nearly reached the climax of its political and economic domination; it could hardly advance much; any change in the situation could bring about a setback. Its policy is to maintain that which has already been conquered. The line of action, at the present time, is limited to the brutal use of force with the purpose of thwarting the liberation movements, no matter what type they might happen to be.

The slogan "We will not allow another Cuba" hides the possibility of perpetrating aggressions without fear of reprisal, such as the one carried out against the Dominican Republic, or before that, the massacre in Panama—and the clear warning stating that Yankee troops are ready to intervene anywhere

Source: Reprinted by permission of Transaction Publishers. "Message to the Tricontinental" by Ernesto "Che" Guevara. Copyright © 1969. In I. Horowitz, et al., *Latin American Radicalism*. New York: Random House, 1969.

in America where the established order may be altered, thus endangering their interests. . . .

But almost every country of this continent is ripe for a type of struggle that, in order to achieve victory, cannot be content with anything less than establishing a government of a socialist nature. . . . There is also such a great similarity among the classes of the different countries that an identification exists among them, as an "international American" type, much more complete than that of other continents. Language, customs, religion, a common foreign master—unite them. The degree and forms of exploitation are similar for both the exploiters and the exploited in many of the countries of Our America. And rebellion is ripening swiftly.

We may ask ourselves: how will this rebellion come to fruition? What type will it be? We have maintained for quite some time now that, owing to the similarity of national characteristics, the struggle in Our America will achieve, in due course, continental proportions. It will be the scene of many great battles fought for the liberation of humanity. Within the overall struggle on a continental scale, the battles which are now taking place are only episodes—but they have already furnished their martyrs, who will figure in the history of Our America as having given their necessary quota of blood in this last stage of the fight for the total freedom of Man. . . .

But if the foci of war grow with sufficient political and military wisdom, they will become practically invincible, obliging the Yankees to send reinforcements. . . . Little by little, the obsolete weapons which are sufficient for the repression of small armed bands will be exchanged for modern armaments and the U.S. military "advisers" will be replaced by U.S. soldiers until, at a given moment, they will be forced to send increasingly greater numbers of regular troops to ensure the relative stability of a government whose national puppet army is disintegrating before the attacks of the guerrillas. It is the road of Viet Nam; it is the road that should be followed by the peoples of the world; it is the road that will be followed in Our America, with the special characteristic that the armed groups may create something like coordinating councils to frustrate the repressive efforts of Yankee imperialism and contribute to the revolutionary cause. . . .

We must carry out a general task which has as its tactical purpose drawing the enemy out of his natural environment, forcing him to fight in places where his living habits clash with the existing reality. We must not underrate our adversary; the U.S. soldier has technical capacity and is backed by weapons and resources of such magnitude as to render him formidable. He lacks the essential ideological motivation which his bitterest enemies of today—the Vietnamese soldiers—have in the highest degree. We will only be able to triumph over such an army by undermining its morale—and that is accomplished by causing it repeated defeats and repeated punishment. . . .

The great lesson of the invincibility of the guerrillas will take root in the dispossessed masses. The galvanizing of national spirit, preparation for harder tasks, for resisting even more violent repressions. Hatred as an element of struggle; relentless hatred of the enemy that impels us over and beyond the natural limitations of man and transforms us into effective, violent, selective, and cold killing machines. Our soldiers must be thus; a people without hatred cannot vanquish a brutal enemy. We must carry the war as far as the enemy carries it: to his home, to his centers of entertainment, in a total war. It is necessary to prevent him from having a moment of peace, a quiet moment outside his barracks or even inside; we must attack him wherever he may be, make him feel like a cornered beast wherever he may move. Then his morale will begin to fall. He will become still more savage, but we shall see the signs of decadence begin to appear. . . .

What a luminous, near future would be visible to us if two, three, or many Viet Nams flourished throughout the world with their share of death and their immense tragedies, their everyday heroism and their repeated blows against imperialism obliging it to disperse its forces under the attack and the increasing hatred of all the peoples of the earth! . . .

Our every action is a battle cry against imperialism, and a call for the peoples' unity against the great enemy of mankind: the United States of America. Wherever death may surprise us, it will be welcome, provided that this, our battle cry, reaches some receptive ear, that another hand be extended to take up our weapons and that other men come forward to intone our funeral dirge with the staccato of machine guns and new cries of battle and victory.

❖

NO. 93

1967

The Tlatelolco Treaty

The Governments of Latin America

On February 14, 1967, the representatives of eighteen Latin American governments made the region the first in the world to declare itself a Nuclear-Weapons-Free Zone. Meeting in Mexico City, they signed the Treaty for the Prohibition of Nuclear Weapons in Latin America, since known as the Tlatelolco

Source: The Agency for the Prohibition of Nuclear Weapons in Latin America and the Caribbean, Mexico City. http://www.opanal.org/ENGLISH/WELCOME/Welcome.htm. December 1998.

Treaty after the site of the meeting; the words *and Caribbean* were added to the official title of the treaty in 1990. Inspired initially by the threat to their nations caused by the Cuban Missile Crisis of 1962, when the United States and the Soviet Union were poised to go to war over Cuba, the framers of the treaty agreed to outlaw the acquisition, testing, manufacture and use of nuclear weapons in their countries. By 1998, all thirty-three states comprising Latin America and the Caribbean had signed the treaty. In addition, the United States, the Russian Federation, France, the United Kingdom, China and the Netherlands signed and ratified Protocols 1 and 2 of the treaty, thus committing themselves to fully respect its provisions. The treaty created the Agency for the Prohibition of Nuclear Weapons in Latin America and the Caribbean (OPANAL—Organismo para la Proscripción de Armas Nucleares en la América Latina y el Caribe), headquartered in Mexico City, to supervise and control its implementation.

Treaty for the Prohibition of Nuclear Weapons in Latin America and the Caribbean

Preamble

In the name of their peoples and faithfully interpreting their desires and aspirations, the Governments of the States which have signed the Treaty for the Prohibition of Nuclear Weapons in Latin America,

Desiring to contribute, so far as lies in their power, towards ending the armaments race, especially in the field of nuclear weapons, and towards strengthening a world at peace, based on the sovereign equality of States, mutual respect and good neighbourliness,

Recalling that the United Nations General Assembly, in its resolution 808 (IX), adopted unanimously as one of the three points of a co-ordinated programme of disarmament "the total prohibition of the use and manufacture of nuclear weapons and weapons of mass destruction of every type";

Recalling that militarily denuclearized zones are not an end in themselves but rather a means for achieving general and complete disarmament at a later stage. . . .

Recalling that the Charter of the Organization of American States proclaims that it is an essential purpose of the organization to strengthen the peace and security of the hemisphere,

Convinced:

That the incalculable destructive power of nuclear weapons has made it imperative that the legal prohibition of war should be strictly observed in practice if the survival of civilization and the survival of mankind itself is to be assured,

That nuclear weapons, whose terrible effects are suffered, indiscriminately and inexorably, by military forces and civilian population alike, constitute, through the persistence of the radioactivity they release, an attack on the integrity of the human species and ultimately, may even render the whole earth uninhabitable,

That general and complete disarmament under effective international control is a vital matter which all the peoples of the world equally demand,

That the proliferation of nuclear weapons, which seems inevitable unless States, in the exercise of their sovereign rights, impose restrictions on themselves in order to prevent it, would make any agreement on disarmament enormously difficult and would increase the danger of the outbreak of a nuclear conflagration,

That the establishment of militarily denuclearized zones is closely linked with the maintenance of peace and security in the respective regions,

That the military denuclearization of vast geographical zones, adopted by the sovereign decision of the States comprised therein, will exercise a beneficial influence on other regions where similar conditions exist,

That the privileged situation of the signatory States, whose territories are wholly free from nuclear weapons, imposes upon them the inescapable duty of preserving that situation both in their own interests and for the good of mankind,

That the existence of nuclear weapons in any country of Latin America would make it a target for possible nuclear attacks and would inevitably set off throughout the region a ruinous race in nuclear weapons which would involve the unjustifiable diversion, for warlike purposes, of the resources required for economic and social development,

That the foregoing reasons, together with the traditional peace-loving outlook of Latin America, give rise to an inescapable necessity that nuclear energy should be used in that region exclusively for peaceful purposes, and that the Latin American countries should use their right to the greatest and most equitable possible access to this new source of energy in order to expedite the economic and social development of their peoples,

Convinced finally:

That the military denuclearization of Latin America—being understood to mean the undertaking entered into internationally in this Treaty to keep their territories forever free from nuclear weapons—will constitute a measure which will spare their peoples from the squandering of their limited resources on nuclear armaments and will protect them against possible nuclear attacks on their territories, and will also constitute a significant contribution towards preventing the proliferation of nuclear weapons and a powerful factor for general and complete disarmament, and

That Latin America, faithful to its tradition of universality, must not only endeavour to banish from its homelands the scourge of a nuclear war, but must also strive to promote the well-being and advancement of its peoples, at the same time co-operating in the fulfillment of the ideals of mankind, that is to say, in the consolidation of a permanent peace based on equal rights, economic fairness and social justice for all, in accordance with the principles and purposes set forth in the Charter of the United Nations and in the Charter of the Organization of American States,

Have agreed as follows:

ARTICLE 1—OBLIGATIONS

1. The Contracting Parties hereby undertake to use exclusively for peaceful purposes the nuclear material and facilities which are under their jurisdiction, and to prohibit and prevent in their respective territories:

(a) The testing, use, manufacture, production or acquisition by any means whatsoever of any nuclear weapons, by the Parties themselves, directly or indirectly, on behalf of anyone else or in any other way; and

(b) The receipt, storage, installation, deployment and any form of possession of any nuclear weapon, directly or indirectly, by the Parties themselves, by anyone on their behalf or in any other way.

2. The Contracting Parties also undertake to refrain from engaging in, encouraging or authorizing, directly or indirectly, or in any way participating in the testing, use, manufacture, production, possession or control of any nuclear weapon. . . .

❖

NO. 94

1967

The Lost Alliance

Eduardo Frei Montalva

The hopes that the Alliance for Progress raised among many Latin American political leaders began to give way to despair long before its promised decade of development had expired. One of the most thoughtful critiques came from Eduardo Frei Montalva (1911–82), a founder of Chile's Christian Democratic Party. Committed to thoroughgoing social and political reform yet staunchly anticommunist, Frei and his party attracted strong support from the U.S. government, including secret funding from the Central Intelligence Agency for his 1964 presidential campaign (see Document No. 102). Promising a "Revolution in Liberty," Frei won election that year to a six-year term, and almost immediately U.S. economic assistance for his reforms climbed to almost 15 percent of the national

Source: Eduardo Frei Montalvo. "The Alliance That Lost Its Way." Reprinted by permission of *Foreign Affairs*, Vol. 45, No. 3, 437–448. Copyright 1967 by the Council on Foreign Relations, Inc.

budget. Although Frei and his party were one of the greatest beneficiaries of U.S. development policy in Latin America, some of the tensions and contradictions inherent in the Alliance for Progress may be detected in the following excerpts from Frei's analysis. It was published midway through his presidential term by *Foreign Affairs,* the organ of the New York–based Council on Foreign Relations, a nongovernmental organization whose members and ideological outlook have been closely associated with the U.S. Department of State.

The Alliance for Progress is committed to the achievement of a revolution which, as a political instrument, should be placed at the service of democratic ideas and the interests of the majority so that it will bring forth a substantial change in the political, social and economic structures of the region. This change must be swift, and the responsibility for bringing it about belongs not just to a group of leaders or to a technocratic elite but to the whole of society. The Latin American origins of the Alliance for progress were especially evident in the non-Marxist political parties which had no links with the national oligarchies and were strongly opposed to the traditional Latin American Right.

The Latin American revolution, as a force for rapid and substantial change, has been germinating for the last decade; it is now a permanent and dynamic torrent which is weakening the political and social institutions of the continent. The form taken by this drastic change will depend on the time which elapses before the forces of revolution are finally released. The greater the delay, the greater will be the accumulated pressure and the greater the violence of the eventual explosion.

The Latin American revolution has clearly defined objectives: the participation of the people in the government and the destruction of the oligarchies; the redistribution of land and the ending of the feudal or semi-feudal regimes in the countryside; the securing of equal access to cultural and educational facilities and wealth, thus putting an end to inherited privilege and artificial class divisions. Finally, a main objective of the revolution is to secure economic development, coupled with a fair distribution of its products and the utilization of international capital for the benefit of the national economy. . . .

Has the Alliance achieved these objectives? Has it preserved democracy and helped to implement substantial changes? Unfortunately the answer is negative; the Alliance has not achieved the expected success. It cannot be said that since 1961 there has been a consolidation of democratic regimes in Latin America. On the contrary, various forces have threatened democratic governments, seeking to overthrow them or to prevent the implementation of their programs. Nor have structural reforms taken place at the expected rate.

This does not mean that the Alliance has failed. It has brought about many beneficial changes. Under its auspices there have been advances in education, in public health services, in communal improvement, in the development of rational economic programs and in better understanding between Latin America and the United States. But these constructive achievements could have been secured simply with the financial assistance of the United States, plus, of course, the demand that these additional resources should be used rationally by the recipient countries. The problem is that what was fundamental to the Alliance for Progress—a revolutionary approach to the need for reform—has not been achieved. Less than half of the Latin American countries have started serious programs of agrarian reform. Drastic changes in the tax system are even scarcer, while the number of genuinely democratic regimes, far from increasing, has actually declined. In other words there has been no strengthening of the political and social foundations for economic progress in Latin America. This is the reason why the ultimate objective of the Alliance—the formation of just, stable, democratic, and dynamic societies—is as distant today as it was five years ago. Several experiences indicate that economic progress alone does not suffice to ensure the building of truly free societies and peaceful international coexistence. The problem does not stem solely from the inadequate flow of internal financial resources. What has been lacking is a clear ideological direction and determination on the part of the political leaders to bring about change. These two factors are intimately related and they involve the collective political responsibility of all the members of the Alliance. . . .

It is unnecessary to point out names or dates, but at some stage the imaginative, dynamic commitment of countries united by a common ideal was gone. The name, Alliance for Progress, became yet another label for all forms of aid. Uncoordinated emergency loans became "Alliance loans"; technical and financial aid freely given to dictatorships was also "Alliance aid." The Alliance in fact became just one more source of assistance instead of a concerted program of mutual cooperation. Even though the aid retained its financial value, its ideological significance was completely lost. The flow of dollars given by the United States was carefully watched, but there was no equivalent effort on the part of Latin Americans to reform and become more democratic. Hence the Alliance has not reached the people of Latin America for whom it was created.

This is one of the most serious criticisms made of the Alliance: that the people have not been able to participate in it. Could it have been otherwise? The people are grateful for the assistance received, but they have no sense of belonging to the scheme. The revolutionary awareness of the Latin American people has evolved in such a way that it can now be considered as a norm—giving direction to their principal activities. The Alliance has failed to channel this awareness, and it has not provided the needed leadership; in fact, it does not belong to this revolutionary mainstream.

The Latin American institutions which collaborate with the Alliance do not include trade unions, student federations, peasant leagues, cooperatives, etc., yet it is vital that such organizations should take part in an enterprise which is essentially popular and whose success depends fundamentally on its capacity to satisfy the demands made by the community. From a political point of view this is one of the weakest aspects of the Alliance; its task is to carry through a revolution which will bring about economic and social development, and for this it is absolutely necessary that the people as a whole be committed to it.

The loyal participation of the community in this effort to build an egalitarian society is the only way in which the objective can be achieved. This is why the Alliance must incorporate all sectors of society in its work of transformation. . . . Another grave problem of the Alliance is its inability to promote the integration of Latin America. . . .

The salvation of the Alliance depends on the implementation of all these measures: the support of integration, the discouragement of the armaments race and the finding of a cooperative solution for the problems of external trade. The problem is not one of financial resources only, though at certain times these have been scant when compared with the legitimate needs of the region. It is essentially a political problem requiring the expression of the will to change, together with the acceptance of the measures needed to bring about this change. People do not support governments because they have dutifully complied with directives from this or that international organization; they support them when they offer a promising political and economic alternative to present frustrations, and the hope of moving into a better future. . . .

❖

NO. 95

1967

Transferring the Tools of Counterinsurgency

Albert H. Smith Jr.

By the mid-1960s, the armed forces of the United States had begun to accumulate a broad body of knowledge about the conduct of military operations against revolutionary guerrilla armies, as a result of the U.S. military's experience not only in Latin America but elsewhere in the world as well, most notably in southeast Asia. By 1967, almost every Latin American country had a U.S. Military Group ("MILGRP" in Pentagon parlance) to administer the programs of U.S. military assistance to the governments to which they were assigned, and to ad-

Source: "Counterinsurgency Operations Objectives." Correspondence from Commander in Chief, U.S. Southern Command, to U.S. Military Assistance Groups, Latin America, Aug. 30, 1967. Archives of the U.S. Army Military History Institute, Carlisle Barracks, Pennsylvania. Smith papers, file 13, "Counterinsurgency," Commander in Chief, U.S. Southern Command.

vise that government's military forces. The groups reported directly to the U.S. Southern Command, the Canal Zone headquarters of U.S. military operations in Latin America. The following memorandum was written by Brigadier General Albert H. Smith Jr., director of operations and training for the Southern Command in 1967–68, and apparently directed to the heads of the U.S. Military Groups in the various Latin American countries.

Based on recent experiences in support of counterinsurgency operations in Guatemala, Colombia and Bolivia, the following counterinsurgency operations objectives in countries faced with guerrilla or potential guerrilla problems were developed.

Counterinsurgency Operations Objectives

Improvement of recruit training. Related specific objectives include the establishment of facilities specifically for basic combat training (BCT) and advanced individual training (AIT). The programs of instruction should be standardized and oriented toward COIN [counterinsurgency] operations.

Development of a professional NCO corps—especially the development of professional NCO's [noncommissioned officers] to serve as fire team leaders, squad leaders and platoon sergeants in Army combat units. This requires the conduct of a realistic NCO training program on a continuing basis.

Establishment of an effective intelligence system. This involves not only creating an appreciation of the need for hard intelligence, but also the development of sources, surveillance means, training at all levels, responsive communication systems and joint action.

Improvement of personnel policies, systems and procedures. Here, a most important advancement is a measured input of inductees, as opposed to the practice in most countries of mass induction and mass release once or twice a year. From an optimum standpoint, new recruits should be taken into the armed forces monthly and veterans discharged monthly—as is the practice in the U.S. military. . . .

Development of a responsive logistics system to support operations in the field. Experience indicates that few Latin American countries have faced up to the problem of supporting combat units in the field, and this capability is absolutely essential for operations against guerrilla forces.

Improvement of joint operations in the field. Effective air/ground operations are based on a mutual understanding of capabilities; continuing liaison; rapid, reliable communications between ground forces and supporting air forces; and competent forward air controllers. Also, there is no substitute for joint training exercises. Periodic practice in the field will promote employment of the full range of air capabilities during anti-guerrilla campaigns.

In summary, MILGPs should emphasize the basic requirement for training fighters who are proficient and confident in their weapons and who have the morale and discipline to participate in combat. Quality training of the individual, improved leadership, intelligence, personnel and logistics systems are essential. . . .

To assist you in promoting and pursuing objectives listed, the staff will provide appropriate guidance materials. . . . Obviously, this is a long term effort. . . .

❖

NO. 96

1967

Songs of Protest from Latin America

The First Protest Song Conference

Latin American "protest song" was an expression that emerged in the late 1960s to encompass such diverse currents in popular music as the *nueva canción* of Chile and Argentina, the *nueva trova* of Cuba and *canción folklórica* of Mexico and Peru. Each country developed its own contribution based upon different musical traditions, and the songs often explored political and philosophical themes as well as sentimental one. Frequently they expressed a shared sense of pan-American solidarity, against and not with the United States. Excerpted below is the "Final Resolution from the Protest Song Conference" adopted at a meeting of fifty musicians from around the world at Havana's Casa de las Américas, a cultural institution, from July 29 to August 10, 1967. It represents one of the first attempts to identify a coherent ideological framework for the fledgling protest-song movement. By the early 1970s the movement's writers and musicians had made the protest song an important part of Latin American popular culture. While Cuba and the leftist government of Chilean president Salvador Allende directly subsidized protest-song musicians, right-wing governments terrorized, exiled and killed musicians, and even banned certain musical instruments associated with the popular-song repertoire. Among the most popular of the movement's musicians were the Cubans Pablo Milanés and Silvio Rodríguez (see Document No.

Source: "Resolución Final del Encuentro de la Canción Protesta." *Casa de las Américas*, 45 (Nov.–Dec., 1967): 143–44. Translation by Robert H. Holden and Eric Zolov.

100), the Chileans Violeta Parra and Victor Jara, Mercedes Sosa of Argentina and Los Folklorístas of Mexico.

The authors, performers and scholars gathered at this First Protest Song Conference, carried out in Cuba, the first free territory of America, salute the initiative of the Casa de las Américas for having allowed us to meet one another, exchange experiences and comprehend the scope of our work, as well as the important role that we are fulfilling in the struggle for the liberation of the people against North American imperialism and colonialism. We hope that this experience might be repeated for the benefit of the union of all those countries that fight with song.

Protest-song workers must be aware that song, by its particular nature, is an enormous force for communications with the masses, to the extent that it breaks down barriers like illiteracy that impede the dialogue of the artist with the people of whom he forms a part. As a result, song must be a weapon at the service of the peoples, not a consumer product used by capitalism to alienate us. Protest-song workers have the duty to deepen their skills, since the search for artistic quality is in itself a revolutionary stance.

The task of protest-song workers must be to develop themselves from a position at the side of their people, confronting the problems of the society in which they live.

Everyone today is a witness to the crimes of imperialism against the people of Vietnam, as shown by the just and heroic struggle of the Vietnamese people for their liberation. As authors, performers and scholars of protest songs, we raise our voices to demand an immediate and unconditional end to the bombing of North Vietnam and the total withdrawal of all the forces of the United States from South Vietnam.

We support the growing struggle of the black people of the United States against all forms of discrimination and exploitation.

We support the proletarian and student struggle which in the capitalist countries is being carried out against workplace exploitation, a faithful ally of imperialism.

We support the Cuban Revolution, which has shown the true path that the peoples of Asia, Africa and Latin America must take to liberate themselves, and we feel honored that Cuba has been the site of the First Protest Song Conference.

[Signed by musicians from: Chile, Argentina, Uruguay, Peru, Paraguay, France, Portugal, Mexico, Haiti, Cuba, Great Britain, Australia, Italy, and Spain.]

1968

Massacre in Mexico

U.S. Department of State

Ten days before the 1968 Olympic Games were scheduled to open in Mexico City, army troops fired on a crowd of several thousand antigovernment protesters, many of whom were students. About two hundred were killed. The massacre at the Plaza de las Tres Culturas in the Tlatelolco district on October 2, 1968, was a turning point in the modern history of Mexico. It revealed the brutality of an authoritarian political system long acclaimed abroad for its tranquil stability as well as the deep currents of discontent that the system had provoked among many Mexicans. Little by little over the next two decades, under continuing popular pressure, the system would be reformed to allow greater freedom of self-expression and genuine political competition. After the Olympic Games the U.S. State Department's Bureau of Research and Intelligence filed a report on the massacre, excerpted below. The report reveals both skepticism of the Mexican government's claim of communist influence and doubts about the future legitimacy of the government sponsored party that monopolized political power in Mexico, the Partido Revolucionario Institucional (Institutional Revolutionary Party), referred to as the PRI.

Student disorders of unusual ferocity have plagued a number of Latin American nations since April 1968. Extensive property damage, hundreds of arrests and injuries and more than one hundred deaths have resulted from police/student clashes in Mexico, Brazil, and Uruguay. Similar but less violent disturbances occurred in Bolivia, Chile, and in several other countries. Political tensions heightened in all five countries and—while tempers have cooled since October 1968—the present atmosphere remains unsettled and the possibility of renewed violence cannot be discounted.

Of all the countries in Latin America Mexico has experienced the highest degree of student unrest. Massive demonstrations by Mexico's university stu-

Source: National Security Archives, Washington, D.C. "Student Violence and Attitudes in Latin America (working draft)." Bureau of Intelligence and Research, Department of State. November 15, 1968.

dents have troubled the Díaz Ordaz government since late July 1968 when communist youths celebrating the July 26 anniversary of Fidel Castro's revolution managed to take over a peaceful student demonstration which had been authorized by the government. When police tried to disperse the crowd, rioting students burned buses and barricaded a four-block area of downtown Mexico City. About 4,000 students again demonstrated on July 29, at which time federal troops were used to restore order after police lost control of the student mob. Press accounts of the deployment of tanks and armored cars against student barricades served to picture Mexico as a battleground, not unlike Paris during the disturbances in the Spring of 1968. Several Mexican students were killed and more than 200 were injured during these battles with security forces.

Demonstrations, accompanied by occasional violence, continued throughout August and September, with the number of participants approaching 100,000 at times. Student grievances at first focused upon local issues of police brutality, release of arrested students, and a recognition of university autonomy which was violated on July 29. Cries were raised for the dismissal of the chief of police and the mayor of Mexico City and some radical students attempted to enlist labor support for their cause by calling for a 40-hour week and better housing. By August 15, however, the first student animus against the President was evident, a criticism which reached unprecedented heights of scathing vulgarity (for Mexico) on August 27 when student poster attacks depicted Díaz Ordaz as dishonoring the Mexican Constitution and openly called for an end to his government.

The student/government conflict grew in intensity and ferocity during September and October. With the October 12 opening of the Olympic Games fast approaching, the government seemed to abandon all hope of resolving the matter through negotiations and opted instead to use whatever force was necessary to put down what was then assuming the proportions of a student revolt. Such tactics had always worked in the past and the government probably assumed that they would be equally as effective again. Moreover, the timing of the student protests was linked to the Olympics and the continued agitation was extremely embarrassing to the Mexican Government which was most anxious to impress the world as a deserving host to the prestigious international games. The occupation of the national autonomous university by government forces on September 18 sparked new violence which continued intermittently until the bloody clashes on October 2 in which perhaps as many as 100 persons lost their lives. The October incident did considerable damage to Mexico's reputation as the most stable and progressive country in Latin America and brought into question the suitability of Mexico City as the Olympic site. Student agreement not to disrupt the games helped to cool tempers and an uneasy calm returned to student/government relations.

Seeking to justify its actions and its inability to resolve the situation, the Mexican Government raised the specter of foreign elements and domestic communists who it alleged were responsible for student activism. The administration seemed not to realize that extremists, even with the aid of foreign elements, could hardly have sustained the unrest over such a long period if student dissatisfaction were not deep and widespread.

The positions of both sides are intransigent and it seems unlikely that a fundamental solution to the problem can be brought about without changing the widespread conviction that the PRI is entrenched, stagnant and primarily self-serving. Despite the enormous graft and dishonesty which have become PRI hallmarks, students will have to be convinced that the party is still, or will again become, a vital force for political and social change as well as economic growth.

❖

NO. 98

1969

The Rockefeller Report

Nelson A. Rockefeller

The day after he took office as president on January 20, 1969, Richard M. Nixon asked one of his rivals for the Republican presidential nomination, Governor Nelson A. Rockefeller of New York, to go to Latin America, consult with its leaders and offer policy recommendations for the new administration. Accompanied by twenty to twenty-five special advisors on each of four separate trips to Latin America over the next six months, Rockefeller was greeted frequently by angry demonstrators. The governments of Peru, Chile and Venezuela asked him not to come. On August 30, Rockefeller submitted his report to President Nixon. It argued that Latin America and the United States were drifting apart and that in order to solve the hemisphere's social and economic problems, a new partnership between Washington and the Latin American governments had to be created. One dimension of that partnership, the report recommended, would have to be more tolerance by the United States for authoritarian rule in Latin America.

Source: Nelson A. Rockefeller. *The Rockefeller Report on the Americas: The Official Report of a United States Presidential Mission for the Western Hemisphere*, pp. 38–41, 58–62. Chicago: Quadrangle Books, 1969.

THE UNITED STATES' NATIONAL INTEREST

The moral and spiritual strength of the United States in the world, the political credibility of our leadership, the security of our nation, the future of our social and economic lives are now at stake.

Rising frustrations throughout the Western Hemisphere over poverty and political instability have led increasing numbers of people to pick the United States as a scapegoat and to seek out Marxist solutions to their socio-economic problems. At the moment, there is only one Castro among the twenty-six nations of the hemisphere; there can well be more in the future. And a Castro on the mainland, supported militarily and economically by the communist world, would present the gravest kind of threat to the security of the Western Hemisphere and pose an extremely difficult problem for the United States. . . .

Today's 250 million people in South and Central America will become 643 million in just thirty years. If the current anti-U.S. trend continues, one can foresee a time when the United States would be politically and morally isolated from part or much of the Western Hemisphere. If this should happen, the barriers to our collective growth would become formidable indeed. . . .

Historically, the United States has had a special relationship with the other American republics. It is based upon long association, geography, and, above all, on the psychological acceptance of a concept of hemisphere community. It is embodied in the web of organizations, treaties, and commitments of the inter-American system. Beyond conventional security and economic interests, the political and psychological value of the special relationship cannot be overestimated. Failure to maintain that special relationship would imply a failure of our capacity and responsibility as a great power. If we cannot maintain a constructive relationship in the Western Hemisphere, we will hardly be able to achieve a successful order elsewhere in the world. Moreover, failure to maintain the special relationship would create a vacuum in the hemisphere and facilitate the influence in the region of hostile foreign powers. . . .

POLICY AND ACTION

. . . Democracy is a very subtle and difficult problem for most of the other countries in the hemisphere. The authoritarian and hierarchical tradition which has conditioned and formed the cultures of most of these societies does not lend itself to the particular kind of popular government we are used to. Few of these countries, moreover, have achieved the sufficiently advanced economic and social systems required to support a consistently democratic system. For many of these societies, therefore, the question is less one of democracy or a lack of it than it is simply of orderly ways of getting along.

There will often be times when the United States will find itself in disagreement with the particular policies or forms of government of other American nations. However, the fundamental question for the United States is how it can cooperate to help meet the basic needs of the people of the hemisphere despite the philosophical disagreements it may have with the nature of particular regimes. It must seek pragmatic ways to help people without necessarily embracing their governments. It should recognize that diplomatic relations are merely practical conveniences and not measures of moral judgment. This can be done by maintaining formal lines of communication without embracing such regimes.

The U.S. should also recognize that political evolution takes time and that, realistically, its long-term interests will be served by maintaining at least minimal diplomatic relationships with other governments of the hemisphere while trying to find ways to assist the people of those countries, and to encourage the governments to move toward democratic processes. Such a policy requires a very difficult balance but is one that must be achieved pragmatically on a case-by-case basis. The U.S. cannot renege on its commitment to a better life for all of the people of the hemisphere because of moral disagreement with regimes which the people themselves did not establish and do not control. . . . If the quality of life for the individual in this hemisphere is to be meaningful, there must be freedom from fear and full respect for the rights and personal dignity of individuals—not just one's own rights and dignity, but everyone's.

Unfortunately, far too many people in the hemisphere—including people in the United States—are denied such freedom and respect. Forces of anarchy, terror, and subversion are loose in the Americas. Moreover, this fact has too long gone unheeded in the United States.

Doubt and cynicism have grown in the other American nations as to the purposefulness of the United States in facing this serious threat to freedom, democracy, and the vital interests of the entire hemisphere.

Many of our neighbors find it incomprehensible that the United States will not sell them military equipment which they feel is required to deal with internal subversion. They have been puzzled by the reduction in U.S. military assistance grants in view of the growing intensity of the subversive activities they face. . . . The subversive capabilities of these communist forces are increasing throughout the hemisphere. . . .

Military leaders throughout the hemisphere are frequently criticized here in the United States. However, we will have to give increasing recognition to the fact that many new military leaders are deeply motivated by the need for social and economic progress. . . . In many cases, it will be more useful for the United States to try to work with them in these efforts, rather than to abandon or insult them because we are conditioned by arbitrary ideological stereotypes. . . .

One other point not clearly understood in the United States is that no one country today can effectively protect its own internal security by itself. The youth that go abroad for training in subversive activities, the money and directives that flow through agents, and the propaganda that comes from outside their borders are all beyond their effective control. Only through hemisphere cooperation can these problems, which so vitally affect internal security, be adequately dealt with. . . .

1969

The Principles of Economic Development— According to the *Dependentistas*

Fernando H. Cardoso and Enzo Faletto

F ollowers of what came to be known as dependency theory argued that the chronic poverty and underdevelopment of Latin America were the historic outcomes of a world economic system that favored the wealthy core countries at the expense of those on the periphery of the system. By the late 1960s, Latin American economists affiliated with the *dependentista* school were refining their argument, grounding it in the region's economic history and building on the views that had been systematically staked out by the U.N. Economic Commission on Latin America (see Document No. 73). As developed by Latin American social scientists, dependency theory would become one of the region's most original contributions to late twentieth century social theory, exerting a strong influence on research in history, sociology, political science and anthropology as well as economics. Probably the single most influential statement of the theory was written by Fernando Henrique Cardoso and Enzo Faletto, between 1965 and 1967 while both worked at the Latin American Institute for Economic and Social Planning, a United Nations organization in Santiago, Chile. The English-language edition of their book, first published in 1979 as *Dependency and Development in Latin America,* was a revised and expanded version of editions published separately in Peru and Mexico. Cardoso was elected president of Brazil in 1995, by which time he had rejected some of the core tenets of dependency theory.

For our historical-structural analysis the crucial methodological question was to delineate moments of significant structural change in countries characterized by different situations of dependency in Latin America rather than criticizing on theoretical grounds either the structural approach to socioeconomic development proposed by ECLA or the structural functionalist models pre-

Source: Fernando Henrique Cardoso and Enzo Faletto. *Dependency and Development in Latin America.* Translated by Marjory Mattingly Urquidi, pp. vii–xxiv. Berkeley: University of California Press, 1971. Reprinted by permission.

vailing in sociological analyses, or blaming vulgar Marxism or the theory of political modernization. . . . We do not see dependency and imperialism as external and internal sides of a single coin, with the internal aspects reduced to the condition of "epiphenomenal." Conceived in this manner, imperialism turns into an active and metaphysical principle which traces out the paths of history on the sensitive but passive skin of dependent countries. . . .

We conceive the relationship between external and internal forces as forming a complex whole whose structural links are not based on mere external forms of exploitation and coercion, but are rooted in coincidences of interests between local dominant classes and international ones, and, on the other side, are challenged by local dominated groups and classes. In some circumstances, the networks of coincident or reconciled interests might expand to include segments of the middle class, if not even of alienated parts of working classes. In other circumstances, segments of dominant classes might seek internal alliance with middle classes, working classes, and even peasants, aiming to protect themselves from foreign penetration that contradicts their interests. External domination in situations of national dependency (opposed to purely colonial situations where the oppression by external agents is more direct) implies the possibility of the "internationalization of external interests."

Of course, imperialist penetration is a result of external social forces (multinational enterprises, foreign technology, international financial systems, embassies, foreign states and armies, etc.). What we affirm simply means that the system of domination reappears as an "internal" force, through the social practices of local groups and classes which try to enforce foreign interests, not precisely because they are foreign, but because they may coincide with values and interests that these groups pretend are their own. . . .

The very existence of an economic "periphery" cannot be understood without reference to the economic drive of advanced capitalist economies, which were responsible for the formation of a capitalist periphery and for the integration of traditional noncapitalist economies into the world market. Yet, the expansion of capitalism in Bolivia and Venezuela, in Mexico or Peru, in Brazil and Argentina, in spite of having been submitted to the same global dynamic of international capitalism, did not have the same history or consequences. The differences are rooted not only in the diversity of natural resources, nor just in the different periods in which these economies have been incorporated into the international system (although these factors have played some role). Their explanation must also lie in the different moments at which sectors of local classes allied or clashed with foreign interests, organized different forms of state, sustained distinct ideologies, or tried to implement various policies or defined alternative strategies to cope with imperialist challenges in diverse moments of history. . . .

Of course, there are common factors in capitalism which affect all economies under consideration and which constitute the starting point of the analysis. But it is the diversity within unity that explains historical process. If the analytical effort succeeds, general platitudes and reaffirmations about the role of capitalist modes of production can turn into a lively knowledge of real processes. . . .

Almost all contemporary national economic systems are articulated in the international system. Superficial or apologetic analysts, in order to minimize exploitative aspects of the international economy, have merely assumed that "modern" economies are "interdependent." By stating this platitude, they often forget that the important question is what forms that "interdependency" takes. While some national economies need raw material produced by unskilled labor, or industrial goods produced by cheap labor, others need to import equipment and capital goods in general. While some economies become indebted to the financial capital cities of the world, others are creditors. Of course, bankers need clients, as much as clients need bankers. But the "interrelationship" between the two is qualitatively distinct because of the position held by each partner in the structure of the relationship. The same is true for the analysis of "interdependent" economies in world markets. . . .

By pointing to the existence of a process of capitalistic expansion in the periphery, we make a double criticism. We criticize those who expect permanent stagnation in underdeveloped dependent countries because of a constant decline in the rate of profit or the "narrowness of internal markets," which supposedly function as an insurpassable obstacle to capitalist advancement. But we also criticize those who expect capitalist development of peripheral economies to solve problems such as distribution of property, full employment, better income distribution, and better living conditions for people. . . . It is not realistic to imagine that capitalist development will solve basic problems for the majority of the population. In the end, what has to be discussed as an alternative is not the consolidation of the state and the fulfillment of "autonomous capitalism," but how to supercede them. The important question, then, is how to construct paths toward socialism. . . .

1969

Playa Girón

Silvio Rodríguez

S ilvio Rodríguez (b. 1946) was Cuba's best-known representative of its *nueva trova* ("new ballad") movement of the late 1960s and '70s. Building on Cuba's tradition of public song, nueva trova helped shape the "protest song" movement in Latin America (see Document No. 96). Unlike some of his contemporaries who rejected all commercialized popular music as "imperialist," Rodríguez openly spoke of his admiration for the Beatles, whose music was banned in Cuba. Rodríguez's politically inspired, poetic verses evoked a strongly sympathetic response from Latin America's middle-class youth. Written in 1969, "Playa Girón" was a song named after a fishing boat on which Rodríguez wrote many of his earliest songs. It was also the name of the beach where a U.S.-backed invasion force of Cuban exiles was defeated in 1961, a site known in English as the Bay of Pigs (see Document No. 84).

Playa Girón

Compañeros poetas,
tomando en cuenta los últimos sucesos
en la poesía, quisiera preguntar
—me urge—,
¿qué tipo de adjetivos se deben usar
para hacer el poema de un barco
sin que se haga sentimental,
fuera de la vanguardia
o evidente panfleto,
si debo usar palabras como
Flota Cubana de Pesca y
"Playa Girón?"

Compañeros de música,

Source: "Welcome to Luaka Bop Records." http://www.luakabop.com/cuba_classics/cmp/album1.html. November 1999. Translated by Eric Zolov.

tomando en cuenta esas politonales
y audaces canciones, quisiera preguntar
—me urge—,
¿qué tipo de armonía se debe usar
para hacer la canción
de este barco
con hombres de poca niñez, hombres y solamente
hombres sobre cubierta,
hombres negros y rojos y azules,
los hombres que pueblan el "Playa Girón?"

Compañeros de historia,
tomando en cuenta lo implacable
que debe ser la verdad, quisiera preguntar
—me urge tanto—,
¿qué debiera decir, qué fronteras debo respetar?
Si alguien roba comida
y después da la vida, ¿qué hacer?
¿Hasta dónde debemos practicar las verdades?
¿Hasta dónde sabemos?
Que escriban, pues, la historia, su historia,
los hombres del "Playa Girón."

*   *   *

My poetic comrades,
taking into account the latest trends
in poetry, I would like to ask
—it's urgent—
what types of adjectives should one use
to write a poem about a boat
without making it sentimental, keeping it avant garde
not sounding like propaganda,
if I am to use words like
Cuban Fishing Fleet and
Playa Girón?

My musical comrades,
taking into account those polytonal
and bold songs, I would like to ask
—it's urgent—
what type of harmony should one use
to write the song of this boat
and its men whose childhood was short, men and only
men on deck
black and red and blue men,
the men who make up the *Playa Girón?*

Comrades in history,
taking into account the implacable nature
of the truth, I would like to ask
—it's really urgent—
what should one say, what borders should I respect?
If someone steals food
and later gives life, what is to be done?
How far do we practice the truth?
How much do we really know?
Then let them write history, their own history,
the men of the *Playa Girón*.

NO. 101

1972

The Culture of Imperialism

Ariel Dorfman and Armand Mattelart

W hen Ariel Dorfman and Armand Mattelart wrote *How to Read Donald Duck: Imperialist Ideology in the Disney Comic,* they were committed to a radical transformation of Chilean society. In this short book, initially banned in the United States because of legal challenges by Walt Disney for copyright infringements, and publicly burned in Chile after the military overthrow of the leftist government of President Salvador Allende, the authors argued that various Disney comics were subtle instruments of U.S. imperialism. First published in Chile in 1971 as *Para Leer el Pato Donald,* the book was widely read in Latin America and translated into fifteen languages, influencing a generation of students and intellectuals. It became a standard reference for studies of cultural imperialism by the mid-1980s, when new theories of mass media reception

Source: Ariel Dorfman and Armand Mattelart. *How to Read Donald Duck: Imperialist Ideology in the Disney Comic,* p. 41ff. Translation and updated introduction by David Kunzle. With appendix by John Shelton Lawrence. 4th printing. New York: International General, 1991. Reprinted by permission of the publisher.

challenged many of the basic assumptions first popularized by Dorfman and Mattelart.

. . . Disney relies upon the acceptability of his world as *natural*, that is to say, as at once normal, ordinary and true to the nature of the child. His depiction of women and children is predicated upon its supposed objectivity, although, as we have seen, he relentlessly twists the nature of every creature he approaches. It is not by chance that the Disney world is populated with animals. Nature appears to pervade and determine the whole complex of social relations, while the animal-like traits provide the characters with a facade of innocence. It is, of course, true that children tend to identify with the playful, instinctive nature of animals. As they grow older, they begin to understand that the mature animal shares some of his own physical evolutionary traits. They were once, in some way, like this animal, going on all fours, unable to speak, etc. . . .

The use of animals is not in itself either good or bad; it is the use to which they are put, it is the kind of being they incarnate that should be scrutinized. Disney uses animals to trap children, not to liberate them. The language he employs is nothing less than a form of manipulation. He invites children into a world which appears to offer freedom of movement and creation, into which they enter fearlessly, identifying with creatures as affectionate, trustful, and irresponsible as themselves, of whom no betrayal is to be expected, and with whom they can safely play and mingle. Then, once the little readers are caught within the pages of the comic, the doors close behind them. The animals become transformed, under the same zoological *form* and the same smiling mask, into monstrous human beings. . . . A simple statistic: out of the total of one hundred magazines we studied, very nearly half—47 percent—showed the heroes confronting beings from other continents and races. If one includes comics dealing with creatures from other planets, the proportion rises well over 50 percent. Our sample includes stories covering the remotest corners of the globe. In these lands, far from the Duckburg metropolis, casual landing grounds for adventurers greedy for treasure and anxious to break their habitual boredom with a pure and healthy form of recreation, there await inhabitants with most unusual characteristics. . . .

Where is Aztecland? Where is Inca-Blinca? Where is Unsteadystan? There can be no doubt that Aztecland is Mexico, embracing as it does all the prototypes of the picture-postcard Mexico: mules, siestas, volcanoes, cactuses, huge sombreros, ponchos, serenades, machismo, and Indians from ancient civilizations. The country is defined primarily in terms of this grotesque folklorism. Petrified in an archetypical embryo, exploited for all the superficial and stereotyped prejudices which surround it, "Aztecland," under its pseudo-imaginary name becomes that much easier to Disnify. This is Mexico recognizable by its commonplace exotic identity labels, not the real Mexico with all its problems. . . .

According to Disney, underdeveloped peoples are like children, to be treated as such, and if they don't accept this definition of themselves, they should have their pants taken down and be given a good spanking. That'll teach them! When something is *said* about the child/noble savage, it is really the Third World one is *thinking* about. The hegemony which we have detected between the child-adults who arrive with their civilization and technology, and the child-noble savages who accept this alien authority and surrender their riches, stands revealed as an exact replica of the relations between metropolis and satellite, between empire and colony, between master and slave. . . . What are these adventurers escaping from their claustrophobic cities really after? What is the true motive of their flight from the urban center? Bluntly stated: in more than seventy-five percent of our sampling they are looking for gold, in the remaining twenty-five percent they are competing for fortune—in the form of money or fame—in the city. . . . [Gold] is to be found in the Third World, and is magically pointed out by some ancient map, a parchment, an inheritance, an arrow, or a clue in a picture. After great adventures and obstacles, and after defeating some thief trying to get there first (disqualified from the prize because it wasn't his idea, but filched from someone else's map), the good Duckburgers appropriate the idols, figurines, jewels, crowns, pearls, necklaces, rubies, emeralds, precious daggers, golden helmets, etc. . . .

In Disney, the working class has therefore been split into two groups: criminals in the city, and noble savages in the countryside. Since the Disney worldview emasculates violence and social conflicts, even the urban rogues are conceived as naughty children ("boys"). As the anti-model, they are always losing, being spanked, and celebrating their stupid ideas by dancing in circles, hand in hand. They are expressions of the bourgeois desire to portray workers' organizations as a motley mob of crazies. Thus, when Scrooge is confronted by the possibility that Donald has taken to thieving, he says "My nephew, a robber? Before my own eyes? I must call the police and the lunatic asylum. He must have gone mad." This statement reflects the reduction of criminal activity into a psychopathic disease, rather than the result of social conditioning. The bourgeoisie convert the defects of the working class which are the outcome of their exploitation, into moral blemishes, and objects of derision and censure, so as to weaken them and to conceal that exploitation. . . .

To defend this type of comic on the grounds that it feeds the "overflowing imagination" of the child who tends, supposedly, by his very nature to reject his immediate surroundings, is really to inject into children the escapist needs of contemporary society. A society so imprisoned in its own oppressive, dead-end world, that it is constrained to dream up perversely "innocent" utopias. . . . The Disney world could be revamped and even disappear altogether, without anything changing. Beyond the children's comic lies the whole concept of contemporary mass culture, which is based on the principle that only entertainment can liberate humankind from the social anxiety and conflict in which it is submerged. . . . Simply to call Disney a liar is to miss the target. Lies are easily exposed. The laundering process in Disney, as in all the mass media, is much more complex. Disney's social class has molded the world in a certain clearly defined and functional way which corresponds to *its* needs. The bourgeois imagination does not ignore this reality, but seizes it and returns it veneered with innocence, to the consumer. Once it is interpreted as a magical marvelous paradigm of his own common experience, the reader then can consume his own contradictions in whitewashed form. This permits him to continue viewing and living these conflicts with the innocence and helplessness of a child. He enters the future without having resolved or even understood the problems of the present. . . .

But how can the cultural superstructure of the dominant classes, which represents the interests of the metropolis and is so much the product of contradictions in the development of its productive forces, exert such influence and acquire such popularity in the underdeveloped countries? Just why is Disney such a threat? The primary reason is that his products, necessitated and facilitated by a huge industrial capitalist empire are imported together with so many other consumer objects into the dependent country, which is dependent precisely because it *depends* on commodities arising economically and intellectually in the power center's totally alien (foreign) conditions. Our countries are exporters of raw materials, and importers of superstructural and cultural goods. To service our "monoproduct" economies and provide urban paraphernalia, we send copper, and they send machines to extract copper, and, of course, Coca Cola. Behind the Coca Cola stands a whole structure of expectations and models of behavior, and with it, a particular kind of present and future society, and an interpretation of the past. As we import the industrial product conceived, packaged and labeled abroad, and sold to the profit of the rich foreign uncle, at the same time we also import the foreign cultural forms of that society, but without their context: the advanced capitalist social conditions upon which they are based. . . .

Underdeveloped peoples take the comics, at second hand, as instruction in the way they are supposed to live and relate to the foreign power center. There is nothing strange in this. In the same way Disney expels the productive and historical forces from his comics, imperialism thwarts real production and historical evolution in the underdeveloped world. The Disney dream is cast in the same mold which the capitalist system has created for the real world. . . .

1975

The Church Committee Report on CIA Covert Action

U. S. Senate Select Committee to Study Governmental Operations

I n the wake of the Watergate scandal of 1972–74 and in response to growing concern about the covert operations of U.S. government intelligence agencies, the U.S. Senate established the Select Committee to Study Governmental Operations with Respect to Intelligence Activities to investigate government intelligence operations and determine the extent to which they were "illegal, improper or unethical," according to the Senate resolution that established the committee. Chaired by Senator Frank Church of Idaho and better known as the Church Committee, the panel held public hearings and issued reports on the activities of the Central Intelligence Agency and the Federal Bureau of Investigation, the two largest intelligence-gathering agencies. Excerpted below are two 1975 interim reports by the Church Committee: one on CIA assassination plots against foreign leaders and another on CIA covert action in Chile between 1963 and 1973. As a result of the committee's findings, as well as those of a House investigating committee, Presidents Ford and Carter issued executive orders to improve presidential control over the CIA's covert operations, while congressional action culminated in the passage of the Intelligence Oversight Act of 1980. In 1981, President Reagan issued Executive Order No. 12,333, which provided that "No person employed by or acting on behalf of the U.S. government shall engage in or conspire to engage in assassination."

Alleged Assassination Plots Involving Foreign Leaders

The events discussed in this Interim Report must be viewed in the context of United States policy and actions designed to counter the threat of spreading Communism. . . . The Committee regards the unfortunate events dealt with in this Interim Report as an aberration, explainable at least in part, but not justi-

Source: U.S. Senate. Select Committee to Study Governmental Operations with Respect to Intelligence Activities. *Alleged Assassination Plots Involving Foreign Leaders: An Interim Report*, November 20, 1975, pp. 1–6, 255–67. Washington, D.C.: GPO, 1975. *Covert Action in Chile 1963–1973: Staff Report*, 1, pp. 15–16. Washington, D.C.: GPO, 1975.

fied, by the pressures of the time. The Committee believes that it is still in the national interest of the United States to help nations achieve self-determination and resist Communist domination. However, it is clear that this interest cannot justify resorting to the kind of abuses covered in this report. . . .

The evidence establishes that the United States was implicated in several assassination plots. The Committee believes that, short of war, assassination is incompatible with American principles, international order, and morality. It should be rejected as a tool of foreign policy. . . .

The Committee believes the truth about the assassination allegations should be told because democracy depends upon a well-informed electorate. We reject any contention that the facts disclosed in this report should be kept secret because they are embarrassing to the United States. Despite the temporary injury to our national reputation, the Committee believes that foreign peoples will, upon sober reflection, respect the United States more for keeping faith with its democratic ideal than they will condemn us for the misconduct revealed. We doubt that any other country would have the courage to make such disclosures. . . .

The Committee finds that the system of executive command and control was so ambiguous that it is difficult to be certain at what levels assassination activity was known and authorized. This situation creates the disturbing prospect that Government officials might have undertaken the assassination plots without it having been uncontrovertibly clear that there was explicit authorization from the Presidents. It is also possible that there might have been a successful "plausible denial" in which Presidential authorization was issued but is now obscured. Whether or not the respective Presidents knew of or authorized the plots, as chief executive officer of the United States, each must bear the ultimate responsibility for the activities of his subordinates. . . .

The Committee finds that officials of the United States Government initiated and participated in plots to assassinate Patrice Lumumba and Fidel Castro.

The plot to kill Lumumba was conceived in the latter half of 1960 by officials of the United States Government, and quickly advanced to the point of sending poisons to the Congo to be used for the assassination.

The effort to assassinate Castro began in 1960 and continued until 1965. The plans to assassinate Castro using poison cigars, exploding seashells, and a contaminated diving suit did not advance beyond the laboratory phase. The plot involving underworld figures reached the stage of producing poison pills, establishing the contacts necessary to send them into Cuba, procuring potential assassins within Cuba, and apparently delivering the pills to the island itself. . . . The poisons intended to use against Patrice Lumumba were never administered to him, and there is no evidence that the United States was in any way involved in Lumumba's death at the hands of his Congolese enemies. The efforts to assassinate Castro failed. . . .

American officials clearly desired the overthrow of [Dominican President Rafael] Trujillo, offered both encouragement and guns to local dissidents who sought his overthrow and whose plans included assassination. American officials also supplied those dissidents with pistols and rifles. . . . The record reveals that United States officials offered encouragement to the Chilean dissidents who plotted the kidnapping of General Rene Schneider [in 1970], but American officials did not desire or encourage Schneider's death. Certain high officials did know, however, that the dissidents planned to kidnap General Schneider. . . .

This country was created by violent revolt against a regime believed to be tyrannous, and our founding fathers (the local dissidents of that era) received aid from foreign countries. Given that history, we should not today rule out support for dissident groups seeking to overthrow tyrants. But passing beyond that principle, there remain serious questions: for example, whether the national interest of the United States is genuinely involved; whether any such support would be overt rather than covert; what tactics should be used; and how such actions should be authorized and controlled by the coordinate branches of government. . . .

No doubt, the CIA's general efforts against the regimes discussed in this report were authorized at the highest levels of the government. However, the record is unclear and serious doubt remains concerning whether assassination was authorized by the respective Presidents. . . . Whether or not the Presidents in fact knew about the assassination plots, and even if their subordinates failed in their duty of full disclosure, it still follows that the Presidents should have known about the plots. This sets a demanding standard, but one the Committee supports. The future of democracy rests upon such accountability.

The various Presidents and their senior advisors strongly opposed the regimes of Castro and Trujillo, the accession to power of Allende, and the potential influence of Patrice Lumumba. Orders concerning action against those foreign leaders were given in vigorous language. For example, President Nixon's orders to prevent Allende from assuming power left [CIA Director Richard] Helms feeling that "if I ever carried a marshall's baton in my knapsack out of the Oval Office, it was that day." Similarly, General Lansdale described the Mongoose effort against Cuba as "a combat situation," and Attorney General [Robert] Kennedy emphasized that "a solution to the Cuba problem today carries top priority." Helms testified that the pressure to "get rid of Castro and the Castro regime" was intense, and [deputy director of planning at the CIA] Bissell testified that he had been ordered to "get off your ass about Cuba."

It is possible that there was a failure of communication between policymakers and the agency personnel who were experienced in secret, and often violent, action. Although policymakers testified that assassination was not intended by such words as "get rid of Castro." Some of their subordinates in the Agency testified that they perceived that assassination was desired and that they should proceed without troubling their superiors. . . .

The perception of certain [CIA] Agency officials that assassination was within the range of permissible activity was reinforced by the continuing approval of violent covert actions against Cuba that were sanctioned at the Presidential level, and by the failure of the successive administrations to make clear that assassination was not permissible. . . .

Covert Action in Chile, 1963–1973

Covert United States involvement in Chile in the decade between 1963 and 1973 was extensive and continuous. The Central Intelligence Agency spent three million dollars in an effort to influence the outcome of the 1964 Chilean presidential elections. Eight million dollars was spent, covertly, in the three years between 1970 and the military coup in September 1973, with over three million dollars expended in fiscal year 1972 alone. . . .

Covert action during the 1964 campaign was composed of two major elements. One was direct financial support of the Christian Democratic campaign. The CIA underwrote slightly more than half of the total cost of that campaign. After debate, the Special Group [of the CIA] decided not to inform the Christian Democratic candidate, Eduardo Frei, of American covert support of his campaign. A number of intermediaries were therefore mobilized to pass the money to the Christian Democrats. In addition to the subsidies for the Christian Democratic Party, the Special Group allocated funds to the Radical Party and to private citizens' groups.

In addition to support for political parties, the CIA mounted a massive anti-communist propaganda campaign. Extensive use was made of the press, radio, films, pamphlets, posters, leaflets, direct mailings, paper streamers, and wall painting. It was a "scare campaign," which relied heavily on images of Soviet tanks and Cuban firing squads and was directed especially to women. Hundreds of thousands of copies of the anti-communist pastoral letter of Pope Pius XI were distributed by Christian Democratic organizations. They carried the designation, "printed privately by citizens without political affiliation, in order more broadly to disseminate its content." "Disinformation" and "black propaganda"—material which purported to originate from another source, such as the Chilean Communist Party—were used as well.

The propaganda campaign was enormous. During the first week of intensive propaganda activity . . . a CIA-funded propaganda group produced twenty radio spots per day in Santiago and on 44 provincial stations; twelve-minute news broadcasts five time [sic] daily on three Santiago stations and 24 provincial outlets; thousands of cartoons, and much paid press advertising. By the end of June [1964], the group produced 24 daily newscasts in Santiago and the provinces, 26 weekly "commentary" programs, and distributed 3,000 posters daily. The CIA regards the anti-communist scare campaign as the most effective activity undertaken by the U.S. on behalf of the Christian Democratic candidate. . . .

❖

1975 and 1978

Human Rights and Foreign Aid

The Congress of the United States

B y the 1970s, the human rights records of governments receiving military and economic assistance from the United States had emerged as one of the core issues in U.S.–Latin American relations. Much of the impetus for this new attention to human rights came out of the U.S. Congress. Its criticism of the Nixon administration's support for repressive foreign governments was part of a general pattern of congressional assertiveness in foreign policy matters during the 1970s. The first major piece of human rights legislation was known as the Harkin amendment (after Representative Tom Harkin, Democrat of Iowa) to the Foreign Assistance Act. Passed in 1975, it greatly strengthened the legal limitations that had been adopted in 1973 on U.S. economic (or "development") aid to repressive governments. In 1978, encouraged by President Jimmy Carter's announcement that human rights would be "the soul of our foreign policy," Congress toughened similar restrictions on military (or "security") assistance that had been passed in 1976. Congressional action to strengthen human rights legislation was strongly resisted by all three presidential administrations of the 1970s—those of Presidents Nixon, Ford and Carter. The laws passed in 1975 and 1978 are excerpted below.

§ 2151n. Human rights and development assistance [1975]

No [development] assistance may be provided . . . to the government of any country which engages in a consistent pattern of gross violations of internationally recognized human rights, including torture or cruel, inhuman, or degrading treatment or punishment, prolonged detention without charges, causing the disappearance of persons by the abduction and clandestine detention of those persons, or other flagrant denial of the right to life, liberty, and the security of person, unless such assistance will directly benefit the needy people in such country. . . .

The Secretary of State shall transmit to the Speaker of the House of Representatives and the Committee on Foreign Relations of the Senate, by January 31 of each year, a full and complete report regarding—

Source: *U.S. Code Annotated.* Title 22, secs. 2151n and 2304. St. Paul, Minn.: West Publishing Co., 1990.

(1) the status of internationally recognized human rights, . . .

(A) in countries that receive [development] assistance . . . and

(B) in all other foreign countries which are members of the United Nations and which are not otherwise the subject of a human rights report under this chapter;

(2) wherever applicable, practices regarding coercion in population control, including coerced abortion and involuntary sterilization . . .

§ 2304. Human rights and security assistance [1978]

(A) OBSERVANCE OF HUMAN RIGHTS AS PRINCIPAL GOAL OF FOREIGN POLICY; IMPLEMENTATION REQUIREMENTS

(1) The United States shall, in accordance with its international obligations as set forth in the Charter of the United Nations and in keeping with the constitutional heritage and traditions of the United States, promote and encourage increased respect for human rights and fundamental freedoms throughout the world without distinction as to race, sex, language, or religion. Accordingly, a principal goal of the foreign policy of the United States shall be to promote the increased observance of internationally recognized human rights by all countries.

(2) Except under circumstances specified in this section, no security assistance may be provided to any country the government of which engages in a consistent pattern of gross violations of internationally recognized human rights. Security assistance may not be provided to the police, domestic intelligence, or similar law enforcement forces of a country, and licenses may not be issued under the Export Administration Act of 1979 [50 App. U.S.C.A. § 2401 et seq.] for the export of crime control and detection instruments and equipment to a country, the government of which engages in a consistent pattern of gross violations of internationally recognized human rights unless the President certifies in writing to the Speaker of the House of Representatives and the chairman of the Committee on Foreign Relations of the Senate and the chairman of the Committee on Banking, Housing, and Urban Affairs of the Senate (when licenses are to be issued pursuant to the Export Administration Act of 1979 . . .) that extraordinary circumstances exist warranting provision of such assistance and issuance of such licenses. . . .

(3) In furtherance of paragraphs (1) and (2), the President is directed to formulate and conduct international security assistance programs of the United States in a manner which will promote and advance human rights and avoid identification of the United States, through such programs, with governments which deny to their people internationally recognized human rights and fundamental freedoms, in violation of international law or in contravention of the policy of the United States as expressed in this section or otherwise.

(B) REPORT BY SECRETARY OF STATE ON PRACTICES OF PROPOSED RECIPIENT COUNTRIES; CONSIDERATIONS

The Secretary of State shall transmit to the Congress, as part of the presentation materials for security assistance programs proposed for each fiscal year, a full and complete report, prepared with the assistance of the Assistant Secretary of State for Human Rights and Humanitarian Affairs, with respect to practices regarding the observance of and respect for internationally recognized human rights in each country proposed as a recipient of security assistance. Wherever applicable, such report shall include information on practices regarding coercion in population control, including coerced abortion and involuntary sterilization. . . .

(D) DEFINITIONS

The term "gross violations of internationally recognized human rights" includes torture or cruel, inhuman, or degrading treatment or punishment, prolonged detention without charges and trial, causing the disappearance of persons by the abduction and clandestine detention of those persons, and other flagrant denial of the right to life, liberty, or the security of person. . . .

❖

NO. 104

1976

Soft Spots in the "Brazilian Model"

G. A. Costanzo

A *golpe de estado* by the armed forces of Brazil against the elected civilian government of President João Goulart in 1964 inaugurated a period of military dictatorship that lasted until 1985. As the military regime's repression of its political opponents intensified after 1968, the Brazilian economy began an extraordinary six-year boom of 11 percent annual growth rates as the government succeeded in holding down inflation, expanding the country's industrial base and diversifying its agricultural export sector. The balance of payments deficit that the military had inherited from Goulart's administration was reversed and did not reappear again until the mid-1970s, when world oil prices shot up, draining Brazil's currency reserves. The government responded by borrowing more and

Source: G. A. Costanzo. "U.S. Foreign Investment in Brazil." In *Brazil–U.S. Business Council Inaugural Meeting August 16–18, 1976, Brasilia: A Report by the U.S. Section Secretariat,* pp. 31–42. Mimeo. Washington, D.C.: Chamber of Commerce of the United States, 1976.

more money from foreign banks. By the early 1980s, the strategy of debt-dependent growth proved to be a ruinous one, not just for Brazil but for all of Latin America. Brazil defaulted on its bank loans and the boom ended abruptly. By then, the United States had become Brazil's largest supplier of capital and technology and its principal trading partner. In 1976, as concerns about Brazil's indebtedness and growth prospects were beginning to occupy U.S. investors and financial institutions, the Brazil–U.S. Business Council was created as a forum for representatives of the private sectors of both countries to discuss trade and investment relations. At the council's inaugural meeting, from August 16 to 18, 1976, in Brasilia, the vice chairman of Citibank, G. A. Costanzo, addressed the gathering of U.S. and Brazilian executives. Costanzo retired from Citibank in 1981.

As an old Brazilian hand, I am proud and happy for the great strides which your country has made in the last decade towards the realization of its tremendous potential.

This is not a bargaining session, but a meeting between very close friends in the pursuit of goals of mutual interest. . . . U.S. business on its part has a large and profitable stake in Brazil. Millions of American shareholders will benefit directly from a thriving and growing Brazilian economy. . . .

There is no doubt in my mind that today Brazil is the most attractive investment climate in the world. This is a great asset, achieved through courageous governmental policies and sacrifices by all Brazilians of the present for the future. The maintenance of this hard-earned confidence is critical to the economic future of the country. Without it the country will not be able to mobilize the huge capital funds required to finance rapid economic growth and the creation of jobs needed for the growing labor force. . . . Since 1974 Brazil has been able to attract from abroad net capital inflows of approximately $7 billion per year. This is by far the highest rate of capital inflow in the world. . . .

This is impressive evidence of the confidence of U.S. investors in Brazil. What is the basis of this confidence? It is important that this be clearly understood by Brazil, because confidence is an elusive thing. It is very hard to come by, but easily and quickly dissipated. The U.S. investor's confidence in Brazil rests basically on the successful execution of the broad spectrum of political and economic policies which have come to be known as the "Brazilian model." The critical elements of this model are the following:

1. Political stability and the prevalence of law and order,
2. Reliance on a market economy and willingness of the authorities to permit the price mechanism to function,
3. A policy of curbing inflation through demand management rather than controls, and to put it in plain language this means controlling the money supply,

4. A policy of realistic exchange rates and export-oriented high growth,
5. Efficient balance of payments and external debt management, and
6. Recognition of the vital role of foreign investments in Brazil's economic growth and policies of active encouragement of such investments.

These are the things that the U.S. investor will be following and will determine the rate of future direct investments and flow of foreign savings to Brazil. . . .

I would be less than frank if I did not face the reality that there are some uncertainties in the mind of the foreign investor as to the future of the Brazilian model. The concerns have to do with Brazil's ability to cope with inflation and the related current balance of payments deficit and external debt service problem. I believe it is of crucial importance for Brazil to show significant progress in the near future in these areas if the confidence of the foreign direct investor and the external financial markets is to be maintained. I believe no one would disagree that the current inflation rate of roughly 45 percent should be reduced as soon as possible. The insidious consequences of such a rate of inflation are well understood in Brazil and require no comments on my part. . . .

The second area of concern is that of the current account deficit and debt service problem. The aim of the Brazilian authorities to reduce the current balance of payments from close to $7 billion in 1975 to about $5.5 billion in 1976 is sound and very encouraging. The achievement of this target, however, should result primarily from domestic demand management coupled with keeping the exchange rate realistic rather than from governmental limitations on imports. . . . Brazil more than most other countries has been particularly hard hit by the quadrupling of oil prices and the world recession of 1974–1975. Brazil's ability to finance its current account deficit in this period has been most gratifying. But the large increase in external debt in Brazil and less developed countries in general has given rise to fears of default. These fears have been aided and abetted by the media and demands by some countries at international conferences for debt forgiveness or moratorium. Brazil, therefore, must face the fact that in this overall environment the question is asked of how Brazil is going to repay all this debt.

You and I, of course, know that is a meaningless question. Debt and economic growth are normal in developing nations such as Brazil. They lack capital to sustain adequate economic growth; therefore, they must import capital in many forms to supplement domestic savings. One form for those eligible is private bank lending. A going and growing concern, whether it is a firm or a country, does not have to reduce its debt as it grows. What it needs to do to maintain its credit is keep its debt and its debt service in proper proportion to its rising debt service capacity. In the case of a country, debt service capacity is fundamentally based on exports and gross national product.

It would be demanding, indeed, to expect Brazil, which by virtue of its stage of development is structurally predestined to be a net importer of capital, to engage in net repayment overnight. What Brazil must do, however, is to restrain borrowing sufficiently to maintain its sound credit rating. That will enable it to continue borrowing even in difficult times. It will also enable Brazil to borrow in times of strong competition for funds as might arise if the current economic expansion in the industrial world should result again in a strong demand for credit. . . .

These, in my opinion, are the more critical areas of concern from the point of view of maintaining the attractiveness of Brazil for U.S. investments. The complaints which I run into most frequently in discussions with our customers are the following:

1. Delays and difficulties in obtaining Industrial Development Council approval for new projects. Since as a practical matter all new industrial projects require Industrial Development Council approval or in other sectors of the economy the approval of a similar agency, delays and restrictions create an often imposing obstacle.

2. Problems with import restrictions. Frequently projects are approved subject to the use of national similar equipment instead of imported equipment. Many times this national equipment is not similar in either quality or price. . . .

4. Difficulties in registering technical assistance and royalty agreements. At present it is virtually impossible for a majority foreign-owned company in Brazil to remit funds in payment of technical assistance received from the head office or to pay royalties on processes to be used. This is a serious impediment for high technology companies.

5. Some investors find Brazil's profit remittance law restrictive. Investors can remit as dividends up to a gross 16 percent of their registered foreign capital with a withholding tax of 25 percent (in other words, a net 12 percent). Anything beyond that is taxed at a confiscatory rate. This is particularly troublesome for high technology companies which are people-intensive rather than capital-intensive (e.g., engineering firms, consulting companies, computer software outfits).

6. Is the cruzeiro-dollar exchange rate realistic? Some investors don't think so. Some investors feel the cruzeiro is overvalued which results in an investor receiving fewer cruzeiros for his incoming dollars than comparative internal-external costs would indicate.

7. Restrictive policy re government sources credit for foreign companies. Most sources of government cruzeiro term credit (usually subsidized) are not available to foreign-controlled companies. This puts them at a disadvantage with respect to local competitors.

8. Shortage of local currency working capital financing. Cruzeiros are chronically in short supply and are very expensive when available. Existing regulations make external sourced working capital financing an unattractive alternative.

9. Difficulties in finding and keeping qualified local managers. Qualified

Brazilian managers are hard to come by and tend to be very expensive. Local remuneration schemes are often difficult to integrate into a multi-national's global personnel program. Management level turnover is high.

10. Frequent changes in laws and regulations in business area [sic] makes long-range planning difficult if not impossible. Progress in these areas would go far in increasing the rate of foreign investments in Brazil. . . .

More countries will be trying to follow the Brazilian example and it will be important that Brazil remedy the soonest possible the soft spots I have previously referred to and remove any uncertainties as to the permanence of the "Brazilian model." I know that this is fully understood by the Brazilian Government. . . .

❖

NO. 105

1977

The Panama Canal Treaties

The Governments of the United States and Panama

Under the Hay–Bunau-Varilla Treaty of 1903 (Document No. 33), the republic of Panama had granted the United States "in perpetuity the use, occupation and control" of the ten-mile-wide Canal Zone, as well as "in perpetuity a monopoly for the construction, maintenance and operation" of a canal. By the mid-1960s, however, it was becoming increasingly difficult for the United States to resist pressure from the governments of Panama and other Latin American countries to give up U.S. control of both the Zone and the Canal. Accordingly, U.S. president Jimmy Carter and Omar Torrijos, the head of Panama's government, signed two treaties on September 7, 1977: "Treaty Concerning the Permanent Neutrality and Operation of the Panama Canal" and the "Panama Canal

Source: U.S. Department of State. *United States Treaties and Other International Agreements.* Vol. 33, Part I, 1979–1981, pp. 1–140. Washington, D.C.: GPO, 1987.

Treaty." The U.S. Senate, reflecting the sharp division of U.S. public opinion on the issue, approved both treaties in March and April 1978 by margins of a single vote. At the Senate's insistence, a special protocol was attached to the first treaty and signed by the two leaders on June 16, 1978. That protocol, besides repeating the paragraph excerpted below, stipulated that all other conditions and reservations that had been contained in the Senate resolutions of approval were accepted by Panama. Among those conditions was the United States's right to use "military force in the Republic of Panama" to reopen the canal should it be closed or its operations interfered with, even after 1999.

Treaty Concerning the Permanent Neutrality and Operation of the Panama Canal

The United States of America and the Republic of Panama have agreed upon the following:

ARTICLE 1. The Republic of Panama declares that the Canal, as an international transit waterway, shall be permanently neutral in accordance with the regime established in this Treaty. The same regime of neutrality shall apply to any other international waterway that may be built either partially or wholly in the territory of the Republic of Panama.

ARTICLE 2. The Republic of Panama declares the neutrality of the Canal in order that both in time of peace and in time of war it shall remain secure and open to peaceful transit by the vessels of all nations on terms of entire equality, so that there will be no discrimination against any nation, or its citizens or subjects, concerning the conditions or charges of transit, or for any other reason, and so that the Canal, and therefore the Isthmus of Panama, shall not be the target of reprisals in any armed conflict between other nations of the world. . . .

ARTICLE 5. After the termination of the Panama Canal Treaty, only the Republic of Panama shall operate the Canal and maintain military forces, defense sites and military installations within its national territory. . . .

Protocol of Exchange of Instruments of Ratification

Pursuant to the resolution of the Senate of the United States of America of March 16, 1978, the following text . . . is repeated herewith:

"Nothing in the Treaty shall preclude the Republic of Panama and the United States of America from making, in accordance with their respective constitutional processes, any agreement or arrangement between the two countries to facilitate performance at any time after December 31, 1999, of their responsibilities to maintain the regime of neutrality established in the Treaty, including agreements or arrangements for the stationing of any United States military forces or the maintenance of defense sites after that date in the Republic of Panama that the Republic of Panama and the United States of America may deem necessary or appropriate."

Panama Canal Treaty

The United States of America and the Republic of Panama, . . . acknowledging the Republic of Panama's sovereignty over its territory, have decided to terminate the prior Treaties pertaining to the Panama Canal and to conclude a new Treaty to serve as the basis for a new relationship between them and, accordingly, have agreed upon the following: . . .

This Treaty shall terminate at noon, Panama time, December 31, 1999.

[T]he Republic of Panama, as territorial sovereign, grants to the United States of America, for the duration of this Treaty, the rights necessary to regulate the transit of ships through the Panama Canal, and to manage, operate, maintain, improve, protect and defend the Canal. . . . The Republic of Panama shall participate increasingly in the management and protection and defense of the Canal, as provided in this Treaty. . . .

The United States of America and the Republic of Panama commit themselves to protect and defend the Panama Canal. Each Party shall act, in accordance with its constitutional processes, to meet the danger resulting from an armed attack or other actions which threaten the security of the Panama Canal or of ships transiting it. For the duration of this Treaty, the United States of America shall have primary responsibility to protect and defend the Canal. . . .

The Republic of Panama shall reassume plenary jurisdiction over the former Canal Zone upon entry into force of this Treaty and in accordance with its terms. . . .

Upon termination of this Treaty, the Republic of Panama shall assume total responsibility for the management, operation, and maintenance of the Panama Canal, which shall be turned over in operating condition. . . . The United States of America transfers, without charge, to the Republic of Panama all right, title and interest the United States of America may have with respect to all real property, including non-removable improvements thereon. . . .

NO. 106

1980

Saving the New World from Communism

The Committee of Santa Fe

As the U.S. presidential election of 1980 approached, the Democratic administration of President Jimmy Carter found itself on the defensive from conservative critics of his foreign policy. They accused Carter of failing to adequately defend the governments of U.S. allies against internal opposition movements and armed insurgencies. One early critic was Jeane Kirkpatrick, a political science professor at Georgetown University, whose 1979 essay, "Dictatorships and Double Standards," charged Carter with being the idealistic dupe of communist forces that were subverting faithful U.S. allies, above all the "traditional autocracies" that had ruled Nicaragua and Iran. A few months after Kirkpatrick's essay appeared, the following document was published by the Council for Inter-American Security. Clearly building on Kirkpatrick's general arguments, it was written by five men who called themselves the Committee of Santa Fe. They were L. Francis Bouchey, Roger Fontaine, David C. Jordan, Lieutenant General Gordon Sumner Jr. and Lewis Tambs. After Carter lost the 1980 election to Ronald Reagan, three of the five (Fontaine, Sumner and Tambs) joined the Reagan administration's foreign policy team, as did Jeane Kirkpatrick, who became U.S. ambassador to the United Nations. This document is widely considered to have served as a blueprint for President Reagan's policy toward Latin America in the 1980s.

The Americas are under attack. Latin America, the traditional alliance partner of the United States, is being penetrated by Soviet power. The Caribbean rim and basin are spotted with Soviet surrogates and ringed with socialist states.

No great power is sufficiently strong to conduct hemispheric foreign policies as if the different regions of the world were isolated and did not impact on each other. Historically the Latin American policy of the United States has never been separated from the global distribution of power, and there is no

Source: The Committee of Santa Fe. *A New Inter-American Policy for the Eighties.* Washington, D.C.: Council for Inter-American Security, 1980.

reason to assume that what happens in the 1980s between great states in one area of the world will not affect power relationships on other continents. The Monroe Doctrine, the historic cornerstone of United States–Latin American policy, recognized the intimate relationship between the struggle for power in the Old World and the New. . . .

U.S. global power projection rests upon a cooperative Caribbean and a supportive South America. The exclusion of Old World maritime powers from Cuba, the Caribbean and Latin America has helped the United States generate sufficient surplus power for balancing activities on European, Asian and African continents.

Latin America, like Western Europe and Japan, is part of America's power base. Any United States power base, be it in Latin America, Western Europe or the Western Pacific, cannot be allowed to crumble if the United States is to retain adequate extra energy to be able to play a balancing role elsewhere in the world. For a balancing state like the United States, there is no possibility of flexible global action if its power is immobilized or checked in any one area. Indeed, in areas vital to any nation's power potential, preservation of the status quo is not enough. The United States must seek to improve its relative position in all its spheres of influence. If there is a loss of will with respect to the importance of improving a nation's relative power position, it will be only a matter of time until the inactive state is replaced by a competitor.

The United States is being shoved aside in the Caribbean and Central America by a sophisticated, but brutal, extracontinental super power manipulating client states. Soviet influence has expanded mightily since 1959. The Soviet Union is now ensconced in force in the Western Hemisphere and the United States must remedy the situation. . . .

The United States is reaping the consequences of two decades of neglect, short-sightedness and self-deception. Now, the Carter Administration faces a Soviet Union entrenched in force in the Caribbean and a possible Marxist and pro-Cuban oriented Central America. In contrast to simplistic U.S. policies, the Soviet Union has employed sophisticated tactics for enhancing international Communist connections in Latin America and for reducing the U.S. presence. Havana accepts Moscow's doctrine that there is no single road to power for Communism, that local Marxists may employ peaceful persuasion, violent means, or a combination of the *via pacifica* and direct action in the drive to power, and that the U.S. government and private financial institutions may be counted on to recognize diplomatically and support financially Latin American Marxist movements if handled properly.

The Kremlin seeks to wed Marxism to Latin American nationalism and anti-Americanism and to exploit the inability or unwillingness of the U.S. Government's policy makers to support alternatives to Marxist movements in the search for a progressive and stable Ibero-America. Having thus defined the intellectual parameter for clients, adversaries and targets, the Soviet Union has managed to expand its ties with Latin American governments, while simultaneously pursuing subversion and revolution as opportunities are fomented or arise. For Soviet foreign policy is based on creating chaos and exploiting opportunities, and the U.S. power base in Latin America is not immune. . . .

The Committee of Santa Fe contends that U.S. foreign policy is in disarray; that the norms of conflict and social change adopted by the Carter Administration are those of the Soviet Union; that the area in contention is the sovereign territory of U.S. allies and Third World trading partners; that the sphere of the Soviet Union and its surrogates is expanding; and that the annual balance sheet of gains and losses favors the U.S.S.R.

The American response of camouflaged escapism to Soviet imperialism must be reversed. The United States must push for an inventive, creative and strategic solution to this situation. Ethical realism provides the underlying moral support to the foreign policy principles the United States has traditionally used to solve the problem of value and power in external affairs. U.S. intervention abroad was only justified for the security of the Republic and was not justified for the shaping of any particular order in any other country unless activities there were tied to an extracontinental threat to the United States. The United States can grant this same nationalistic perspective to all Latin American nations which do not develop a semi-vassalage-like relationship with an extracontinental super power. Such a semi-colonial connection introduces a sterilizing intenationalism into the culture and countries of the Western Hemisphere and undercuts a Latin American policy based on reciprocity. . . .

A United States–Latin American policy which fosters American and Ibero-American security, based on mutual national independence and inter-American dependence, promotes autonomous economic and political development based on our cultural and religious heritages, accepts limits on U.S. impulses to promote internal reforms in Ibero-America, and recognizes and respects that the dignity and sensibilities of our neighbors should be pursued. . . .

Defense of a nation's sovereignty and preservation of a people's cultural identity are basic to survival. Both of these elements are being suppressed and sterilized by international Communism. Only a U.S. policy aimed at preserving the peace, promoting production and achieving political stability can save the New World and salvage the U.S. global power position which rests upon a secure and sovereign Latin America. The Americas are under attack. Whither Washington?

NO. 107

1984

Central America in Revolt: A Reagan Administration View

The National Bipartisan Commission on Central America

A s public debate over U.S. policy in Central America sharpened in the wake of President Ronald Reagan's strong commitment to military intervention to stem what he identified as a tide of communist subversion, the administration sought means to win more public and congressional support for its policies. On July 19, 1983, President Reagan created the National Bipartisan Commission on Central America to "study the nature of United States interests in the Central American region and the threats now posed to those interests." Chaired by former secretary of state Henry A. Kissinger, the largely conservative twelve-man panel presented its report to President Reagan on January 10, 1984. The report, whose analysis and recommendations coincided with those of the administration, was called "magnificent" by President Reagan but severely criticized by opponents of his policy. Its concluding chapter is presented here in full.

Conclusion

We have concluded this exercise persuaded that Central America is both vital and vulnerable, and that whatever other crises may arise to claim the nation's attention the United States cannot afford to turn away from that threatened region. Central America's crisis is our crisis.

All too frequently, wars and threats of wars are what draw attention to one part of the world or another. So it has been in Central America. The military crisis there captured our attention, but in doing so it has also wakened us to many other needs of the region. However belatedly, it did "concentrate the mind." In the case of this Commission, one effect of concentrating the mind has been to clarify the picture we had of the nations of Central America. It is a common failing to see other nations as caricatures rather than as portraits, exaggerating one or two characteristics and losing sight of the subtler nuances

Source: U.S. National Bipartisan Commission on Central America. *The Report of the President's National Bipartisan Commission on Central America,* pp. 150–52. New York: Macmillan Publishing Company, 1984.

on which so much of human experience centers. As we have studied these nations, we have become sharply aware of how great a mistake it would be to view them in one-dimensional terms. An exceptionally complex interplay of forces has shaped their history and continues to define their identities and to affect their destinies.

We have developed a great sympathy for those in Central America who are struggling to control those forces, and to bring their countries successfully through this period of political and social transformation. As a region, Central America is in midpassage from the predominantly authoritarian patterns of the past to what can, with determination, with help, with luck, and with peace, become the predominantly democratic pluralism of the future. That transformation has been troubled, seldom smooth, and sometimes violent. In Nicaragua, we have seen the tragedy of a revolution betrayed; the same forces that stamped out the beginnings of democracy in Nicaragua now threaten El Salvador. In El Salvador itself, those seeking to establish democratic institutions are beset by violence from the extremists on both sides. But the spirit of freedom is strong throughout the region, and the determination persists to strengthen it where it exists and to achieve it where it does not.

The use of Nicaragua as a base for Soviet and Cuban efforts to penetrate the rest of the Central American isthmus, with El Salvador the target of first opportunity, gives the conflict there a major strategic dimension. The direct involvement of aggressive external forces makes it a challenge to the system of hemispheric security, and, quite specifically, to the security interests of the United States. This is a challenge to which the United States must respond.

But beyond this, we are challenged to respond to the urgent human needs of the people of Central America. Central America is a region in crisis economically, socially and politically. Its nations are our neighbors, and they need our help. This is one of those instances in which the requirements of national interest and the commands of conscience coincide.

Through the years, there has been a sort of natural progression in this nation's ties with other parts of the world. At first they were almost exclusively with Europe. Then, without diminishing those ties with Europe, we expanded our trans-Pacific bonds. Now the crisis in Central America has served as a vivid reminder that we need to strengthen our ties to the south, as well as east and west.

Our response to the present crisis in Central America must not be a passing phenomenon. The United States was born of a vision, which has inspired the world for two centuries. That vision shines most brightly when it is shared. Just as we want freedom for ourselves, we want freedom for others. Just as we cherish our vision, we should encourage others to pursue their own. But in fact, what we want for ourselves is very largely what the people of Central America want for themselves. They do share the vision of the future that our ideals represent, and the time has come for us to help them not just to aspire to that vision, but to participate in it.

Our task now, as a nation, is to transform the crisis in Central America into an opportunity: to seize the impetus it provides, and to use this to help our neighbors not only to secure their freedom from aggression and violence, but also to set in place the policies, processes and institutions that will make them both prosperous and free. If, together, we succeed in this, then the sponsors of violence will have done the opposite of what they intended: they will have roused us not only to turn back the tide of totalitarianism but to bring a new birth of hope and of opportunity to the people of Central America.

Because this is our opportunity, in conscience it is also our responsibility.

❖

NO. 108

1984

The Fear of Communism in Central America

Ronald Reagan

A popular uprising led by the Frente Sandinista de Liberación Nacional (Sandinista National Liberation Front, or FSLN) overthrew the U.S.-backed dictator of Nicaragua, Anastasio Somoza Debayle, on July 19, 1979. The front's platform for radical social and economic reforms, its Marxist-nationalist ideology, and its assertion of a foreign policy independent of the Cold War policies of the United States, made the FSLN's leadership of the new government an unwelcome development for Washington. The United States had not confronted a similar challenge to its hegemony in Central America since the presidency of Jacobo Arbenz in Guatemala (see Document Nos. 74 and 75). By spring 1984 the Reagan administration was deeply committed to removing the Sandinista government. It was supporting the Honduran-based military force known as the contras (see Document No. 109), had imposed a crippling economic and financial embargo on Nicaragua, and was seeking to convince the U.S. public that Nicaragua posed a national security threat. Excerpted below is a transcript of a televised speech by President Reagan on May 9, 1984.

Source: U.S. Department of State. "President Reagan: U.S. Interests in Central America." *Current Policy* No. 576 (May 9, 1984): 1–5.

. . . I asked for this time to tell you of some basic decisions which are yours to make. I believe it is my constitutional responsibility to place these matters before you. They have to do with your national security, and that security is the single most important function of the Federal Government. In that context, it's my duty to anticipate problems, warn of dangers, and act so as to keep harm away from our shores.

Our diplomatic objectives will not be attained by good will and noble aspirations alone. In the last 15 years the growth of Soviet military power has meant a radical change in the nature of the world we live in. This does not mean, as some would have us believe, that we're in imminent danger of nuclear war. We're not.

As long as we maintain the strategic balance and make it more stable by reducing the level of weapons on both sides, then we can count on the basic prudence of the Soviet leaders to avoid that kind of challenge to us. They are presently challenging us with a different kind of weapon: subversion and the use of surrogate forces—Cubans, for example. We've seen it intensifying during the last 10 years as the Soviet Union and its surrogates moved to establish control over Vietnam, Laos, Kampuchea, Angola, Ethiopia, South Yemen, Afghanistan, and recently, closer to home in Nicaragua and now El Salvador. It's the fate of this region, Central America, that I want to talk to you about tonight.

The issue is our effort to promote democracy and economic well-being in the face of Cuban and Nicaraguan aggression, aided and abetted by the Soviet Union. It is definitely not about plans to send American troops into combat in Central America. . . .

The defense policy of the United States is based on a simple premise: we do not start wars. We will never be the aggressor. We maintain our strength in order to deter and defend against aggression—to preserve freedom and peace. We help our friends defend themselves.

Central America is a region of great importance to the United States. And it is so close—San Salvador is closer to Houston, Texas, than Houston is to Washington, D.C. Central America is America; it's at our doorstep. And it has become the stage for a bold attempt by the Soviet Union, Cuba, and Nicaragua to install communism by force throughout the hemisphere.

When half of our shipping tonnage and imported oil passes through Caribbean shipping lanes, and nearly half of all our foreign trade passes through the Panama Canal and Caribbean waters, America's economy and well-being are at stake. . . .

What we see in El Salvador is an attempt to destabilize the entire region and eventually move chaos and anarchy toward the American border.

As the National Bipartisan Commission on Central America, chaired by Henry Kissinger, agreed, if we do nothing or if we continue to provide too little help, our choice will be a communist Central America with additional communist military bases on the mainland of this hemisphere and communist subversion spreading southward and northward. This communist subversion poses the threat that 100 million people from Panama to the open border on our south could come under the control of pro-Soviet regimes.

If we come to our senses too late, when our vital interests are even more directly threatened, and after a lack of American support causes our friends to lose the ability to defend themselves, then the risks to our security and our way of life will be infinitely greater. . . .

We can and must help Central America. It's in our national interest to do so; and, morally, it's the only right thing to do. But, helping means doing *enough*—enough to protect our security and enough to protect the lives of our neighbors so that they may live in peace and democracy without the threat of communist aggression and subversion. . . .

But making this choice requires a commitment from all of us, our Administration, the American people, and the Congress. So far, we have not yet made that commitment. We've provided just enough aid to avoid outright disaster but not enough to resolve the crisis; so El Salvador is being left to slowly bleed to death.

Part of the problem, I suspect, is not that Central America isn't important, but that some people think our Administration may be exaggerating the threat we face. Well, if that's true, let me put that issue to rest. . . .

The Sandinista rule is a communist reign of terror. Many of those who fought alongside the Sandinistas saw their revolution betrayed; they were denied power in the new government; some were imprisoned, others exiled. Thousands who fought with the Sandinistas have taken up arms against them and are now called the *contras*. They are freedom fighters.

What the Sandinistas have done to Nicaragua is a tragedy. But we Americans must understand and come to grips with the fact that the Sandinistas are not content to brutalize their own land. They seek to export their terror to every other country in the region. . . .

The role that Cuba has long performed for the Soviet Union is now also being played by the Sandinistas. They have become Cuba's Cubans. Weapons, supplies, and funds are shipped from the Soviet bloc to Cuba, from Cuba to Nicaragua, from Nicaragua to the Salvadoran guerrillas. . . .

The simple questions are: will we support freedom in this hemisphere or not? Will we defend our vital interests in this hemisphere or not? Will we stop the spread of communism in this hemisphere or not? Will we act while there is still time? . . .

We Americans should be proud of what we're trying to do in Central America, and proud of what, together with our friends, we can do in Central America, to support democracy, human rights, and economic growth, while preserving peace so close to home. Let us show the world that we want no hostile, communist colonies here in the Americas: South, Central, or North.

❖

1984

Teaching Sabotage

The U.S. Central Intelligence Agency

Overthrowing the Sandinista government of Nicaragua became one of the prime foreign policy objectives of the administration of President Ronald Reagan (1981–89). Among the methods employed by the Reagan administration to unseat the Nicaraguan government were an economic embargo and the organization and financing of an insurgent military force, based in neighboring Honduras, known as the contras (for *contra revolucionario,* the Spanish for "counterrevolutionary"). The contra army was supported by the Central Intelligence Agency, which also funded a propaganda war against the Nicaraguan government from inside Nicaragua. One result was the production and distribution of a *Freedom Fighter's Manual,* a sixteen-page cartoon-format handbook for carrying out small acts of sabotage against the Nicaraguan government, ranging from failing to turn out the lights (and thus wasting electrical energy) to the building of small incendiary bombs. The manual's distribution was first exposed in the U.S. news media in August 1984. It was subsequently translated and published by Grove Press in 1985, whose edition is excerpted below. In October 1984, a second CIA-produced contra manual, *Psychological Operations in Guerrilla Warfare,* was exposed by the U.S. news media and dubbed "the murder manual" because it advocated the assassination of Nicaraguan public officials.

What the Free Nicaraguan Can Do In Order to Tie Down the Marxist Tyranny

All Nicaraguans who love their country and cherish liberty—men, women, young and old people, farmers and workers alike—surely ask themselves what they can do with the means at their disposal, in order to participate in the final battle against the usurpers of the authentic sandinista revolution for which the people of Nicaragua have fought and shed their blood for so many years. Some might think that today's armed struggle requires military supplies and economic re-

Source: *The Freedom Fighter's Manual: Practical Guide to Liberating Nicaragua From Oppression and Misery by Paralyzing the Military-Industrial Complex of the Traitorous Marxist State Without Having to Use Special Tools and With Minimal Risk for the Combatant.* New York: Grove Press, 1985.

sources only available to states or terrorist bands armed by Moscow. There is an essential economic infrastructure that any government needs to function, which can easily be disabled and even paralyzed without the use of armaments or costly and advanced equipment, with the small investment of resources and time.

The following pages present a series of useful sabotage techniques, the majority of which can be done with simple household tools such as scissors, empty bottles, screwdrivers, matches, etc. These measures are extremely safe and without risk for those who use them, as they do not require equipment, skill or specialized activities that can draw attention to the doer.

One combatant can perform many of them, without having to turn to collaborators or having to make a detailed plan beforehand. These are acts that can be done practically in an improvised way every time an occasion presents itself. Our sacred cause needs to have more men and women join its ranks in order to perform these sabotage tasks. However, necessary caution should be taken, and only when the task requires it, should another person or persons participate in or have knowledge of a given act. As mentioned above, the techniques found in this manual correspond to the stage of individual sabotage, or at the most cellular—with cells of no more than two individuals—of the clandestine struggle.

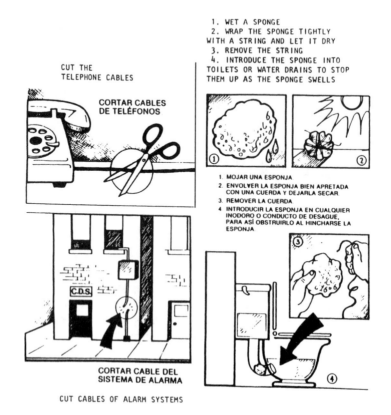

CUT THE
TELEPHONE CABLES

CORTAR CABLES
DE TELÉFONOS

CORTAR CABLE DEL
SISTEMA DE ALARMA

CUT CABLES OF ALARM SYSTEMS

1. WET A SPONGE
2. WRAP THE SPONGE TIGHTLY WITH A STRING AND LET IT DRY
3. REMOVE THE STRING
4. INTRODUCE THE SPONGE INTO TOILETS OR WATER DRAINS TO STOP THEM UP AS THE SPONGE SWELLS

1. MOJAR UNA ESPONJA
2. ENVOLVER LA ESPONJA BIEN APRETADA CON UNA CUERDA Y DEJARLA SECAR.
3. REMOVER LA CUERDA
4. INTRODUCIR LA ESPONJA EN CUALQUIER INODORO O CONDUCTO DE DESAGUE, PARA ASÍ OBSTRUIRLO AL HINCHARSE LA ESPONJA.

LEAVE LIGHTS ON

DEJAR LAS LUCES ENCENDIDAS

PLANT FLOWERS ON STATE FARMS

**SEMBRAR FLORES EN
LAS GRANJAS DEL ESTADO**

**DEJAR ABIERTOS
LOS GRIFOS
DE AGUA**

LEAVE WATER
TAPS ON

HOARD AND STEAL
FOOD FROM THE
GOVERNMENT

**ACAPARAR
Y ROBAR
ALIMENTOS
DEL GOBIERNO**

PUT NAILS ON ROADS
AND HIGHWAYS

**REGAR CLAVOS
EN LOS
CAMINOS Y
CARRETERAS**

PUT DIRT INTO GASOLINE TANKS

**ECHARLE TIERRA
AL TANQUE DE GASOLINA**

**COLOCAR CLAVOS JUNTO A LOS
NEUMÁTICOS DE VEHÍCULOS
ESTACIONADOS**

PUT NAILS NEXT TO THE TIRES
OF PARKED VEHICLES

**ECHAR AGUA EN EL TANQUE DE
GASOLINA**

PUT WATER IN GASOLINE TANKS

NO. 110

1986

The United States Condemned

The International Court of Justice

The government of Nicaragua sued the U.S. government in the International Court of Justice on April 9, 1984, charging it with illegally using military force against Nicaragua and intervening in its internal affairs. Nicaragua asked the court to order Washington to stop the intervention and to pay damages of $370.2 million. The United States initially responded that its activities against Nicaragua were justified by the principle of "collective self-defense" because Nicaragua was supporting guerrilla warfare against the governments of El Salvador, Honduras and Costa Rica. In 1985, however, the United States declared that it would no longer participate in the case and that it would ignore any further proceedings of the court. On June 27, 1986, the court issued its judgment in favor of Nicaragua. The court rejected the U.S. claim to collective self-defense, found the United States guilty of violating both international law and its treaty obligations to Nicaragua, and ordered Washington to stop the intervention and negotiate a reparations settlement with Nicaragua. After the U.S.-backed government of President Violeta Chamorro defeated the Sandinista government in the elections of February 1990, Washington urged President Chamorro to withdraw the suit and the associated damage claims, which had by now risen to $17 billion. President Chamorro complied with the U.S. request on September 12, 1991; two weeks later Washington forgave $260 million in loans to Nicaragua.

. . . It appears to the Court to be clearly established first, that the United States intended, by its support of the *contras*, to coerce the Government of Nicaragua in respect of matters in which each State is permitted, by the principle of State sovereignty, to decide freely . . . and secondly that the intention of the contras themselves was to overthrow the present Government of Nicaragua. The 1983 Report of the Intelligence Committee [i.e., the Permanent Select Committee on Intelligence of the U.S. House of Representatives] refers to the *contras'* "openly acknowledged goal of overthrowing the Sandinistas." Even if it be accepted,

Source: International Court of Justice. *Military and Paramilitary Activities in and Against Nicaragua (Nicaragua v. United States of America). Merits, Judgment, I.C.J. Reports 1986*, pp. 124–35.

for the sake of argument, that the objective of the United States in assisting the *contras* was solely to interdict the supply of arms to the armed opposition in El Salvador, it strains belief to suppose that a body formed in armed opposition to the Government of Nicaragua, and calling itself the "Nicaraguan Democratic Force," intended only to check Nicaraguan interference in El Salvador and did not intend to achieve violent [sic] change of government in Nicaragua. The Court considers that in international law, if one State, with a view to the coercion of another State, supports and assists armed bands in that State whose purpose is to overthrow the government of that State, that amounts to an intervention by the one State in the internal affairs of the other, whether or not the political objective of the State giving such support and assistance is equally far-reaching. . . .

The Court therefore finds that the support given by the United States, up to the end of September 1984, to the military and paramilitary activities of the *contras* in Nicaragua, by financial support, training, supply of weapons, intelligence and logistic support, constitutes a clear breach of the principle of non-intervention. The Court has however taken note that, with effect from the beginning of the United States governmental financial year 1985, namely 1 October 1984, the United States Congress has restricted the use of the funds appropriated for assistance to the *contras* to "humanitarian assistance" . . . . There can be no doubt that the provision of strictly humanitarian aid to persons or forces in another country, whatever their political affiliations or objectives, cannot be regarded as unlawful intervention, or as in any other way contrary to international law. . . .

The effects of the principle of respect for territorial sovereignty inevitably overlap with those of the principles of the prohibition of the use of force and of non-intervention. Thus the assistance to the *contras*, as well as the direct attacks on Nicaraguan ports, oil installations, etc. . . . not only amount to an unlawful use of force, but also constitute infringements of the territorial sovereignty of Nicaragua, and incursions into its territorial and internal waters. Similarly, the mining operations in the Nicaraguan ports not only constitute breaches of the principle of the non-use of force, but also affect Nicaragua's sovereignty over certain maritime expanses. The Court has in fact found that these operations were carried on in Nicaragua's territorial or internal waters or both . . . and accordingly they constitute a violation of Nicaragua's sovereignty. The principle of respect for territorial sovereignty is also directly infringed by the unauthorized overflight of a State's territory by aircraft belonging to or under the control of the government of another State. The Court has found above that such overflights were in fact made. . . .

These violations cannot be justified either by collective self-defence, for which, as the Court has recognized, the necessary circumstances are lacking, nor by any right of the United States to take countermeasures involving the use of force in the event of intervention by Nicaragua in El Salvador, since no such right exists under the applicable international law. They cannot be justified by the activities in El Salvador attributed to the Government of Nicaragua.

The latter activities, assuming that they did in fact occur, do not bring into effect any right belonging to the United States which would justify the actions in question. Accordingly, such actions constitute violations of Nicaragua's sovereignty under customary international law. . . .

The Court now turns to the question of the application of humanitarian law to the activities of the United States complained of in this case. . . . The Court has . . . found the United States responsible for the publication and dissemination [to the *contras*] of the manual on "Psychological Operations in Guerrilla Warfare". . . . The Court takes note of the advice given in the manual on psychological operations to "neutralize" certain "carefully selected and planned targets", including judges, police officers, State Security officials, etc., after the local population have been gathered in order to "take part in the act and formulate accusations against the oppressor". In the view of the Court, this must be regarded as contrary to the prohibition in Article 3 of the Geneva Conventions, with respect to non-combatants, . . . and probably also of the prohibition of "violence to life and person, in particular murder of all kinds. . . ."

. . . The publication and dissemination of a manual in fact containing the advice quoted above must therefore be regarded as an encouragement, which was likely to be effective, to commit acts contrary to general principles of international humanitarian law reflected in treaties. . . .

The finding of the United States Congress [of July 29, 1985, linking U.S. support for the *contras* with alleged breaches by the Nicaraguan Government of its "solemn commitments to the Nicaraguan people, the United States, and the Organization of American States"] also expressed the view that the Nicaraguan Government had taken "significant steps towards establishing a totalitarian Communist dictatorship." However the regime in Nicaragua be defined, adherence by a State to any particular doctrine does not constitute a violation of customary international law; to hold otherwise would make nonsense of the fundamental principle of State sovereignty, on which the whole of international law rests, and the freedom of choice of the political, social, economic and cultural system of a State. Consequently, Nicaragua's domestic policy options, even assuming that they correspond to the description given of them by the Congress finding, cannot justify on the legal plane the various actions of the [United States] complained of. The Court cannot contemplate the creation of a new rule opening up a right of intervention by one State against another on the ground that the latter has opted for some particular ideology or political system. . . .

Similar considerations apply to the criticisms expressed by the United States of the external policies and alliances of Nicaragua. . . . [I]t is sufficient to say that State sovereignty evidently extends to the area of its foreign policy, and that there is no rule of customary international law to prevent a State from choosing and conducting a foreign policy in co-ordination with that of another State. . . .

The Court also notes that Nicaragua is accused by the 1985 finding of the United States Congress of violating human rights. . . . In any event, while the

United States might form its own appraisal of the situation as to respect for human rights in Nicaragua, the use of force could not be the appropriate method to monitor or ensure such respect. With regard to the steps actually taken, the protection of human rights, a strictly humanitarian objective, cannot be compatible with the mining of ports, the destruction of oil installations, or again with the training, arming and equipping of the *contras*. The Court concludes that the argument derived from the preservation of human rights in Nicaragua cannot afford a legal justification for the conduct of the United States. . . .

The Court now turns to another factor which bears both upon domestic policy and foreign policy. This is the militarization of Nicaragua, which the United States deems excessive and such as to prove its aggressive intent, and in which it finds another argument to justify its activities with regard to Nicaragua. It is irrelevant and inappropriate, in the Court's opinion, to pass upon this allegation of the United States, since in international law there are no rules, other than such rules as may be accepted by the State concerned, by treaty or otherwise, whereby the level of armaments of a sovereign State can be limited, and this principle is valid for all States without exception. . . .

NO. 111

1986

The Pentagon Prepares for Prolonged War

The U.S. Department of Defense

In the early 1980s, as the U.S. government stepped up its political and military involvement in Central America, the Defense Department ordered a comprehensive study of what it identified as a new type of unconventional warfare: low-intensity conflict. A "steering group" composed of seven military officers plus one representative each from the Central Intelligence Agency and the Department of State oversaw the creation of the Joint Low-Intensity Conflict Project and the pub-

Source: U.S. Joint Low-Intensity Conflict Project, United States Army Training and Doctrine Command, Fort Monroe, Virginia. *Joint Low-Intensity Conflict Project Final Report: Executive Summary.* 1 August 1986.

lication of its *Final Report* August 1, 1986. The "Executive Summary" of the *Report,* excerpted here, reflected the concern within the Reagan administration that the United States was inadequately prepared to fight "low-intensity" wars of the kind that it was conducting in Central America. "Low-intensity conflict," Secretary of State George P. Schultz commented in 1986, "is the prime challenge we will face, at least through the remainder of this century. The future of peace and freedom may well depend on how effectively we meet it."

This report addresses a major United States foreign policy and defense issue: how to defend threatened United States interests in conflict environments short of conventional war. Increasingly, our adversaries are confronting us with political violence short of conventional war to achieve their goals. If most forecasts are correct, this is precisely the form of conflict that will confront us in the years ahead.

Numerous senior leaders have expressed concern that we do not understand low-intensity conflict; that we are unable to fully use United States capabilities in this form of conflict; that we are not adequately organized to cope; and that our current efforts fall short of what is required for a prudent national defense. . . .

Ironically, our concentration on the need to deter nuclear and conventional war has given rise to a lack of focus on low-intensity conflicts around the globe. Our adversaries have consciously turned to political violence to advance their political objectives. . . . Many government departments and agencies of the United States fail to comprehend the nature of this type of conflict. They do not understand the special socioeconomic environment in which it occurs; the strategy employed by our adversaries; the relationship of political violence to other forms of violence; and the futility of reacting with policy and instruments developed for other forms of conflict.

Among the factors contributing to this lack of understanding are our perceptions that the nation and the world are either at war or at peace, with the latter being the normal state; and the existance [sic] of a well-resourced campaign by our adversaries to create and support misunderstanding of the means and ends of this confrontation. However, the greatest obstacle to an institutionalized understanding is our tendency to think and act in a manner appropriate to more traditional forms of conflict. We attempt to make the various forms of low-intensity conflict fit the same successful prescriptions we use to deter conventional and nuclear war. Our reliance upon these traditional structures and solutions impedes the development of specific policies and policy instruments.

How does one begin to bring understanding to this complex issue? Where does one start? How, in a world that is crowded with demands on our limited personal and national resources, a world of rival priorities, does one strike the balance that will provide the requisite defense? One of the project's major goals was to demonstrate that this ambiguous form of warfare can, in fact, be understood. It began by tackling the contentious issue of defining the term "low-intensity conflict."

During the conduct of the project, the JCS [Joint Chiefs of Staff] approved the following definition. While the definition does not specifically mention military objectives, it does provide a foundation to focus on both civil and military activities, to include the employment of special forces and tailored conventional forces in low-intensity conflict.

"Low-intensity conflict is a limited politico-military struggle to achieve political, social, economic, or psychological objectives. It is often protracted and ranges from diplomatic, economic, and psychosocial pressures through terrorism and insurgency. Low-intensity conflict is generally confined to a geographic area and is often characterized by constraints on the weaponry, tactics, and level of violence."

Low-intensity conflict is not an operation or an activity that one or more of the departments of the United States government can conduct. Rather, it is, first, an environment in which conflict occurs and, second, a series of diverse civil–military activities and operations which are conducted in that environment. While low-intensity conflict may be ambiguous, the specific activities are not. Despite their diversity, these activities, which fall outside the realm of conventional combat, share significant commonalities in their operational environment.

The project found that the low-intensity conflict activities could be identified and grouped into four distinct categories: insurgency/counterinsurgency, terrorism counteraction, peacetime contingency, and peacekeeping operations. Through these activities the United States can provide the following capabilities: diplomatic, economic, and military support for either a government under attack by insurgents or an insurgent force seeking freedom from an adversary government; in cooperation with our allies, protection of personnel, property, and institutions from terrorism; military presence, humanitarian assistance, noncombatant emergency evacuation, limited strike, and similar operations; and support or participation in peacekeeping operations. . . .

Second only to our lack of understanding is our lack of unity in responding to the threats to our interests. Our adversaries combine a substantial collection of military, diplomatic, economic, and psychological forces to inspire and support low-intensity conflict. Therefore, we must counter ideas with ideas, force with force, diplomacy with diplomacy, and all must flow from a strategy implemented through a strong national unity of effort. Nevertheless, a degree of unity exists only at the individual country level. At the national level and on a regional basis, unity is lacking.

Regional and national unity is dependent on clearly stated policy and well-established strategy. . . . Such strategy, clearly detailed for traditional warfare, is conspicuously absent in our response to various low-intensity conflicts. Who, for example, is responsible for a national effort in Central America? Ambassadors of specific countries? The unified commander responsible for the land mass? The unified commander responsible for the islands and oceans? The regional Assistant Secretary of State? The ad hoc interdepartmental task force? The National Security Council? Our responses to this threat are often piecemeal, disjointed, short ranged, and focused on a single event as opposed to the larger whole.

Without national direction it is futile to expect unity of effort. Lack of unity at the national and regional levels hampers every effort to defend threatened interests in the low-intensity conflict environment. A strong, synchronized civil-military effort is essential. . . . A comprehensive civil-military strategy must be developed to defend our interests threatened by the series of low-intensity conflicts around the globe. It must be crafted in comprehensive terms, not focused on a single conflict or on a single department. It must integrate all the national resources at our disposal, military and nonmilitary, lethal and non-lethal. . . .

1986

Solidarity

Audrey Seniors

During the 1980s, thousands of U.S. citizens challenged their government's policies in Central America by writing letters to public officials, demonstrating, going on hunger strikes, initiating court action and offering sanctuary in their homes and churches to Central Americans who were displaced by war. In Nicaragua, where the revolutionary Sandinista government sought to defend the country against the U.S-backed contra forces in neighboring Honduras, thousands of people from the United States (as well as those from many other nations) demonstrated their support for the Nicaraguan government by helping to harvest coffee and cotton, teach in the public school system, provide medical assistance and work on construction projects. For an older generation, these efforts hearkened back to the Abraham Lincoln Brigades of the 1930s in Spain and solidarity with Cuba in the early 1960s. For a younger generation, Central America helped to shape a new experience with political activism. Excerpted below is an interview with Audrey Seniors, one of the volunteers or "brigadistas." Seniors, a forty-four-year-old African American woman with twenty-five years of experience as a political activist, worked as a legal secretary for the Center for Constitutional Rights in New York City.

In June 1984, I made my first visit to Nicaragua, meeting with the Mothers of Heroes and Martyrs, a group of mothers whose children had been killed in the fight against Somoza or by the contras. A statement made by a mother whose daughter had been killed by the contras stands out in my mind. She asked us to tell the mothers in the United States not to let their sons come to invade Nicaragua: "We know what it is like to lose a child and we do not wish it to happen to anyone else. But if your sons come here to invade us, they will be killed."

Source: *Brigadista: Harvest and War in Nicaragua: eyewitness accounts of North American volunteers working in Nicaragua*, Jeff Jones, ed., pp. 132–35. Copyright © 1986 by Praeger. Reproduced with permission of Greenwood Publishing Group, Westport, CT.

Many times since I have reflected on these words and what they mean for Black and Latino mothers and families here. History has shown, in Vietnam and most recently in Grenada, that it is Blacks and the poor who are on the front line fighting the United State's dirty wars. Black mothers must bury our sons, and all of us suffer the emotional and economic hardship of their loss to our communities.

The Reagan administration has spent over 100 million dollars in its attempt to overthrow the Nicaraguan government. It is lobbying for 14 million dollars more for this year alone. At the same time, in Black communities across the country, we have been faced with tremendous cutbacks: in health care, day care, education, food stamps, grants to higher education. Our teenagers have the highest unemployment rate in the nation. Our rate of infant mortality has risen to almost twice the rate of white infants since Reagan started cutting social programs.

On December 18, 1984, I returned to Nicaragua for the second time, one of a group of seventy-four North Americans going to work in the coffee fields. To show my support for the Nicaraguan people and the revolution, as well as my opposition to the Reagan administration's support of the contras, I was to spend three weeks in Nicaragua cutting [sic] coffee.

In the Miami airport, I sat looking around at what was to become the Jean Donovan Brigade, named after one of the Church women who was killed in El Salvador by a right-wing death squad in 1980. Anxious to return, I wondered what it would be like living and working with so many different people from so many different parts of North America.

The week before, someone had attempted to snatch my bag off my shoulder, and someone else had robbed my daughter's apartment. I looked forward to three weeks of feeling safe and secure, even though I knew I would be in a country at war.

After two and a half days of orientation in Managua, we boarded buses and began a seven hour trip to Matagalpa in the North. As we traveled into the mountains and beautiful countryside, passing through the picturesque city of Matagalpa, night began to overtake us. I thought of the murders of the TelCor (telecommunications) workers, who were on their way to cut coffee, of the mothers who were murdered on the way to visit their sons and daughters at the front. I also thought of the brothers and sisters in Southern Africa; the young, the old, murdered, dying, and suffering there. I thought of the atrocities carried out in Third World countries, supported with weapons and monies supplied by the United States government.

Finally, we reached our destination. As we climbed off the trucks we were greeted with applause, songs, and chants. What a welcome from the people of La Lima. There were speeches of greeting, revolutionary songs and chants, and tears in my eyes.

La Lima is a coffee farm that was once privately owned. The owner had allowed the coffee fields to grow wild, the hacienda and the land around it to deteriorate from years of neglect. Within the last year the government has taken control, the workers and families have begun rebuilding the farm and its coffee fields, now theirs.

To reach La Lima's coffee fields, you have to climb the mountains. The highest places I had ever climbed previously were the subway stairs of New York. I was determined to climb those mountains and either to lose my fear of heights or at best ignore it.

Each morning we were awakened at 4 a.m. to wash, dress, breakfast, and leave for the fields by 6 a.m. We were summoned to line up by the sound of a large sea shell being blown. There were approximately 130 brigadistas from Argentina, Australia, Colombia, Guatemala, Ecuador, France, Spain, and North America. We were told then who were the top cutters of the previous day, what today's production goals were, and where we would be cutting. We were led to the fields by Nicaraguan workers and some militia people for our protection.

At noon we returned from the fields for lunch, all starving. By 12:30 we were on our way back to finish the day's cutting. Between 4 and 4:30 p.m. we returned again, with our coffee sacks on our shoulders, ready for weigh-in. We were happy, tired, wet, and muddy. Even though the rainy season was supposedly over, someone forgot to tell Mother Nature—it rained every day.

We celebrated Christmas eve with the other internationalists and the families of La Lima. We prepared gifts and made a piñata for the children. The foreman slaughtered a cow for the holiday meal.

Before returning to Managua, we made a stop at one of the coffee plants to see how the coffee was processed. Later we were told that our brigade had surpassed the amount of coffee the Nicaraguans had predicted we would cut. That made us happy, and the happiness was the hope that we were of some help to the people and the economy of Nicaragua.

Nicaragua is a beautiful country: the lushness of the countryside is a wonder. The people are friendly, pleasant, and helpful. The Nicaraguans should have the right to determine their own future without interference from the United States. My experience cutting coffee was a good one—and my stay away from Nicaragua will be a short one.

NO. 113

1987

The Esquipulas II Accords

The Governments of Costa Rica, El Salvador, Guatemala, Honduras and Nicaragua

After the violent overthrow of the Nicaraguan government of Anastasio Somoza Debayle in 1979 by the Sandinista Front for National Liberation, the United States became increasingly engaged in the political and military conflicts that divided the nations of Central America. As the violence intensified during the early 1980s, the search for peace was led by the governments of Colombia, Mexico, Panama and Venezuela. Known as the Contadora Group after their foreign ministers met on Panama's Contadora Island in 1983, representatives of these governments began to mediate negotiations among the Central American countries aimed at ending the fighting in the region. The Contadora effort resulted in a draft agreement in 1984 that failed to win the full support of all five countries or of the United States. Attempts by the Contadora Group to restart the peace process continued, without success, into 1987. A turning point came in February 1987, when Oscar Arias, the newly elected president of Costa Rica, convened a meeting of the presidents of El Salvador, Guatemala and Honduras in San José, Costa Rica, in February 1987. He presented them with a plan that built on the Contadora draft agreement but went beyond it by requiring the signatories to take specific steps toward democratization and to negotiate with insurgent forces. The outcome of what became known as the Arias Peace Plan was the "Procedure for Establishing Firm and Lasting Peace in Central America," better known as Esquipulas II (after the name of the Guatemalan town where the presidents held a summit meeting in 1986), signed by the presidents of all five governments in Guatemala City on August 7, 1987. In recognition of his efforts, President Arias was awarded the Nobel Peace Prize that year.

The governments . . . have agreed on the following procedures to establish firm and lasting peace in Central America.

Source: International Commission for Central American Recovery and Development. *Poverty, Conflict and Hope: A Turning Point in Central America.* "App. 3: Esquipulas II Accords." Np. February 1989.

1. National Reconciliation

A. DIALOGUE. To undertake on an urgent basis, in those cases where deep divisions have occurred in society, actions for national reconciliation that will permit the participation of the people, with full guarantees in genuine democratic political processes, on the bases of justice, freedom and democracy, and to that end, to establish mechanisms that will make dialogue with opposing groups possible under the law.

To that end, the governments involved shall initiate a dialogue with all disarmed internal political opposition groups and with those that have availed themselves of amnesty.

B. AMNESTY. In each Central American country, except where the International Committee for Verification and Follow-up determines that it is not necessary, decrees for amnesty shall be issued that will establish all of the provisions to ensure inviolability of life, freedom in all of its forms, material property and safety of the persons to whom those decrees are applicable. Simultaneously with the issuance of the amnesty decrees, the irregular forces of the country concerned shall release all persons in their power.

C. NATIONAL RECONCILIATION COMMITTEE. To verify compliance with the commitments that the five Central American Governments undertake by signing this document, regarding amnesty, cease-fire, democratization and free elections, a National Reconciliation Committee shall be established that will have the duties of verifying the real effectiveness of the national reconciliation process, and the unrestricted respect for all the civil and political rights of Central American citizens that are guaranteed in this document. . . .

2. Urging the Cessation of Hostilities

The governments strongly urge the countries in the area that are now undergoing attacks by irregular or insurgent groups to agree to ceasing hostilities. The governments of those countries undertake to carry out all actions required to achieve an effective cease-fire under their constitutions.

3. Democratization

The governments undertake to encourage an authentic participatory and pluralistic democratic process involving promotion of social justice, respect for human rights, sovereignty, territorial integrity of the States, and the right of all countries to determine freely and without outside interference of any kind their economic, political and social models, and they shall take in a verifiable manner measures that are conducive to the establishment, and where necessary, the improvement of democratic, representative and pluralistic systems that guarantee the organization of political parties and effective participation of the people in decision-making and that ensure free access of holders of divergent political groups to honest periodic elections, based on the full observance of the rights of citizens.

To verify good faith in carrying out this process of democratization, it shall be understood that:

a. There shall be freedom of the press, radio and television. This complete freedom shall include opening and keeping in operation mass media for all ideological groups and operating those media without subjecting them to prior censorship.

b. There shall be total pluralism of political parties. In this regard, political groups shall have full access to the mass media, shall enjoy fully the rights of association and the right to public assembly in the unrestricted exercise of oral, written and televised publicity, and freedom of movement of the members of political parties in their efforts to win support. . . .

4. Free Elections

Having established the conditions inherent in any democracy, they shall hold free, pluralistic and honest elections. . . .

5. Cessation of Aid to Irregular Forces or to Insurrectional Movements

The Governments of the five Central American countries shall request the Governments in and outside the region that openly or covertly provide military, logistic, financial, propaganda, manpower, armament, munitions, and equipment assistance to irregular forces or insurrectional movements, to cease such assistance, as an essential element for achieving stable and durable peace in the region. Not included in the foregoing is assistance and the aid necessary for return to normal life of those persons who were members of such groups or forces. In addition, irregular forces and insurgent groups operating in Central America shall be requested to refrain from receiving such assistance, in order to maintain a true Latin Americanist spirit. . . .

6. Non-Use of Territory for Aggression Against Other States

The five countries signing this document reiterate their commitment to deny the use of their territory to, and not to provide or permit logistic military support for, persons, organizations or groups that seek to destabilize the governments of Central American countries. . . .

9. Cooperation, Democracy and Freedom for Peace and Development

In the climate of freedom that democracy ensures, the Central American countries shall take decisions to accelerate development in order to achieve societies that are more egalitarian and free from poverty. Consolidation of democracy involves the establishment of an economy of well-being and an economic and social democracy. To reach those objectives, the governments shall jointly make arrangements to obtain special economic assistance from the international community.

10. International Follow-Up and Verification

An International Committee for Verification and Follow-up shall be established with the following members: the Secretary Generals [sic], or their representatives, of the Organization of American States and the United Nations, and the Foreign Ministers of Central America, the Contadora Group and the Support Group. This Committee shall have the duty of verification and follow-up on compliance with the commitments set forth in this document. . . .

❖

NO. 114

1987

A School of the Americas "Study Manual"

The U.S. Department of Defense

The U.S. Army began offering courses to Latin American military personnel at Fort Amador in the Panama Canal Zone in 1946. Shortly renamed the U.S. Army Caribbean School, and finally the U.S. Army School of the Americas in 1963, the school had trained almost 60,000 Latin American military and police personnel by 1996. Under the Panama Canal treaties of 1977 (see Document No. 105), the United States agreed to close the school, and as a result it was moved to Fort Benning, Georgia, in 1984. Seven U.S. Army training manuals used by the school between 1989 and 1991 were declassified by the U.S. government in 1996 following allegations of improper Central Intelligence Agency links to Guatemalan military officers accused of torture and murder. The U.S. Army intelligence officers who wrote the manuals compiled them from U.S. Army documents produced in the 1960s and from lesson plans that had been used at the School of the Americas since 1982. The manuals, all in Spanish, provided instruction on the detection and suppression of antigovernment political and military activities and were used in the school's intelligence training courses. As many as 1,000 copies of the manuals had also been distributed directly to mili-

Source: National Security Archive, Washington, D.C. *Manual de Estudio: Manejo de Fuente.* Pp. 1–10; 29–32; 79–81. Translation by Robert H. Holden and Eric Zolov.

tary personnel and intelligence schools in Colombia, Ecuador, El Salvador, Guatemala and Peru by U.S. Army trainers working in those countries between 1987 and 1989. The Department of Defense said it had investigated the use of the manuals in 1991–92, concluded that they contained "objectionable" material and ordered all copies destroyed except for an archival copy of each manual. Excerpted below are passages from one of the handbooks, the 174-page *Manejo de Fuente,* translated by the Defense Department as *Handling of Sources*; passages that were considered "objectionable and questionable" by the Department of Defense are italicized.

The purpose of this chapter is to present the procedures one must follow in the recruitment and utilization of the personnel needed to gather intelligence for the government. . . .

We can define "employee" as that person who lends services in exchange for remuneration or compensation. Because insurrectionary movements can emerge in different zones of economic, political, and geographic influence, the government cannot depend only upon information given voluntarily by loyal citizens or on *information obtained involuntarily from insurgents who have been captured.* Some incentive must exist in order to assure the continued supply of information to the government. Consequently, it is necessary to disseminate throughout all segments of society informers whose services can be paid for. An employee is that person who can provide useful intelligence information in exchange for some compensation, whether it is monetary or of another nature. This person might be a village peasant, a cell member of the insurgent organization, or a person in charge of propaganda.

The informers should be dispersed in all places considered important, in every mass organization, regardless of its size, and in every place where there might appear any outbreak of insurrection. . . .

In planning operations it is very important to realize that even when one does not perceive any guerrilla activity, an insurrectionary movement might be in gestation. Every countermeasure that is focused solely on guerrilla activity without taking into consideration the secret organization and the great preparation necessary before the outbreak of violence is destined to fail.

The mere elimination of the guerrillas will not alter in any way the basic organization of the insurgents. If one is to achieve permanent victory, internal defense operations must be planned with the goal of attacking the insurgent organization before the guerrillas can initiate their operations, an attack that encompasses both the secret subversive elements and the military wing once the movement begins its second phase. . . .

During the initial phases, the insurgents are feverishly occupied with the formation of front organizations and the infiltration of institutions with large numbers of people. We have already seen how a relatively small number of people can manage to control an organization by means of infiltration and rigged elections. The government can learn about insurgent activity within these organizations in a timely way by distributing its employees in every organization suspected of being of interest to the insurgent group. Among the principal organizations of this type are political parties, unions, and student and youth groups. Since the insurgents' tactics follow a continuously repeated pattern, the government's employees can warn about their behavior. . . .

The insurgents will necessarily have to make contacts with certain people in the local area like merchants and vendors in order to obtain supplies and other goods. When they can be persuaded to become government employees, these merchants can help to identify the liaisons used by the insurgents in these operations. . . .

Insurrection is an evil which cannot be tolerated. A secret organization can be identified and made use of. However, a CI [counterintelligence] agent must know how and where to look in order to locate the foci of insurrection, and therefore must have the necessary information. The agent must also know the characteristic weaknesses of the insurgent organization and how to proceed in order to take advantage of them. . . .

Probably the most common motives for mercenaries is the desire for profit. Often the potential employee already has a job, but wishes to enhance his earnings. Even when money is the commonly used medium for transactions, the individual may ask to be paid with certain goods that are difficult to obtain. . . .

The possibilities of finding people disposed to collaborate with the government in an area where an insurrectionary movement is developing are immense. *Specific individuals, organizations, and commercial firms should be targeted for infiltration by employees of the government, with the goal of gaining information about the guerrillas.* . . .

A vital part of this program is the educational system established for indoctrinating and compensating government employees who become informers when approached by guerrillas seeking to recruit them. *The CI agent might arrange for the arrest or detention of the employee's relatives, jail the employee, or give him a beating as part of the plan for placing the employee within the guerrilla organization.* Of course, [the CI agent] will have to plan all of these demonstrations carefully, and utilize them at the exact moment in order to bolster the assertions of the employee. . . .

The CI agent can increase the value of the employee by destroying the guerrilla organizational structure that surrounds the employee. *This can be done by means of arrests, executions, or raids, making sure not to expose the employee as the source of information.* If the employee is one of the few survivors, he could become the key member of a new or different guerrilla organization. In this situation, the employee's reputation might be reinforced by fabricating stories, documents, and witnesses that would not only be credible, but difficult to refute, given that few guerrillas will have survived. . . .

There are other methods of providing outside help with the goal of assuring the promotion of an employee [within a guerrilla organization]. One method is through the influence of an employee higher up in the guerrilla organization; another is by eliminating a potential guerrilla rival. . . .

It is much more difficult to locate an employee in an area or an organization after the guerrillas have seized control. The CI agent can place an employee beforehand, during, or after the guerrillas have gained control of an area; however, the earlier it is done, the better the chances are for success. . . .

❖

NO. 115

1988

"We Say No"

Eduardo Galeano

B orn in Montevideo, Uruguay, in 1940, Eduardo Galeano worked as a magazine editor and writer until 1973, when he went into exile in Argentina for three years and then moved to Spain before returning to Uruguay in 1985. One of the best known of Latin America's public intellectuals, Galeano first established himself as a writer with a worldwide reputation with the publication of *Las venas abiertas de América Latina* (*Open Veins of Latin America*), a lyrical and biting historical analysis of the continent. First published in Mexico in 1971, *Venas abiertas* has sold more than 400,000 copies in Latin America alone. That book and the many others that Galeano has written since then have been translated into English and many other languages. What follows is the opening speech by Galeano at an international meeting in Chile from July 11 to 16, 1988, to support the restoration of democracy in that country. The title of the speech refers to the campaign, led by opponents of the military dictatorship of General Augusto Pinochet, encouraging Chileans to vote no in a plebiscite scheduled by Pinochet for October 5, 1988. Confident of his own popularity, the general had asked Chileans to vote yes or no on whether he should serve eight more years as president. Prodemocracy forces organized a "Command for the No" that succeeded in defeating the proposition with 55 percent of the vote, stunning Pinochet and opening the way for presidential and congressional elections in 1989, the first since Pinochet's overthrow of the government of President Salvador Allende in 1973.

Source: From *We Say No: Chronicles 1963–1991* pp. 241–44. Copyright © 1992 by Eduardo Galeano; original Spanish edition copyright © 1989 by Eduardo Galeano. Translation copyright © 1988 by Cedric Belfrage. Published in English by W.W. Norton & Company, Inc. Reprinted by permission of Susan Bergholz Literary Services, New York. All rights reserved.

We have come from different countries, and we are here—reunited under the generous shade of Pablo Neruda—to join the people of Chile, who say no.

We also say no.

We say no to the praise of money and of death. We say no to a system that assigns prices to people and things, within which he who has the most is hence he who is most worthy, and we say no to a world which spends two million dollars each minute on arms for war while each minute it kills thirty children with hunger or curable illnesses. The neutron bomb, which saves things and annihilates people, is a perfect symbol of our times. To the murderous system that converts the stars of the night sky into military objectives, the human being is no more than a factor of production and of consumption and an object of use; time, no more than an economic resource; and the entire planet a source of income that must yield up to the last drop of its juice. Poverty is multiplied in order to multiply wealth, and the arms that guard this wealth—the wealth of very few—are multiplied and keep all others on the brink of poverty. Meanwhile, solitude is also multiplied: we say no to a system that neither feeds its people nor loves them, that condemns many to a hunger for food and many more to a hunger for the embrace.

We say no to the lie. The dominant culture, which the mass media irradiates on a universal scale, invites us to confuse the world with a supermarket or a racetrack, where one's fellow man can be merchandise or competition, but never a brother. This culture of lies, which vulgarly speculates with human love in order to extract its appreciation, is in reality a culture of broken bonds: its gods are its winners, the successful masters of money and of power, and its heroes are uniformed "Rambos" who use their influence while applying the Doctrine of National Security. By what it says and what it fails to say, the dominant culture lies when it claims that the poverty of the poor is not a result of the wealth of the wealthy, but rather the daughter of no one, originating in a goat's ear or in the will of God, who created the lazy poor and the donkey. In the same way, the humiliation of some men by others does not necessarily have to motivate shared indignance [sic] or scandal, because it belongs to the natural order of things: let us suppose that Latin American dictatorships form part of our exuberant nature and not of the imperialist system of power.

Disdain betrays history and mutilates the world. The powerful opinion-makers treat us as though we do not exist, or as though we are silly shadows. The colonial inheritance obliges the so-called Third World—populated by third-class people—to accept as its own the memory of the victors who conquered it and to take on the lies of others and use them as its own reality. They reward our obedience, punish our intelligence, and discourage our creative energy. We are opinionated, yet we cannot offer our opinions. We have a right to the echo, not to the voice, and those who rule praise our talent to repeat parrot fashion. We say no: we refuse to accept this mediocrity as our destiny.

We say no to fear. No to the fear of speaking, of doing, of being. Visible colonialism forbids us to speak, to do, to be. Invisible colonialism, more efficient, convinces us that one cannot speak, cannot do, cannot be. Fear disguises itself as realism: to prevent realism from becoming unreal, or so claim the ideologists of impotence, morals must be immoral. Confronted with indignity, misery, lies and deceit, we have no alternative other than that of resignation. Marked by fatality, we are born irresponsible, violent, stupid, picturesque, and condemned to military bondage. At best, we can aspire to convert ourselves into model prisoners, to be able to conscientiously pay our share of a colossal foreign debt contracted to finance the luxury that humiliates us and the club that beats us.

And within this framework, we say no to the neutrality of the human word. We say no to those who invite us to wash our hands of the crucifixions we witness daily. To the bored fascination of an art that is cold, indifferent, contemplative of its mirrored reflection, we prefer a warm art, one that celebrates the human adventure in the world and participates in this adventure, an art that is incurably enamored and pugnacious. Would beauty be beautiful if it were not just? Would justice be just if it were not beautiful? We say no to the divorce of beauty and justice, because we say yes to the powerful and fertile embrace they share.

As it happens, we are saying no, and by saying no we are saying yes.

By saying no to dictatorships, and no to dictatorships disguised as democracies, we are saying yes to the struggle for true democracy, one that will deny no one bread or the power of speech, and one that will be as beautiful and dangerous as a poem by [Pablo] Neruda or a song by Violeta [Parra].

By saying no to the devastating empire of greed, whose center lies in North America, we are saying yes to another possible America, which will be born of the most ancient of American traditions, the communitarian tradition that the Chilean Indians have defended, desperately, defeat after defeat, during the last five centuries.

In saying no to a peace without dignity, we are saying yes to the sacred right of rebellion against injustice and its long history, as long as the history of popular resistance on the long map of Chile. By saying no to the freedom of money, we are saying yes to the freedom of people: a mistreated and wounded freedom, a thousand times defeated as in Chile and, as in Chile, a thousand times arisen.

To say no to the suicidal egotism of the powerful, who have converted the world into a vast barracks, we are saying yes to human solidarity, which gives us a universal sense and confirms the power of a brotherhood that is stronger than all borders and their guardians: the force that invades us, like the music of Chile, and like the wine of Chile, embraces us.

And by saying no to the sad charm of disenchantment, we are saying yes to hope, the famished and crazy and loving and loved hope of Chile, the obstinate hope, like the sons of Chile shattering the night.

❖

V.

AFTER THE COLD WAR: CONFLICT IN THE SEARCH FOR COMMON GROUND

1990

The United States Invades Panama: "We Never Heard The Truth"

Ramsey Clark

Central America continued to maintain its unusually prominent role on the U.S. foreign policy agenda in 1989, the year that George Bush, vice president during the administration of Ronald Reagan (1981–89), succeeded to the presidency. Still preoccupied with forcing the Sandinistas out of office in Nicaragua and shoring up the regime that Washington was sustaining against a guerrilla insurgency in El Salvador, the Bush administration ordered a U.S. military invasion of Panama on December 20, 1989. With 13,000 troops flying into Panama to join the 13,000 already in place at U.S. bases in the Canal Zone, this was the largest U.S. force sent into battle since the Vietnam War, and the largest in Latin America since the war with Spain in 1898. President Bush announced the four goals of the invasion, code-named Operation Just Cause: "to safeguard the lives of Americans, to defend democracy in Panama, to combat drug trafficking and to protect the integrity of the Panama Canal treaty." In thirteen hours, more than four hundred bombs were dropped by U.S. war planes. Large areas of Panama City were burned to the ground, between 10,000 and 18,000 people were left homeless and nearly 5,000 prisoners were taken. The most important objective of the invasion, however, was not achieved until January 4, 1990, when U.S. forces finally captured General Manuel Antonio Noriega, the commander of the Panamian Defense Forces. Noriega, who had been indicted by a U.S. grand jury in 1988 for conspiring to smuggle drugs into the United States, was arrested, stood trial in Miami and was sentenced to forty years in prison. In the course of the U.S. invasion, the Panamanian Defense Forces were destroyed, and later replaced by a new, U.S.-created National Police. Critics of the invasion challenged the official U.S. estimate that only 202 Panamian civilians were killed by U.S. forces. Among the most prominent of the critics was Ramsey Clark, former U.S.

Source: Ramsey Clark. "We Never Heard the Truth." In the Independent Commission of Inquiry on the U.S. Invasion of Panama, *The U.S. Invasion of Panama: The Truth Behind Operation "Just Cause."* Pp. 9–14. Boston: South End Press, 1991.

attorney general (1967–69). Excerpted below is a speech Clark made on April 5, 1990, in New York City.

. . . During this century there was a major U.S. intervention in Panama every time independence was seriously asserted. And for all of those years, across that beautiful bracelet that links the continents, there was this terrible scar, like a chain across the human heart, the intrusion on sovereignty and fundamental political, economic and human rights: the canal. It has dominated the lives of the people of Panama for all of this century.

And finally we come to December 20, 1989. We waited. We shouldn't have. We watched when action was called for. We were silent though many enjoyed the demonization period that we've witnessed so many times in so many places. We heard all of the false reasons being developed for what was going to happen, something anyone could sense.

We heard nothing said about the purpose of the invasion being instruction in absolute obedience to authority. We heard nothing about how "There will be no sovereignty in this hemisphere but ours." We heard nothing about the Southern Command being very comfortable in its quarters in Panama. We heard nothing about keeping the Canal, and our investment there. We heard nothing about the real reasons. We saw domestic politics, face saving and all those pitiful things impel us toward the invasion of Panama and its celebration.

We heard a bunch of lies. We never heard the truth.

There is no need to cite article and verse of the laws prohibiting the invasion. It would only distract from the obvious. Of course the invasion of Panama violated international law. One nation cannot invade another because of its displeasure with policies, or leadership there. Of course it violated the laws of the United States. We cannot under our law deploy military force in time of peace; killing civilians at the whim of the executive. And as you can imagine it violated the laws of the sovereign Republic of Panama which intend to protect its independence. But it also violated the human rights of millions of people, not just Panamanians but everyone affected and implicated, then, now and hereafter.

It was a physical assault of stunning violence. It was a time for testing new equipment with no concern for human lives. It was a time for measuring the worth of technology against the life of a child. The Stealth fighter in Panama! And now we hear, well, they didn't mean to hurt anybody.

How many times will we accept that sort of misinformation? You go to Panama right after the invasion, you go to a place, El Chorrillo, "a little stream" or "rush of water." At one time it was El Chorro, a lot of water. The people there before Cristobal Colón and the Mayflower enjoyed that water, it was *pura*, it was *sabrosa*, it was healthy. After the cut for the canal it came down to a trickle, and it's where the poor people were left to live.

I stayed in El Chorrillo in 1946 for a few weeks, just shortly after I got out of—yes!—the United States Marine Corps as a corporal. Like some of the older people from Panama, I spent some good nights in Kelly's Ritz and a few other places and I loved El Chorrillo and I loved its people—their diversity, their beauty, their joy, their music and their poetry. I couldn't believe it when I went back two weeks after our invasion and saw it in utter ruin: 15 blocks or more, home to at least 30,000 people, destroyed or so badly damaged that no one could possibly live there.

Try to imagine being there in the middle of the night, in the poor part of town, perhaps in a highrise, and all of a sudden the power is off. And then you hear artillery. And then you hear helicopters. And then you hear rockets. And then you hear heavy caliber automatic gunfire.

What do you do? You get under the bed. You hide where you can. How do you get out? Where do you go? What's going on? Where is it safe?

How many died? Doesn't anybody care how many people we killed in Panama?

General Stiner—who seemed to be the source of most public utterances on the subject of the invasion, how fine it was, how surgical and all the rest—was telling the press 84 Panamanian civilians killed as late as January 4th. Voltaire, you remember, argued the terrible thought that "history is fiction agreed upon." Napoleon loved that. He thought Voltaire was a pretty smart fellow.

The U.S. military wanted to make 84 Panamanian civilian deaths a fiction that history would agree on. But it's not going to work.

I estimated when I left in early January at least a thousand killed. There were probably several thousand. The people of the United States have an absolute moral obligation to demand the most thorough account possible.

Let me wind up with two things.

I kept hearing about a place called Jardín de Paz. Sounded nice—the garden of peace. And I went out there the last evening I was in Panama, which was the first Saturday of January of this year, and found a couple of little children who played in the cemetery because it was the best place they had to play. I gave one of them a dollar (Americans should know that the currency in Panama is the dollar; they don't have a currency of their own) and asked if he had seen anybody burying any bodies around there. And he took me and several Panamanian companions over to what seemed to be the gravesite. I paced it off. The grave was 18 feet wide—six paces. It was 120 feet long—40 paces. The earth hadn't been filled in for an additional 26 paces. The unfilled cut was five feet deep.

We need to know how many Panamanians were killed in the invasion. The families are entitled to know what's happened to their loved ones, to their children, to their women, to their men. And most of all, and I say this to the people from the United States, we live in a country that functions to some minor degree under democratic institutions, and whether it does or not, we are responsible for the acts of our agents. We need to pull up our socks, we need to find out everything that happened here. Then we must resolve that it shall never happen again!

Not in Panama, not in Nicaragua, not in Cuba, not in Haiti, not in Syria or Iraq. Nowhere!

We have some folks at home that need help. Let's lend a hand here. They are victims of the same false values. But we must recognize that we have a responsibility to see that the anthem of Panama is fulfilled and that victory belongs to the people of Panama at last.

❖

NO. 117

1992

The Rio Declaration on Environment and Development

The Delegates to the U.N. Conference on Environment and Development

In 1989, the United Nations General Assembly voted to convene the United Nations Conference on Environment and Development in Brazil for two weeks in June 1992. After four international negotiating sessions that took place over the intervening two and one-half years, the "Earth Summit," as the Rio de Janeiro meeting came to be known, was seen as an important forum for the shaping of a new international post–Cold War order. It attracted more than 100 heads of state and government, the delegates of more than 1,500 officially accredited nongovernmental organizations and some 7,000 journalists. Two major international treaties, on biodiversity and climate change, were opened for signature at Rio. One setback was the failure to negotiate a treaty to protect the forests of the world, owing largely to concerns among the less developed countries that such a treaty might limit their freedom to exploit their forests. Some of the tensions that emerged at the meeting between the more developed and the less developed countries (or the North and the South, as they were frequently referred to) may be detected in a close reading of a document that had been agreed to at

Source: United Nations. *The Earth Summit: The United Nations Conference on Environment and Development (UNCED)*, pp. 117–24. London: Graham & Trotman/Martinus Nijhoff, 1993.

one of the preliminary conferences, the Rio Declaration on Environment and Development, excerpted below. It was formally approved at the Rio meeting, with the United States announcing its formal reservations to Principles 3, 7, 12 and 23.

Principle 1

Human beings are at the centre of concerns for sustainable development. They are entitled to a healthy and productive life in harmony with nature.

Principle 2

States have, in accordance with the Charter of the United Nations and the principles of international law, the sovereign right to exploit their own resources pursuant to their own environmental and developmental policies, and the responsibility to ensure that activities within their jurisdiction or control do not cause damage to the environment of other States or of areas beyond the limits of national jurisdiction.

Principle 3

The right to development must be fulfilled so as to equitably meet developmental and environmental needs of present and future generations.

Principle 4

In order to achieve sustainable development, environmental protection shall constitute an integral part of the development process and cannot be considered in isolation from it. All States and all people shall cooperate in the essential task of eradicating poverty as an indispensable requirement for sustainable development, in order to decrease the disparities in standards of living and better meet the needs of the majority of the people of the world. . . .

Principle 6

The special situation and needs of developing countries, particularly the least developed and those most environmentally vulnerable, shall be given special priority. International actions in the field of environment and development should also address the interests and needs of all countries.

Principle 7

States shall cooperate in a spirit of global partnership to conserve, protect and restore the health and integrity of the Earth's ecosystem. In view of the different contributions to global environmental degradation, States have common but differentiated responsibilities. The developed countries acknowledge the responsibility that they bear in the international pursuit of sustainable development in view of the pressures their societies place on the global environment and of the technologies and financial resources they command.

Principle 8

To achieve sustainable development and a higher quality of life for all people, States should reduce and eliminate unsustainable patterns of production and consumption and promote appropriate demographic policies.

Principle 9

States should cooperate to strengthen endogenous capacity-building for sustainable development by improving scientific understanding through exchanges of scientific and technological knowledge, and by enhancing the development, adaptation, diffusion and transfer of technologies, including new and innovative technologies.

Principle 10

Environmental issues are best handled with the participation of all concerned citizens, at the relevant level. At the national level, each individual shall have appropriate access to information concerning the environment that is held by public authorities, including information on hazardous materials and activities in their communities, and the opportunity to participate in decision-making processes. States shall facilitate and encourage public awareness and participation by making information widely available. Effective access to judicial and administrative proceedings, including redress and remedy, shall be provided.

Principle 11

States shall enact effective environmental legislation. Environmental standards, management objectives and priorities should reflect the environmental and developmental context to which they apply. Standards applied by some countries may be inappropriate and of unwarranted economic and social costs to other countries, particularly developing countries.

Principle 12

States should cooperate to promote a supportive and open international economic system that would lead to economic growth and sustainable development in all countries, to better address the problems of environmental degradation. Trade policy measures for environmental purposes should not constitute a means of arbitrary or unjustifiable discrimination or a disguised restriction on international trade. Unilateral actions to deal with environmental challenges outside the jurisdiction of the importing country should be avoided. Environmental measures addressing transboundary or global environmental problems should, as far as possible, be based on an international consensus.

Principle 13

States shall develop national law regarding liability and compensation for the victims of pollution and other environmental damage. States shall also cooperate in an expeditious and more determined manner to develop further international law regarding liability and compensation for adverse effects of environmental damage caused by activities within their jurisdiction or control to areas beyond their jurisdiction.

Principle 14

States should effectively cooperate to discourage or prevent the relocation and transfer to other States of any activities and substances that cause severe environmental degradation or are found to be harmful to human health. . . .

Principle 22

Indigenous people and their communities, and other local communities, have a vital role in environmental management and development because of their knowledge and traditional practices. States should recognize and duly support their identity, culture and interests and enable their effective participation in the achievement of sustainable development.

Principle 23

The environment and natural resources of people under oppression, domination and occupation shall be protected.

Principle 24

Warfare is inherently destructive of sustainable development. States shall therefore respect international law providing protection for the environment in times of armed conflict and cooperate in its further development, as necessary.

Principle 25

Peace, development and environmental protection are interdependent and indivisible. . . .

NO. 118

1994

The North American Free Trade Agreement

The Governments of Canada, the United States and Mexico

In 1990, the governments of Mexico, the United States and Canada began to negotiate a comprehensive trade treaty that was intended to gradually move the three countries toward unfettered commercial relations, creating a single huge trade bloc. From the beginning of the negotiation process, however, it was clear that the proposed treaty would have the greatest impact on Mexico. Long protected from foreign competition and heavily controlled by the Mexican state, the economy was in a shambles. It was crippled by a staggering load of foreign debt, continuous inflationary pressures, currency instability, undercapitalization and low productivity. President Carlos Salinas de Gortari had already begun to radically reshape the economy by bringing it into line with the worldwide trend toward neoliberalism. He negotiated a slight reduction in Mexico's foreign debt, sold off billions of dollars worth of state enterprises and loosened state controls over the economy. But the centerpiece of his government's shift to a more market-oriented economy was the North American Free Trade Agreement (NAFTA). A preliminary agreement was signed by Salinas, U.S. president George Bush and Canadian prime minister Brian Mulroney on December 17, 1992. Intense negotiations over the final form of the treaty continued following the inauguration of President Bill Clinton in January 1993. After ratification by the legislative bodies of the three nations, the agreement went into effect on January 1, 1994. Excerpts from the main agreement and two "side" agreements dealing with labor and environmental issues follow.

The Government of Canada, the Government of the United Mexican States and the Government of the United States of America . . . have agreed as follows:

The Parties to this Agreement, consistent with Article XXIV of the General Agreement on Tariffs and Trade, hereby establish a free trade area.

The objectives of this Agreement, as elaborated more specifically through

Source: Official home page of Organization of American States, Foreign Trade Information System, http://www.sice.oas.org/trade/nafta/naftatce.stm. December 1998.

its principles and rules, including national treatment, most-favored-nation treatment and transparency, are to:

(a) eliminate barriers to trade in, and facilitate the cross-border movement of, goods and services between the territories of the Parties;

(b) promote conditions of fair competition in the free trade area;

(c) increase substantially investment opportunities in the territories of the Parties;

(d) provide adequate and effective protection and enforcement of intellectual property rights in each Party's territory;

(e) create effective procedures for the implementation and application of this Agreement, for its joint administration and for the resolution of disputes; and

(f) establish a framework for further trilateral, regional and multilateral cooperation to expand and enhance the benefits of this Agreement. . . .

This Agreement shall enter into force on January 1, 1994, on an exchange of written notifications certifying the completion of necessary legal procedures. . . . Any country or group of countries may accede to this Agreement subject to such terms and conditions as may be agreed between such country or countries. . . .

A Party may withdraw from this Agreement six months after it provides written notice of withdrawal to the other Parties. . . .

North American Agreement on Labor Cooperation Between the Government of Canada, the Government of the United Mexican States and the Government of the United States of America

The objectives of this Agreement are to:

(a) improve working conditions and living standards in each Party's territory;

(b) promote, to the maximum extent possible, the labor principles set out in Annex 1;

(c) encourage cooperation to promote innovation and rising levels of productivity and quality;

(d) encourage publication and exchange of information, data development and coordination, and joint studies to enhance mutually beneficial understanding of the laws and institutions governing labor in each Party's territory;

(e) pursue cooperative labor-related activities on the basis of mutual benefit;

(f) promote compliance with, and effective enforcement by each Party of, its labor law; and

(g) foster transparency in the administration of labor law. . . .

Affirming full respect for each Party's constitution, and recognizing the right of each Party to establish its own domestic labor standards, and to adopt or modify accordingly its labor laws and regulations, each Party shall ensure that its labor laws and regulations provide for high labor standards, consistent with high quality and productivity workplaces, and shall continue to strive to improve those standards in that light.

North American Agreement on Environmental Cooperation Between the Government of Canada, the Government of the United Mexican States and the Government of the United States of America

The objectives of this Agreement are to:

(a) foster the protection and improvement of the environment in the territories of the Parties for the well-being of present and future generations;

(b) promote sustainable development based on cooperation and mutually supportive environmental and economic policies;

(c) increase cooperation between the Parties to better conserve, protect, and enhance the environment, including wild flora and fauna;

(d) support the environmental goals and objectives of the NAFTA;

(e) avoid creating trade distortions or new trade barriers;

(f) strengthen cooperation on the development and improvement of environmental laws, regulations, procedures, policies and practices;

(g) enhance compliance with, and enforcement of, environmental laws and regulations;

(h) promote transparency and public participation in the development of environmental laws, regulations and policies;

(i) promote economically efficient and effective environmental measures; and

(j) promote pollution prevention policies and practices. . . .

Each Party shall, with respect to its territory:

(a) periodically prepare and make publicly available reports on the state of the environment;

(b) develop and review environmental emergency preparedness measures;

(c) promote education in environmental matters, including environmental law;

(d) further scientific research and technology development in respect of environmental matters;

(e) assess, as appropriate, environmental impacts; and

(f) promote the use of economic instruments for the efficient achievement of environmental goals. . . .

Each Party shall consider prohibiting the export to the territories of the other Parties of a pesticide or toxic substance whose use is prohibited within the Party's territory. When a Party adopts a measure prohibiting or severely restricting the use of a pesticide or toxic substance in its territory, it shall notify the other Parties of the measure, either directly or through an appropriate international organization. . . .

❖

1994

Insurgency After the Cold War

The Zapatista Army of National Liberation

On January 1, 1994, the day the North American Free Trade Agreement (Document No. 118), took effect, Mexicans woke up to discover that an armed, largely indigenous rebel group had declared war on the government from the southern state of Chiapas. Taking their name from Mexico's famed revolutionary peasant leader, Emiliano Zapata (1879–1919), the Ejército Zapatista de Liberación Nacional (Zapatista Army of National Liberation, or EZLN) denounced the neoliberal economic policies of President Carlos Salinas de Gortari (1988–94) and authoritarian rule by the Partido Revolucionario Institucional (Institutionalized Revolutionary Party or PRI), which had controlled political power in Mexico for more than sixty years. The article excerpted below was published in the first issue of the official newspaper of the EZLN, *El Despertador Mexicano*, on December 31, 1993. Most of the Zapatistas' public pronouncements were drafted by an EZLN leader who only identified himself as "Sub-comandante Marcos."

Declaration of War

TODAY WE SAY ENOUGH IS ENOUGH! TO THE PEOPLE OF MEXICO: MEXICAN BROTHERS AND SISTERS: We are the product of 500 years of struggle: first against slavery, then during the War of Independence against Spain led by insurgents, then to avoid being absorbed by North American imperialism, then to promulgate our constitution and expel the French Empire from our soil, and later the dictatorship of Porfirio Díaz denied us the just application of the Reform Laws, and the people rebelled and leaders like Villa and Zapata emerged, poor people just like us. We have been denied the most elemental preparation so that they can use us as cannon fodder and pillage the wealth of our country. They don't care that we have nothing, absolutely nothing, not even a roof over our heads: no land, no work, no health care, no food, no education. Nor are we able to freely and democratically elect our political

Source: General Command of the Ejército Zapatista de Liberación Nacional [EZLN], "Declaration of War," *El Despertador Mexicano*, 31 December 1993. In *¡Zapatistas! Documents of the New Mexican Revolution (31 December 1993–12 June 1994)*, pp. 49–51. Brooklyn, N.Y.: Autonomedia, 1994.

representatives, nor is there independence from foreigners, nor is there peace nor justice for ourselves and our children.

But today, we say ENOUGH IS ENOUGH. We are the inheritors of the true builders of our nation. The dispossessed, we are millions, and we thereby call upon our brothers and sisters to join this struggle as the only path, so that we will not die of hunger due to the insatiable ambition of a 70-year dictatorship led by a clique of traitors who represent the most conservative and sell-out groups. They are the same ones who opposed Hidalgo and Morelos, the same ones who betrayed Vicente Guerrero, the same ones who sold half our country to the foreign invader, the same ones who imported a European prince to rule our country, the same ones who formed the "scientific" Porfirista dictatorship, the same ones who opposed the Petroleum Expropriation, the same ones who today take everything from us, absolutely everything.

To prevent the continuation of the above, and as our last hope, after having tried to utilize all legal means based on our Constitution, we go to our Constitution, to apply Article 39, which says: "National Sovereignty essentially and originally resides in the people. [. . .]" Therefore, according to our Constitution, we declare the following to the Mexican Federal Army, the pillar of the Mexican dictatorship that we suffer from, monopolized by a one-party system and led by Carlos Salinas de Gortari, the supreme and illegitimate federal executive who today holds power.

According to this Declaration of War, we ask that other powers of the nation advocate to restore the legitimacy and the stability of the nation by overthrowing the dictator.

We also ask that international organizations and the International Red Cross watch over and regulate our battles, so that our efforts are carried out while still protecting our civilian population. . . . We have the Mexican people on our side, we have the beloved tri-colored flag, highly respected by our insurgent fighters. We use black and red in our uniform as a symbol of our working people on strike. Our flag carries the following letters, "EZLN," Zapatista National Liberation Army, and we always carry our flag into combat.

Beforehand, we reject any effort to disgrace our just cause by accusing us of being drug traffickers, drug guerrillas, thieves or other names that might be used by our enemies. Our struggle follows the Constitution, which is held high by its call for justice and equality.

Therefore, according to this declaration of war, we give our military forces, the EZLN, the following orders:

First: Advance to the capital of the country . . . protecting in our advance the civilian population and permitting the people in the liberated area the right to freely and democratically elect their own administrative authorities.

Second: Respect the lives of our prisoners and turn over all wounded to the International Red Cross.

Third: Initiate summary judgments against all soldiers of the Mexican Federal Army and the political police who have received training or have been paid by foreigners, accused of being traitors to our country, and against all those who have repressed and treated badly the civilian population, and robbed, or stolen from, or attempted crimes against the good of the people.

Fourth: Form new troops with all those Mexicans who show their interest in joining our struggle. . . .

Fifth: We ask for the unconditional surrender of the enemy's headquarters. . . .

Sixth: Suspend the robbery of our natural resources in the areas controlled by the EZLN.

To the People of Mexico: We, the men and women, full and free, are conscious that the war that we have declared is our last resort, but also a just one. The dictators have been waging an undeclared genocidal war against our people for many years. Therefore we ask for your participation, your decision to support this plan that struggles for work, land, housing, food, health care, education, independence, freedom, democracy, justice and peace. We declare that we will not stop fighting until the basic demands of our people have been met by forming a government of our country that is free and democratic. JOIN THE INSURGENT FORCES OF THE ZAPATISTA NATIONAL LIBERATION ARMY!

❖

NO. 120

1994

Proposition 187

The Voters of California

On November 8, 1994, 59 percent of California voters approved a ballot initiative, Proposition 187, that would have ended access to health, education and social services for the state's illegal aliens, the vast majority of whom were Latin Americans. The measure, which was supported by Governor Pete Wilson, would also have required state employees to identify suspected illegal aliens to law enforcement authorities for arrest and deportation. Opponents of Proposition

Source: California. Secretary of State. *1994 General Election. 1994 California Voter Information: Proposition 187. Text of Proposed Law;* http://ca94.election.digital.com/e/prop/187/txt.html. December 1998.

187 immediately challenged it in federal court, and in 1998 the measure was declared unconstitutional by a U.S. District Court. The state of California dropped its appeal of that ruling in 1999, effectively burying Proposition 187.

Proposed Law

Section 1. Findings and Declaration.

The People of California find and declare as follows:

That they have suffered and are suffering economic hardship caused by the presence of illegal aliens in this state.

That they have suffered and are suffering personal injury and damage caused by the criminal conduct of illegal aliens in this state.

That they have a right to the protection of their government from any person or persons entering this country unlawfully. . . .

Section 5. Exclusion of Illegal Aliens from Public Social Services. . . .

(b) A person shall not receive any public social services to which he or she may be otherwise entitled until the legal status of that person has been verified as one of the following:

(1) A citizen of the United States.
(2) An alien lawfully admitted as a permanent resident.
(3) An alien lawfully admitted for a temporary period of time.

(c) If any public entity in this state to whom a person has applied for public social services determines or reasonably suspects, based upon the information provided to it, that the person is an alien in the United States in violation of federal law, the following procedures shall be followed by the public entity:

(1) The entity shall not provide the person with benefits or services.
(2) The entity shall, in writing, notify the person of his or her apparent illegal immigration status, and that the person must either obtain legal status or leave the United States.
(3) The entity shall also notify the State Director of Social Services, the Attorney General of California, and the United States Immigration and Naturalization Service of the apparent illegal status, and shall provide any additional information that may be requested by any other public entity.

Section 6. Exclusion of Illegal Aliens from Publicly Funded Health Care. . . .

(b) A person shall not receive any health care services from a publicly-funded health care facility, to which he or she is otherwise entitled until the legal status of that person has been verified as one of the following:

(1) A citizen of the United States.
(2) An alien lawfully admitted as a permanent resident.
(3) An alien lawfully admitted for a temporary period of time.

(c) If any publicly-funded health care facility in this state from whom a person seeks health care services, other than emergency medical care as required by federal law, determines or reasonably suspects, based upon the information provided to it, that the person is an alien in the United States in violation of federal law, the following procedures shall be followed by the facility:

(1) The facility shall not provide the person with services.
(2) The facility shall, in writing, notify the person of his or her apparent illegal immigration status, and that the person must either obtain legal status or leave the United States.
(3) The facility shall also notify the State Director of Health Services, the Attorney General of California, and the United States Immigration and Naturalization Service of the apparent illegal status, and shall provide any additional information that may be requested by any other public entity.

(d) For purposes of this section "publicly-funded health care facility" shall be defined as specified in Sections 1200 and 1250 of this code as of January 1, 1993.

Section 7. Exclusion of Illegal Aliens from Public Elementary and Secondary Schools. . . .

(a) No public elementary or secondary school shall admit, or permit the attendance of, any child who is not a citizen of the United States, an alien lawfully admitted as a permanent resident, or a person who is otherwise authorized under federal law to be present in the United States.

(b) Commencing January 1, 1995, each school district shall verify the legal status of each child enrolling in the school district for the first time in order to ensure the enrollment or attendance only of citizens, aliens lawfully admitted as permanent residents, or persons who are otherwise authorized to be present in the United States.

(c) By January 1, 1996, each school district shall have verified the legal status of each child already enrolled and in attendance in the school district in order to ensure the enrollment or attendance only of citizens, aliens lawfully admitted as permanent residents, or persons who are otherwise authorized under federal law to be present in the United States.

(d) By January 1, 1996, each school district shall also have verified the legal status of each parent or guardian of each child referred to in subdivisions (b) and (c), to determine whether such parent or guardian is one of the following:

(1) A citizen of the United States.

(2) An alien lawfully admitted as a permanent resident.

(3) An alien admitted lawfully for a temporary period of time.

(e) Each school district shall provide information to the State Superintendent of Public Instruction, the Attorney General of California, and the United States Immigration and Naturalization Service regarding any enrollee or pupil, or parent or guardian, attending a public elementary or secondary school in the school district determined or reasonably suspected to be in violation of federal immigration laws within forty-five days after becoming aware of an apparent violation. . . .

Section 8. Exclusion of Illegal Aliens from Public Postsecondary Educational Institutions.

(a) No public institution of postsecondary education shall admit, enroll, or permit the attendance of any person who is not a citizen of the United States, an alien lawfully admitted as a permanent resident in the United States, or a person who is otherwise authorized under federal law to be present in the United States.

(b) Commencing with the first term or semester that begins after January 1, 1995, and at the commencement of each term or semester thereafter, each public postsecondary educational institution shall verify the status of each person enrolled or in attendance at that institution in order to ensure the enrollment or attendance only of United States citizens, aliens lawfully admitted as permanent residents in the United States, and persons who are otherwise authorized under federal law to be present in the United States.

(c) No later than 45 days after the admissions officer of a public postsecondary educational institution becomes aware of the application, enrollment, or attendance of a person determined to be, or who is under reasonable suspicion of being, in the United States in violation of federal immigration laws, that officer shall provide that information to the State Superintendent of Public Instruction, the Attorney General of California, and the United States Immigration and Naturalization Service. . . .

❖

1994

The Summit of the Americas

The Heads of State of Thirty-Four American Nations

I n December 1994, one year after the implementation of the North American Free Trade Agreement (Document No. 118), the heads of state of thirty-four American nations (with the single prominent exception of Cuba) met in Miami and agreed to create a "Free Trade Area of the Americas" encompassing North America, the Caribbean, Central America and South America. The Miami "Summit of the Americas" adoped a Declaration of Principles, excerpted below, to guide the process of negotiating a hemisphere-wide trade bloc, which the delegates agreed to conclude by 2005. Negotiations were officially launched at the second summit in Santiago, Chile, April 18-19, 1998.

Declaration of Principles

Partnership for Development and Prosperity: Democracy, Free Trade and Sustainable Development in the Americas

The elected Heads of State and Government of the Americas are committed to advance the prosperity, democratic values and institutions, and security of our Hemisphere. For the first time in history, the Americas are a community of democratic societies. Although faced with differing development challenges, the Americas are united in pursuing prosperity through open markets, hemispheric integration, and sustainable development. We are determined to consolidate and advance closer bonds of cooperation and to transform our aspirations into concrete realities. . . .

To Preserve and Strengthen the Community of Democracies of the Americas

The Charter of the OAS establishes that representative democracy is indispensable for the stability, peace and development of the region. It is the sole politi-

Source: Official home page of the Free Trade Area of the Americas process, maintained by the Tripartite Committee, which consists of the Inter-American Development Bank (IDB), the Organization of American States (OAS) and the United Nations Economic Commission for Latin America and the Caribbean (ECLAC). http://www.ftaa-alca.org/EnglishVersion/miami_e.htm. December 1998.

cal system which guarantees respect for human rights and the rule of law; it safe-guards cultural diversity, pluralism, respect for the rights of minorities, and peace within and among nations. Democracy is based, among other fundamentals, on free and transparent elections and includes the right of all citizens to participate in government. Democracy and development reinforce one another.

We reaffirm our commitment to preserve and strengthen our democratic systems for the benefit of all people of the Hemisphere. We will work through the appropriate bodies of the OAS to strengthen democratic institutions and promote and defend constitutional democratic rule, in accordance with the OAS Charter. We endorse OAS efforts to enhance peace and the democratic, social, and economic stability of the region.

We recognize that our people earnestly seek greater responsiveness and ef-ficiency from our respective governments. Democracy is strengthened by the modernization of the state, including reforms that streamline operations, re-duce and simplify government rules and procedures, and make democratic in-stitutions more transparent and accountable. Deeming it essential that justice should be accessible in an efficient and expeditious way to all sectors of soci-ety, we affirm that an independent judiciary is a critical element of an effec-tive legal system and lasting democracy. Our ultimate goal is to better meet the needs of the population, especially the needs of women and the most vul-nerable groups, including indigenous people, the disabled, children, the aged, and minorities.

Effective democracy requires a comprehensive attack on corruption as a fac-tor of social disintegration and distortion of the economic system that under-mines the legitimacy of political institutions.

Recognizing the pernicious effects of organized crime and illegal narcotics on our economies, ethical values, public health, and the social fabric, we will join the battle against the consumption, production, trafficking and distribu-tion of illegal drugs, as well as against money laundering and the illicit traf-ficking in arms and chemical precursors. We will also cooperate to create viable alternative development strategies in those countries in which illicit crops are grown. Cooperation should be extended to international and national programs aimed at curbing the production, use and trafficking of illicit drugs and the re-habilitation of addicts.

We condemn terrorism in all its forms, and we will, using all legal means, combat terrorist acts anywhere in the Americas with unity and vigor.

Recognizing the important contribution of individuals and associations in ef-fective democratic government and in the enhancement of cooperation among the people of the Hemisphere, we will facilitate fuller participation of our people in political, economic and social activity, in accordance with national legislation.

To Promote Prosperity Through Economic Integration and Free Trade

Our continued economic progress depends on sound economic policies, sus-tainable development, and dynamic private sectors. A key to prosperity is trade without barriers, without subsidies, without unfair practices, and with an increasing stream of productive investments. Eliminating impediments to market access for goods and services among our countries will foster our economic growth. A growing world economy will also enhance our domestic prosperity. Free trade and increased economic integration are key factors for raising standards of living, improving the working conditions of people in the Americas and better protecting the environment.

We, therefore, resolve to begin immediately to construct the "Free Trade Area of the Americas" (FTAA), in which barriers to trade and investment will be progressively eliminated. We further resolve to conclude the negotiation of the "Free Trade Area of the Americas" no later than 2005, and agree that concrete progress toward the attainment of this objective will be made by the end of this century. . . .

Aware that investment is the main engine for growth in the Hemisphere, we will encourage such investment by cooperating to build more open, transparent and integrated markets. In this regard, we are committed to create strengthened mechanisms that promote and protect the flow of productive investment in the Hemisphere, and to promote the development and progressive integration of capital markets. . . .

To Eradicate Poverty and Discrimination in Our Hemisphere

It is politically intolerable and morally unacceptable that some segments of our populations are marginalized and do not share fully in the benefits of growth. With an aim of attaining greater social justice for all our people, we pledge to work individually and collectively to improve access to quality education and primary health care and to eradicate extreme poverty and illiteracy. The fruits of democratic stability and economic growth must be accessible to all, without discrimination by race, gender, national origin or religious affiliation.

In observance of the International Decade of the World's Indigenous People, we will focus our energies on improving the exercise of democratic rights and the access to social services by indigenous people and their communities.

Aware that widely shared prosperity contributes to hemispheric stability, lasting peace and democracy, we acknowledge our common interest in creating employment opportunities that improve the incomes, wages and working conditions of all our people. We will invest in people so that individuals throughout the Hemisphere have the opportunity to realize their full potential.

Strengthening the role of women in all aspects of political, social and economic life in our countries is essential to reduce poverty and social inequalities and to enhance democracy and sustainable development. . . .

1995

Drugs and Democracy in Bolivia

Human Rights Watch

When William J. Bennett, the director of the U.S. Office of National Drug Control Policy in the administration of President George Bush (1988–93) declared that "drugs are a major threat to our national security," he was referring to the fact that most of the illegal drugs consumed in the United States were imported from other countries. And the principal source by far of two of those drugs—cocaine and marijuana—was Latin America. As a result, the U.S. government's "war on drugs" took on a strongly military character, as the United States undertook programs to eradicate coca and marijuana fields in Latin America while supplying the region's armed forces with equipment and training services intended to help them suppress the drug trade. Some critics said the drug war was little more than a pretext for Washington to maintain its Cold War military presence in the region. At best, they charged, the militarization of the U.S. antidrug campaign in Latin America was undermining progress toward human rights and democracy. Human Rights Watch, a New York–based group that has been investigating and exposing human rights abuses since 1978, published the results of its inquiry into U.S. support for Bolivian antidrug activities in 1995.

President Clinton, like his Republican predecessors, has made the Andean countries of Bolivia, Colombia and Peru a focus of his international counternarcotics strategy. Within this trio, Bolivia—second to Peru as a producer of coca leaf and to Colombia as a producer of refined cocaine—has been the largest recipient of U.S. counternarcotics aid. The impact of U.S. counternarcotics pressure on Bolivia cannot be overstated: Bolivia has passed laws, created institutions and adopted antinarcotics strategies shaped by U.S. concerns and dependent on U.S. funding. The United States funds and equips Bolivia's special antinarcotics police, and has stationed a large contingent of Drug Enforcement Administration (DEA) personnel within Bolivia to train and guide

Source: Human Rights Watch. *Human Rights Violations and the War on Drugs.* "Introduction." New York: Human Rights Watch, 1995.

them. The United States also funds and provides technical assistance to all other Bolivian agencies involved in counternarcotics activities.

Assistant Secretary of State for the Bureau for International Narcotics and Law Enforcement Affairs, Robert Gelbard, insists that U.S. "counternarcotics assistance can be a powerful force in advancing, rather than retarding, human rights objectives in the hemisphere. . . ." In Bolivia, however, U.S. counternarcotics assistance has supported programs and policies deeply flawed by human rights abuses:

Under the country's anti-drug law, Law 1008, Bolivians charged with drug offenses—no matter how minor—are imprisoned without the possibility of pretrial release and must, if acquitted, remain in prison until the trial court's decision is reviewed by the Supreme Court, a process that takes years. During that time, prisoners are held in appallingly overcrowded and miserable prisons.

In the Chapare, the rural area in which most of Bolivia's coca is grown and cocaine base produced, the antinarcotics police run roughshod over the population, barging into homes in the middle of the night, searching people and possessions at will, manhandling and even beating residents, stealing their goods and money. Arbitrary arrests and detentions are routine.

A number of Bolivians detained on drug trafficking charges allege torture by Bolivian law enforcement personnel. They also allege DEA complicity with abusive interrogations. DEA personnel acknowledge that they do not intervene to stop abuse.

Impunity for abuses by the antinarcotics police is the norm. Even complaints of serious human rights violations, including torture, are rarely investigated. Charges of human rights abuse by DEA agents are left unanswered. A mantle of diplomatic immunity and agency secrecy impedes public investigation and accountability.

Bolivian and U.S. public officials make excuses for or attempt to justify human rights violations in the context of the drug war. Senior Bolivian officials concede that there are profound problems with Law 1008, but insist that the United States, which had encouraged the enactment of the law, would oppose reform. U.S. officials acknowledge that aspects of Law 1008 are inconsistent with principles of liberty and due process, but are concerned that any legislative reform of the offending legal provisions would be accompanied by efforts to weaken the law's substantive framework, which undergirds Bolivia's entire antinarcotics effort.

U.S. officials dismiss or downplay abuses by the U.S.-supported Bolivian counternarcotics forces. . . . But the U.S. attitude . . . appears to reflect a determination not to be distracted from the principal goal of combating drug trafficking, and a willingness to overlook human rights violations that arise in pursuit of that goal. When questioned by Human Rights Watch about abusive interrogations by the Bolivian police, a senior DEA official in Bolivia acknowledged the problem but said simply that "the Bolivians have their own way of doing business" and that it is "not our job to interfere." U.S. officials are well aware of the reputation of the rural antinarcotics police, the UMOPAR, as "thieves and thugs," but have failed to use U.S. leverage to press for adequate reform. U.S. efforts to improve the UMOPAR's human rights record have consisted primarily of including a human rights component in the UMOPAR's basic training; trying to ensure that "good men" are placed in senior positions; and engaging in ad hoc monitoring, necessarily limited to the more egregious cases.

Human Rights Watch believes the United States should pay more attention to the problem of abusive conduct by the antinarcotics police. . . .

Recent events in Bolivia underscore the dangers posed to democracy and respect for human rights by counternarcotics efforts—and the unfortunate role of the United States in exacerbating those dangers. On March 2 [1995], the United States informed Bolivia that it would cut off aid and oppose multilateral bank loans to Bolivia if the government did not immediately undertake certain counternarcotics efforts, including the eradication of 1,750 hectares of coca by June 30. This ultimatum, which prompted political furor in Bolivia, came at a time when the Bolivian government was already being sorely tested by other domestic political battles. On April 18, in the midst of escalating political tensions, the government declared a state of siege, suspended certain constitutional rights, and began to round up labor leaders who were prominent in the public opposition to government initiatives. Precise figures are not available, but estimates are that approximately 400 individuals were arrested; most were administratively detained and banished without charges or access to judicial review to public facilities including military barracks in remote areas of the country. . . .

The state of siege illustrates, we believe, a broader pattern in Bolivia by which U.S. pressure to yield results in the war on drugs can subvert the rule of law. Pressed by the U.S.—under penalty of forfeiting crucial economic support—to combat coca cultivation, but lacking a strong domestic constituency in favor of such action, the Bolivian government has reacted by skirting its international obligation to protect the human rights of its people. . . .

NO. 123

1996

Sweat-Shop Labor

The Organización Regional Interamericana de Trabajadores

The growth of Export Processing Zones (EPZs) expanded dramatically throughout Mexico, Central America and the Caribbean in the 1980s and '90s as U.S. pressures to reduce trade barriers coincided with cost-saving measures pursued by transnational corporations. Labor-intensive assembly operations were being moved to plants abroad where wages were a fraction of those in the United States. Employing mostly women, these assembly plants (*maquiladoras* in their Mexican usage) re-export finished manufactured products—apparel, furniture, toys, electronics—back to the United States. For the host country the EPZs provide employment, but workers often confront abusive managers and hostility toward union organizing. At the same time, lax enforcement of environmental laws leads to the degradation of the environment. The report excerpted below was published by the International Confederation of Free Trade Unions (ICFTU), whose regional affiliate in Latin America is the Organización Regional Interamericana de Trabajadores (ORIT), based in Caracas. ORIT was established in 1951 with the support of the giant U.S. labor federation, the AFL-CIO, and received the backing of the U.S. government, which considered ORIT a potential bulwark against Marxist influence in the Latin American labor movement. Today ORIT-affiliated unions claim a membership of more than forty-five million workers in twenty-nine hemispheric countries.

One of the most disturbing aspects of the growth of the global market is the increasing number of Export Processing Zones where millions of workers, mainly young women, are employed in grossly repressive conditions. . . . It is a shocking revelation of the dark underside of globalization and a call for action by the international trade union movement, governments and employers to end a major scandal. . . . The enterprises go to these zones because

Source: International Conference of Free Trade Unions. "Behind the wire: Anti-union repression in the export processing zones" (April 1996), http://www.icftu.org/english/tncs/etnexpzo. html#Antiunionrepression. Reprinted by permission.

they can take advantage not only of adequate infrastructure, exemptions from tax and customs duties, and low wages but also from the "anti-union" climate which enables them to reduce production costs and multiply their value added. . . .

Widespread poverty in the zones' host countries, and the high levels of unemployment and underemployment are all major obstacles to union organising. Employers can use unemployment as a form of blackmail, and have an almost inexhaustible reserve to choose from, particularly given that the tasks performed in the factories require very little training. Thousands of workers are concentrated in clearly demarcated zones subjected to the close and often brutal surveillance of private guards preventing the entry of any trade union officials. The dispersion of workers in family workshops, in the "submaquilas" (subsubcontracting), also weakens trade union action. The employers often consider themselves omnipotent and untouchable. . . .

During the second international conference on export processing zones, held in Miami in October 1991, the representative of Panama distributed brochures which highlighted the limitations imposed on trade union activities in the zones. Panama hosts the second largest zone in the world, the Colón zone at the Atlantic end of the canal. Governments bear much of the responsibility for this antiunion repression. They do not only exonerate enterprises from paying taxes and customs duties, they also exempt them from applying the host country's labour legislation. . . .

In El Salvador, the legislation appears to protect the freedom of association: article 47 of the Constitution grants workers in the private sector the right to "associate freely in order to defend their respective interests by forming occupational associations or trade unions." This right is reinforced by article 248 of the labour code under the terms of the "fuero sindical" which bans the dismissal of trade union officials (unless on legal grounds determined by a judge) at the time of their election, during their mandate and for the year following their mandate.

"The reality endured by trade unionists however differs substantially from the letter of the law" notes an AFL-CIO report. "The list of sacked trade union members and leaders is getting longer. Not only are these workers dismissed for no reason, they are also refused any form of compensation or reintegration. Despite these abuses, the Salvadorian Labour Ministry maintains his complacent attitude and if an enterprise is found to be at fault, the Labour Minister often refrains from applying the law or even imposing a fine."

This laxity often hides the collusion between the public authorities and the enterprises. According to information collected from Korean owners, the Foreign Affairs ministry of Honduras, under the Callejas presidency, promised Korean investors that if they came to the EPZs trade unions would not be tolerated and the labour code would not be strictly applied. A parliamentary report published in May 1994 commented on "the slowness and sometimes apathy of labour inspectors called on to investigate workers' complaints."

The report made several proposals, including the expulsion of foreign employers found guilty of ill-treatment, but the suggestions were never acted upon.

The Honduran authorities, already very hostile towards any social protest, consider enterprises in the zones as strategic industries. The EPZs have the same status as a public enterprise, making all strike action illegal. The progovernment press is also part of the antiunion campaign. For many weeks, says an AFL-CIO report published in June 1995, the daily papers accused, without giving the slightest proof, the U.S. trade unions of sending money to the Honduran unions, with a view to destabilising the maquila industry and bringing clothing jobs back to the United States. . . .

In Mexico, the authorities have multiplied the obstacles facing the organisation of independent unions in the maquiladoras. According to the daily *La Jornada* some towns on the border with the United States do not have a labour tribunal. "Attempts to set up a tribunal in the towns of Sabinas, San Pedro and Muzquiz were blocked by a member of parliament from the PRI (the ruling Institutional Revolutionary Party) who also owns one of the biggest firms running factories in these towns."

These practices confirm the fact that most of the countries that are host to export processing zones also appear regularly in the reports of human rights organisations. It shows that the repression against the trade unions comes not only from the employers but also from the public authorities. . . .

In Central America, *solidarismo,* a movement sponsored by the employers and conservative circles and supported by the official U.S. development aid agency (USAID), is openly favoured in the zones. This is particularly the case in Costa Rica where workers belonging to these associations almost outnumber the trade union membership for the whole country. A document from the U.S. Labour department shows that 90 per cent of workers from U.S. firms operating in Costa Rica are members of solidarist associations. The associations, favoured by the country's legislation, also claim to help workers by involving them in a "profit-sharing" scheme and by granting them extralegal advantages, but their real objective is to break the trade unions and prevent collective bargaining.

A survey published in the ICFTU newspaper, *Free Labour World,* in November, 1992, showed that the advantages offered to workers, such as loans, consumer goods, canteens, etc. were always lower than those obtained by trade unions through collective bargaining, and that their sole purpose was to bind the employee to the enterprise and undermine any possible opposition. . . .

Some enterprises use violence to get their way. Death threats against trade union activists are not unusual and the employers have no scruples about using security guards who act as a veritable militia. In August 1994, in Honduras, during a dispute at the King Star company in the Buffalo Park, fifty guards with batons and tear gas attacked workers protesting peacefully against the management. "Hit them. Kill them if you can" yelled the head of the security guards. Shots were fired in the air and close to the workers' feet. Pregnant women were brutally attacked. According to the *El Tiempo* newspaper, one of the guards tried to rape one of the women workers after making her get into a lorry. . . .

The enterprises based in the export processing zones are sometimes nicknamed "companies on wheels" or "swallow" companies, because they are quick to close down and fly towards more clement skies when they see their advantages wearing thin, which usually means when it gets harder for them to exploit their workers. The history of the maquiladoras is strewn with the empty shells of factories abandoned by their former owners when the workers succeeded in organising. . . .

In 1991, according to an AIFLD [American Institute for Free Labor Development] document, a representative of the Westinghouse company said they would rather leave the Dominican Republic than accept a trade union in their factory. The result of all this pressure is obvious: the rate of unionisation in the EPZs is extremely low. In Honduras, in May 1995, of the 45,000 workers employed in the 103 factories in the EPZs, there were only seven trade unions in a position to sign collective agreements. They were all based in the Puerto Cortes zone, controlled by the government. In private enterprises, all fledgling unions have been broken by the management, despite legislation which theoretically protects trade union leaders from management reprisals. . . .

NO. 124

1997

The First Americans

The Inter-American Commission on Human Rights

In 1989, on the eve of the 500th anniversary of the European encounter with the indigenous inhabitants of the New World, the General Assembly of the Organization of American States asked the OAS's Inter-American Commission on Human Rights to prepare a legal instrument dealing with the rights of native Americans. The Commission adopted a "Proposed American Declaration on the Rights of Indigenous Peoples" on February 26, 1997. An example of the broadening scope of interamerican relations after the end of the Cold War, the proposed declaration clearly had far-reaching implications for the member states of the OAS as they considered whether to sign it. The commission submitted the declaration to the General Assembly with a recommendation for prompt approval. The assembly resolved to study the matter before proceeding further, and it was still under consideration in 1999.

The member states of the OAS (hereafter the states) . . . declare:

Section One. Indigenous Peoples

ARTICLE 1. SCOPE AND DEFINITIONS

1. This Declaration applies to indigenous peoples as well as peoples whose social, cultural and economic conditions distinguish them from other sections of the national community, and whose status is regulated wholly or partially by their own customs or traditions or by special laws or regulations.

2. Self identification as indigenous shall be regarded as a fundamental criterion for determining the peoples to which the provisions of this Declaration apply. . . .

Source: Organization of American States. Inter-American Commission on Human Rights. "Proposed American Declaration on the Rights of Indigenous Peoples." http://www.oas.org/EN/PROG/indigene.htm. December 1998.

Section Two. Human Rights

ARTICLE 2. FULL OBSERVANCE OF HUMAN RIGHTS

1. Indigenous peoples have the right to the full and effective enjoyment of the human rights and fundamental freedoms recognized in the Charter of the OAS, the American Declaration of the Rights and Duties of Man, the American Convention on Human Rights, and other international human rights law. . . .

2. Indigenous peoples have the collective rights that are indispensable to the enjoyment of the individual human rights of their members. Accordingly the states recognize *inter alia* the right of the indigenous peoples to collective action, to their cultures, to profess and practice their spiritual beliefs, and to use their languages. . . .

ARTICLE 5. NO FORCED ASSIMILATION

1. Indigenous peoples have the right to freely preserve, express and develop their cultural identity in all its aspects, free of any attempt at assimilation.

2. The states shall not undertake, support or favour any policy of artificial or enforced assimilation of indigenous peoples, destruction of a culture or the possibility of the extermination of any indigenous peoples. . . .

Section Three. Cultural Development

ARTICLE 7. RIGHT TO CULTURAL INTEGRITY

1. Indigenous peoples have the right to their cultural integrity, and their historical and archeological heritage, which are important both for their survival as well as for the identity of their members.

2. Indigenous peoples are entitled to restitution in respect of the property of which they have been dispossessed, and where that is not possible, compensation on a basis not less favorable than the standard of international law.

3. The states shall recognize and respect indigenous ways of life, customs, traditions, forms of social, economic and political organization, institutions, practices, beliefs and values, use of dress, and languages.

ARTICLE 8. PHILOSOPHY, OUTLOOK AND LANGUAGE

1. Indigenous peoples have the right to indigenous languages, philosophy and outlook as a component of national and universal culture, and as such, shall respect them and facilitate their dissemination. . . .

ARTICLE 9. EDUCATION

1. Indigenous peoples shall be entitled: a) to establish and set in motion their own educational programs, institutions and facilities; b) to prepare and implement their own educational plans, programs, curricula and materials; c) to train, educate and accredit their teachers and administrators. The states shall endeavor to ensure that such systems guarantee equal educational and teaching opportunities for the entire population and complementarity with national educational systems.

2. When indigenous peoples so decide, educational systems shall be conducted in the indigenous languages and incorporate indigenous content, and

they shall also be provided with the necessary training and means for complete mastery of the official language or languages.

3. The states shall ensure that those educational systems are equal in quality, efficiency, accessibility and in all other ways to that provided to the general population. . . .

ARTICLE 10. SPIRITUAL AND RELIGIOUS FREEDOM

1. Indigenous peoples have the right to freedom of conscience, freedom of religion and spiritual practice, and to exercise them both publicly and privately.

2. The states shall take necessary measures to prohibit attempts to forcibly convert indigenous peoples or to impose on them beliefs against their will. . . .

ARTICLE 11. FAMILY RELATIONS AND FAMILY TIES

1. The family is the natural and basic unit of societies and must be respected and protected by the state. Consequently the state shall recognize and respect the various forms of indigenous family, marriage, family name and filiation. . . .

ARTICLE 12. HEALTH AND WELL-BEING

1. Indigenous peoples have the right to legal recognition and practice of their traditional medicine, treatment, pharmacology, health practices and promotion, including preventive and rehabilitative practices.

2. Indigenous peoples have the right to the protection of vital medicinal plants, animals and minerals in their traditional territories. . . .

Section Four. Organizational and Political Rights

ARTICLE 14. RIGHTS OF ASSOCIATION, ASSEMBLY, FREEDOM OF EXPRESSION AND FREEDOM OF THOUGHT

1. Indigenous peoples have the right of association, assembly and expression in accordance with their values, usages, customs, ancestral traditions, beliefs and religions.

2. Indigenous peoples have the right of assembly and to the use of their sacred and ceremonial areas, as well as the right to full contact and common activities with their members living in the territory of neighboring states.

ARTICLE 15. RIGHT TO SELF-GOVERNMENT

1. Indigenous peoples have the right to freely determine their political status and freely pursue their economic, social, spiritual and cultural development, and accordingly, they have the right to autonomy or self-government with regard to *inter alia* culture, religion, education, information, media, health, housing, employment, social welfare, economic activities, land and resource management, the environment and entry by nonmembers; and to determine ways and means for financing these autonomous functions. . . .

ARTICLE 16. INDIGENOUS LAW

1. Indigenous law shall be recognized as a part of the states' legal system and of the framework in which the social and economic development of the states takes place.

2. Indigenous peoples have the right to maintain and reinforce their indigenous legal systems and also to apply them to matters within their com-

munities, including systems related to such matters as conflict resolution, crime prevention and maintenance of peace and harmony. . . .

Section Five. Social, Economic and Property Rights

ARTICLE 18. TRADITIONAL FORMS OF OWNERSHIP AND CULTURAL SURVIVAL Rights to land, territories and resources

1. Indigenous peoples have the right to the legal recognition of their varied and specific forms and modalities of their control, ownership, use and enjoyment of territories and property.

2. Indigenous peoples have the right to the recognition of their property and ownership rights with respect to lands, territories and resources they have historically occupied, as well as to the use of those to which they have historically had access for their traditional activities and livelihood. . . .

7. Indigenous peoples have the right to the restitution of the lands, territories and resources which they have traditionally owned or otherwise occupied or used, and which have been confiscated, occupied, used or damaged, or when restitution is not possible, the right to compensation on a basis not less favorable than the standard of international law. . . .

ARTICLE 21. RIGHT TO DEVELOPMENT

1. The states recognize the right of indigenous peoples to decide democratically what values, objectives, priorities and strategies will govern and steer their development course, even where they are different from those adopted by the national government or by other segments of society. Indigenous peoples shall be entitled to obtain on a non-discriminatory basis appropriate means for their own development according to their preferences and values, and to contribute by their own means, as distinct societies, to national development and international cooperation. . . .

Index